THE LIFE OF
D. MARTYN LLOYD-JONES
1899–1981

THE LIFE OF
D. MARTYN LLOYD-JONES
1899–1981

Iain H. Murray

THE BANNER OF TRUTH TRUST

THE BANNER OF TRUTH TRUST

Head Office
3 Murrayfield Road
Edinburgh
EH12 6EL
UK

North America Office
PO Box 621
Carlisle
PA 17013
USA

banneroftruth.org

First published 2013
© Iain H. Murray 2013
Reprinted 2013, 2014, 2016, 2020

*

ISBN
Print: 978 1 84871 180 8
Epub: 978 1 84871 220 1
Kindle: 978 1 84871 221 8

*

Typeset in 11/13 Adobe Garamond Pro
at The Banner of Truth Trust, Edinburgh

Printed in the USA by
Versa Press Inc.,
East Peoria, IL.

'Fellowship with God is the only worthwhile thing in life and it makes us new.'

'I gave up nothing; I received everything, I count it the highest honour that God can confer on any man, to call him to be a herald of the Gospel.' [Spoken after he had been commended for 'the sacrifice' of leaving medicine for the work of the ministry.]

'The two greatest meetings in my life were both prayer meetings.'

'My whole life experiences are proof of the sovereignty of God and his direct interference in the lives of men. I cannot help believing what I believe. I would be a madman to believe anything else — the guiding hand of God! It is an astonishment to me.'

'Do not waste too much of your time in worrying about the future of the Christian church.'

'We are sinners saved by grace. We are debtors to mercy alone.'

'Love is the greatest thing in religion, and if that is forgotten nothing can take its place.'

D. MARTYN LLOYD-JONES

Contents

Illustrations

Preface

This book is a re-cast, condensed and, in parts, re-written version of my two volumes *D. Martyn Lloyd Jones: The First Forty Years* (1982) and *The Fight of Faith* (1990). Since those dates, the life of Dr Lloyd-Jones has been the subject of comment and assessment in many publications and I have taken that into account. The main purpose of a further biography, however, is to put Dr Lloyd-Jones' life before another generation in a more accessible form. The two original volumes remain in print, and they preserve fuller documentation, but the big story is here for those hindered by the prospect of 1,200 pages. The omissions have to do chiefly with his overseas visits, and with a shortening of quotations. While almost a lifetime has passed since I first began to love and benefit from Martyn Lloyd-Jones, my appreciation of the ministry God gave him has only deepened with the years.

Today it is immensely encouraging that so many who never knew him personally now share in the benefits of his ministry. This has been possible because the greater part of what he preached is currently read across the world. The publication figures of his books run into millions. One of those titles alone, *Preaching and Preachers,* went through fourteen printings in twenty years, and last year went out in a new edition. Given the number of his books now available, a word of advice may help some who are about to read him for the first time. Go for the hard backs which he chose first for publishing! At their head is, *Studies on the Sermon on the Mount* (IVP). A number of his most influential addresses were published individually in his lifetime; they are brought together in, *Knowing the Times* (Banner of Truth) and give the best introduction to his thinking. For his expositions in series, start with his *Ephesians*.

Sixteen hundred of his sermons are now available for free down-loading at www.mljtrust.org. These are being heard by far larger numbers than those who heard him in his lifetime, and they consti-tute a great resource. But it would be wise, in ML-J's own opinion, not to put recordings before books. A listing of his sermons may be found in my title, *Lloyd-Jones: Messenger of Grace* (2008), which is not a biography but a fuller account of his thinking on such subjects as 'Preaching and the Holy Spirit'.

Sometimes too much comment is given to Martyn Lloyd-Jones as a Welshman and not enough to the tradition of Welsh Calvinistic Methodism from which he came. What was said of William Wil-liams, one of the leaders in that tradition, can be said of ML-J: 'These four things were marked in him: viz. the strength and abundance of his natural gifts; his great diligence in the use of them, night and day; the very great extent to which he enjoyed the influence and power of the Holy Spirit in his own work; and the immense blessing which the people received through him.'[1] Happily what can take us to the heart of that heritage is to be found in the current titles, *Thomas Charles' Spiritual Counsels*, *John Elias, Life and Letters*, and *The Cal-vinist Methodist Fathers of Wales* (all Banner of Truth Trust).

These pages could not have been written without the help of the late Mrs Bethan Lloyd-Jones and her daughters, Lady Catherwood and Mrs Ann Beatt. To them I am also indebted for most of the pho-tographs used. The Rev. Graham Harrison, and my wife, have given much valued assistance with the final proofs, and, as ever, the input and care of the publishers have been indispensable.

Preparing a book of this kind has been a forceful reminder to the author of the brevity of life. Few who figure in these pages still belong to the present scene. The once great congregation of Westminster Chapel, which I still see in my mind's eye, is now for the most part re-assembled in a better world. For every one of us 'the time is short', and the call is to live for the Lord Jesus Christ. May the testimony of these pages serve to that end!

IAIN H. MURRAY
Edinburgh,
November 24, 2012

[1] D. E. Jenkins, *The Life of Thomas Charles of Bala* (Denbigh: Jenkins, 1910), vol. 2, p. 57.

ONE

'A Welshman Now!'

In the spring of the year 1906 a pony and trap brought a family to their new home in the village of Llangeitho, Cardiganshire. They were Henry Lloyd-Jones, then in his early forties; his wife, Magdalene; and their three boys, Harold, Martyn, and Vincent. Martyn, separated by some two years in each case from his older and younger brothers, was aged five years and three months. He was to remember little of the life they had left behind in Donald Street, Cardiff, where he had been born on December 20, 1899. A flag hung from one of their windows to celebrate some victory in the Second Boer War, a fall downstairs from top to bottom, and a dancing lesson which he suffered at a small private school in Connaught Road — these things were almost all that he was to recall in later life from the days before he reached Llangeitho.

The Lloyd-Joneses felt no grief in exchanging Wales's largest city and port for the sixty or so houses which made up this village in the upper valley of the Aeron. Both parents were native to Cardiganshire. After only indifferent success with his Cardiff grocery shop, and a growing impression that town life did not suit his health, Henry had determined to move back to the country. When, therefore, a favourable opportunity arose, he sold his business, together with the home that went with it, and removed his family to a nearby boarding house until the general store at Llangeitho came on the market. His offer for the store was accepted and a new chapter in their lives began.

By temperament Henry Lloyd-Jones was an optimist and the soul of honour and uprightness. He was once called 'a proper Mr Micawber', ever waiting for something advantageous to turn up, and undoubtedly he felt that there were reasons for hopefulness in the spring of 1906. Wales herself, it seemed to him and to many others, was awakening after a long winter. Certainly times had changed since the days of his own childhood, spent at Cefn-Ceirw, his parents' farm in the Rhydlewis district of Cardiganshire, where Elizabeth, his strong-minded mother, better known as Betty-Cefn, had been famous for her participation in the 'tithe-wars'. Now, as the landslide victory for the Liberals in the General Election of that same year 1906 demonstrated, the Established Church and the landowners could no longer quieten the people with admonitions to 'know their betters'. New political thinking was stirring, the days of privilege were over and reforms certain. With brilliant eloquence, David Lloyd George, Liberal MP for Caernarvon Boroughs, chastised the forces of tradition which had long ruled Wales on behalf of England, and shortly, as Chancellor of the Exchequer, he was even to turn 11 Downing Street into a kind of Welsh embassy.

No doubt comparatively little of the change was being registered in Llangeitho in 1906. As a local centre of the Welsh-speaking farming community, it had long stood aloof from much that was going on elsewhere. Its very name was a reminder of how tradition lingered in inland Cardiganshire for, in truth, it ought not to have been called Llangeitho at all, but Capel Gwynfil. Llangeitho parish actually lay on the other side of the river Aeron. The explanation of the anomaly lay in an occurrence two centuries back. Llangeitho ('church of Ceitho') had no fame in the annals of Welsh history until a certain Daniel Rowland became curate there in the 1730s. Thereafter it was to become the centre of a series of evangelical revivals which transformed large areas of the Principality and brought Calvinistic Methodism to birth. At an open-air communion service in Rowland's remote parish in 1742, George Whitefield believed that he saw 'perhaps ten thousand from different parts'. When the authorities of the Church of England, in an attempt to suppress Calvinistic Methodism, ejected Rowland from the parish church in 1763 a 'new church' (*Yr Eglwys Newydd*) was built for him in Capel Gwynfil and the village, considering itself honoured by such a change, was equally pleased to adopt the name of the old parish itself!

For the most part, by 1906, religion existed in Llangeitho in tradition only, and though the population continued to clean the road in front of their homes and to scrub the front-door step every Saturday night in preparation for Sunday, when all went to the chapel, it was hard indeed to imagine how Calvinistic Methodism had ever given such alarm to the bishops. In some parts of Wales the denomination had been touched afresh by a breath of true revival as recently as 1904-05, but in Llangeitho chapel all was as motionless as the statue of Daniel Rowland which the Lloyd-Jones boys passed each morning on their way to school. Martyn's memories of that state of lifelessness were to remain vivid in later years:

> Our minister was a moral, legalistic man — an old schoolmaster. I do not remember that he ever preached the gospel, and none of us had any idea of the gospel. He and the head deacon, John Rowlands, looked upon themselves as scholars. Neither had any sympathy for the Revival of 1904-05, and both of them were not only opposed to any spiritual stress or emphasis, but were equally opposed to every popular innovation. Those who came home for their holidays from Glamorganshire, who spoke of their having been 'saved', were regarded as hot-heads and madmen from the South. We did not have annual preaching meetings in our chapel, and the eminent preachers of the day were never invited. We would not have heard Dr John Williams and T. C. Williams of Menai Bridge [two leading Calvinistic Methodists of the time] if it were not for the Association Meeting which was held at Llangeitho in June 1913. The only reason for its coming was that the Association itself had asked to come to Llangeitho to celebrate the bicentenary of the birth of Daniel Rowland. Although there is a statue of Daniel Rowland in the village, his influence had long since disappeared from the place, and 'Ichabod' had been written across everything. While large congregations still met to worship on Sundays, morning and evening, it was the strong sense of tradition which accounted for it. Llangeitho had lost the fire and the rejoicing of the Methodist Revival to the same extent as Westminster Abbey had lost the life and vitality of the Early Church — 'The glory had departed from Israel'.

3

It was certainly not the Calvinistic Methodist chapel which drew Henry Lloyd-Jones to Llangeitho. Hitherto his attachment had been with the Congregationalists: he now joined the Calvinistic Methodists because there was no real alternative and it was to suffer rather than to sympathise with what Rowland's old congregation had become. Among the Congregationalists in Rhydlewis he had learned to think that such dullness arose from the dead hand of outworn creeds, and he was a warm advocate of the so-called 'New Theology' of R. J. Campbell (Congregational minister of the City Temple in London) which raised a storm among the orthodox in Wales in 1907. Henry Lloyd-Jones had encountered nothing which led him to question whether the 'new' was better than the old. Rather, like so many others, he had been misled into identifying the lifeless traditionalism of Calvinistic Methodism with the real Christianity which it had once represented, and in his reaction to that kind of formal religion he had come to imagine that Christianity's best work lay in achieving social change through education and political action. He was as committed as was his favourite religious weekly, the *Christian Commonwealth,* to an alliance between Liberal politics and religious Nonconformity. At Westminster, Lloyd George gloried in the claim that one had to go back to Cromwell's day to find a Parliament composed of so many Nonconformists. But Lloyd George knew no more than did Henry Lloyd-Jones about what Nonconformity had once been.

At this point 'Maggie' Lloyd-Jones — as everyone called Henry's wife — was in no position to help her husband. Her step-mother had given her an attachment to the Church of England, but there had been little religion of any kind in her parents' home. In fact, David Evans, Martyn's maternal grandfather, was a thorough pagan who made no secret of his indifference to both church and chapel. In many respects David Evans was a remarkable man, not least in his powers of memory: in any market-day debate among his fellow farmers none was his equal in recalling with effortless accuracy the details of sales of cattle and horses which others had long since forgotten. With rising prosperity, he had moved from his farm near Aberystwyth to a rather grander establishment, Llwyncadfor, near the border of south Cardiganshire. In his grandson's first memories of the place, Llwyncadfor, with its big house standing at the junction of three roads, and called after the name of an ancient Welsh prince *(Cadifor),* was virtually a village: four uncles helped to direct the many grooms and farm-hands, while the house itself bustled with aunts, servants and maids.

But to return to Llangeitho, an initial problem for the Lloyd-Jones boys on their arrival was the language. Although their parents spoke nothing but Welsh to each other, they had used English only in bringing up the children. The explanation for this lay in their mother's own experience. Magdalene was still a child when her mother died and fourteen when her father, David Evans, married again. His second wife was English and so, thereafter, English was the language which the children of the home always heard from their step-mother. When Maggie later had her own children she simply carried on what she had known at Llwyncadfor. Martyn felt his lack of Welsh keenly and determined to remedy it:

> I well remember, about a year after we moved to Llangeitho, as I was playing with a number of children outside the school, that I begged them not to speak English to me any more, 'Speak Welsh to me — I'm a Welshman now!'

Some two years later the point was well proved when Martyn spoke for the first time in public. One of the old Calvinistic Methodist practices which survived in Llangeitho down to the time of the First World War, was the exercise of catechising on the Sunday School lesson in the chapel. At one such catechising in 1909, the minister, with reference to the resurrection of Lazarus, asked, 'Why did Jesus say, *"Lazarus,* come forth"?' Silence followed until there burst out a reply in Welsh from the second Lloyd-Jones boy which was to be repeated around Cardiganshire. 'In case', Martyn declared, 'they all came forth!'

Under Henry Lloyd-Jones, the General Store at Llangeitho soon developed a retail business with surrounding farms and there was nothing which Martyn enjoyed more in his childhood than to accompany his father on such journeys in the trap, pulled by one of the two horses which they owned. Henry Lloyd-Jones was a cheerful man. As a youth he had competed for the bass solo prize at singing festivals and singing was still one of his favourite recreations. His neighbours knew him as a busy, inventive and honest figure. Many years later Martyn was to speak of his father as 'the best natural man I've ever known and the kindest character I've ever met'. His first memories of his mother were of her charm, her activity and her friendliness. In character she was 'very impulsive, generous, and open-hearted'. She delighted in entertaining visitors, whether invited or uninvited. On some points her judgment was fixed; she remained a churchwoman and a Tory; on others she relied on her not inconsiderable intuition. 'I would say that my mother was highly intelligent but not intellectual, she did not read; she was a very quick thinker and could take up a point at once. She was more intelligent than my father.'

Henry Lloyd-Jones showed great wisdom in bringing up the boys. Martyn's greatest desire in life was to be a man, to be grown-up, and, as one sign of manhood was to smoke, he longed for the day when he could join the older lads in this so manly custom.

One day, his father and mother were to be away for the day, and to Martyn's pride and great delight his father entrusted him with all the keys of the house and business — after all he was the practical one, Harold was always reading, and Vincent was too young. So the honour fell to him and the keys were safe in his pocket. But this temporary freedom from the presence of authority gave him an idea. He would buy a packet of cigarettes! Away he went to the appropriate shop and bought a packet of Woodbines. They were not his first smoke but they were the first packet he ever had of his own and he was full of pride and joy. With the responsibility of the keys and the packet of cigarettes, he had arrived!

The boys were asleep when their parents returned, but their father needed the keys and went to get them from Martyn's pocket where he found the packet of cigarettes with them! Whatever else Martyn might forget, he would never forget his father's arrival in his bedroom the next morning. It was the weight of his words rather than his hand which hurt him. He had, his father said, felt he could trust him. He had thought that he was old enough to take responsibility, that he could be relied upon, and he went on to speak of his own deep hurt and disappointment in such a manner that Martyn could bear no more and wept. 'Now get up and get dressed,' said his father. 'We are going down to the shop.' Down to the cigarette shop they went, where Henry Lloyd-Jones announced his displeasure that the shop-keeper had sold the cigarettes to a young boy, and Martyn handed the packet back!

1. Martyn as an infant.

2. Martyn, aged six, on a pony.

There was another indelible memory of those early days in Llangeitho. Christmas was coming with all its delights and surprises. The carol-singers were out every night, but the Lloyd-Jones boys were not encouraged in that money-raising activity. One night, however, Martyn could resist the temptation no longer and he attached himself to a group of children on their rounds — singing at one door after the other and collecting and sharing the odd pennies which they received right through the village. He never forgot — not to old age — his feelings, when at the end of the round, he learnt that these poor children were collecting money for their mother's funeral. The wound to his conscience was deep and lasting and meant many sleepless hours until the shock faded somewhat, though never the memory.

Here, in his own words, are more of Martyn's own memories of his Llangeitho childhood:[1]

> Our family life was extremely happy. The clearest recollection I have is that of always having a houseful of people. The main reason for this — apart from the fact that my father and mother were very pleased to welcome friends and others to the house for a meal and a chat — was that our house was also a business establishment. Like other shops in the country areas we used to sell all sorts of goods and my father was also a pioneer in selling machines such as ploughs, separators, haymaking machines and binders for the hay. And quite soon he also began a sort of creamery — a dairy. We had two manservants who toured the surrounding countryside to collect unsalted butter. Then it was all mixed together, salt was added, and finally the butter was placed in boxes and sent to various shops and co-operatives in Glamorganshire. The butter was sold as 'Vale of Aeron Blend'.
>
> I say this to explain why there were always so many people in our house. We dealt not only with the farmers of the Llangeitho district but also with those of Tregaron, Llanddewi Brefi, Penuwch, Bwlchyllan, Abermeurig, Llwynygroes, and even further. Travellers selling various goods would also call regularly and everyone who came had to have tea or supper. There is no need to say that

[1] From the 'Reminiscences of his early life', given on Radio 4 (Wales) April 21, 1971, and published in Welsh in *Y Llwybrau Gynt*, ed. Alun Oldfield-Davies, vol. 2, Llandysul, 1972. To the same source belong other quotations in this chapter.

such a life was exceptionally interesting for children. We took great interest in the different characters and their peculiarities. I remember how we looked forward to some of them coming because of their remarkable sayings. For example, whatever was said, one of these characters would always reply, *'Be chi'n siarad'* ('You don't say'). Another one, *'Cerwch ona'* ('Get away with you'). And yet another, *'Fo'lon marw nawr'* ('I'm willing to die now') as a protestation of the truth of what he was saying.

A subject which was often discussed at home was 'politics'. My father was a staunch Liberal and in those days he was an avid admirer of Lloyd George, although he turned against him from 1915 onwards. It wasn't often that a Tory would call in, but my mother supported that dogma. When she had some measure of support from a visitor there would be a heated argument. Today it is difficult to realise the faith that our fathers had in politicians. I remember one afternoon immediately after the 1909 Budget when I was in the trap with my father and one of our neighbours. This man had been brought up in central Cardiganshire and was therefore a Unitarian. I still remember the shock that I had when I heard him tell my father that he was certain that Lloyd George would do more good than Jesus Christ, because he had a better chance. I pity them! I have a vivid memory of the two elections in 1910. In one of them — if not both — the man who later became Sir George Fossett Roberts stood for election for the Tories against Mr Vaughan Davies [Lord Ystwyth], our MP. Mr Roberts was a brewer from Aberystwyth. I remember nothing of the speeches but I remember well that Mr Fossett Roberts was not allowed to speak at all when he came to address the meeting held one evening in the day school. The moment he opened his lips some of the Liberal boys started to sing — and many joined in with them.

> Vaughan Davies is the man,
> Vaughan Davies is the man,
> Farewell to the man of the barrel,
> Vaughan Davies is the man.

Mr Roberts persevered in his attempt to speak for some twenty minutes and then gave up. I am afraid that I was one of those that followed him, still singing the rhyme until he left the village in his car.

Llangeitho, like many other villages, was rich in characters. Time will only allow me to mention three of them. One of the most original was a shoemaker — or Ianto Crydd ('the boot') as he was known by some. His workshop was always full and that was for several reasons. One reason was that he talked so much that he tended to neglect his work, and the only way to make sure of retrieving one's shoes was to stay in the workshop until he finished the work!

He was a kind creature and dear to many. Here is one sample of his ability. One day a farmer went to the shoemaker in great distress. His eldest daughter had failed an examination at the Tregaron Intermediate School and the poor girl was nearly heart-broken. This wasn't the first time for her to fail, and every time she failed in the same subject, namely, algebra. He, the father, did not understand, and he came to the shoemaker and asked, 'What is this algebra that this lass always fails in? What is it?' Immediately the shoemaker began to explain and said, 'Oh! algebra! Think now of a train leaving Aberystwyth with thirty passengers on it. It comes to Llanrhystyd Road and two get out and one steps in. On arriving at Llanilar, three get out and no one enters. Tregaron, five get off and six enter. Then from station to station until they arrive at Bronwydd Arms where twelve enter. At last the train reaches Carmarthen. Now this is the problem, this is the question — What was the guard's name?' 'Dear me,' said the farmer, 'no wonder the poor lass fails.' And he went home to sympathise with his daughter. The shoemaker was very discerning and he knew his customers inside out.

I must speak of another place which plays a big part in my child-hood memories, until I reached my thirteenth birthday — and that is Llwyncadfor. This was the name of my grandfather's home on my mother's side. That is where I would spend all my holidays apart from Christmas time, and nothing gave me greater pleasure than this. Llwyncadfor is a fairly large farm not far from Newcastle Emlyn, but in those days it was not only a farm; Llwyncadfor was a stud farm, i.e. a farm for breeding horses. My grandfather was an expert in this matter, and after starting with the Welsh cob, he began to keep both heavy, or shire, horses and the light, or hackney, horses. It was he who was responsible for bringing these two latter breeds into Cardiganshire. There were a number of horses of dif-ferent breeds at Llwyncadfor, and individual stables called boxes

3. Henry Lloyd-Jones with Martyn outside the shop at Langeitho.

4. Llwyncadfor.

had been built for them here and there along the farmyard and also in the fields near the house. He had bred many horses which were shown in the different shows, some in harness and others under saddle or in hand. By my time there were three or four uncles and four or five aunts too, as well as five or six grooms to care for the horses, not to mention the farm hands who worked on the land. Llwyncadfor indeed looked more like a small village than a farm. I can see the servants sitting round the table in the living room — a whole tableful of them, with the family eating in another dining room and my grandfather eating by himself in the best living room. My inclination and ambition in those days was to become a groom and I spent my time carrying buckets of water and horsemeal. Sometimes I would have the extraordinary pleasure of sitting in the four-wheeler with my uncle Tom as he was training one of the best horses for the big show — the Welsh National or the United Counties in Carmarthen, or the Bath and West of England. I remember often leading some of the quietest horses to Henllan station and putting them in a horsebox to go by rail to one of the larger shows. Llwyncadfor farm staff would hire a train for themselves — because they had so many horses in the competition. And almost without exception they would take the chief prizes in all classes and many other prizes as well.

At night after supper most of the Llwyncadfor family used to sit in the living room around the open-hearth fire, with the chimney open to the sky. This is when they would tell stories and recount happenings, and often they would sing and entertain themselves in various ways. Then, again, there would always be a number of strangers in the company, because the stallions would travel each year throughout the counties of South Wales, apart from Brecknock and Radnor. The place would be ablaze with interest and to be part of it all was a great experience for a little boy. I remember my breast swelling with pride in shows, say at Aberystwyth or Carmarthen or Newcastle Emlyn, when I saw Llwyncadfor horses win cups and medals, and rosettes being placed on their necks.

Martyn's childhood in Llangeitho was comparatively uneventful until a night in January 1910 which was to influence the life of the whole family. Early in that month Henry Lloyd-Jones had sent out bills to a number of farmers who came to pay them — in old sovereigns and half-sovereigns — on the evening of Wednesday, January

19. The business was done in the clothing section of the shop where the men stood, talking and smoking. Mrs Lloyd-Jones and the eldest boy, Harold, happened to be away from home. About 1 A.M., the next morning, long after everyone had retired for the night, Martyn and Vincent, who shared a room, were half-aroused from their sleep by the smell of fumes, but sensing no danger they merely pulled the blankets higher over their heads. It seems that tobacco ash which had fallen to the floor of the store below, amidst millinery goods, had smouldered and then ignited. Once the building itself caught alight, the wind blowing that winter's night fanned the fire almost immediately into a terrific blaze. Just in time, the cries of the family's maid and the milliner, and their banging fists, awakened the father — a heavy sleeper — who was able to reach the boys' bedroom. 'I was thrown', recalled Martyn, 'by my father from one of the upstair windows into the arms of three men who were standing in their nightshirts in the road. Then they got hold of a ladder so that my father and brother could climb down.' They were scarcely out when the floor collapsed behind them and everything went up in flames.

Speaking of that early morning of January 20, 1910, ML-J was later to comment in the memories which he gave on radio:

> Somehow things at Llangeitho were never the same after the fire. Although we built a new home and started living in it within the year [1910] things were different. Certainly as a building the new house was a great improvement on our former home, but there was something missing, and more than anything the feeling of home was lacking. I felt as if I were in a strange house and that living there was a temporary matter. I always prefer old houses, although I appreciate many of the modern amenities.

In fact the effects of the fire went deeper than those few remarks reveal. For one thing, on the material level it brought his father into great difficulties. When they had gone through the ruin the next morning, Martyn had discovered a cracked and discoloured mug (which in later years stood on the mantelpiece of his study), and his father the sovereigns — melted into a solid mass of gold — but otherwise the loss was virtually complete. Thereafter Henry Lloyd-Jones was rarely free of financial problems. These were carefully hidden from the boys until David Evans of Llwyncadfor broke the secret to Martyn in 1911. Well able to rule a farm, under the influence of drink the old man could not always rule himself and there were times when as he drove his gig back to Llwyncadfor, after a convivial meeting, at the end of a market day perhaps, the safest thing to do was to hand the reins over to Martyn. On one such occasion David Evans told his grandson of his father's financial distress and though, when sober the next morning, he sought to whittle down what he had said, the damage was done in the boy's mind: 'It left a deep impression upon me. Before then I used to buy a pennyworth of sweets every week, now I reduced it to a half-penny. It was my contribution to the family problem.' For the next three years Martyn was not to share with anyone the burden which this news had laid upon him.

It may well have been the case that the fire of January 1910, and its consequences, also influenced Martyn's attitude to school. Probably Llangeitho school was typical of many a Welsh village school in days before rural depopulation emptied many parts of the countryside. With a headmaster and three lady teachers, education was carried up to grade six. For many it would be all the education they were likely to have and for a while it seemed possible that Martyn would fall into that group. Harold was quiet and studious, but Martyn seemed of a more practical and businesslike bent. Until the age of eleven he had no interest in books. Football and other pursuits possessed far more attraction.

About the year 1910 one of the lady teachers at Llangeitho retired, and her place was taken by a man, and it was this assistant schoolmaster who one day interrupted a game of football in the village square to express his serious concern at Martyn's inattention to his work. Unless he settled down, the teacher warned him, he would never get a scholarship to the County Intermediate School at Tregaron. Knowing his father's financial position, Martyn did not need telling that, if he failed to get a scholarship place in 1911, it might well mean an end to his further education. The warning was heeded and in the scholarship examination of 1911 Martyn Lloyd-Jones took second place, close behind the boy who stood first. This convinced him, for the first time, that he could do something with his mind and securing a place at Tregaron County School also opened the way to a new chapter in his life.

TWO

School-days: Tregaron and London

Only four miles from Llangeitho, Tregaron was nevertheless a different world for an eleven-year-old boy. He would not have agreed with the first part of the description given in one guide-book, 'Tregaron is a comfortable old town with a host of local legends'. The market town, situated at a point where a tributary of the Teifi ceases to be a mountain stream, marks a boundary between the fertile west of Cardiganshire and the wild hinterland of the north and east from whence the wind often blew in winter. But what made Tregaron and its school of 120 pupils so different for him was the fact that it was no longer possible to live at home. At the time of his arrival to join his brother Harold, who was already accustomed to spending Monday to Friday in lodgings, Martyn was the youngest in the school.

The greatest influence upon Martyn in the school was undoubtedly S. M. Powell who first awakened his interest in history. As well as being an able teacher, Powell had a shrewd ability at setting the pupils on making their own discoveries. 'Find out the date of the beginning of the 'cause' or Chapel where you belong', would be a typical piece of homework set for the weekend. Or again, 'Find out from the hymns of William Williams of Pantycelyn the profession which he had originally intended to follow.' This latter duty caused considerable dismay when it was given out, for the class knew that, while the author of 'Guide me, O Thou great Jehovah' had few hymns translated into English, the prospect of reading through all his Welsh hymnal was daunting! In reality the answer was not hard to find. Williams had been a medical student when the evangelical revival of the 1730s changed the course of his life and led him into the ministry. The love of medicine was supplanted by something higher and his hymns often speak of Christ as the better physician. Even so, that weekend none of the boys came back to school with the right answer.

Mr G. T. Lewis, the headmaster, had fewer personal dealings with the younger boys although he left an impression of his wisdom by actions which were not always predictable. When Martyn won a prize for Mathematics he was surprised to find himself presented with a book on woodwork, a subject for which he had no aptitude or interest! As he later came to see, that was precisely why the old Head had given it to him. It was a first lesson in the need for balance.

We continue with Martyn's own account of this period of his life:

> What shall I say about Tregaron and the time I spent in that school? These are the things which stand out in my memory. The first is an impression of how cold the town was. Tregaron is still to me the coldest place on the face of the earth. This can be attributed to the fact that the town lies between Cors Caron [Tregaron Bog] with its dampness, and the pass of Cwm Berwyn in the mountains, which is like a funnel drawing the cold easterly winds on to the town — all so different from Llangeitho which nestles cosily in the Vale of Aeron with the kind hills sheltering it from nearly all directions. But one has to be fair to Tregaron, although I suffered so much there. To judge from the state of the blood circulation in my body, I am much to be pitied, and as a result I have suffered a great amount of discomfort every year from chilblains for which we had our own local name *maleithe*. If that happened in Llangeitho with all its home comforts, then it was far worse in Tregaron where I stayed in lodgings from Monday morning until teatime on Friday. I can remember now the terrible burning sensation and then the itching which nearly drove me mad, and that happening not only on my hands but also on my toes. I was not able to run or play to lessen the complaint because of the pain; there was nothing to do but to suffer.
>
> But, in addition to this, I must add that I suffered at the same time from a far greater sickness, and a more painful one, which has remained with me all along life's path — and that was *hiraeth* [longing or home-sickness]. I am pleased to tell my friends at

Tregaron that I do not hold them or the place responsible for this. What is the reason for it? The psychologists cannot explain it. I believe that this again, like the circulation of the blood, belongs to a man's constitution, and that it is decided in part by the functioning of the ductless glands! Be that as it may, *hiraeth* is an awful thing, as also is the feeling of loneliness, and of being destitute and unhappy which stem from it. It is difficult to define *hiraeth*, but to me it means the consciousness of man being out of his home area and that which is dear to him. That is why it can be felt even among a host of people and amidst nature's beauty.

My three years in Tregaron County School were very unhappy and that was only because of this longing. I had bosom companions there, like Dai Williams and others, and I enjoyed the lessons . . . but I remember as if it were yesterday sitting in our pew in chapel at Llangeitho before the service on Sunday night and suddenly being hit by the thought — 'This time tomorrow night I shall be in my lodgings in Tregaron' — and all at once I would be down in the depths. And if it was like that on Sunday night, when still able to go home from the service, what about being in Tregaron with the chilblains on top of everything else!

Every Tuesday a market was held at Tregaron, and once a month the monthly market. This was before the time of marts as such, of course. My father and many of the farmers from the Llangeitho area came to Tregaron therefore nearly every Tuesday. Rather than being any consolation to me, this knowledge merely added to my hurt. I would sometimes go in the pony and trap with my father to Trecefel Bridge, about a mile out of the town, in order to lessen the pain, although I knew, like the poor drunk, that I was making things worse, because I would have to leave him and return by myself. Sometimes I would stand close to the school to see some of the farmers returning home — while I had to remain in Tregaron.

I suffered in this way for a year without any lessening of the complaint. Through the first two terms of the second year I was also in the same state — indeed in a worse state. And then in the summer term 1913, I persuaded my parents to allow me to return home every night. The journey was only about four and a half miles, and when the weather was fine I would travel on a bicycle. On very wet days I used to walk. This was heavenly for me, and I could reflect on that summer term without a shadow or cloud, apart from the fact that I happened to read *David Copperfield* about the same time. That caused me a great deal of unhappiness, like all the works of Dickens, because of the suffering and the unhappiness, especially among children, which is found in them.

Well, that's how it was with me. In September 1913 my youngest brother started at Tregaron, and so we were three brothers in the lodgings. But I failed to get over my malady even by this remedy, though it did ease a little of the heartache.

Time does not allow me to talk at length, as I would wish, of Tregaron School, but I would be willing to challenge the world that there were never two such teachers together in the same school as G. T. Lewis, the headmaster, and S. M. Powell, his chief assistant: the first was a 'character' verging upon the eccentric, the other was a genius. Both were Welshmen to the core and spoke a great deal of Welsh in the classroom. Mr Lewis would sometimes break out into a sermon in Welsh, and that might happen halfway through a geometry lesson. S. M. Powell was famous for his pioneering work in the field of drama — he wrote many plays himself and was a born actor. I remember his giving us a lesson on the *Merchant of Venice* and taking the part of Shylock himself. I see him now taking a knife from his pocket, opening it and sharpening it on his shoe, declaiming the words 'three thousand ducats' and 'one pound of flesh', the while.

The mention of 1913 causes me to mention two other providential happenings in my story. The first is that this was the year in which I decided to be a doctor. I am not quite sure what caused me to take this course. The fact that my mother's father's father had been a doctor could be one element in the reason perhaps, but I believe that my admiration for David Davies, Birchill — a local boy who had returned home to practise his profession — was even greater. Whatever lay behind it, it was my personal choice to be a doctor, and I received every support and encouragement from my parents.

The other truly important event in 1913 was that our Chapel had invited the Summer Association of the Calvinistic Methodists to Llangeitho. As I have already said, the reason for this was the bicentenary of Daniel Rowland's birth. This Association had a deep impact on me. I had never seen or heard open-air preaching before, but because of the number of people expected, the main meetings were held in a field at the bottom of, and to the left side of, the hill which leads down into Llangeitho from the direction of Tregaron. A stage had been erected, with a pulpit at the front for the preacher and seats for the leading ministers behind him. And then the congregation of about four to five thousand sat on benches facing the preacher. I well remember the meeting held to celebrate Daniel Rowland on the Wednesday afternoon, when we had addresses by Dr Thomas Charles Williams, Dr John Morgan Jones, Cardiff (the historian), Dr John Williams, Brynsiencyn, and the Rev. W. E. Prytherch of Swansea. That Association had a deep effect upon me, and possibly the most important thing it did was to create in me an interest in the Calvinistic Methodist Fathers which has lasted until today.

* * *

This regular routine of childhood came to a sudden end one Sunday night in January 1914. As the three brothers were sitting reading, as they usually did after supper, their parents came into the room,

and my father started to say that he had something extremely important to tell us, and that he was sure that we would receive what he had to say like men.

The message was that we were to leave Llangeitho within a few weeks and that it would be for ever. Difficulties had arisen in the business and there was nothing to do but to sell everything and face a new life. As we look back in the terms of today, I can see clearly that there were two elements in that crisis, over-expansion and under-capitalisation. The business in its varying aspects had grown too big and the machines were expensive and costly. Added to that, our customers were short of money and were very slow in paying their bills. There was no Milk Marketing Board; and no quotas or subsidies in those days. It is obvious that my father was about twenty years and more before his time. He also, on principle, refused to bargain in the usual way — and between everything we were in a crisis and there was nothing for it but to try to collect the debts and to hold an auction. So in February everything was sold during two whole days in the Jubilee Hall — everything, the horses, the contents of the shop, and even the furniture from our home, apart from a few minor items. This came as a great shock to us as boys, but I remember that our main reaction was that we felt a challenge in the situation and that we were willing to do anything in order to help. I remember saying that I would forgo the chance of becoming a doctor, and that I would become a bank clerk when I was old enough.

The bankruptcy which Martyn had secretly feared for the past three years had become a reality. To some extent it was probably a relief to him, after listening to his father's sad words on that January Sunday evening, to be able to exclaim, 'I knew all about this.' Henry Lloyd-Jones was astonished and very grieved to realise the burden which his second son had been carrying.

The head of the household was not, however, a man to sit down in despair. He meant to find other work, concerned for the best for his family, and also determined that outstanding debts would be repaid. The best course of action, he came to believe, was to emigrate to Canada and to start a new life. But there were practical difficulties. Harold was due to sit the Senior Central Welsh Board examination in June and July of that same year and Martyn's own ability was by now clearly established. His powers of memory — inherited from David Evans — were exceptional. As one of the Tregaron teachers told his father, 'What Martyn knows, he *knows!*' It was important, therefore, that Martyn should sit the Junior Central Welsh Board examination in the summer before leaving the district. Henry Lloyd-Jones resolved the dilemma by deciding that he would go himself to prepare the way as soon as the auction had taken place and that Maggie and the boys would live in part of a house near the school of Tregaron until July when they also could sail for Canada. Martyn recalled:

The most heart-breaking moment in the whole process for me was the morning my father bade us all farewell, and began his journey. After that we used to try to imagine what sort of life would be waiting for us in Canada, and we played with various fantasies. But before the end of the three months it became obvious that we were not to go to Canada. My father wrote regularly, about twice a week from Winnipeg, where he was staying with one of my mother's brothers. The refrain in his letter was that he could see clearly that there was no hope for us there. He was by then past fifty years of age and could not find suitable work. His opinion on the situation was: 'A wonderful country for young people, and a great chance for the boys, but hopeless for a man of my age.'

By the end of May, 1914, Henry Lloyd-Jones had decided to return to Britain and to try to restart life in London. His hope was that Maggie might be able to arrange something through relatives and that meanwhile he would attempt to earn a little by occasional work in Winnipeg. These must have been deeply perplexing months for Mrs Lloyd-Jones, with Harold and Martyn facing important examinations, pressure from creditors in the Llangeitho area, and her husband eagerly awaiting news of some opening in London. All the enquiries she attempted from Tregaron ended in failure. Understandably, Henry Lloyd-Jones was hardly his old buoyant self when on notepaper headed 'Memo. from H. Lloyd-Jones, General Merchant, Albion Stores, Llangeitho', he wrote from Winnipeg on July 1, 1914:

My dear Maggie and Children

I am writing today again. I am doing nothing now and am quite miserable. I very much hope you will be able to hit on something in London very soon, I do not think it is any use thinking of staying here, things are too bad here. I cannot get anything to go on with, the place is so much overdone. I am trying every day but there is nothing to be had. I only want something until you fix in London. We are all of the same opinion that it is safer there than here on the whole. One may have a job here today and be out of it tomorrow, that is the way of the country. There is no such thing as being given notice here. Please do not lose any time as I am getting so uneasy — spending every day and nothing coming in for me anywhere. Perhaps when the school is broken up for holidays the children can go somewhere for a week or so. Keep it strictly to yourselves about going to London, I hope I shall not be bothered there. We can live there quite as good as here, I mean as private if we only think of it for few years. I am anxiously expecting to hear from you on the matter, all we want is a support for a little while.

I do hope you can get something in London, no doubt we can do well there once we can have a start, and get good posts for the children as well.

I am anxious to know what the children are thinking of it. Do they prefer going to London than coming over here? I am sick of this country on account of its uncertainty, and everyone would come back tomorrow if they could.

Please write me at once. I am quite miserable here now, nothing coming in. I have no news. I have asked Willie for my money back;

he cannot pay me now, he said, and I do not know what to do. If I had a month's work at $80 or $100 I could manage it very well without, but I cannot do it as things are now.

Mind to keep everything entirely to yourselves and let me hear from you at once.

No news, only my very best and warmest love to you and children.

Your loving
Dada.

Mrs Lloyd-Jones must have read these lines with a feeling of utter helplessness, but shortly after that, another letter brought the news that her husband was about to begin his return journey and expected to be in London on August 3. No doubt his hope was that Maggie would be there to meet him, with the boys left at Llwyncadfor, until a new home could be found. In the event Mrs Lloyd-Jones made what proved to be a providential decision. Martyn, with his practical skills, would be the best one to help his father look for a business, so on Saturday, August 1, she put him on a train at Tregaron, bound for London, and went herself, with the other two boys, to Llwyncadfor.

There could scarcely have been a more memorable moment to arrive in London than that Bank-holiday weekend. At Paddington station Martyn was met by his mother's brother and as they made their way back to the uncle's home in Bermondsey, the fourteen-year-old boy noticed more than the shops and great buildings, the tram cars and some of the quarter-of-a-million toiling horses still present in the streets of the capital. Tension filled the air. England, which had sent no troops across the English Channel since 1815, was poised ready for the shock of the war against Germany which would be declared the following Tuesday.

On the Monday, which brought a hot, dry morning, Henry Lloyd-Jones' boat was due at the Surrey Docks. But, not wishing to bring a passenger ship through the English Channel because of the international crisis, the shipping company had ended the voyage at Plymouth, and so in the afternoon Martyn was once more back at a railway station to meet his father. In the evening of the same day he walked from Bermondsey to the Elephant and Castle, surveying the crowds of people, many, no doubt, returning from their Bank-holiday outings. Few anticipated the scale of the war that was about

to begin, or knew that London's halcyon Edwardian period was at
its end. Taking up the story on the day that war broke out, Martyn
Lloyd-Jones recalled:

> On Tuesday, August 4, my father took me to Westminster in the
> morning. We succeeded in joining the crowd which had gathered
> in Downing Street, and there we stayed for hours watching the
> various members of the Cabinet going in and out of No. 10. At
> last the moment we had been waiting for arrived, namely, that of
> seeing the door of No. 10 opening, and Mr Asquith leaving the
> house and getting into his car and starting off to Parliament, where
> he was to hear Sir Edward Grey making his never-to-be-forgotten
> speech. I remember the thrill I felt to see the man that was so much
> of a hero to my father, the man of whom I had heard so much. The
> only disappointment that day was that we had not caught sight,
> for some reason, of the 'little man', Lloyd George.
>
> Every day, straight after breakfast, we went in the direction of
> Westminster and stood outside the Palace Yard or Downing Street
> to catch a glimpse of the giants. And we were particularly for-
> tunate. It is impossible to try to describe the people of London
> at that time. The fever of war had taken a firm grip of them, and
> they sang and waved banners both large and small. They possessed
> a confident spirit, and a certainty that we would conquer the Ger-
> mans in a short time. We heard somehow that a regiment of our
> soldiers who were about to cross over to France, were to march
> through the city, setting out from the Tower. We went there early,
> and we caught sight of them marching by in their red coats and the
> band playing 'It's a long way to Tipperary'. The people nearly lost
> control of themselves in their enthusiasm, and while most of them
> were shouting and clapping their hands, others would break into
> song, and many wept.
>
> Strange days, fearful days — nothing was the same after that. I
> pity my father and his contemporaries with their unfailing loyalty
> to those political leaders. I'm glad that they are not alive to read
> the diaries of C. P. Scott, which I read recently, and to realise that
> their idols had feet of clay.

For Mr Lloyd-Jones and his second son that first week in August
was the beginning of a great trial which had nothing to do with the
war. It was not the spirit of sight-seeing which took them up each
day into the heart of London but the urgent need to find a small

business and a new home. Together they tramped the streets, looked at notices in shop windows, and read the advertisement columns of newspapers. The difficulties were immense, especially his father's lack of money and the unwillingness of relatives and friends to lend him any. Of those days Martyn Lloyd-Jones once said, 'I will never forget the discouragement and the depression. We had endless disappointments. My father and I, to save money, walked and walked and walked.' On the days when Mr Lloyd-Jones found it necessary to go alone in his search for work he was concerned not to leave Martyn at Bermondsey lest he should be a burden on their none-too-sympathetic relatives. So Martyn recalled how, to fill the time, he 'used to walk from Bermondsey to St James's Park and buy a sandwich at a booth there and a cup of tea'.

There were, however, times when Martyn's uncle did want him at home. Mr Evans carried on a milk and dairy business which enabled him to do well enough without a great deal of personal effort. But during August some of his roundsmen, anxious to be among the victorious troops who were expected to push the Germans back to the Rhine before winter, suddenly joined the army without any warning. Unless milk deliveries were to be curtailed there was no choice but to do a round himself, and to lessen the work he took Martyn with him. A milkman's job in those days was not as simple as it became when milk was bottled. Each roundsman either on a horse-drawn cart, or on a barrow which he pushed, carried a large churn of milk from which, at each household, the correct quantity had to be measured into little cans or jugs which might be brought to him. This was all new to Martyn and it was to prove one of the most valuable lessons of his school-days.

After many disappointments, by the end of September 1914, Mr Lloyd-Jones was settled in his plans. Another dairy and milk business at 7 Regency Street, Westminster, was on the market and the price asked was extremely attractive. Perhaps, at the time, Henry Lloyd-Jones did not know the reason for the low asking-price. The fact was that a fellow-countryman, M. D. Williams, having run this business for a number of years, was alarmed at the possible effects of the war recently declared. Williams remembered that during the Boer War of 1899–1902, when he had contracts with the troops at Chelsea and Wellington barracks, his profits had slumped when most of these men had been sent to South Africa and the barracks left comparatively empty. This time he decided to get out in good time and, to make sure of doing so, he had set the price which attracted the attention of Henry Lloyd-Jones. When all was weighed up, the latter found that he only needed £50 to secure the dairy, with its home above the shop and the business. And yet no such sum could be found in London. His brother-in-law in Bermondsey would not lend a halfpenny. In the end it was a groom at Llwyncadfor, who had long admired Henry Lloyd-Jones, who offered the necessary sum. Thus, after Martyn had spent two months at Bermondsey with his father, the family was again reunited as they set up home in Westminster's Regency Street in October 1914.

Meanwhile, during all the heartache of September, one bright piece of news had arrived from Tregaron via Llwyncadfor. It was in the handwriting of the headmaster of the boys' former school:

The County School,
Tregaron
14 Sept. 1914

My dear Mr Evans

I do not know where to send the results of the exams which your two grandsons, Harold and Martyn, entered.

Harold is through in all, with conversational power in French. Martyn is through in all, with distinction in arithmetic, maths and chemistry, and conversational power in French. Tell the boys they have done remarkably well — 29 certificates besides 4 supplementary.

You will, I feel sure, be kind enough as to forward this note on to them.

Yours in a hurry
G. T. Lewis

Notwithstanding these results, it was not immediately apparent to Henry and Maggie Lloyd-Jones, in their very straitened circumstances, that Martyn would be able to return to school.[1] His elder brother, Harold, became an articled clerk in a solicitor's office. Some thought that Martyn was the natural lawyer of the three, but for the

---

[1] Not until 1918 was education to the age of fourteen made compulsory. In September 1914 Martyn had already passed the normal school-leaving age.

moment there was talk of his becoming a bank clerk. Meanwhile in the initial days at Regency Street, Martyn's help was invaluable, for (after his experiences at Bermondsey) he was the only one who understood the business of milk rounds. No small part of that work was done before the average person's day had even begun. Between 4.30 and 5 in the morning, milk was delivered to their premises in huge churns by wholesalers. This had then to be divided into the deliveries for the four rounds, a horse-drawn cart for one round and barrows for the remainder. While the driver of the milk-cart arrived regularly every morning, this was by no means the case with the rest of the roundsmen and Martyn would often be required. In his own words: 'I would be sleeping, with my brothers, and suddenly hear my father whistling. That meant a roundsman had not turned up and I had got to do the round — half-past five in the morning!'

The name of the dairy was not immediately changed and as Martyn soon became familiar to customers (who recognised that he was not the usual milkman), he was surprised to be addressed as 'Mr Williams'!

Mr Lloyd-Jones' new business made a successful beginning and the fears of the former owner were never realised. The dairy was to flourish and in due course the debts which had brought such a shadow over the family were all repaid. Perhaps it was because he sensed that relief was in sight that Henry Lloyd-Jones sent Martyn back to school, along with Vincent, in January 1915. In any case, Martyn could still do a round, if necessary, before leaving for Marylebone Grammar School. Not infrequently it was necessary, and on at least one occasion some confusion at the dairy even led his father to send an urgent message to the school asking that his son be sent home!

The shop at 7 Regency Street brought many interesting customers, among them a near-neighbour by the name of Miss Brandon who enthusiastically proposed her church to the Lloyd-Joneses — Westminster Chapel, in Buckingham Gate — and only a short walk away. When Martyn delivered milk to the Wellington Barracks he passed its imposing Victorian front. For Henry Lloyd-Jones it had recommending features: it was Congregational, for example, and its fifty-one-year-old minister, George Campbell Morgan, was famous for the way in which he had turned a cause which had been the despair of the denomination into the city's foremost Nonconformist

5. *Henry Lloyd-Jones at 7 Regency Street, Westminster.*

6. *Dairy roundsmen.*

pulpit. But the family was already committed to continuing with the Calvinistic Methodists or Welsh Presbyterians (a synonymous term) and had joined one of the oldest and best-known chapels of that denomination, at Charing Cross Road. The ardent Miss Brandon, however, was not to be easily put off and Martyn recalled the day in 1915 when she arrived at their home 'to try to persuade us as a family to join Westminster Chapel'. Her visit to Regency Street was a failure, and yet, perhaps, not entirely so, for in the course of 1915 Martyn, along with one of his brothers, made one visit to Westminster Chapel. One of Campbell Morgan's friends was Dr Thomas Charles Williams, the great contemporary Welsh preacher, who, as already noticed, had attended the Association at Llangeitho in 1913. He normally preached at Westminister at least once a year (commonly staying with Lloyd George in Downing Street!) and it was on such an occasion that Martyn made his first visit to Westminster Chapel. After the service the congregation was invited to meet Dr Williams in the large Institute Hall and the two boys were gratified to speak to him in Welsh!

Thereafter, once or twice, Martyn heard sermons by Campbell Morgan. He also tried to go to Westminster Chapel whenever Williams was visiting there, but Charing Cross Chapel was his decided preference. If this Welsh Calvinistic Methodist Chapel was not Cardiganshire, at least it provided a cross-section of London's Welsh-speaking community and a centre for both religious and social life. In the fine building erected in 1887 there were Literary and Debating Society meetings on Friday nights in which he was subsequently to join, and on Sundays, besides the usual services, Sunday School for all age groups (in the Welsh tradition) and the practising of hymn tunes at the end of the day. There was no choir, for the whole congregation was expected to sing!

There was much about the minister at Charing Cross, the Reverend Peter Hughes Griffiths, which appealed to Martyn. For one thing, he was an original character and an individualist. With his shock of black, well-groomed hair, his morning coat, his Gladstone collar and flat, black, cravat type of tie with a gold pin in the centre, Griffiths did not look much like the average Welsh minister. Out of doors he wore a silk hat. He certainly did not wear such things out of deference to London's higher circles, for respect for the establishment was an attitude from which the minister of Charing Cross was wholly free. While still at college he had amazed his fellow students by his indifference to the drudgery of Greek syntax, and when examination time came round, instead of giving the required answer, he calmly wrote, 'See *North and Hillard,* page x!'

Prior to the war, Griffiths was a pacifist (as were many other Non-conformist ministers): once the conflict 'for King and country' had begun pacifism fell silent, but though having to make some adjust-ment to the times, Griffiths never shared in the euphoria which led the country to turn every soldier into a hero. He was shocked at the blasé confidence with which troops sang,

> Pack up your troubles in your old kit bag
> And smile, smile, smile!

At the beginning of the First World War, when county cricket continued as usual, men did not know that it would require five mil-lion Britons in arms before it could end, and that the pre-1914 *'Pax Britannica'* was never to return. Yet even before the slaughter of the Somme and of Passchendaele Martyn's mind was made up:

Those days were horrific days for me; I was glad that I was young enough not to have to face the situation personally. I have never understood the minds and constitutions of men who see war as a romantic thing and who are anxious to join the forces to have a chance to fight and kill. The fact that I had started as a medical student at the age of sixteen years was why I was spared the hor-rible fate. By then there was a scarcity of doctors to such an extent that the boys who had started a course but who had joined the army, were being sent back from France to resume their medical studies. I have given thanks a hundredfold that I was never forced to live in a barracks — that would have been even worse than my lodgings at Tregaron.

One side-effect of the War was to heighten the interest in politics in the Lloyd-Jones' home. Now, however, there was no need to wait for newspapers from London with the latest speeches of the country's leaders, for little more than a quarter of a mile away was the House of Commons itself, and Harold and Martyn were often to be found in the Strangers' Gallery. The Liberals still virtually headed the country in a coalition government formed in 1915, but their leaders, Asquith (the Prime Minister) and Lloyd George, were plainly divided. In that rivalry, which was to lead to the Welshman's becoming Prime Minister, the Lloyd-Jones household, with the exception of his mother, opposed Martyn's enthusiasm for Lloyd George.

Given Martyn's keenness for politics, his parents may have wondered whether the present emphases of his school work were the best for him. When he started at Tregaron he had enjoyed History and English, the novels of Sir Walter Scott being special favourites. By this date, however, almost all his attention was given to science and to subjects related to his anticipated career in medicine.

The results of his summer examinations in 1916 were to show that neither the dairy, nor the House of Commons, had distracted him from his main purpose. A Welsh newspaper, under the heading 'Llangeitho', announced that 'an old Llangeitho boy, David Martyn Lloyd-Jones, at the London University Senior School examination, passed in seven subjects and gained distinction in five'. With such results it was probable that he could gain a place for medical training in any of the best teaching hospitals in London. On his own initiative he wrote to several hospitals for information and then made up his own mind to apply to St Bartholomew's. A preliminary examination and an interview with the Dean proved enough, even at the age of sixteen, to secure him a place among the eighty-two students who began their course on October 6, 1916.

In later years ML-J was never to sympathise with those who looked back to their school-days as the happiest years of their lives. In his memory the time at Tregaron County School and at Marylebone Grammar School was associated with the family difficulties with which he had felt so closely involved after his grandfather's disturbing disclosure in 1911. After that event he was never the carefree footballer who had so troubled the assistant master at Llangeitho by his lack of application. It was as though he by-passed much that is common to youth, which is what he meant when he sometimes said, 'I was never an adolescent.' How uncertain his future life appeared to him is probably illustrated by a verse of Matthew Arnold from *Sohrab Rustum*, which he wrote in the album of his school-friend William Evans at Tregaron, in July 1914:

> For we are all, like swimmers in the sea,
> Pois'd on the top of a huge wave of Fate,

Which hangs uncertain to which side to fall.
And whether it will heave us up to land,
Or whether it will roll us out to sea . . .
We know not.

7. Martyn in a characteristic position.

8. *The Square at St Bartholemew's Hospital, London.*

THREE

The World of Medicine

A short walk from St Paul's, from Newgate and Aldersgate Streets, St Bartholomew's Hospital stood in the centre of the old city of London. Within its buildings Cromwell's injured troops had been nursed in the 1640s; outside its walls, at the time of the Reformation, the Protestant martyrs had died in Smithfield, and it was more than a hundred years before that when the hospital first began its work of healing among London's poor. In 1916 the principal part of the hospital, with some 600 beds, still consisted of the four buildings around a square, built in the mid-eighteenth century. To enter its 1702 gateway was to enter a world quite as distinct and influential as that of any ancient university.

But it was Bart's doctors, not mere antiquity, which made the hospital what it had become, with a distinguished line of physicians and surgeons going back to the sixteenth century. John Abernethy was the first to give a regular programme of lectures to students and by the time of his death in 1831 Bart's had the largest Medical School in London. New buildings for the school were put up in 1879–80. Abernethy, and the hospital 'chiefs' who followed him, had airs and habits of pungent speech which placed them rather above the common race of mortals. It was not only students who could receive their summary treatment. Once when the famous Duke of Wellington, intent on seeing Abernethy and arriving at his room unannounced, was asked how he got in, 'By the door', was the reply. 'Then,' said the doctor, 'I recommend you to make your exit by the same way.' The same man is said to have refused to attend King George IV until he had first delivered a lecture! Both the medical brilliance and the authoritarian manners of the Bart's chiefs contributed in no small measure to the ethos into which each new generation of students entered. The biographer of one of the hospital's chiefs, writing about the period when Lloyd-Jones was a student, says:

> Bart's doctors, like graduates of Trinity College, Cambridge, acquire a feeling that membership of their institution is alone enough to set them somewhat apart, that they are not as other men are; but even allowing for this 'consciousness of effortless superiority', the galaxy of medical talent deployed at Bart's during the first forty years of the twentieth century was an exceptionally splendid one.[1]

Martyn Lloyd-Jones' first impressions of Bart's are unrecorded. Almost all we know is that his friendships made in these early years were warm and lasting, even though opportunities of meeting were later to be few and far between. He was popular among his fellow-students and respected for his undoubted ability. One early photo from this period — hardly printable except in a medical text-book — shows him at work in the post-mortem room. He clearly imbibed the common Bart's opinion that, in the words of Sir Norman Moore, 'the best physicians were all morbid anatomists, who regarded the post-mortem room as the place from which, after the wards, a physician should fill his mind, and where he should acquire a familiarity with the interpretation of symptoms and the course of diseases'. Even when he was only on the first rungs of the ladder he knew clearly where he wanted to be.

Martyn's commitment to medicine gave him exemption from military service, unlike his elder brother, Harold, who, having begun to study law at Aberystwyth, was called up to join the Royal Welsh Fusiliers. But to some extent the War itself came to London. He recalled:

> We saw many things happening for the first time ever during the War. One event was seeing the first Zeppelin to attack London. Strangely enough, instead of looking for a hiding place, we all used to run out into the street to stare at the Zeppelin and the

[1] Mervyn Horder, *The Little Genius, A Memoir of the First Lord Horder*, 1966, pp. 15-16.

searchlights playing on it, making it look like a huge illuminated cigar in the sky. I also remember the first daylight raid by an aeroplane. The first bomb fell on a Saturday morning quite close to St Bartholomew's Hospital where I was a student, and I rushed there to give a helping hand. Then there was one memorable Sunday night. We had gone upstairs to bed when suddenly the northern sky became as red as a sunset for some minutes and then the colour faded out. Simultaneously there was a victorious shout to be heard with people running out into the streets rejoicing. Lieut. Leif Robinson had managed to shoot down the first Zeppelin above Cuffley, near Potters Bar.

Next to home and hospital, the most important thing in his life at this date was Charing Cross Chapel. It had so happened that on the very first Sunday that the Lloyd-Jones family came to their new church they occupied a pew immediately in front of the Phillips family who were to play such a major part in subsequent events. Dr Tom Phillips belonged to Newcastle Emlyn, where his father, the Rev. Evan Phillips, had been the much-esteemed minister of Bethel Calvinistic Methodist Chapel for more than fifty years and among the foremost leaders in the 1859 Revival in Wales. By the autumn of 1914 Tom Phillips had been in London for more than twenty years and had become a well-known eye specialist. David Lloyd George was one of his patients. With his wife, their eighteen-year-old son, Ieuan, their sixteen-year-old daughter, Bethan, and ten-year-old son, Tomos John, they were never missing from their seats at Charing Cross, even though their home at Harrow was some twelve miles out of London. Bethan was to remember the appearance of the three boys as the new family arrived in the pew in front of them, Vincent, in the younger style, wearing his Eton collar outside his jacket. She was unaware that Martyn had already admired her from a distance at Newcastle Emlyn, probably on some market-day in his early youth, while accompanying his grandfather from Llwyncadfor.

Bethan was to start the study of medicine at University College the same day that Martyn started at Bart's in 1916: over the next nine years there were to be periods of friendship and association between them interspersed with considerable intervals. For one thing, despite their initial parity in medicine, it was difficult for her to forget that Martyn was eighteen months her junior. He was to find friendship with Ieuan Phillips an easier proposition and before long the two were to become close friends. In the first instance, however, it was Dr Tom Phillips who was to play a major part in Martyn's life once the young medical student joined his Sunday School class in 1917. Henry Lloyd-Jones had always encouraged his sons to debate public issues amongst themselves in the home, and in the open kind of class which Tom Phillips conducted Martyn was soon in his element. Speaking of Dr Phillips' class (in which he was to remain until 1924) he said:

> The arguing was keen and sometimes fierce every Sunday afternoon, and very often he and I were the main speakers. I have argued a lot, and with many men during my lifetime, but I can vouch that I have never seen his like from the point of view of debate and the swiftness of his mind. He, my brother Vincent, and Dr David Phillips of Bala, are the three best debaters that I have ever met and my debt to the first two is very great. There is nothing better for the sharpening of wits and to help a man to think clearly and orderly, than debating, and especially to debate on theological and philosophical topics.

Before the end of the War the family circle was again complete as Harold had been invalided out of the army on account of a heart condition. His condition soon improved and he looked forward to the legal career upon which he now embarked. Verses from his pen, which appeared in the well-known periodical, *John o' London's Weekly*, also revealed his considerable poetical gifts.

One Sunday morning in June 1918 Martyn awoke to find himself dizzy and unable to stand up. He was a victim of the great flu epidemic which was to claim so many lives. On the Tuesday Harold went down with the same infection and never recovered. At the age of twenty he was buried in a parish graveyard near Llwyncadfor on July 1, 1918. A new grave, that of David Evans, his grandfather, was alongside. The master of Llwyncadfor, with whom the boys had spent so many memorable childhood days, had died the previous year.

Four months later came the end of the War. As soon as Martyn Lloyd-Jones heard of the signing of the Armistice on November 11 he laid aside any more thought of work that day at Bart's:

> I went at once from the hospital in the direction of Westminster. I heard, after arriving there, that the members of the House

of Commons intended crossing the road to a short service of thanksgiving in St Margaret's Church. I, like many others, was allowed by a policeman to stand and watch the procession, and at about three o'clock they came, with Lloyd George and Asquith walking together at the front. In December I stood on my feet for about four hours to catch a glimpse of President Woodrow Wilson of the USA going past in an open carriage with King George V. I was a bit of a hero worshipper in those days, and I still tend to be so. But alas! the heroes have become scarce.

The earliest letter of Martyn's to survive was written to his mother, who was on holiday near Newcastle Emlyn, on July 18, 1919. Its contents are of little moment but they give some idea of the horizons of every-day thought in the life of a medical student:

> St Bartholomew's Hospital London, E.C.
> Friday

My dear Mamma

Again I am writing without having much news to give you. I would have written earlier in the week but for the fact that I have been extremely busy. As I think I pointed out before, I was on duty over the weekend so that I was kept very busy until Wednesday. Since then also, I have been very busy with operations to attend etc. Added to these I caught another nasty cold last weekend, so that I have been feeling very tired. However, it is much better by now; with the rest over this weekend, I hope to be all right once more.

I am very glad to hear that you are enjoying yourself so much, and I suppose that you have been to Llangeitho by now.

I do not know exactly how I am going to spend tomorrow. I feel that in view of my cold it would perhaps be advisable for me not to play tennis as it might get worse. At the same time I do not feel like standing in the crowd watching the procession. Of course, the peace celebrations will not make much difference to you down there . . .

Martyn Lloyd-Jones reached the first goal of his medical studies in 1921, taking his M.R.C.S. and L.R.C.P. degrees in July and his Bachelor of Medicine and Bachelor of Surgery (M.B., B.S.) in October, with distinction in Medicine. There was another reason, besides examinations, which was to make the year 1921 a vital one in his whole medical career. For the first time he began to work under Sir Thomas Horder, a doctor whose name must stand in any list of Bart's most brilliant men.

While still in his thirties, Horder's call to the sickroom of King Edward VII in 1910 had established him as one of the most sought-after men in private practice in Harley Street. This practice he conjoined with duties at Bart's where he became Physician to the Hospital in the same year that Lloyd-Jones qualified. It was, as Horder's biographer says, the entrance to the peak years of his life and work in clinical teaching. Prior to that date the medical student from Regency Street, Westminster, had seen comparatively little of Horder, as he had worked in a different firm from that of which the latter was chief.

An incident in 1920 first brought Lloyd-Jones to Horder's notice. According to the usual practice, Lloyd-Jones had one day examined and made a diagnosis of a patient allocated to him as a student in the out-patient department. The same patient was later seen by Horder on a teaching round with a group of students, and he expressed surprise at the diagnosis which Lloyd-Jones proposed. Its correctness was dependent upon being able to feel the patient's spleen — something which Lloyd-Jones professed to be able to do even when Horder twice failed. Not surprisingly the gathered students supported their chief's judgment, in part, no doubt, because they knew that a mistake could bring down upon them some caustic witticism quite as pungent as anything ever uttered by Abernethy. 'Let me see, Mr Smith', Horder said one day to a student. 'What is the cause of this disease?' 'Well, sir,' the young man responded, 'I did know but I have forgotten.' 'A pity,' exclaimed the chief, 'because now no one knows!'

For a different reason Lloyd-Jones had himself had a similar uncomfortable encounter with Horder on an earlier occasion. It was one of those days, which still occurred, when some emergency at the dairy had caused him to rise very early before he went on to Bart's. There one of his first duties was attendance at Horder's out-patients' clinic where he arrived half asleep only to be faced with one of the chief's piercing questions which he scarcely heard. To the merriment of his fellow students Horder at once pulled his leg as he hesitated and dithered. It was different, however, on the day to which we are now referring in 1920. In full possession of his senses, Lloyd-Jones

stood by his diagnosis, and when a few days later he was proved correct by the course of the patient's illness, Horder's interest in him was
established.

In 1921, when it came to the time of making hospital appointments,
which was before the results of the October M.B., B.S. examination
were known, Horder took the unusual step of going outside his own
firm to appoint Lloyd-Jones as his Junior House Physician. Two previous house physicians of Horder's were disappointed that he had
overlooked another man whom they had advised him to choose.
'Wouldn't I have looked a fool if I had appointed your man instead of
mine', the Chief told them, once the distinction which Lloyd-Jones
had gained in his M.B., B.S. became known.

Lloyd-Jones' subsequent years with Horder were to make a deep
impression upon him. After a year as House Physician there followed two years, 1923–24, as Horder's Chief Clinical Assistant, by
which time he was also associated with his private practice. In 1924
at Horder's instigation he was the first to benefit from a scholarship
from the R. L. St John Harmsworth Memorial Research Fund, in
order to undertake important research work on sub-acute bacterial
endocarditis, a condition affecting the inner lining of the heart which
Sir William Ostler and Horder had first described in 1909. It was this
research work[2] which later gave rise to the often repeated misunderstanding that he had been a heart specialist. In fact, like his chief, it
was always his first love to be a general physician.

Horder's influence upon him lay chiefly in the manner in which he
thought and taught. Notwithstanding the number of distinguished
men — physicians, surgeons, and professors — whom Dr Lloyd-
Jones had met at Bart's it was his opinion that 'Horder was quite on
his own.'

> The most astute and clear thinker that I ever knew was my old
> teacher, Lord Horder. This was the chief element in his outstanding
> success as a doctor. He was a thorough diagnostician and after he
> had collected his facts, he would reason until he reached his diag-
> nosis. His method was to work always from first principles, never
> jumping to conclusions. Having gathered all the data on a patient

[2] Part of the results of his research was published under the title, 'An Experimental
Study of Malignant Endocarditis', as an appendix in *Bacterial Endocarditis*, C. Bruce
Perry, 1936.

he would then set up all possible explanations for his illness like a group of skittles. These he proceeded to 'knock down' one by one, as objections were applied to them, until there was only one left.

Often, in dealing with cases, Horder was able to go through this process with such speed that he became known, in the words of the poet T. S. Eliot, as 'The Little Genius'. This was the case, for example, in 1910 when, after one of the royal physicians, Dr Samuel Jones Gee, had called him in to advise on the chest condition of King Edward VII, it had seemed as though a mere glance at the King's full ash-trays had been enough to lead him to identify the cause as nicotine poisoning. There were far more difficult cases which Lloyd-Jones was to see his chief deal with effectively. When, for instance, four or five distinguished specialists had failed to diagnose the gasping for breath of a rich Welsh coal-owner in 1923, Horder — by no means univer-sally popular among his colleagues — was called in. As he arrived to make his examination one of these men was heard to exclaim with some relish, 'Well, Horder will soon find this is where he gets off.' Instead within a few minutes, the Bart's physician was pointing to the evidence for a pleural effusion.

The Chief Assistant, who was frequently with him on such cases, knew that Horder's success was not the result of any magic. As usual, Horder was working from first principles. On his teaching rounds Horder would constantly demonstrate the process with his students — often 'grooming' them by close questioning in the 'Socratic' trad-ition of instruction. He aimed to demonstrate that mastering 'the elements of precise thinking and precise expression of thought' was equally important with mastering the elements of clinical medicine. In the extent to which he did this he exceeded many of his older colleagues, and it was characteristic of him that one book which he constantly urged on his students was not a medical text-book but William Stanley Jevons' *The Principles of Science: a Treatise on Logic and Scientific Method.* It was a mark of Horder's affection for Lloyd-Jones that he was to pass on to him his own copy of Jevons, bought in 1893 and carefully annotated in pencil.

For Dr Lloyd-Jones the benefits of working with Horder abun-dantly compensated for the excessive demands on junior colleagues which the chief could sometimes make. There was one occasion, for example, when Sir Thomas was so late in preparing the material for some important public lectures which he was giving, that Lloyd-Jones and another junior member of staff had to have permission to remain in the Bart's library late into the night pursuing quotations and references which would be needed the next day. The work was not completed before the research colleague collapsed with exhaustion and had to be removed to a ward where Lloyd-Jones revived him with brandy! A considerably larger task Lloyd-Jones had to take on single-handed in 1923 when Horder, now aged fifty-two, found his powerful memory was not always reliable in recalling the names of the patients suffering from the many and varied diseases which he had treated. Hitherto all Horder's case histories were grouped under the patients' names. What he now wished to have was a second classification under the diseases, and many of Lloyd-Jones' evenings and Saturday afternoons were to be given to the work of preparing this second index.

Yet life was not all hard work at this date. Lloyd-Jones could enjoy lunch-hour musical recitals at St Sepulchre's Church opposite Bart's, or evening theatre or opera visits. The financial difficulties of earlier years were now behind him — a fact perhaps, which his father had in mind on his death in 1922, when he exhorted his sons 'not to forget the poor'. New avenues of social life were also opened up, as Horder, whose patients included many celebrities and national figures, frequently invited him to join the circle who enjoyed the stimulating conversation and the *bonne vie* of Ashford Chace, his country estate at Petersfield, Hampshire. One early invitation to 'Dear Lloyd-Jones' (August 24, 1924) read:

> The time flies away and I must not delay asking you to come to see us for a night, — because I am due to go to Scotland on the night of 28th can you come here on Tuesday evening, to return with us on Wednesday, or, if we are too full in the car, by train? There is a good train leaving Waterloo 4.50 and arriving Petersfield 6.23. I will meet that train in the car if I hear that you can come.

Before Lloyd-Jones took his postgraduate examination for the Membership of the Royal College of Physicians in April 1925, the final examination which it was possible for him to take, his reputation in the medical world was already beginning to be established. Other Bart's chiefs, including Sir Thomas P. Dunhill and Sir Bernard

Spilsbury, took a close interest in his future. Spilsbury, who was Chief Pathologist to the Home Office, sought to draw him into his own private practice. The invitation was declined, though Lloyd-Jones admired the man whom he met so often in the post-mortem room.

Contemporaries of Dr Lloyd-Jones at Bart's have recorded memories of his days in medicine. Dr C. Langton Hewer, then a junior anaesthetist, recalls: 'I got to know Dr Lloyd-Jones as a brilliant scholar and teacher of medicine and also as a music lover. I used to go with him sometimes in the lunch hour to St Sepulchre's Church opposite Bart's where they had a first-class organist.' Sir Geoffrey L. Keynes, one of Bart's leading surgeons of the twentieth century, wrote in 1980: 'I was very friendly with Martyn Lloyd-Jones when we were both working as Chief Assistants at St Bartholomew's Hospital in the early 1920s, he on the medical side, I on the surgical. I greatly admired his intellectual approach to Medicine as a profession. I was not the only one of his friends to have these feelings and to appreciate also his humanity as a doctor.'

9. A firm at Bart's, ML-J second from left, middle row.

FOUR

'All Things New'

Psychology, in which Martyn Lloyd-Jones became interested at Bart's, taught him that the opinions which a man expresses, instead of being purely the results of his voluntary decisions, are rather the consequence of prejudices which arise from previous conditioning factors. Thus in his own case, it might be said, he was ready to argue for Christian opinions because of the formulating influences present throughout his upbringing. In February 1914, at the suggestion of their minister, all three Lloyd-Jones brothers had professed their faith and become communicant members of the Calvinistic Methodist denomination before they left Llangeitho. Once in London, as we have seen, the affiliation was strongly maintained and Martyn, at the unusually early age of eighteen, was Superintendent of the whole Sunday School at Charing Cross Road for one year. He was certainly conditioned to think of himself as a Christian. Of course, neither he, nor his religious teachers, would have expressed this in merely psychological terms. They would have seen it as a God-appointed process in virtue of which we become Christians by family ties and by church connections.

In fact, as Martyn Lloyd-Jones entered his early twenties, he was brought to an entirely new opinion. It was an opinion which owed virtually nothing to the events in his life which we have so far considered. Contrary to the thought of both home and chapel, he was now to come to the belief that so far he had never been a Christian at all. 'For many years I thought I was a Christian when in fact I was not.

It was only later that I came to see that I had never been a Christian and became one. But I was a member of a church and attended my church and its services regularly.'

To his contemporaries the conditions producing such a major change of opinion were not easy to see. As we have already said, his spiritual change, far from being the product of his regular religious education, was clean contrary to the assumptions which that education had instilled. Peter Hughes Griffiths, the minister at Charing Cross, had more sympathy with evangelical Christianity than the minister of Llangeitho, yet he had the same propensity to treat all his hearers as Christians and in consequence his preaching also made little appeal to the mind or conscience. Instead of theology or exposition, Griffiths supplied an abundance of anecdotes and illustrations. Feeling and sentiment were what he aimed at, and not without effect; as, for example, with such themes as 'A Mother's View of Things' based on Isaiah 66:13 ('As one whom his mother comforteth, so will I comfort you'). On that occasion Martyn Lloyd-Jones saw the whole congregation dissolve into tears.

Commenting on this situation, Martyn Lloyd-Jones was later to say: 'What I needed was preaching that would convict me of sin and make me see my need, and bring me to repentance and tell me something about regeneration. But I never heard that. The preaching we had was always based on the assumption that we were all Christians, that we would not have been there in the congregation unless we were Christians.'

If chapel life does not explain Martyn Lloyd-Jones' spiritual change, far less does any influence which he encountered at Bart's. That he became a Christian while at the hospital, and about the time that he was Horder's Chief Clinical Assistant, was in spite of his location, not because of it. William Hogarth's painting of the pool of Bethesda still adorned the main staircase of the eighteenth-century buildings, but not much of the influence of the Scriptures remained at Bart's in the 1920s. Medicine and biblical Christianity had parted company. None of the chiefs to whom Lloyd-Jones was closest was a Christian. Horder was an avowed rationalist and a vigorous exponent of what would now be called scientific humanism. The common belief was that modern knowledge, not least the recognition of evolution, had made historic Christianity untenable. Even in the Christian

Union at Bart's (at that time run by the Student Christian Movement) the concessions made to modern thought were so large that Lloyd-Jones, even before he was a Christian, regarded attendance there as worthless.

It might seem, then, that in Dr Lloyd-Jones' case, the argument that 'belief' is the result of a prior 'conditioning' breaks down. But was this really so? Though his new faith did not come from the areas we have mentioned, yet he was *led* to it. It was no mere voluntary and irrational whim which was to make him different, rather he had been prepared and brought by influences which at length proved irresistible.

The earliest of these 'influences' had to do with the events which even as a child impressed upon him the very uncertain and changing character of life in this world. The home which he saw burned down in the night when he was ten years old was the third in which he had lived, and, not only did he never feel 'settled' in the new house which followed, he became conscious that this world itself can provide 'no continuing city'. After the sudden death of his brother Harold, with whom he had done so much, in 1918, he could say, as Edmund Burke once said in similar circumstances, 'What shadows we are and what shadows we pursue!' The death of his much-loved father, four years later, reinforced the same truth.

A further powerful factor in his life was an acute awareness, of which he had been conscious from childhood, of 'destiny' standing behind events. Shakespeare's famed axiom, 'There's a divinity that shapes our ends, rough hew them how we will', he understood, and he could never doubt that his deliverance from the fire of January 1910 was all part of a higher purpose. In the words of a Welsh hymn which he used to sing in Llangeitho Chapel,

> There must have been some silent providence . . .

He also began to see this same destiny in past history and especially in the story of the Christian church. The Llangeitho Association meetings of 1913 first awakened his attention. Just a few weeks after that event, as he had stood in the playground at Tregaron at the end of the summer term, his history master, S. M. Powell, thrust something into his pocket with the abrupt instruction, 'Read that!' It was a penny booklet on the ministry of Howell Harris, one of the foremost figures in the eighteenth-century revival in Wales. This was his first reading in the history of Calvinistic Methodism — a history from which he was to gain a distinct view of the majesty and power of God. This new interest was greatly confirmed when, while reading the Scriptures at the age of seventeen, he came to see the truth of predestination — that doctrine which places all things under the rule of God's eternal throne. Thereafter he was eager to expound his 'discovery' both to his family and in the Sunday School class of Dr Tom Phillips at Charing Cross Chapel, where it often came to be debated. Once, on a holiday with his brother Vincent and a friend at Craven Arms, in the home of an uncle, a discussion on predestination began after lunch one day. It was still continuing when tea was brought in and finally concluded late in the evening, but only after Vincent had lost his voice!

Early in 1923 Dr Lloyd-Jones began to hear sermons which, though not distinctly evangelical, added something to his understanding. This was at Westminster Chapel. After Campbell Morgan resigned in 1917, his successor John Henry Jowett (1863–1923) had struggled with poor health and a declining congregation before preaching for the last time on December 17, 1922. Shortly after that date ML-J made one of his periodic visits to hear Dr T. C. Williams who was again filling the Westminster Chapel pulpit. At this service he was interested to learn of the new minister, a Scot by the name of Dr John A. Hutton, who was due to begin his pastorate on the following Sunday. Martyn again varied his customary church attendance to hear Hutton the next week and he was at once impressed with the fifty-three-year-old Scot — indeed so gripped was the entire congregation that an unintentional wave of the preacher's hand as the sermon closed brought everyone to their feet! 'This man's preaching appealed to me tremendously,' Lloyd-Jones later recalled. 'I often listened to him. I think I listened to him most of the Sunday mornings that he was here.' Hutton's preaching was uneven in effect. He was not expository, and his best efforts were occasional rather than regular; but he added something more to Lloyd-Jones' thinking, 'He impressed me with the power of God to change men's lives.' He believed in rebirth and regeneration. Hutton's young medical hearer already knew that God plans and purposes, he was now becoming aware that he also acts and intervenes. At Westminster Chapel he was aware of a sense of spiritual reality which he missed at Charing Cross.

The most powerful influence of all in Dr Lloyd-Jones' complete change of direction has still to be stated. It was the fact of sin, the evidence that something is profoundly wrong with man himself. He observed it among London's poor with whom he had often to mix while at Bart's. In particular, while undertaking his student training in obstetrics in some of the roughest areas of Islington he met with conditions of ungodliness of which he had no conception in rural Cardiganshire. And yet what he saw in Islington was by no means so decisive in affecting his thinking as was the close contact which he came to have in the 1920s with people at the opposite end of social life. After all, wrong-doing among the poorer classes was, so it was said, readily explicable: it was merely a problem of education, housing and economic improvement. Change their conditions and their environment and all would be well! Precisely the same philosophy, taken up by politicians and by the League of Nations, was going to reconstruct the world and prevent any future war. But if that theory were correct — that is, that man is morally neutral and only needs help and education in order to be good — it ought to have been demonstrated among Horder's patients who often represented the best of the land from among the wealthy and the great. Certainly the patients of the King's Physician who came to Horder's rooms at Harley Street were neither deprived nor uneducated. Three Prime Ministers were to be numbered among them, and many of the leading intellectuals, writers and musicians of the day. As Lloyd-Jones moved with his chief in these circles he found such people altogether as needy as any whom he had seen in Islington. Their basic need was still untreated; for once, Horder's diagnoses did not go far enough. This lesson never came home to Lloyd-Jones more forcefully than it did in 1923 when, as mentioned earlier, he had to spend a number of weeks re-classifying his chief's case histories under their respective diseases. Horder's notes revealed that perhaps as many as 70 per cent of his private cases could not be classified under recognised medical criteria at all. 'Eats too much', 'Drinks too much' and similar comments, pointed to signs and symptoms with origins normally outside the province of medicine. Strange though it may sound, it was in a temple of scientific humanism — Horder's clinic — that Lloyd-Jones was helped to see the fallacy of the argument that modern man is so different from his forebears that historic Christianity is no longer relevant. He discovered that man in his fundamental need of a changed relation to God had not changed at all: 'All the changes about which men boast so much are external', he observed. 'They are not changes in man himself, but merely in his mode of activity, in his environment.' The real problem which he now saw written large on Horder's case notes was neither medical nor intellectual. It was one of moral emptiness and spiritual hollowness. Horder's card index was to him almost what the vision of a valley of dry bones was to the prophet Ezekiel.

Nor did it escape his attention that nominal religion gave no help to these patients. The idol of his youth, David Lloyd George, had ceased to be Prime Minister in 1922, by which time his faith in him was already dead. Lloyd George was followed in the premiership by Andrew Bonar Law — another of Horder's patients whose very Christian names reflected his upbringing. At the time of his birth in 1858, his mother, the wife of a Free Church of Scotland minister, had been reading Andrew Bonar's *Memoir of R. M. M'Cheyne.* But when, shortly after coming to power, Law lay dying in 1923, his biographer reports that 'there are no signs that he ever sought consolation in the sombre faith of his ancestors . . . He had too much intelligent integrity to turn in sickness to a creed which had long ceased to carry conviction to him.' Horder's patients indeed represented the mood of the 1920s. What was lacking, as C. S. Lewis has written in a criticism of Rudyard Kipling (another of Horder's circle), was 'a doctrine of Ends'. Life in Kipling's eyes, said Lewis, had lost all cosmic context. 'He has a reverent Pagan agnosticism about all ultimates. "When man has come to the turnstiles of Night," he says in the preface to *Life's Handicap,* "all the creeds in the world seem to him wonderfully alike and colourless."' [1]

Parallel with Lloyd-Jones' observance of the world around him, but ultimately more decisive, was the growing recognition which came to him of his own sinfulness. He began to recognise that sin was much more profound than such acts as are commonly recognised as immoral: there is a wrongness in man's very desires. What the Apostle Paul calls 'the lusts of the mind' — pride, jealousy, envy, malice, anger, bitterness — are all part of the very same disease. Even in the mind, his highest faculty, man has become a fool. As this fact

[1] C. S. Lewis, *Selected Literary Essays,* ed. W. Hooper, 1969, pp. 243-48.

slowly dawned upon Lloyd-Jones at about the age of twenty-three, his estimate of his whole life was changed. The very debates which he had so enjoyed on religious subjects he discovered to be nothing but evidence of his depravity. Preaching in later years on the 'lusts of the mind', he made one of his rare personal allusions when he declared: 'As I was preparing this sermon it filled me with a loathing and a hatred of myself. I look back and I think of the hours I have wasted in mere talk and argumentation. And it was all with one end only, simply to gain my point and to show how clever I was.' He was thinking of the years prior to 1923–24.

But the diagnosis had to go further still. He learned from both Scripture and his own experience that he was actually dead to God and opposed to God. He found the ruling principle of self-centredness and self-interest in his own heart the final proof of his fallen nature and of his wrong relationship to God. 'Sin is the exact opposite of the attitude and the life which conform to, "Thou shalt love the Lord thy God with all thy heart, and with all thy soul, and with all thy mind, and with all thy strength." If you are not doing that you are a sinner. It does not matter how respectable you are: if you are not living entirely to the glory of God you are a sinner.' Giving testimony to his own experience of this truth he was to say:

> I am a Christian solely and entirely because of the grace of God and not because of anything that I have thought or said or done. He brought me to know that I was dead, 'dead in trespasses and sins', a slave to the world, and the flesh, and the devil, that in me 'dwelleth no good thing', and that I was under the wrath of God and heading for eternal punishment.
>
> He brought me to see that the real cause of all my troubles and ills, and that of all men, was an evil and fallen nature which hated God and loved sin. My trouble was not only that I did things that were wrong, but that I myself was wrong at the very centre of my being.

In other words, Dr Lloyd-Jones came to see that his outward life had been little more than play-acting: the real truth was that he had been seeking to escape from God. This knowledge did not come to him in days, nor even weeks. He put no date to his conversion. It was progressive. His later comment was: 'The prerequisite of a path is that it leads to a road. I strayed, I got lost and I grew tired on many paths, but I was always aware, as was Francis Thompson, that the "Hound of Heaven" was on my tracks. At last he caught me and led me to the "way that leads to life".'

It is possible to trace Lloyd-Jones' growing spiritual awareness and understanding in two addresses which he gave at the Chapel in Charing Cross Road in 1924 and 1925 at the Friday evening meeting of the Literary and Debating Society. He had first spoken at these meetings in 1921 on the subject of Modern Education. The meeting of March 1924 is the first address of which his manuscript survives and it gives us direct access to his thinking at that date. With a title, 'The Signs of the Times', his theme was basically serious, namely, the moral chaos of the times, which he proceeded to illustrate from eight different areas: dress (female and male); bathing ('the modern method of installing a bath in each house is not only a tragedy but has been a real curse to humanity'); the rage for degrees and diplomas; newspapers and advertising; the wireless craze; the women of today; nationalism; and finally, the position of the church. By any standards it was a scintillating speech, yet despite its general intention there was probably too much of the personal tastes and humour of the young advocate to subdue and convince those who listened.

The address had included an earnest plea for serious thought, and a charge that the degeneration of the pulpit was the real cause of the weakness of the church; but, spiritually, there was an element of vagueness and indistinctness. The truth seems to be that the young Lloyd-Jones was as yet only half-alert to the message of Scripture. Perhaps, like the blind man at Bethsaida, when partially restored to sight, he might have said, 'I see men as trees, walking' (*Mark* 8:24). Hesitatingly, it may be, faith was in exercise but was not yet professing with Charles Wesley

> Thou, O Christ, art all I want,
> More than all in Thee I find.

When another eleven months had passed and he spoke again to the Literary and Debating Society on February 6, 1925 (shortly after taking the diploma which made him a Member of the Royal College of Physicians), the change was marked. His first intention on this occasion, he told the gathering, had been to give a biblical paper on the subject of predestination, but instead he felt compelled to take up

'The Tragedy of Modern Wales'. The title itself was startling among a people who, as he had alleged the previous year, made such 'great play of nationalism'. The fact was that, in the light of his own spiritual experience, he had gone back to his national history with new insight and was now surer of the message without which Wales, he believed, could not be true to herself. 'It is my love and my devotion to the Wales of the past that makes me talk about the tragedy of Modern Wales.' To give blind praise to Wales and to Welsh virtues might be the habit of politicians but 'to state the truth as it is, is the duty of the true patriot'. Wales' spiritual need, he declared, was his absorbing concern: 'My waking hours are filled with thoughts about her, and in my dreams I cannot escape from her; indeed everything else seems to be relative and subsidiary.'

The address contains many of the features which were to become so common in his later public speaking — a unified argument, penetrating analysis, and forceful application. He saw six principal signs of his country's degeneration:

1. The tendency to judge a man by his degrees and diplomas rather than by his character. 'What degrees,' he asked, 'had Daniel Rowland (Llangeitho), Howell Harris, William Williams (Pantycelyn), John Elias? Is it not pathetic that the nation which produced such men should be found today worshipping at the altar of degrees? That it should have crept into our chapels is still worse.' Education in Wales had replaced real Christianity.

2. The enthronement of financial success as the ultimate goal in life and the love of position and power which is its constant concomitant. 'One of the first remarks you hear these days almost about any man or, at least, one of the first questions asked is, "Is he doing well?" which, being interpreted means, as you well know, "Is he making money?"'

3. The proneness of the Welsh press to blazon forth 'the smallest achievements'. 'We are all "brilliant", at least so the Welsh newspapers say. The form of the paragraphs is well-known to you and reads somewhat as follows: "His numerous friends will be delighted to hear of the success of Mr Johnny Jones in passing the entrance examination into the London and Wales bank. This brilliant young man, etc., etc." — then follows an almost complete genealogical table of the prodigy.'

The speaker then turned, in the fourth and fifth places, to the evidence of national degeneration in the making of public appointments and in the misuse of hymnody. The sanctity of worship, he believed, was disappearing: 'Hymn-singing is to us what a glass of beer is to the Englishman.' Instead of being for God's praise, singing had become an expression of mere sentimentality: 'Is it not time that we sang less and began to think more seriously about life?'

The sixth sign of degeneration he drew from the state of the pulpit, as he had done a year before, but now his words are fuller and stronger:

A nation given wholly to worldly success cannot possibly produce a great pulpit. Preaching today — again please note the glorious exceptions — has become a profession which is often taken up because of the glut in the other professions. I have already referred to the method adopted in the choice of ministers and we are reaping what we have sown. It is not at all surprising that many of our chapels are half-empty, for it is almost impossible to determine what some of our preachers believe. Another great abomination is the advent of the preacher-politician, that moral-mule who is so much in evidence these days. The harm done to Welsh public life by these monstrosities is incalculable. Their very appearance in public is a jeer at Christianity. Is it surprising that the things I have already mentioned are so flagrant with all these Judases so much in evidence? We get endless sermons on psychology, but amazingly few on Christianity. Our preachers are afraid to preach on the doctrine of the atonement and on predestination. The great cardinal principles of our belief are scarcely ever mentioned, indeed there is a movement on foot to amend them so as to bring them up-to-date. How on earth can you talk of bringing these eternal truths up-to-date? They are not only up-to-date, they are and will be ahead of the times to all eternity.

It was this address which first brought Martyn Lloyd-Jones to public attention in Wales, for a reporter of the *South Wales News* had been present and the paper's columns in its issue of February 7 and 9, 1925, deplored the speaker's 'wild and indiscriminate abuse of fellow-countrymen'. A Bank Manager was also given space to voice his protests and, despite a supportive letter from the Reverend Peter Hughes Griffiths, the editor closed the subject on February 14 with renewed censure of the 'young firebrand': 'If Dr Martin Lloyd-Jones talks like this at twenty-five, we tremble to think what he will say about us when he is fifty.'

There was, however, something far more important about this Literary and Debating Society address of February 1925 than anything noticed by the press. Some, at least, who were present could recognise that the lecturer was really preaching and that a living experience lay behind his words. The fact that he was speaking in the basement beneath the church made no difference: there was now a prophetic, authoritative element in his mode of speech which led these hearers to wonder whether the hospital and Harley Street were the right place for him. They did not know that Martyn Lloyd-Jones had already reached a decision upon that subject. A pull far more powerful than that of medicine had entered his life. God had become real to him. The truths which now thrilled him he had rarely heard preached and yet he knew that the same grace which had come to him could bring people everywhere to real Christianity. 'The kingdom of God' was in the world in 1925. In the opening words of Francis Thompson's poem which has that title, Martyn Lloyd-Jones could now say,

> O world invisible, we view thee,
> O world intangible, we touch thee.

Later he would write:

> If you were to ask me to give a definition of a Christian I should say that he is one who, since believing in Christ, feels himself to be the happiest man in the world and longs for everyone else to be equally happy.

10. *The family at Regency Street: Henry and Magdalene Lloyd-Jones, with Harold [front] and Martyn [left] and Vincent.*

FIVE

The Call to the Ministry

O n the Tuesday following his address on 'The Tragedy of Modern Wales' in February 1925, he wrote in a letter to his older friend and future brother-in-law, Ieuan Phillips, then studying at Aberystwyth for the ministry of the Calvinistic Methodist Church:

> You are probably well aware of the fact that I really have a good excuse this time for not answering your exceptionally nice letter long before this. I assume you have seen the *South Wales News* the last few days and can therefore understand that what with people calling and phoning I have had very little time to myself.
>
> Last week, of course, I was well occupied with my paper and I want to tell you some of the facts.
>
> I have already made up my mind as to my future, in fact I did it as soon as I finished with the exam, and I have already had one lesson in Greek. My paper was prepared therefore without any restraint or restriction apart from the fact that I withheld the fact that I intend to practise what I have preached . . .
>
> At Charing Cross on Friday, the paper was received extraordinarily well, better than I had anticipated, for I really felt that it did not do justice to my theme and was in any case necessarily incomplete. The whole of my future life will be devoted to its completion and then I shall not have finished.
>
> The criticisms that appeared in yesterday's paper have naturally served to strengthen my belief in what I have done and what I

propose to do. Oh that I could see you now and talk to you for several hours. I thought of you several times this evening while I was with Bethan. I really think that she is now about as determined about Wales as I am — Ieuan, she almost makes a vital difference to me and yet when she asked me the other day whether she or Wales came first, I had to say that Wales came first. That was certainly the most awful question I have yet been asked during my life. She was great enough to say that she thought still more of me for saying that.

I am now longing for the time to come so that I may start on the way. The beginning which I had intended to be quiet and unobtrusive has, to say the least, been dramatic, hasn't it? It was the very last thing I wished for — but there you are, I have sufficient faith to believe that it is all for the best. They can heap all the personal abuse they like on me, it will make no difference, but I will not tolerate any misrepresentation of the truth . . .

I must now end with a request. Would you be kind enough to send to the hospital some of the papers that have been set in the first paper in Greek, in the entrance examination? The man who is coaching me would like to see them.

Good night, Ieuan, and may he who has guarded you and blessed you until this moment, be with you for ever.[1]

As this letter to his future brother-in-law indicates, ML-J was already learning Greek, with the intention of being able to enter his denomination's Theological College at Aberystwyth. With that in view he went there for an interview in March 1925. But although the Principal, Dr Owen Prys, was delighted to see him, the prospective theological student had not finished his return railway journey to London before he knew that the training offered at Aberystwyth was not for him. Despite the welcome he had received, instinctively he was not drawn to that situation.

Others at Martyn's church at Charing Cross soon came to know of his desire to become a preacher. Some rejoiced, as Ieuan Phillips undoubtedly did. One of this number was a man belonging to the congregation who had been blessed in Wales at the time of the 1904 Revival and who now ran a small hotel near King's Cross. He was among the first to tell him, 'You have got a message for this

[1] *D. Martyn Lloyd-Jones: Letters 1919–1981* (Edinburgh: Banner of Truth, 1994), pp. 4-8.

generation.' Another encourager was a Miss Ellen Roberts who ran a tumble-down mission hall in Poplar, close to East India docks, in the rough East End of London, for the help of down-and-out Welsh people. It was at Poplar about this date that he preached his first sermon. Shortly afterwards he preached again at the Poplar Mission and twice in Welsh in a schoolroom rented in Walthamstow where a Welsh dairy-owner was seeking to start a new cause for his fellow-countrymen.

There were now pressures to face from various directions. His nearest counsellors were not in favour of the radical change in occupation which he was proposing. Peter Hughes Griffiths bluntly told him, 'If I had my time again I would be a doctor'! More serious still, his mother was equally uncomprehending at such an unexpected turn of events. Generally confident that Martyn's judgment was sound, the possibility of his exchanging Harley Street for a pulpit was more than she could accept.

Martyn now found himself in the throes of an intense struggle over whether or not he was right to abandon medicine. It was true he was already established in private practice at Harley Street (with the use of one of Horder's rooms) and he was also still in the midst of important research work at Bart's, the conclusion of which was not in sight. There was also to be considered the Christian influence which he could exercise in the higher ranks of the medical profession open before him. On the other hand, he knew what it was to have experiences which rendered all questions of position and self-interest utterly insignificant. One such experience occurred at Easter 1925 in the small study which he shared with Vincent at their Regency Street home. Alone in that room on that occasion he came to see the love of God expressed in the death of Christ in a way which overwhelmed him. Everything which was happening to him in his new spiritual life was occurring because of what had first happened to Christ. It was solely to that death that he owed his new relationship to God. The truth amazed him and in the light of it he could only say with Isaac Watts,

> Were the whole realm of nature mine,
> That were a present far too small;
> Love so amazing, so divine,
> Demands my soul, my life, my all.

It was in this spirit that he went to a congress of the Union of Welsh Societies at Pontypridd on a Saturday in April 1925 to speak on 'The Problem of Modern Wales'. His address — his first in Wales and delivered from the pulpit of the Pontypridd Baptist Tabernacle — was largely a restatement of what he had said at Charing Cross two months earlier, for, as he reminded the congress at the outset, they had invited him 'to reiterate and to re-emphasise' what he said on that occasion. Before going over his main points, he did, however, comment on some criticisms which had followed his earlier address.

The first concerned the doubts expressed about his patriotism and his alleged incompetence as a resident of London to talk about 'Modern Wales'. Responding to these charges he said: 'It is because I love Wales passionately and devotedly, it is because I am proud of her glorious past and jealous of her future, that I talk about the *tragedy* of Modern Wales . . . I am proud of the fact that I was born and bred in Wales, that I attend a Welsh Chapel in London every Sunday and that I spend every holiday in Wales. These are my credentials — I think they entitle me to an opinion.'

The second criticism was one which he was often to hear in later life, namely, an expression of sympathy with his views followed by a complaint that he was 'too negative' in the way in which those views were expressed, 'We quite agree with you in what you say, but we do not agree with your method of redressing the evil.' Addressing himself to this point he told the congress:

It is a criticism which I can understand and with which I have a certain amount of sympathy. Indeed it appealed to me to this extent, that I hesitated and pondered over the question for some time before I decided or realised that it also was based on a fallacy. Now what is the fallacy? It is, that people who hold that view no longer remember that conviction of sin is the essential prelude to salvation. In other words, I believe that it is one of the most vital functions of all preaching to demonstrate that necessity. It is not sufficient merely to tell a man that he is a sinner — you must prove it to him — give him examples and make him think, then there may be some hope for him.

As Lloyd-Jones went on to review the charges which he had made in February, his statements were sharpened rather than moderated.

On the move away from the Bible which was becoming increasingly prominent in the education given in the University Colleges of Wales he said:

> Our education may teach us that hell does not exist, but death is a surer and sterner master. How much will our degrees and diplomas avail us then? My friends, do let us return to the stern realities of life before it is too late.

Further, he urged that the high regard paid to financial success was evident even in the church itself:

> The possession of wealth counts more even in our chapels these days than does a simple faith in God. If you do not believe me, I ask you all to look in the direction of the *Set Fawr* [2] when you are in chapel tomorrow. It has permeated right through our religious system and, speaking of the Calvinistic Methodists to whom I belong, I have no hesitation in saying that, as a financial organisation, it will bear comparison with the Bank of England itself.

As he had done in London, he treated the state of the church as the ultimate cause of the national degeneration and with the pulpit as supremely at fault. Nonconformity was now in the same kind of mechanical and stereotyped condition as the Church of England was before the eighteenth-century revival:

> Preaching has very largely become a profession. Instead of real Christian sermons we are given second-hand expositions of psychology. The preachers say that they give the congregations what they ask for! What a terrible condemnation both of the preachers themselves and their congregations! Daniel Rowland, Llangeitho used to preach hell. Has there been preaching which has had anything like the effect of his preaching since those days? We know quite well that there has not been. I am one of those who believe that until such men rise again in our midst, our condition — far from improving — will continue to deteriorate. Our pulpit today is effete and ineffective. It is the final touch in the tragedy of Modern Wales!

Before he concluded, Dr Lloyd-Jones introduced one new note, which was not likely to please some of his hearers at this gathering of

---

[2] The 'big seat' or platform beneath the pulpit where the elders sat.

Welsh Societies. After referring to the inability of all political parties to restore a nation's soul, he spoke specifically of the auspices under which they were gathered:

> This movement is out for Welsh Home Rule and in some cases for a Welsh Republic. It believes that the restoration of the Welsh language as the universal language in Wales is vital, is indeed the most important point of all. If we all speak Welsh we shall all be happy . . .
>
> Let us get rid of all injustices by all means, let us fight for the right to manage our own local affairs in our way, but do not let us delude ourselves into believing that we shall be better Christian men and women merely because we speak Welsh and have a parliament of our own. No, what Wales needs above everything today is not a republic but a revival, a revolution in the sense that we turn back to the things, to the one thing that has made us great. By a revival I do not mean a wave of emotionalism, but a great spiritual awakening such as took place in the eighteenth century under the influence and guidance of the Methodist Fathers.

Once the address was over, it was not only the more ardent Welsh republicans who considered that they had reason to be aggrieved. The twenty-five-year-old speaker had first to listen to some criticism from two members of the conference and then an onslaught from the Rev. W. A. Williams whom the chairman had asked to second a vote of thanks to Dr Lloyd-Jones. One Welsh paper, under the heading, 'No Longer a Christian Nation', was to give full coverage to the collision between the two men:

> A devastating indictment of modern Welsh tendencies was made by Dr Martin Lloyd-Jones, a young man of penetrating mind and fearless disposition, hailing from Cardiganshire, but now residing in London. Against him arose a man of mature years and extensive experience of life in the industrial districts of Wales, the Reverend W. A. Williams.
>
> The scene at the close will not soon be forgotten by those who observed it — the young doctor in the pulpit proclaiming the degeneration of modern Wales and the grey-haired preacher in the pew protesting vehemently against what he considered to be a false view of things. It was not a mere battle of words, but a

confident clash of opinions, representing the struggle between the old and the new in the Welsh life of today.

From what he knew of the Welsh pulpit, the Reverend W. A. Williams declared seriously and sincerely that the speaker's conclusions were wrong. There were as good and honest preachers as Daniel Rowland in Wales today, but they preached to a different kind of people and had to face vastly different problems.

There was 'vigorous applause' as Williams at length resumed his seat and still more as Lloyd-Jones rose to reply: 'If', as Mr Williams believed, 'there were as good preachers as Daniel Rowland in Wales today where was the effect produced by their preaching?' Before he could continue, Williams was on his feet with the reply, 'Welsh life is not the same today.' But the objection was swept aside: 'It is not a question of changed conditions. The teaching of Jesus Christ does not vary from age to age. Name me one preacher of the standard of Daniel Rowland?' 'There is Evan Roberts', Williams confidently answered, as he gave the name of the man who had suddenly become famous in the Revival of 1904. Dr Lloyd-Jones' response, 'I would not compare Evan Roberts with Daniel Rowland', brought interruptions from others and the intervention of an astonished chairman who had to remind the conference that discussion was not in order while the speaker was replying to 'the vote of thanks'. But Dr Lloyd-Jones was not prepared to leave the point at issue and pressed on with his challenge to W. A. Williams. Let him point to a preacher in Wales whose ministry was accompanied by anything like the effect produced by Rowland, Harris, and Williams, Pantycelyn: 'I am surprised,' he went on, 'that a minister of religion should say here seriously that there are men of that type in Wales today. Where are the results? They are not to be seen. The membership of most chapels is dwindling and Sabbath observance is rapidly going out of our lives. We see things today that were unknown in the Wales of the past.'

Some of his hearers were far from pacified. The newspaper account reported that at this point:

There were more interruptions from several quarters, and the chairman, declaring that the meeting was going out of hand, said he had never been in a meeting, not even a political meeting, where such interruptions had taken place.

Not a few who heard the visitor from London giving his first address in Wales at the Pontypridd meeting of April 1925 must have recognised that his main emphasis came fresh from his own experience. He knew that God himself must bring men to the truth. We are in God's hands : 'You can never reason at Truth, you can never find it by looking for it. Truth is revealed to us, all we do is to reason about it after having seen it.'

* * *

If the ability to speak, and the readiness of others to listen, had been all that was needed, Dr Lloyd-Jones would have been confirmed by this time in his decision to leave the medical profession. But his difficulties were much deeper than those considerations. He feared that his initial decision to turn to the ministry had lacked the clear guidance of God. Enough had happened since he had written to Ieuan Phillips on February 10 to give him cause to doubt, and how could doubts be consistent with a divine call? Not without much difficulty, he came to the conclusion that he must remain in his present career. In his own words, 'I went through a great crisis and decided I would not do it. I made a solemn decision to go on with medicine.'

There were those around him who felt that he was distressing himself needlessly in viewing the future in terms of either medicine or preaching. The ideal solution, they urged, was to do both: he should remain a physician and preach as opportunities arose. This advice never appealed to him. His view of the ministry was such that he could not conceive of that calling having a second-place in the life of any man. His whole background was against lay-preaching. Calvinistic Methodism had arisen in a generation of men who interpreted literally the apostolic injunction and gave themselves 'continually to prayer and to the ministry of the word'. Whatever he was, he knew he could not be a part-time preacher. Accordingly, the next time he was asked to speak at the Poplar Mission he declined the invitation.

For the greater part of another year, until the early summer of 1926, the issue which he thought was settled in the spring of 1925 would not leave him. In his own words, 'It was a very great struggle, I literally lost over 20 pounds in weight.' Involved in that struggle, and its final outcome, were several incidents of which Dr Lloyd-Jones rarely spoke. Although he was not conscious of it at the time, and despite the spiritual blessing of Easter 1925, an element in his hesitation had come from the degree of attachment which he still felt to the life which he had formerly found so appealing. Experiences through which he had now to pass were to bring home to him yet more powerfully the emptiness of the world's glamour. One of these occurred during the visit of a family friend who had just married and was busy showing his bride the sights of London. 'One night', Martyn recalled, 'they wanted to go to a theatre in Leicester Square and they persuaded me to go with them. I have no idea what the play was about at all, but they were very excited about it. What I remember is this: as we came out of the theatre to the blare and glare of Leicester Square, suddenly, a Salvation Army band came along playing some hymn tunes and I knew that *these* were my people. I have never forgotten it. There is a theme in Wagner's opera *Tannhäuser,* the two pulls — the pull of the world and the chorus of the pilgrims — and the contrast between the two. I have very often thought of it. I know exactly what it means. I suppose I had enjoyed the play. When I heard this band and the hymns I said, "These are my people, these are the people I belong to, and I'm going to belong to them."'

But it was in medicine that Dr Lloyd-Jones had felt the pull of the world most keenly and it was this pull which, in these months of struggle, was finally overcome as he came to see still more clearly the futility of all earthly ambitions. Once more, in this connection, his closeness to Horder was to prove a help. Although the last thing which Sir Thomas intended was to assist Lloyd-Jones spiritually, his actions unintentionally served that end. As Lloyd-Jones explains: 'Horder was very kind to me. He would take me now and again to medical dinners where the top people were present, and I used to hear the mutterings, the criticisms, and the jealousies. It sickened me.' What he saw of life at 'the top' killed any ambition to get there.

There was also an occasion of a different nature, not connected with Horder, which enforced the same lesson. One of the most famous of the chiefs at Bart's was closely attached to a lady friend on the hospital staff and Lloyd-Jones was one of a small circle aware of their relationship. Then with scarcely any warning the woman died. Shortly afterwards Dr Lloyd-Jones was surprised to find the bereaved chief standing at the door of his research room and asking if he might come in and sit by his fire. Probably it was a corner where he knew he would be undisturbed. For some two hours, without a word, the distraught man stared vacantly into the grate until every aspect of the scene was indelibly fixed upon Lloyd-Jones' memory. In his own words, 'That event had a profound effect upon me. I saw the vanity of all human greatness. Here was a tragedy, a man without any hope at all.'

These experiences did more than mortify ambition; they added to the compassion which he now felt for those around him and for those whom he saw daily as he walked the crowded streets of London. Though he might decline to preach at Poplar or elsewhere, Dr Lloyd-Jones found that, as he worked alone at his research bench, he was often preaching to himself. The Bible itself had come alive and its arguments pursued him. If, as he believed, bodily suffering justifies care for people, what kind of concern is warranted for those who are shut out from the presence of God? However much sickness can be alleviated, men must still die, and die deserving hell, unless they be first reconciled to God through Christ. Possibly he had not yet thought much of the words of the Apostle Paul, 'I am debtor both to the Greeks and to the Barbarians . . .' (*Rom.* 1:14), but he felt their meaning and the sense of responsibility which they express. 'A debtor', he once said in a comment on that text, 'is a man who is conscious of certain pressures being brought to bear upon him. He is a man who feels that he has got something to which other people have a right. Paul is a man who has got something to give. He has been given it by the Lord. He has received it; he has got it. It has transformed his life, and he feels that he must give it to others.'

In 1925 Lloyd-Jones knew the same constraint of spirit and it troubled him deeply. A few years later he was to say: 'I used to be struck almost dumb sometimes in London at night when I stood watching the cars passing, taking people to the theatres and other places, with all their talk and excitement, as I suddenly realised that what all this meant was that these people were looking for peace, peace from themselves.'

As already mentioned, it was Dr Lloyd-Jones' custom during these years to go frequently to Westminster Chapel for one service on a Sunday. This he was doing as usual in the summer of 1925, and when Dr Hutton preached for the last time on July 12 before leaving for a preaching tour in the United States, he looked forward to the resumption of his ministry in September. But, to the surprise of all at Westminster Chapel, John Hutton's ministry among them was almost over, because of the death in August of the Editor of the *British Weekly*,[3] the Reverend J. M. E. Ross. The issue of the *British Weekly* for October 8, 1925, announced that Hutton had accepted the editorship and would enter upon his new work the following week. Once more Westminster Chapel was vacant. Dr Lloyd-Jones ceased to attend but his appreciation for Hutton was such that he now became a regular reader of *The British Weekly*, and it was this which brought him to a new area of reading.

He came to this reading, however, not through the principal columns of *The British Weekly*, many of which had little appeal to him, but rather through a few scattered references to the English Puritans which he found in that journal. On the front page of the issue of the *British Weekly* announcing Hutton's appointment was a publisher's advertisement of a new edition of *The Autobiography of Richard Baxter* and this led Dr Lloyd-Jones to read F. J. Powicke's *Life of Richard Baxter 1615–91*. 'The Puritans', wrote Powicke, 'were men sure of God, sure of his will, sure of the absolute duty to act in his sight and for his approval. Nothing else mattered by comparison. Consequences were of no account. Obedience alone held the secret of freedom, courage, peace, power, happiness and salvation. Essentially they were right.' Such was his first introduction to the Puritans and his affinity with them was instant. Baxter's earnestness stirred him deeply and so when Peter Hughes Griffiths asked him to speak again at the final session of the winter meetings of the Literary and Debating Society at Charing Cross in March 1926 he agreed and stated that his subject would be 'Puritanism'.

Despite the youthfulness of the speaker on that occasion, and the small range of his Puritan reading as yet, the address contained a number of perceptive thoughts. The Puritan, he argued, is not 'the

---

[3] The *British Weekly* (founded in 1886) still possessed great influence at this date, being read throughout the British Empire. John A. Hutton (1868–1947) was to remain its Editor until 1946. A first reference to ML-J in its pages was on Feb. 19, 1925 when J. Hugh Edwards MP rejected the case the young man had argued in his address on 'The Tragedy of Modern Wales'.

strong man'. He is: 'a very weak man who has been given strength to realise that he is weak. I would say of all men and women that we are all weak, very weak, the difference being that the sinners do not appreciate the fact that they are weak, whereas the Christians do.' It was this knowledge of their own frailty, he believed, which made the Puritans careful how they lived and led them to avoid all that is doubtful. 'Soberness and restraint are the key-notes of the character of the Puritans. Have you any objection to them? If you have, you cannot regard yourself as a Christian because these are two essentially Christian virtues.'

But this address on Puritanism in March 1926 is chiefly important as an indication of what was going on in the speaker's own spirit at a time when he was in the midst of his struggle over the question of his life work. Had any stranger dropped into Charing Cross Chapel that Friday evening he could have been forgiven for supposing that the slimly built, dark-haired young man was a preacher rather than a medical doctor. And yet it was not preaching which fitted into any type which was common to the 1920s. The main challenge was for a Christianity which exists not in belief only but in 'vital force'; a Christianity which 'does not merely improve a man but rather completely changes him'. Such Christianity, he argued, is not to be found without 'the baptism of the Holy Spirit' and a personal experience of God.

Clearly in Baxter and the Puritans ML-J found an echo of something which he already knew in his own spirit. His deepening sense of sin was a key to the interpretation of their 'soberness and restraint'. In a letter to a friend in 1926, after speaking of the love he received from his mother and from Vincent, he contrasted what 'they think of me' with the reality:

> They see only that which is good in me, they see me only at my best. I shudder when I realise how unworthy I am and how ignorant they are of the dark and hidden recesses of my soul where all that is devilish and hideous reigns supreme, at times breaking through on to the surface and causing a turmoil that God and I alone know of.

There is reason to think that it was this sense of unworthiness before God which was one of the ultimate obstacles to his clear conviction that he was indeed being called to the ministry of the gospel.

And the final resolution of that difficulty was not the removal of his sense of unworthiness, but the persuasion that God loved him, and had saved him, in spite of all that he deserved. Salvation is bestowed wholly apart from any human merit. He saw the gospel more clearly as 'the power of God unto salvation to everyone that believeth', and it was that very sight which led him to understand the Pauline and Puritan 'passion for saving souls'. He knew the real meaning of 2 Corinthians 5:14:

> Paul is like a man in a vice, and the vice is being screwed up and tightened so that he is pressed. What is pressing him? The love of Christ! 'For the love of Christ constraineth us'. This amazing thing — this gospel of reconciliation! This love of God that sends his only Son and even makes *him* to be sin for us. He has seen it, and he wants *everybody* to see it, to participate in it, to rejoice and glory in it![4]

No words explain better than the above what took Dr Lloyd-Jones into the ministry. As well as knowing conviction of sin and a profound sense of unworthiness, he drank at the fountain-head of redeeming love. Speaking of what that love meant to him in the critical years 1925–26 he testified at the end of his life: 'I must say that in that little study at our home in Regency Street, and in my research room next to the post-mortem room at Bart's, I had some remarkable experiences. It was entirely God's doing. I have known what it is to be really filled with a joy unspeakable and full of glory.'

By June 1926 the struggle was over. He knew what the future must be. It was almost as though the decision was made for him and he could resist it no longer. He would later say: 'Whatever authority I may have as a preacher is not the result of any decision on my part. It was God's hand that laid hold of me, and drew me out, and separated me to this work. A preacher is not a Christian who decides to preach, he does not just decide to do it. It is God who commands preaching.'

---

[4] *God's Ultimate Purpose, An Exposition of Ephesians 1:1-23* (Edinburgh: Banner of Truth, 1978), p. 92. The preacher's personal reference is briefer in the printed version than it was at the time the sermon was preached in 1954. On the call to the ministry see his *Preaching and Preachers,* (London: Hodder and Stoughton, 1971), pp. 103-20.

11. Martyn and Bethan on their wedding day.

SIX

Bethan and Aberavon

Along with his commitment to give up medicine there was a second great decision which Dr Lloyd-Jones took in 1926 and which was to influence profoundly his future life and ministry. In June the girl whom he had, from the first, so admired from afar, but whose affections had proved so difficult to secure, accepted his proposal of marriage. Had the choice been solely his the matter would have been settled long before. Bethan Phillips, however, was in no hurry to commit herself to anyone, for her interests and friends were many. Besides, she did not forget that the fourteen-year-old second son of the Lloyd-Joneses who had arrived in the pew in front of the Phillips family in the late summer of 1914 was eighteen months younger than she was, and differences between them did not stop there. Although, for example, Martyn was a moderately competent tennis player — at least at doubles — he did not share her enthusiasm for the game, and his strictures on the 'craze' for tennis left her unimpressed. Through nine years their friendship was never more than occasional, and it was an 'off' period when Martyn spoke to the Literary and Debating Society meeting in 1924. Bethan was not even present on that occasion.

About the summer of 1925 the two happened to meet in Euston Road, Bethan with a tennis racquet under her arm, and the amicable conversation which ensued (without a single argument!) left her wondering. It was a more significant meeting than Martyn perhaps recognised, for he failed to follow it up, as he said he would, with 'an epistle to the Philippians one of these days'! But, when the Easter week-end of 1926 came, he invited Bethan, with two other friends, to hear Dr Hutton who was supplying the pulpit that day in Westminster Chapel. The invitation being accepted, he lost no time that same Sunday in enquiring whether Bethan was free on the following day — a Bank holiday. She was! So on the Monday they went off to visit a country park and, according to Bethan Phillips, never had another argument!

With a mother's insight, Mrs Phillips was the first to recognise that something was happening and she was a ready supporter of Martyn's case. So also was Ieuan Phillips who had never allowed his sister to forget what he thought of the character and abilities of her suitor. After the sole objection that he did not approve of Bethan's absenting herself from Charing Cross for Westminster Chapel — a practice she was not to repeat — Dr Phillips was equally satisfied when he perceived the direction of events! In the week preceding their engagement, Bethan, already qualified (M.R.C.S., L.R.C.P.), obtained her Bachelor of Surgery. On the Thursday of that week (June 16, 1926) Martyn wrote to Ieuan, a letter which speaks first of his trials concerning his call to the ministry and of the forthcoming marriage:

I need not assure you that I have since thought of you daily and longed for your society and your encouragement. For I have indeed passed through trying, not to say crushing experiences. I have been tried to the very marrow but, thank God, I still stand where I have always stood and my faith remains unshaken and unconquerable.

You must have gathered from my last letter that great developments were about to take place. I gave you all details as I well knew that your knowledge of me and of my circumstances would enable you to fill in all the blanks. I therefore merely write to tell you how happy I was, and to let you know that I was prepared and preparing for whatever might happen, full of hope and of faith.

I have been more conscious of the hand of God during the last month than I have ever been before — we count, Ieuan, and count tremendously. Nothing is trivial, nothing is unimportant, everything matters and matters vitally. There is no responsibility except within the kingdom.

Bethan is writing to tell you about our intentions. We are going to get married. That really does not express what is going to happen but you know all that I want to say and somehow cannot.

I know that I am beyond a doubt the luckiest man on the face of the earth at the present moment. It will make no difference to you and me. Being already your brother, that I shall soon be your brother-in-law makes no difference, and yet, as you know, it makes all the difference! I want to preach more than ever and am determined to preach. The precise nature of my future activities remains to be settled, but nothing can or will prevent my going about to tell people of 'the good news'.

I spent a very happy afternoon at Harrow yesterday and I am going there to have a long talk with your father on Saturday. I am indeed overwhelmed with the love and the kindness of your father and mother.

While parental approval was readily given, Martyn meant no official engagement to be announced until he could purchase a ring on the following Tuesday. But at Charing Cross on Sunday, June 18, Bethan's elation was too much to be explained solely by her University success: before the evening service the secret was out and round the whole chapel!

His long struggle over his future calling now ended, ML-J was conscious of several special indications of God's help at this point. For one thing, his mother and Vincent gave him their support. 'They have been simply wonderful', he told Ieuan Phillips. Further, he had found that Bethan Phillips, far from being disappointed at the knowledge that she would not be marrying a Harley Street Consultant, was herself delighted to face a very different future.

In June 1926 the location and precise nature of that future remained unknown. Some things, however, were certain to Dr Lloyd-Jones. He believed that he was not meant to pursue his denomination's course of theological education, leading in a regular way to the pulpit of some well-to-do and long-established congregation. He was also preoccupied with the need for evangelistic work among poorer, working-class people. This conviction arose not simply out of interest in them as people, but equally out of a persuasion that modern Christianity, unlike the apostolic faith (which was as relevant to the 'Barbarians' and to the 'unwise' as to the 'Greeks' and to 'the wise'), seemed to appeal largely to only one social and cultural group. That was evidence to him that the transforming power of real Christianity was largely absent. He wanted to see the message which he believed had been given to him of God tested in a place where social habits did not support church-going. And one more thing was clear to him, namely, that, if it were possible, his first endeavours should be with the spiritual concerns of his own country.

This was hardly a normal mixture of motives in a candidate for the ministry. As he talked the matter over with Peter Hughes Griffiths (his minister at Charing Cross Chapel) the one work which appeared to them as a possibility, if these particular hopes were to be realised, was in the home-mission agency of the Calvinistic Methodist Church, known as 'The Forward Movement'. The minister of Charing Cross undertook to write to the Superintendent of The Forward Movement, the Rev. Richard J. Rees, and ML-J himself wrote requesting an interview.

It happened that Rees was soon to be in London and it was arranged that they should both meet over a cup of tea in a London café at the beginning of the following week.

The work of the Forward Movement had begun in South Wales towards the end of the nineteenth century in an attempt to reverse the dwindling influence of the denomination upon the unchurched. Although it gave financial help and direction to causes which were too weak to be regular charges, it had experienced little success in its principal objective. The early enthusiasm to make the Forward Movement 'a great evangelical instrument' had 'cooled down', as Rees discovered after he was made the General Superintendent in 1922. 'We need men', he pleaded with the Denomination's General Assembly in 1923. This being so, it might have been expected that he would have given an enthusiastic welcome to this unexpected approach from Lloyd-Jones but he had been too long in the ministry to be swept off his feet. Evangelists, it is true, had normally been either men without theological training or divinity students who had failed to get pastorates. Men with University degrees were not expected to be applicants for mission work. Indeed, of the thirty students training for the regular ministry at the denomination's Aberystwyth College in 1925, only eleven were graduates; yet here was a man with four degrees, already working with some of the foremost medical authorities in the country, enquiring if he could be an evangelist! In a Forward Movement cause he might not even have the status of a regular minister for, despite attempts to change the situation, most of the causes were still 'halls' rather than chapels, and were governed by local committees rather than by presbytery-ordained elders.

Thus, when the two men met on June 28, 1926, and Lloyd-Jones spoke further of his concern to volunteer for service in Wales, it was not long before Rees gently expressed his surprise and indicated that the wisdom of the proposal scarcely commended itself to him. But he was pulled up short when his young enquirer exclaimed, 'Really, Mr Rees, why should you be surprised? Don't you believe what you preach?' It was a situation the Superintendent had never been in before — a doctor from Harley Street appealing for a church-extension charge! Perhaps it required a degree of effort on his part to remain non-committal in the face of such earnestness. In any case, the normal procedures necessary for a man to be recognized as a candidate for the ministry had to be followed and it was arranged that the minister of Charing Cross would raise the matter at the forthcoming meeting of the London Presbytery of the Calvinistic Methodists on July 21, 1926.

As usual, that summer, Martyn Lloyd-Jones and Bethan Phillips were both down in the Newcastle Emlyn area for holidays but with a difference. This time they spent most of the days together and the farmhouses which wanted to see the young couple for tea seemed to be endless — on one day alone there were seven or eight such calls to make! There was also time for many walks in the hills and long conversations together about the future. Of these conversations Bethan was to remember, particularly, his commitment to break through the rut of religious respectability, how on fire he was to tell people what Christianity meant, and his wish to be in some 'raw place' where people were conscious of their need. When she asked him what the answer should be for those who said, 'He can do medicine, but how does he know that he can preach?' the immediate reply was, 'I can preach to myself, I know *what* I want to preach and believe I will be able to say it.'

There being no further word from R. J. Rees, Lloyd-Jones wrote to him again on August 24 and received a reply on September 14. The Superintendent did not intend to hurry, nor indeed could he. For, as he repeated in his letter of September 13, the next step lay with the London Presbytery:

Whatever comes of the matter in the future stages outlined by me, I shall be quite prepared, on hearing what the decision and resolution of the London Presbytery are (concerning your application to it for the status of a Preacher) to go further into the matter, if the above is favourable, and arrange an interview here with me and the Directors at the earliest possible opportunity afterwards.

I hope you keep well and that the Divine guidance is being given you fully and clearly. Thanking you for all your confidence and assuring you of my kindest greetings and wishes in all your ways.

Three days later, on Thursday, September 16, following a decision taken on July 21, two members of the London Presbytery visited Charing Cross Chapel to hear the mind of the people on Dr Lloyd-Jones as a candidate for the ministry. In the presence of a good congregation he gave, in the language recorded by the Presbytery, 'a clear and firm statement of his intention and decision to preach Christ's Gospel'. This course was unanimously approved by the members present. That same month he preached once more in his first pulpit, the Poplar Mission in the East End, and it was arranged that he would preach for the first time at Charing Cross on October 10.

The London Presbytery now gave their approval, and although Rees had not formally heard that news when he next wrote, he was now ready to be more definite. He proposed that Lloyd-Jones should take the forthcoming 21st anniversary services of Beechwood Presbyterian Church, Newport, a congregation currently without a minister.

Dr Lloyd-Jones went to Newport and thus preached for the first time in Wales on November 11, 1926. No record survives of the congregation's response but, for his part, Dr Lloyd-Jones was not drawn to the situation. It was more respectable and affluent than the one which he envisaged. Meanwhile another invitation had arrived, this time from E. T. Rees, the Secretary of Bethlehem Forward Movement Church in Aberavon, Port Talbot, asking him to preach for them on Sunday, November 28. A brief reply, accepting the invitation, was to prove the beginning of a new era.

Thus far, Dr Lloyd-Jones — with no definite prospect yet in view — had said nothing to his colleagues at Bart's concerning his intention to leave medicine. Earlier that autumn he was one day crossing the Square at Bart's when Geoffrey Evans, the Assistant Professor of

Medicine, stopped him and disclosed that his post was becoming vacant and that it was almost certain he would be approached and offered the job. ML-J was glad that his mind was already made up before hearing this news. To have succeeded to Evans' post would have led right to the top, but the twenty-five-year old had no regrets.

* * *

The train from Cardiff across Mid Glamorgan to Swansea offers little to attract the attention of the average passenger, not, at least, until that part of the journey begins where the line reaches the coastal strip on the east-side of Swansea Bay and passes through Port Talbot. Here, with the steam and smoke rising in great columns, is one of the largest steel-works in Wales, placed between the sea and the town's narrow streets and brick-built homes. These works of men are necessarily compressed, for immediately behind the town, bracken-covered hillsides sweep steeply skywards in unspoiled beauty. Mountains, town and sea thus lie side by side in impressive contrast.

Port Talbot is very much a nineteenth-century town. A harbour and docks built in the 1830s, importing iron ore and exporting coal, established its reputation. The ore went up the valleys until Port Talbot's own steel works were opened in 1900. By 1926 the industry of Port Talbot had so overshadowed the neighbouring town of Aberavon that the two were virtually one. Houses and streets simply merged together at the western end of Port Talbot. The latter provided work while Aberavon, with its empty sand-hills and beach, gave space for recreation and for more buildings as they became necessary.

Aberavon might scarcely have been known to the rest of the United Kingdom in 1926 had it not been that it gave its name to a Parliamentary constituency. Its Member of Parliament had made history in 1924 by becoming the first Socialist Prime Minister of the United Kingdom. South Wales in the 1920s was in the throes of a revolution of political opinion, and in that revolution the constituency of Aberavon had proved to be a pace-setter when it elected James Ramsay MacDonald, the Socialist Scot, as its representative to Parliament in 1922. The theological liberalism of former years and the broken promises of Lloyd George had opened the way for the post-war generation who came to believe that Socialism and the New Jerusalem belonged together.

Three men stood on the platform of the railway station at Port Talbot on Saturday, November 27, 1926, awaiting the train due at 5.27 P.M. from London. They were E. T. Rees, the Church Secretary of Bethlehem Forward Movement, Trefor Jones (another member of the congregation who had brought his Ford car to the station in honour of the occasion) and the former minister, the Reverend T. J. Lewis, now serving a pastoral charge at nearby Sketty. E. T. Rees was in many respects a personification of Welsh Socialism. Apart from a period during the World War he had lived in Aberavon since his birth, thirty-six years before.

E. T. Rees and Martyn Lloyd-Jones met for the first time when the train pulled in from London. 'We nearly missed him', the former recalled in later years. 'I expected to see some august person in Saville Row clothes and passed by him in his over-coat and bowler hat.' A few minutes' journey took them to the Church Secretary's home on the hillside overlooking the town. The two men, ten years apart in age, presented a considerable contrast, but both could talk, and debate continued late into the evening as Rees steered through such favourite subjects as economics and politics. Rather to his surprise his visitor could both keep up with him and, at certain points, get the better of the argument. At last the different ways in which they both saw the future was wrapped up in a question to Rees from Lloyd -Jones. '"After death what?" he said to me, and the topic we finished with was everlasting life.' The candidate-preacher had already seen what Rees was later to confess, 'I put politics before the gospel and environmental change before personal change.'

Before they walked down to the church together for the first time on the Sunday morning Dr Lloyd-Jones had already received a fair amount of information about the state of the work in correspondence with Mr Rees. Bethlehem Forward Movement Mission[1] had commenced with a school hall, opened in 1897, as a result of the endeavours of two local Presbyterian churches (one Welsh and the other English) which did not see themselves able to reach the large navvy population brought into the district with the building of new docks. The history of the Mission — by 1926 commonly known as 'The Forward' or 'Sandfields' by those who belonged, after the name

---

[1] Although still a Home Mission of the Forward Movement, its 'Mission' title was slowly giving way to 'Church' in the 1920s.

of the district — had been far from even. Seven pastors and one 'evangelist' had come and gone. After an initial success the two pastorates which followed had to be recorded as failures. Again things had advanced in 1907–08, only to fall back under a fifth man until the membership in 1912 had dwindled to 31. With another pastor from 1913 to 1917, there was renewed spiritual quickening. A permanent church building had been erected in 1914 and the membership rose to 130. Once more, however, a set-back followed with a well-intentioned minister who became drawn into politics. When he left in 1921 most of the politically minded who had joined the church because of his influence also departed. Of a diaconate, established in 1907, only one man remained, and what was worse, despite the monthly help from the Forward Movement, the debt which had existed on the church accounts since the beginning was as serious as ever.

It was the financial position which had driven an anxious E. T. Rees to Cardiff early in November 1926, to solicit an increased monthly grant from his namesake, the Superintendent of the Forward Movement. Besides the outstanding debt of £3,000 there was now an overdraft of £220 at the bank. Yet other things beside Sandfields had been on his mind. The same day Wales was to play a leading overseas side in a much anticipated rugby match at Cardiff Arms Park and the interview was so timed as to allow him to do both. Things did not turn out as E. T. Rees expected. He was enthralled to hear from the Rev. R. J. Rees of a young doctor who wished to evangelise in a hard district in Wales, and responded with alacrity to the proposal that Lloyd-Jones should be invited for a Sunday. The Superintendent was far from promising that his settlement with them was likely, or even possible, but (perhaps wishing to discourage the Church Secretary from setting his sights any higher) he was sure a visit would be beneficial: 'Get him to preach at Sandfields, he will be a draw, and this will mean a good collection!' The same afternoon — without seeing any rugby match — the rejuvenated Church Secretary went straight back to Aberavon. In response to Mrs. Rees' query, 'Why are you home so early?' he poured out what he had heard, ending up with, 'Where's the writing pad, my dear?'

Such was the background to the morning of Sunday, November 28. From the moment of his arrival at the station the previous day Dr Lloyd-Jones was drawn to the place and one night was enough to cement the relationship with E. T. Rees. The latter recalls his young visitor warning him quietly on the Sunday morning, 'I hope you don't expect anything great of me.' The truth was that hitherto he had not preached more than some dozen times in all. But Lloyd-Jones was not so quiet as they reached the church and saw a huge poster which the enthusiastic Secretary had put up, advertising their important visitor: 'I don't like that, don't do it again', he told E. T. Rees in authoritative tones that the older man was to hear more of in the memorable service of that first Sunday.

The morning congregation, normally around seventy, was unusually large to hear the unknown visitor preach on 1 Corinthians 2:9, 'Eye hath not seen, nor ear heard, neither have entered into the heart of man, the things which God hath prepared for them that love him.'

At night the congregation was larger still when the text was 1 Corinthians 2:2, 'For I determined not to know any thing among you, save Jesus Christ, and him crucified.'

Contrary to all good Presbyterian procedures although it was, Dr Lloyd-Jones' future pastorate at Aberavon was virtually if unofficially settled that same day. At an 'after-meeting' (customarily held after the evening service) the people were delighted to hear him say, 'I feel this is the place I would like to work in. Will you have me?'

E. T. Rees remembers: 'We came home that night rejoicing. He said to me, "Well, would you like me to be a preacher in Sandfields?" and the impetuous Secretary said, "Like you, certainly! When will you come again?"' Before he left the next day it was agreed he would return, with his fiancée, to preach on Sunday, December 12. Meanwhile in a letter of December 3, E. T. Rees wrote:

This week has been a never-to-be-forgotten one in my life. Your visit last weekend did it. It has passed so quickly, and has been crowded with wonderful things. On Wednesday night we had a church committee and it was unanimously decided — after many kind things had been said concerning you — to recommend you to the church for the 'call', and the following night the Joint Committee (representing the C. M. Churches of the town) adopted you as the man for Sandfields.

Acknowledging this letter on December 6, Dr Lloyd-Jones confirmed what he had already told them and continued:

I am looking forward to our work together with great eagerness. Your letter of this morning has naturally filled me with joy and hope. Of course, I realise fully the seriousness of the commission which I am taking up, but it is a high adventure and a crusade of hope. Whatever may happen, our cause must triumph, and if we fail (which God forbid!) what we stand for will go on and will in the end prove supreme. That is the spirit in which I am taking up the task, realising that human endeavour at its highest is only feeble and that our only hope is that we shall be given of the Holy Spirit freely.

The second visit to Sandfields — where Bethan now heard Martyn preach for the first time — proved as encouraging as the first and plans commenced for the preparation of the manse to be ready after the wedding which was now fixed for January 8. There was only one difficulty, occasioned by a local newspaper reporter by the name of Lewis. After Dr Lloyd-Jones, who was not staying with E. T. Rees on this occasion, refused to give Lewis an interview on Saturday morning, the man proceeded to the Church Secretary for help, believing that he had a story likely to catch the interest of many in Wales and beyond. As a result, when the couple reached London again on the Monday they were astonished to find themselves in the midst of a blaze of publicity. Several papers for Tuesday, December 14, carried such headings as 'Leading Doctor Turns Pastor: Large Income Given Up for £300 a Year'; 'Harley-Street Doctor to become a Minister'; and 'Specialist to take Aberavon Pastorate'. While ML-J's hearers the previous Sunday might not have taken him for a shy man, the truth is that he was. He also hated the carnal way in which the newspapers handled spiritual things.

But another reason why Dr Lloyd-Jones was so disturbed at these press reports was that he had still not yet mentioned his impending change of career to some of his chiefs at Bart's. Spilsbury and Horder both heard of it first from the newspapers. The former, who was also about to terminate his work at the Hospital, wrote:

> I am exceedingly sorry to see in the Press that you have decided to leave Bart's and to enter the Ministry. I can appreciate the deep conviction which has led you to take this step, but I regret the loss to Medicine and in particular to the hospital.
>
> It lessens my regret at leaving that several whom I have come to regard as friends should have gone already.

Horder was not so placid: understandably he felt entitled to know what was happening before seeing a newspaper announcement, and he suspected that his junior colleague's disinclination to have any discussion with him prior to making the decision was a reflection upon his capacity to judge such matters. 'Your brother is a fool,' he was to exclaim to Vincent Lloyd-Jones, 'he thinks I am only interested in bellies.' That was Martyn's view, but he was mortified at hurting the man to whom he owed so much. In a letter, Dr Lloyd-Jones sought to explain how unintentional, on his part, the press notices had been. Sir Thomas' reply was not lacking in kindness. He wrote:

> It has all been very unfortunate and, as you say, damaging. As to the main issue, disappointed as I am, I have faith in you and what you do — that you follow your best light, and will continue to do so. I think you know my creed — that it is the *man* that matters: his calling is almost an accident.

Despite the temporary strain, the friendship with Horder was to remain intact.

Not without difficulty, for so many things were happening at once, Dr Lloyd-Jones continued to work at Bart's until the end of December. Meanwhile, at Aberavon, E. T. Rees, as well as being heartily involved in preparing the manse, was seeking to regularise the procedures for calling the new minister. The arrangements were little more than a formality, but in his next letter the Church Secretary of Bethlehem Forward Movement Church fulfilled the Presbytery's requirements in the following words.

9 Glen View Terrace
Aberavon
Port Talbot
20 December 1926

My dear Friend

On behalf of the above church I have great pleasure in extending to you a very hearty invitation to become its pastor. The decision was taken by the Glamorgan West Presbytery representatives at a well-attended meeting of members last night. We sincerely pray that God will abundantly bless you and us in the very important step taken.

I beg to submit the following terms for your consideration:

(1) Salary £225 per annum plus manse and rates.

(2) 13 Sundays per annum free.

With the heartiest greetings and best wishes of the church.

Yours sincerely

E. T. Rees (Secretary)

Along with a personal letter to E. T. Rees, Dr Lloyd-Jones sent an 'official' acceptance of the call on December 22.

The expectation was that after their wedding on January 8, 1927, the future minister and his wife should spend a fortnight's honeymoon at Torquay before travelling to Aberavon where he would preach on Sunday, January 30. In the event it proved impossible to crowd all the arrangements necessary for this schedule into the time allowed. There was his research work at Bart's which finally ended only after the Christmas holidays, furniture to buy, packing and removal to arrange, and innumerable letters requiring attention, not to speak of all the preparations for the wedding itself. Amidst it all, what was uppermost in his mind comes out clearly in another letter to E. T. Rees on December 29, 1926:

> Many thanks for all your excellent letters, particularly the one I received on Monday morning . . .
>
> I preached twice on Sunday in Welsh. My theme was the wonder and the amazement that are inherent in the gospel message and our tragic failure to appreciate this. If we could but see the real wonder in the Incarnation, the Crucifixion and the Resurrection, what powers we should be! The Son of God himself dying for *us* — how can we remain so silent and so passive? Do we spend enough time in prayer and silent meditation? Are we not concentrating too much on what we can do in public and depending too much on our own abilities?
>
> Those are the thoughts that have been moving through my mind during the past few days, and above all I have applied them to my personal case.

There were three more letters to the enthusiastic Secretary of Sandfields before January 8 and they included such items as the plans for the 'Welcome Meeting', Bethan's decision on the colour for fireplace tiles, the non-existent electricity supply at the manse (to be rectified later in 1927) which did not bother them, and the lorry belonging to Trefor Jones which was to come to London to collect their belongings. He reports humorously: 'I am by now an absolute authority on furniture, as well as wallpaper'! On the eve of his wedding, and still needing 'to rush off to make a few final purchases', Martyn confesses: 'This has been a terrible week — I scarcely know what I am doing. Oh! for Aberavon!'

The wedding, at 2.15 P.M. on the second Saturday in January, 1927, was conducted at the Charing Cross Chapel by Peter Hughes Griffiths and John Thickens (Calvinistic Methodist minister at Willesden Green, London), with the members of Dr Lloyd-Jones' Sunday School class acting as ushers.

Long before Martyn and Bethan were at last able to relax at Torquay, on the South Devon coast, it was apparent that there was too much left unfinished in London for them to proceed to Aberavon as early as they had hoped. Wednesday, January 26, thus became their revised date of arrival, but that, also, was not to be. Back in London after the honeymoon, Martyn went down with influenza and was running a high temperature and living in a continual bath of perspiration on the day they had expected to reach their new home. Clearly he could not possibly preach at Sandfields, as arranged, on the following Sunday. In the event it was only three days before the 'Welcome Meeting' arranged for Friday, February 4, that they arrived in Aberavon.

Their first night might have been their last. As their future home at 57 Victoria Road was not entirely ready for them, they were to be guests for a few days with one of the church families, the Robsons. Before retiring for the night Martyn and Bethan were standing talking in front of the fireplace in their bedroom when suddenly the light went out. Thinking nothing of it, they went to bed and slept soundly until early next morning when Mrs Lloyd-Jones awoke conscious of a rushing noise in the room and of a strange sensation in her head. She was attempting to alert her husband — who only responded by going further under the blankets — when she suddenly realised that the room was full of gas and, jumping out of bed, threw open a window! Their light of the night before had been a gaslight and when Mr Robson, thinking them to be in bed, had turned off the main supply, they, being used to electricity, had not turned off the gas in their own room! Because of the children in the house, it was Mr Robson's practice to do this last thing every night and then to turn the gas on again early in the morning when he rose to go out to work.

12. *A group at Induction Service, Feb. 4, 1927. Behind Dr Lloyd-Jones [centre], E. T. Rees [behind and to his immediate left], Richard J. Rees (Superintendent of the Forward Movement); [further to the left], T. J. Lewis (the former pastor). [Extreme right, second row], David Williams (minister of Carmel Calvinistic Methodist Chapel).*

13. *Bethlehem Forward Movement Church, 'Sandfields'.*

The Welcome Meetings, or Induction Services, were made up of a preaching service in the afternoon and an evening meeting addressed by several speakers. It was an event which gained much more attention in newspapers, both Welsh and English, than was usual in such cases. Nor was it merely the reporters who felt it to be an unusual occasion. Some of the ordained members of the Presbytery of West Glamorgan had mixed feelings at the prospect of receiving a new colleague who had spent not a single week in a theological college, and they did not intend to give way to the euphoria which possessed others. Dr Collins Lewis of Swansea, welcoming Dr Lloyd-Jones on behalf of the Presbytery, caused a smile by reminding the congregation 'that Dr Lloyd-Jones was after all only human', the proof being that 'he has just had a dose of influenza!' There was a veiled caution in the remark which, at least for the ministers present, would not be lost.

At the conclusion of the day, in the words of one of the newspaper reports:

> Dr Lloyd-Jones said he was truly astonished at the warmth of the welcome which he had received. When he took his step he had not counted on either welcome or support. He looked upon it as the only step he could have taken. Seeing the truth as he saw it, there was only one thing to do, and that was to follow it. If in the future he stood alone in the pulpit, and there was one in the church to listen to him, he would still go on. He had no use for the type of man who was always trying to produce a revival; there were men in the churches today who seemed to regard a revival as a hobby, they were always waiting for it and trying to produce it. No man had ever produced a revival, and he was not foolish enough to think or hope for a moment that anything he did or said would produce such an effect, but he hoped to live in such a way that if, and when, a revival came through the grace of God from heaven, they would be worthy of it. That was the spirit in which he took up the ministry.

SEVEN

A Different Preaching

In February 1927 a frequently discussed subject among those in
South Wales who reflected on Dr Lloyd-Jones' settlement at
Aberavon was the question, 'What does he propose to do?' Not
all were even agreed that his arrival had primarily a religious significance. There were ardent Socialists who, hearing rumours of his
family's connections with the Liberal Party, seriously believed that
he was preparing to recover Aberavon for the Liberals by standing
for Parliament at the next election. After all, such a procedure was
not unknown among Nonconformist ministers. Others of the medical fraternity in South Wales, incredulous of his alleged motives for
leaving London, expressed the view that, once he had become known
in South Wales, he would set up in general practice or as a consultant. Not long after his settlement, ML-J was returning home in a
bus from a meeting at which he had spoken on the other side of Port
Talbot, sitting unrecognised behind two ladies who had been to hear
him. He was highly amused to hear one saying to the other: 'Oh, yes,
I have heard that the doctors are doing very badly in Harley Street
just now, so no doubt he was glad to get away and take up this work'!

But, assuming that the new pastor at Sandfields had come to
engage in work for church extension, it was still unclear to many
how he would proceed. Where did he stand, men wondered, on the
much debated issue of how the decline in Christian influence was to
be arrested? With good reason, no subject was more frequently discussed in the contemporary religious press. Before 1914, not far away

from Aberavon, in the Rhondda Urban District, 151 Nonconformist churches had often held congregations whose aggregate number equalled three-quarters of the entire population. Such days were past. The Forward Mission church building at Sandfields, opened in the year that the First World War broke out, with seating for 400, only had some 70 seats occupied on Sunday mornings, with rather more at night. In Calvinistic Methodism as a whole, with 1,497 churches, an increase of only 353 people was reported in 1926, with Sunday School attendance falling in the same period by 1,169.[1] Throughout much of Britain conditions were similar. In 1925 the Wesleyan Methodists and the Congregationalists both reported losses in Sunday School attendance of well over 100,000 since 1905, the Wesleyans losing 14,000 in 1924–25 alone. It was no wonder, then, that such subjects as 'The Lost Confidence of Nonconformity' often occupied the correspondence columns of the *British Weekly*.

Reactions to this situation were manifold. A number in Nonconformity sought to arrest the drift by a change in church services. There were those, for instance, who, critical of the plainness of congregational worship, looked for some kind of liturgy, with choir, anthem, and organ given a major role. Others, believing that people would not come to church 'to be preached at', wished to turn the sermon into an address 'relevant' to the time, or into an essay replete with many allusions to authors, poets and novelists.

In South Wales there was added weight to the argument that traditional methods would not bring the people back to the chapels. No part of Britain had suffered more from the General Strike of 1926, for while others had gone back to work on May 12 the coal miners — a considerable percentage of the working population of South Wales — had 'remained out' for another six months. Only the threat of starvation finally took them back. During those months the only action taken by the government was to provide two meals per day for children (breakfast and at noon) and for this purpose the church hall at Sandfields was one of the many taken over for use as a communal 'soup kitchen'. A letter by an Aberavon minister under the title, 'Is the Miner's Family Starving?', published

[1] Counting preaching stations, the buildings of the denomination could seat nearly 560,000. The membership in 1926 was 189,323. How many non-members were in attendance is not recorded.

in September 1926, gives a graphic description of the seriousness of the situation. 'In our homes,' he writes, 'we do not think of keeping a child from mid-day to the next morning without food', yet this was being expected in many homes in the Aberavon area. The same writer reported that one soup kitchen in a nearby village had to be closed for lack of coal.

These events were still very much in the public consciousness in February 1927. Unemployment and dole queues were to remain a feature of the Port Talbot area in the 'Great Depression' which was only then beginning. An extract from a letter which E. T. Rees was to write to Mrs Magdalene Lloyd-Jones the following year gives an idea of conditions in some families at this date:

> Oh! how the little ones are suffering in South Wales these days. Not far from where I am writing this I have deposited a heap of shirts, trousers, jerseys, etc., which I am collecting from friends in order to clothe the poor children in my school who are half naked. Only on Wednesday I had a little fellow almost 'trouserless', toes protruding from his broken boots, and cold and hungry in my room, and his brother unable to come because he had *nothing to put on*. There are hundreds and hundreds of miners' children in this sorry plight in the neighbourhood of Aberavon in J. Ramsay MacDonald's constituency. I am determined to do what I can to help. Only this morning I was with Mr MacDonald's agent at the station where he was directing many parcels sent from various parts of the country.

Amid such conditions the case was clearly strong for the many who argued that political and economic measures were the first priority. Even those disposed to give a higher place to religion were tempted to suppose that a population with so many material needs would hardly give attention to anything being preached in chapels.

To bridge the gap with those outside, Sandfields for some years had maintained various activities, including football, musical evenings, a dramatic society, and a 'Brotherhood' on Saturday nights, although with small success, as we have seen. At Dr Lloyd-Jones' induction, the former pastor, T. J. Lewis, after referring to the fact that he had been unable to reverse the non-church-going habit, advised the newcomer that 'he used to go into the streets round about their church and found he could always minister to about six times as many people as he had in his church'. There were others in Sandfields who seemed to think that the best hope lay in the area of children's work: 'Our work amongst the children is capable of great expansion', E. T. Rees reported to Forward Movement headquarters in 1926: 'If we had the teachers, a Sunday School of 500 juniors would be obtained within a month.'

In the event, Dr Lloyd-Jones had nothing to say about any new programme. To the surprise of the Church Secretary he seemed to be exclusively interested in the purely 'traditional' part of church life, which consisted of the regular Sunday Services (at 11 A.M. and 6 P.M.), a prayer meeting on Mondays and a mid-week meeting on Wednesdays. Everything else could go, and thus those activities particularly designed to attract the outsiders soon came to an end. The demise of the dramatic society posed a practical problem, namely, what to do with the wooden stage which occupied a part of the church hall? 'You can heat the church with it', the new minister told the Committee.[2] They demurred and gave it to the local Y.M.C.A.! After some hesitation on Dr Lloyd-Jones' part, the 'Brotherhood', which met on Saturday nights, was allowed to continue.

The Sunday sermons were, indirectly, to indicate the meaning of these and other changes. The church was to advance, not by approximating to the world, but rather by representing in the world the true life and privilege of the children of God. The fundamental need was for the church to recover an understanding of what she truly is. 'The business of preaching is not to entertain but to lead people to salvation, to teach them how to find God.'[3]

Such was the note which was foremost on Martyn Lloyd-Jones' first Sunday as pastor in the Sandfields pulpit, February 6, 1927. The text of the sermon which he most fully prepared for that day was 2 Timothy 1:7, 'For God hath not given us the spirit of fear; but of power, and of love, and of a sound mind.' In the course of his introduction he said:

Young men and women, my one great attempt here at Aberavon, as long as God gives me strength to do so, will be to try to prove to you not merely that Christianity is reasonable, but that ultimately,

[2] The Committee was an elected body and acted as a diaconate would do in the regular Nonconformist churches.

[3] ML-J on Psalm 34:8 (June 28, 1931).

faced as we all are at some time or other with the stupendous fact of life and death, nothing else is reasonable. That is, as I see it, the challenge of the gospel of Christ to the modern world. My thesis will ever be, that, face to face with the deeper questions of life and death, all our knowledge and our culture will fail us, and that our only hope of peace is to be found in the crucified Christ. May I make an appeal to you here and now at the very outset of my work among you? And in appealing to you, I pledge myself to you that I also will reciprocate in kind if you respond to what I ask of you. My request is this: that we all be honest with one another in our conversation and discussions and never profess to believe more than is actually true to our *experience.*

Our chapels and churches are crowded with people nearly all of whom take the Lord's Supper without a moment's hesitation, and yet, without judging harshly or unjustly, do you imagine for a moment that all those people believe that Christ died for them? Well then, you ask, why are they church members, why do they pretend to believe? The answer is that they are afraid to be honest with themselves, afraid of what their parents and friends would say of them if they got up and said that they couldn't honestly say that Christ meant anything to them. I do not know what your experience is, my friends, but as for myself, I shall feel much more ashamed to all eternity for the occasions on which I said that I believed in Christ when in fact I did not, than for the occasions when I said honestly that I could not truthfully say that I did believe. If the church of Christ on earth could but get rid of the parasites who only believe that they ought to believe in Christ, she would, I am certain, count once more in the world as she did in her early days, and as she has always done during times of spiritual awakening. I ask you therefore tonight, and shall go on asking you and myself, the same question: Do you know what you know about the gospel? Do you question yourself about your belief and make sure of yourself?

From this starting-point, the preacher went on to deal with the Pauline description of real religion, not 'the spirit of fear; but of power, and of love, and of a sound mind'. 'If you haven't this,' he concluded — speaking of 'a sound mind' — 'then your religion is probably nothing more than emotionalism, love of tradition, force of habit, or a sense of fear and awe.'

This sermon was a clear indication of the direction Dr Lloyd-Jones intended to take. As he understood the times, the first need was to begin with the church herself. Once real Christian experience was recovered she would find little problem in gaining a hearing from the world. Two weeks later, on Sunday, February 20, he continued the same theme with a sermon on 'Called to be Saints'. The introductory argument was that Paul regards everyone who believes in Christ as a saint:

> The people to whom St Paul wrote were not exceptional people in any sense in which we are not exceptional. To me, every Christian is an exceptional man; at least, if a man is not an exceptional man, then he cannot possibly be a true Christian. For, remember, a Christian is one who believes in the death of Christ and the resurrection, one who has been born again, is a new creation, has become a son of God and is therefore a brother of Christ. Yes, every Christian is an exceptional person, and those who lived in the time of St Paul were no more exceptional than we are, who are followers of Christ at the present time. Christians throughout the years have always been the same and have been called from all classes, Jews and Gentiles, bondmen and free. Their antecedents do not count, everything that has gone before does not matter, in Christ they are all one and are all exceptional. If you do not stand out in your street and in your neighbourhood as an exceptional person then I tell you seriously that you cannot possibly be a Christian. I do not mean by that that you should adopt attitudes and pose before your fellow men, because that would be hypocrisy. What I do mean is this, that the power of the Holy Spirit working in you and through you, makes such a difference to you that you become so completely changed from your former self that all those around you cannot help noticing the difference.

There was much to be said in the coming months on the nature of the life of the Christian and the uselessness of merely nominal religion. Often Dr Lloyd-Jones' approach was staggeringly different from that to which congregations were accustomed. Preaching in July 1927, after a Sunday away from his own pulpit, he said:

> People complain about the dwindling congregations and how the churches are going down. Why are people ceasing to attend places of worship? Why is it, that last Sunday night I noticed that,

while the places of worship in Cardiff were only sparsely attended, the trains coming from Porthcawl and other seaside places were packed out. Why did these people spend their day at the seaside and in other places rather than in the house of God worshipping? Well, the answer is perfectly plain. They obviously prefer to be at the seaside and feel that they get more benefit there than they do in their chapels and churches. Now it is no use our arguing with people like that, it is no use our telling them that they really do not get greater benefit there, because they honestly believe that they do . . . What I feel like saying to these trippers is this: If you honestly believe (and remember it is your responsibility) that you derive greater benefit by spending your day in the country than you do by attending a place of worship, well then, go to the country. Don't come here if you honestly feel that you could do better elsewhere. Unless you feel that something is being offered and given to you here which no other institution can offer or equal, well then, in the name of Heaven, go out into the country or to the seaside. The church of Christ is a church of believers, an association of people banded together by a common belief and a common love. You don't believe? Well, above all, do not pretend that you do, go to the country and the seaside. All I ask of you is, be consistent. When someone dies in your family, do not come to ask the church in which you do not believe to come to bury him. Go to the seaside for consolation . . .

Taken alone, such a statement might have been misunderstood, but it came in the midst of many sermons which showed the church as incomparably different in her privileges, and demonstrated that when she truly enjoys these privileges she conquers the world. There are things for which the church should weep, but confronted with 'the self-righteous, the important, the mighty of the world' she is able to laugh. The unvarnished gospel, possessed by 'a little group of men and women having apparently no influence or power', challenged the great Roman Empire so that it began 'to totter and to shake until it eventually fell, while this small body of people continued to grow and increase and spread throughout the world!'

Generally speaking, it was Dr Lloyd-Jones' habit from the outset of his ministry to devote one sermon each Sunday to teaching and the other to more direct evangelism, although there was often a considerable overlap and, as we shall note, both types of sermon were used to bring people to conversion. The evangelistic sermons, from his first Sunday in February, often dealt with the errors and the misrepresentations of the gospel which men confused with Christianity. Christianity is not a scheme of morality, nor a plan for social and political change, and organisations which propose improvements along such lines are only 'tinkering with the problems'. 'We may be made better men, but before we can face God we must be new men.' All by nature are dead in sin and to all men equally salvation can only come as 'the gift of God'. In no sense at all does salvation depend upon man. So on his third Sunday at Sandfields, preaching from Romans 6:23, he can say:

> It is a gift that is as open to the very worst man in Aberavon tonight as it is to the very best, for no one can ever get it because he deserves it. I have met men sometimes who have said to me that they know that they are beyond hope, that they have sunk so far into sin and iniquity that nothing can save them. My reply to them is just this, that the gifts of God are infinite gifts and that, were you ten times worse than you are already, God could still save you, and do so without realising that his resources had been called upon at all. The most respectable sinner in Aberavon tonight has no more claim on it than the worst and when you both avail yourselves of it you will be doing so on an equal footing. Hold on, my friends, all is not lost, no one is too bad — all are invited.

His evangelistic sermon for the first Sunday in March — with the five foolish virgins in the Parable of the Ten Virgins as his text (*Matt.* 25:1-3) — brought another emphasis to the fore, the folly of being unprepared for eternity. On the previous Tuesday an explosion had occurred in a South Wales coal mine at Ebbw Vale, killing many men. From the moment that he heard the terrible news, he confessed, in beginning his sermon, that his thoughts had come back repeatedly to these words of Christ and his purpose was to ask his hearers how they had reacted:

> Reading the account in the newspapers, a hundred thoughts came rushing into one's mind — the dreadful nature of the calamity with its terrible loss of life, the extreme danger associated with the work of a coal-miner. Whatever one may have thought during the coal-strike, one must have felt this week that no work can possibly be

much more dangerous and that all men doing such work should be adequately paid. The thoughts of the fatherless homes, and women suddenly becoming widows, wives who were planning things for the future for their husbands and their children suddenly being told their fathers were dead! Dreams and hope of future happiness suddenly dashed to the ground! Aged mothers mourning after their sons and wondering why young lives should have been taken before theirs, and little children in the same cases left orphans! . . .

Well, each of you knows his own thoughts, but, for myself, I cannot remember any event which has brought home to me so forcibly the uncertainty of life. No sooner do we think that all is well, than something dreadful happens; no sooner do we feel that certain dangers have been removed once and for all, than they reappear in all their horror. Only just a fortnight ago one of the inspectors of mines had said in a lecture that 'we had seen the last of pit explosions, in all probability'. We boast of our advance of knowledge and of the way we have been able to harness the forces of nature to our own uses, but every now and again we are summarily reminded of their strength and our own impotence. Of everything that is uncertain in life, the most uncertain of all is life itself. No one can predict what will happen next, no one knows at what moment that final blow will come and we shall cease to be.

A fortnight later, on March 20, the brevity and uncertainty of life was again his emphasis as he preached from Hebrews 13:14, 'For here have we no continuing city, but we seek one to come.' The introduction this time dealt with the compromise into which the church had fallen as she sought to attract the world:

Our Christianity has the appearance of being an adjunct or an appendix to the rest of our lives instead of being the main theme and the moving force in our existence . . . We seem to have a real horror of being different. Hence all our attempts and endeavours to popularise the church and make it appeal to people. We seem to be trying to tell people that their joining a church will not make them so very different after all. 'We are no longer Puritans,' we say, 'we believe that they over-did things and made Christianity too difficult for people. They frightened people with their strictness and their unnecessarily high standards. We are not so foolish as to do that', we say, and indeed we do not do so.

We have lost that idea and view of life which was so forcefully stressed and emphasised by the Puritans and the founders of the churches to which we belong, the idea that life is a pilgrimage and that while here on earth we are nothing more than travellers. The fathers wrote about life in that way, talked and preached about it like that, and sang of it in their hymns in that way. They were but 'pilgrims in this barren land'. . . Now this idea has almost vanished out of our vocabulary and sounds strange to us . . .

If you have faith in Christ you will not resent the fact that life is a pilgrimage, but will rather rejoice that it is so, because you will know that the pilgrimage is but a part of your exodus — an exodus from Egypt into Canaan, from bondage into freedom, and that an everlasting freedom. Your only regret will be that it takes such a long time, but even while you are here you will know a peace of mind and a comfort that no one else can possibly feel.

It was preaching like this which explained the changed course of the church life at Sandfields and the quiet dismantling of much that hitherto had been taken for granted.[4] Writing to the Forward Movement headquarters in the time of their former pastor, E. T. Rees had said, 'Our Sunday services are warm, hearty and helpful, and many find their way to the Master. The Penitent Form and the Total Abstinence Pledge are the ways of approach.' But now both 'the penitent form' and 'the pledge' were also gone! No one was summoned to 'come forward' in the brief meeting which took place after the Sunday evening service. Rather, the message was, 'Ye must be born again.' Preaching on June 12, 1927, the minister declared: 'Many churches these days make a new member sign a pledge of total abstinence from alcoholic liquors. Now I do not believe in pledges of any sort. If a man tells me he believes in Christ and desires to be a member of the church, I feel I have no right to question him. I take him at his word and leave it to his honour, but there are times when I almost feel like advocating that all members should sign another pledge, and that is, "a pledge of total abstinence from politics", for I believe that it is causing greater harm in our churches in these days than almost anything else.' E. T. Rees — still an enthusiastic supporter of the Labour

---

[4] Two books of ML-J's sermons at Sandfields, both from his own MSS, have been published: *Evangelistic Sermons at Aberavon* (Edinburgh: Banner of Truth, 1983); *Old Testament Evangelistic Sermons* (Edinburgh: Banner of Truth, 1995).

Party — was astonished! Despite his enthusiasm for the new minister, he had been absent from the station when the Lloyd-Joneses had arrived at Port Talbot station from their honeymoon on February 1, as it coincided with a meeting being held by Ramsay MacDonald. 'If we must send resolutions to Parliament,' the preacher continued in the same sermon, 'I propose that we send this one, drafted by the gentle mind of St John, "He that believeth in him is not condemned; but he that believeth not is condemned already, because he hath not believed in the name of the only begotten Son of God."'

The first newspaper account of this different preaching in Aberavon came from the pen of a Sam Jones who was present on Sunday July 3, 1927, and reported his impressions for his papers:

> Mine was a human failing of curiosity on visiting the Bethlehem Forward Movement Church, Aberavon, last Sunday. Curiosity soon vanished, however. The presence of the young doctor in the pulpit, the tremendous zeal revealed in his preaching, the air of great faith and certainty that he carried, all combined to sweep it away. I remained to wonder and to respect.
>
> I do not crave the reader's pardon for abandoning my usual manner of writing my impressions and for giving to the best of my ability, as much of the sermons as possible. I do this simply because the sermons in themselves were stirring, because Dr Lloyd-Jones has something to say, and because they are the words of one who has felt himself forced to speak by a greater than human power.

The morning sermon, Sam Jones went on to report, was on the words of Nahum 2:1, 'He that dasheth in pieces is come up before thy face [against thee]' — words threatening Nineveh with the wrath of God and with destruction. Nineveh had sinned before but, having been reformed under the preaching of Jonah, had been spared. Now they had forgotten Jonah and turned from the God who can both create and destroy. Nahum, with irony, advised the people to prepare to defend themselves against divine *wrath* — 'keep the fortress, watch the way, make thy loins strong, fortify thy power' — and so the preacher said, 'in the name of God, the church ought to warn the people, 'If you will not worship God, be ready to fight and attempt to defend yourselves against the One who has power to "dash in pieces"!' We were the people of Nineveh — we had lost the reverence. The Sabbath meant nothing — the Bible was the Good Book no longer. We had turned our backs on God. But there was a limit to his forgiveness. God was not going to stand by and allow all the sins of this age.

Sam Jones 'left the church on Sunday morning wondering', and returned in the evening to hear a sermon on, 'The wind bloweth where it listeth' (*John* 3:8). The theme was God's sovereign control of all things — mysterious to us, yet absolutely sure. Man in the arrogance of unbelief supposes he is certain in his opinions. Yet, the preacher said, he is not even able to control his own mind: 'We think a man owns his brain. But you cannot command and order your own brain — the more you do so, the more it refuses to work.' The person who has experienced the life-giving power of the Holy Spirit, and seen God in Christ, the preacher declared, has lost his confidence in himself. He depends upon God and owns the mystery of God's ways. The great difference between the Christian and the non-Christian is that the former speaks with humility and meekness. As with the wind, the evidence of which we see in the results — the rustle of leaves and the sway of branches — so the way in which the Holy Spirit moves men. Though certain and sure, it is beyond analysis. It is the glory of the wind of the Spirit that it is beyond human control. 'It was God's saving grace and we had to go down on our knees and pray that we might share in it . . . At present it seemed that the gale was blowing away from our country — it seemed to have vanished . . . "Let us pray,"' added the preacher, "that the wind comes again, that we experience it. But it all rests with him."'

Sam Jones seems to have been one of the first to recognise in print that what was most unusual about the young preacher was not his change of career but his message itself and the manner in which it was delivered. Thus he closed his column with the question: 'Has the future marked him down as a great leader of the nation? Of this I am certain, if ever a man was called to the ministry it is Dr Martyn Lloyd-Jones.'

* * *

One thing that was clearly recognisable about this preaching was that it was based upon no contemporary models. Most of the preaching which Dr Lloyd-Jones had heard throughout his life had only convinced him what he must not do. He did not stand in the traditional Welsh succession which for some years past had confused emotionalism and sentiment with the genuinely prophetic. He shunned the *hwyl* which J. Hugh Edwards, in the *British Weekly*, described as 'that combination of ecstatic emotion and of musical intonation which has held vast congregations absolutely spellbound with its mesmeric effect'. According to Edwards the *hwyl* was 'the distinctive and exclusive characteristic of Welsh preaching'. Dr Lloyd-Jones viewed it as an artificial contrivance to secure effect, just as he did the multitude of illustrations and anecdotes which the preachers had taught the people to expect. In contrast to this, his sermons were closely reasoned, with the main theme carefully analysed. He was certain that true preaching makes its impact, in the first instance, upon the mind. Yet he did not belong to that more intellectual type of Welsh preaching which announced a text and proceeded at once to exposition. Perhaps the most unusual feature about the form of his sermons was the importance which he gave to the introductions. He once observed:

> I am not and have never been a typical Welsh preacher. I felt that in preaching the first thing that you had to do was to demonstrate to the people that what you were going to do was very relevant and urgently important. The Welsh style of preaching started with a verse and the preacher then told you the connection and analysed the words, but the man of the world did not know what he was talking about and was not interested. I started with the man whom I wanted to listen, the patient. It was a medical approach really — here is a patient, a person in trouble, an ignorant man who has been to quacks, and so I deal with all that in the introduction. I wanted to get the listener and *then* come to my exposition. They started with their exposition and ended with a bit of application.

But beyond the form and structure of Dr Lloyd-Jones' sermons the chief difference lay in the content of the message. Certainly there were aspects of that message which he had heard others preach. John Hutton on the power of God to intervene in life, for example. Yet the combination was his own and among the elements which distinguished it from much of the best-known preaching of that period was its absolute dependence upon the authority of the Scriptures. The Bible was not merely the starting-point, from which he might proceed to Browning, Tennyson or the latest novel; it was the sole source of infallible truth and the final judge of all religious experience. To preach from such a standpoint in the 1920s was to do what the pulpit in general professed to be impossible without extreme obscurantism. Church leaders almost universally conceded that higher criticism had discredited the verbal inspiration of the Bible and brought a change in faith which could never be reversed. Speaking of the rejection of the 'dogmas of revealed religion' which had become commonplace in the 1920s, one historian has written: 'This was as great a happening as any in English history since the conversion of the Anglo-Saxons to Christianity.' And yet, as discussion on 'The Lost Confidence of Nonconformity' in the *British Weekly* in 1925 showed, a majority of ministers were willing to treat rank unbelief as a sign of progress rather than as a setback.

Although it meant standing against the whole tide of respectable modern opinion Dr Lloyd-Jones had recognised that there could be no true recovery of preaching without a prior return to biblical certainties. Without this, 'the revival of preaching' for which Dr J. D. Jones of Bournemouth as Chairman of the Congregational Union had pleaded in 1925, would never occur. The whole tendency of contemporary ministerial training, as Dr Lloyd-Jones had been reminded when he went to Aberystwyth as a prospective student in that same year, involved not submission to Scripture but rather judgment upon it. Even motivation for studying the Bible (as distinct from what scholars said *about* the Bible) was disappearing.

There is one further feature of Dr Lloyd-Jones' preaching which needs to be added. It was customary among evangelical Christians at this date to encourage the practice of giving 'testimonies' as a form of evangelistic witness, and equally common for ministers to include personal references of various kinds in their sermons. Given Dr Lloyd-Jones' unusual career and its interest for the general public; given also the spiritual experience which had so changed his life; it might well be supposed that references to his own story would have appeared frequently in his preaching. The case was exactly the opposite. References to himself in his sermons were brief and rare. Anything in the way of a testimony to his conversion experience was almost wholly absent. The omission was not an oversight on his part but the result of deep convictions.

For one thing, he noticed that the giving of testimonies tended to reduce all conversions to a similar pattern, to standardise experience in a way which went beyond Scripture. And yet, at the same time, testimony-givers were prone to emphasise what made their story noteworthy. No doubt the motives were often well-intentioned, but the effect could easily be carnal and man-centred. Hearers readily became impressed with the dramatic and unique features of a story, instead of with the grace of God which is identical in every conversion. In his own case — as the newspapers reporting his change of career had found — it was easy to emphasise the unusual and to speak of 'the great sacrifice' he had made in leaving medicine, but he disliked such language intensely. To speak of any 'loss' in the context of being a Christian amounted, in his eyes, to a denial of the gospel. He never forgot the shock of once hearing a man say, 'I have been a Christian for twenty years and have not regretted it'! Further, his view of preaching was such that to talk of 'sacrifice' in relation to that work was virtually absurd. 'I gave up nothing,' he said on one such occasion, 'I received everything. I count it the highest honour that God can confer on any man to call him to be a herald of the gospel.'

There was, however, a still more fundamental reason behind his divergence from normal evangelical practice. It was that he knew that the argument from experience could be matched by the claims and apparent results of other 'gospels'. Do Christians claim to have obtained happiness and deliverance from fears? So do the converts to Christian Science and to other cults. 'Our case,' he was never to tire of saying, 'is not based upon experience, it is based upon great external facts.' The business of preaching is the proclamation of the revealed truths of gospel history — truths indeed confirmed by experience, but independent of experience in their objective reality. Compared with those truths concerning Christ, as he said on the first Sunday he visited Sandfields, all else is as worthless 'as paper is to gold'. His text that first November evening of 1926 remained his pole-star: 'I determined not to know anything among you, save Jesus Christ, and him crucified.'

14. Bethan Lloyd-Jones' Sunday School class.

15. ML-J on a Brotherhood outing to Llangeitho.

EIGHT

Early Days at Sandfields

The first home of Martyn and Bethan Lloyd-Jones, situated a few hundred yards from the church, was scarcely the 'dockside cottage' which one newspaper reported, yet it was nothing more than the housing typical of many of the industrial parts of South Wales. 57 Victoria Road was a single-fronted terrace house, larger in its depth than in its breadth. There was a parlour or best-room at the front, a 'middle room' behind it (with a French window opening on to a small yard), and a living room and scullery-kitchen occupying the narrow oblong extremity of the house which lay furthest back from the front door. Up a staircase near the front-door there were three bedrooms and, in the eyes of some visitors, an amazingly small bathroom. The front of the house was almost immediately on the street and behind there was a small garden.

The accommodation suited the young couple admirably. Dr Lloyd-Jones' conviction that a pastor should live among his people and be dependent upon the means which they provide was so strong that he had given all his savings to his mother before leaving London. It meant that for some years Bethan was to count every penny of her house-keeping money, an exercise which she did not regret. The 'middle room' at 57 Victoria Road, ten feet by twelve, at once became the study, where the 300 to 400 books which Dr Lloyd-Jones had brought with him from London soon lined the walls. In a real sense that room was to become the centre of the work, not only as the place where young converts were to visit him in the years ahead, but more as his place of retreat where prayer, study and preparation for the pulpit occupied the best part of the hours of each day. Mornings, and often afternoons as well, were spent in the study, and though he did not work there after supper (about 8 P.M.) there would always be a book in his hands as he sat with Mrs Lloyd-Jones in the living room later in the evening.

In his judgment, this degree of time given to the preparation of his own mind and spirit was not a matter of mere preference but an absolute necessity for an effective ministry. Many years later he was to assert: 'You will always find that the men whom God has used signally have been those who have studied most, known their Scriptures best, and given time to preparation.'[1]

Initially at Aberavon he attempted to write both sermons for Sunday in full — an average of nine, ten or more pages, closely written on both sides. The reason for the full manuscript was not a concern for a literary form, still less for something to read in the pulpit, it was rather to be sure that he was clear in the substance of his message. He believed that a preacher should be prepared for what he was going to say from the beginning to the end. Within weeks, however, he found it impossible to write two sermons in full and thus his settled habit for many years became to write one sermon fully, and the other — though he thought it out in detail — only to record in outline.[2] At first the full sermon manuscript went with him into the pulpit, but he soon found that practice inhibiting, and his custom became to read the fully-written sermon through some three times, and then to have no more than an outline of it with him when he was preaching. In his judgment, the evening sermons (which were more specifically intended for non-Christians) were the hardest to prepare; it was therefore generally these which were written in full. Once or twice when, relying on his 'feeling'

---

[1] 'The Spirit generally uses a man's best preparation. It is not the Spirit *or* preparation; it is preparation *plus* the unction and the anointing and that which the Holy Spirit alone can supply', *The Christian Soldier, An Exposition of Ephesians 6:10-20* (Edinburgh: Banner of Truth, 1977), p. 135.

[2] On writing sermons see *Preaching and Preachers,* pp. 215-16, where he says: 'I believe that one should be unusually careful in evangelistic sermons. That is why the idea that a fellow who is merely gifted with a certain amount of glibness of speech and self-confidence, can make an evangelist is all wrong. The greatest men should always be the evangelists.'

for a text, he preached with an inadequately thought-out plan, and failed miserably.

By no means all his hours in the study were directly concerned with the pulpit. Chief place went to reading the Bible itself, and in the first instance, for his own spiritual help, not to 'find texts'. He aimed to go through the Scriptures every year, omitting nothing — 'That should be the very minimum of the preacher's Bible reading' — and his ability to quote Scripture from memory in the course of preaching was one consequence of the time given to this practice. It could be said of him, as John Foster said of Robert Hall, one of the greatest English preachers of the nineteenth century, 'He maintained through life so assiduous a practice of studying the Bible, that he had acquired a remarkable facility for citing from every part of it, in the course of his preaching, the passages most pertinent for evidence or enforcement of whatever he was advancing.' In his reading of theology the Puritans already had a major place. His 'discovery' of Richard Baxter in 1925 had been followed by other seventeenth-century acquisitions purchased in second-hand bookshops in London, and notably in R. D. Dickinson's. Wedding presents from friends had included second-hand sets of the *Works* of John Owen and of Richard Baxter. In the course of time, Owen was to be preferred; but he always valued Baxter's *Christian Directory.*

Biography and church history were also constantly pursued from the time of his settlement at Sandfields. For sheer stimulus and enjoyment there were no volumes which he prized more highly than *Y Tadau Methodistaidd* which relate (in Welsh) the lives of the fathers of Welsh Calvinistic Methodism.[3] They were constantly in his hands in the early years. In 1926 his interest in the eighteenth century had also been increased with the discovery that English Methodism revealed the same spiritual lessons as were evident in Wales. This interest was awakened through Southey's very inadequate biography of John Wesley, but this book led him on to Wesley's *Journals* which he was always to acknowledge helped him much at the outset of his ministry. Before his settlement at Sandfields he wrote to E. T. Rees on December 29, 1926:

[3] He read them in Welsh. They were reprinted in English, *The Calvinistic Methodist Fathers of Wales,* J. W. Jones and W. Morgan, trans. John Aaron, 2 vols (Edinburgh: Banner of Truth, 2008).

I have been reading, recently, Southey's *Life of John Wesley* and have been greatly impressed with it. I see more clearly than ever that every true spiritual revival is not the result of man's witness, but is determined by God. Again I say that what we have to do is to prepare ourselves, and live in such a way that we shall not be found wanting when that time arrives.

In the course of his reading it was Dr Lloyd-Jones' habit to make very few notes. He relied largely upon his memory. Because he had already made up his mind that he was not going to be a writer, he made no attempt to build up a stock of references for subsequent literary use, 'I have always believed,' he once said, 'that the business of reading is to make one *think,* to stimulate; the idea of obtaining quotations was almost repulsive to me.'

The one thing which he never failed to write down was any suggestion for a future sermon which came to him in the course of reading. He would record the idea at once in skeleton form and in this way was constantly accumulating 'a little pile of skeletons'. No preacher, he believed, should 'be frantic on a Saturday with no texts or sermons for the Sunday, and trying desperately to get hold of something'.

Naturally, the new pastor at Sandfields had no experience or instruction in the running of a church. There were many practical matters, ranging from the conducting of weddings to presbytery responsibilities, upon which he needed help. At his first wedding service he was still waiting for a bride in white to enter and walk down the aisle, with her bridesmaids, when he became aware that the lady was already standing before him, quietly dressed in a navy-blue suit! Happily, the truth had dawned upon him before the pause caused panic! It was in this practical area that the friendship of David Williams, minister of the Welsh-speaking Carmel Calvinistic Methodist Church in Aberavon, contributed much. Williams introduced his young neighbour to many details of church order and procedure with which he was unfamiliar. He also provided him with a service book in Welsh and English and guided him through such technicalities as would normally have been learned at college.

In addition to the Sunday services Dr Lloyd-Jones took a Bible Class during Sunday School on Sunday afternoons. One man who joined the class in 1928 recalled that it met in the small kitchen down some steps from the church hall, and although there were only about a dozen present at that time, the space was so confined that he had to sit on a board placed across the sink!

While there was no mid-week preaching at Sandfields there were three evening meetings during the course of the week. They were, a Prayer Meeting at 7.15 P.M. on Monday, a Fellowship meeting on Wednesday, and 'the Brotherhood' for men on Saturday.

From the outset the Prayer Meeting was a gauge of the spiritual life of the church. At one point before the First World War, Robert Lady, one of the older members, remembered how only five of them had gathered round the stove in the hall for prayer on Monday evenings. In February 1927 the number was perhaps around 40 and included about half-a-dozen who had been converted in the Salvation Army and were the brightest Christians in the church. 'They had very little understanding,' Dr Lloyd-Jones recalled of this half-dozen, 'but they were warm-hearted and a great help to me.' This was for him an important qualification. Despite the discouragement which the former pastor had experienced, ML-J knew that he had 'something to build on'.

The Wednesday evening meeting and the Saturday Brotherhood both took on an entirely new form. The Fellowship was an adaptation of the old Methodist *Seiat* when Christians met together to speak of their spiritual experiences and of experimental religion, yet it was more than that, for one primary intention in ML-J's mind was to convey instruction by open discussion on a question which anyone could propose at the beginning of the meeting. The only stipulation was that the question should concern a practical area of Christian living, such as 'What is growth in grace?' 'How do we deal with temptation and sin?' 'How should we read the Bible?' Once Dr Lloyd-Jones, as chairman, had accepted the question, instead of proceeding to propose answers he would encourage either the questioner himself or others in the meeting to speak. If any in attendance attempted to short-circuit the discussion by a simplistic answer which ignored difficulties, he would quickly bring the speaker to see that the question had aspects of which he was not yet aware. Only one question was taken each evening. Unused though the people were to such a meeting, it soon aroused much interest and began to teach people how to think about the Scriptures with much greater care and intelligence.

The Fellowship Meeting was not a catechising exercise and yet it provided the minister with most valuable insight into the various spiritual needs which existed among the people. One early practical result was that he devised a daily Bible-reading plan for members of the church. This was only to last until he discovered what he considered to be the superior plan of Robert Murray M'Cheyne, which he adopted and urged upon the people.[4]

Although Dr Lloyd-Jones had at first been hesitant about continuing the Brotherhood, it was to become one of the most important of all the meetings. It had originated in the desire to provide an alternative to men who might otherwise go to a public house, or who, no longer wishing to go to such a place, had time on their hands on a Saturday night. They might sing, talk or pray together in an informal manner. From the outset Dr Lloyd-Jones determined that it should be a teaching meeting, and initially it appears that, with this in view, he sometimes gave an address. One evening his subject was 'Purity'. Instead of dealing with the form of moral behaviour normally associated with that subject he went to the foundations with an exposition of the meaning of original sin. Despite the slender education of some of his hearers it was teaching they could all follow:

> The problem of life, my friends, is not individual sins but Sin itself, the whole background — the thing itself, the desire process which is the cause of all these local and minor manifestations and eruptions. And that is our problem. We are not here to teach and lecture men and women about individual sins you may control and conquer. You are still a sinner, your nature is still evil and will remain so, until by the death of Christ and the resurrection you are born again and receive a new nature. Our trouble is that our nature is evil; it really does not matter how it may manifest itself.
>
> What is our duty then? Well, it is this. Before we talk to anyone we must find out first whether he believes in Christ or not. Is he a new man? If he is not, then he is still struggling with flesh and blood. Are we to lecture him on his sins and to preach morality to him? No, we are to preach Christ to him and do all we can to convert him, for what he needs is a new nature, a new outlook, a new mind. It is no use our expecting to find figs on a thorn bush, however much we may treat and tend and care for it. The trouble

[4] Copies of this plan can be obtained from Banner of Truth Trust offices.

is the root. We are wasting our time and neglecting our duty by preaching morality to a lost world. For what the world needs is life, new life, and it can be found in Christ alone.

For purity, as I say, is something for Christians only, it is impossible to anyone else. Sanctification is impossible without conversion, and first things must come first everywhere.

Addresses like this, however, were not continued at the Brotherhood as Dr Lloyd-Jones decided to follow the same discussion practice as on Wednesdays, with one difference: amongst the men on Saturday nights he would encourage a wider range of questions, particularly problems more directly theological. So while practical Christian living was foremost on Wednesdays, the Saturday meeting centred on matters of doctrine and biblical understanding. It was intellectually demanding — in the words of one attender, 'a kind of spiritual University' — and yet the opposite, it should be added, of anything purely scholastic. Unimportant questions of mere theological interest were given no hearing by the chairmen. 'Under the Doctor's leadership,' one of the members recalled, 'the Saturday meeting truly became *the* Brotherhood.' A deeper bond developed among the men which began to be reflected in the whole life of the church. When the summer of 1927 came, the day-outing of the Brotherhood was anticipated with new enthusiasm, and with Llangeitho as the destination it turned out to be the first outing with a serious purpose: their leader had devised a way to give the men an insight into the church history of which they knew so very little.

So there was a guided tour of Daniel Rowland's village with on-the-spot-descriptions of what had happened there two centuries before. From that time onwards, for many of the men, the name 'Calvinistic Methodist' ceased to be a mere denominational label.

Among the things dropped by Dr Lloyd-Jones during his first year at Sandfields was a candidates' class for church membership. This institution existed throughout the denomination and almost automatically numbers of young people passed through it into the communicant membership of the church. Sometimes they joined the class at the suggestion of the minister, sometimes at their own suggestion, but seldom did their approach arise out of any spiritual concern, or out of any evidence of a saving knowledge of Christ. Moreover, Dr Lloyd-Jones came to see the candidates' class as not only spiritually unprofitable but — by its identification of entrance into church membership with teenage years — positively erroneous.

The truth is that there were no means employed at Sandfields to *bring* people to confess Christ. The new pastor believed that, if that work was to be done truly, then only God could do it. At the same time, however, he thought it well to continue the 'after meeting' on Sunday evenings. At this meeting, which lasted for only a few minutes at the conclusion of the service, he indicated that if any who were present wished to become members of the church they should raise their hand. There was no singing and no pressure of any kind. If any did so indicate, Dr Lloyd-Jones would subsequently speak to them alone.

A number of months were to pass after Dr Lloyd-Jones' settlement at Sandfields before there was any apparent response to his preaching. From the outset the congregations had quietly increased, but eighteen months were to pass before the gallery came into use. The real break-through, in fact, was to come from among those who were already within the membership of the church and this was led by E. T. Rees, the Church Secretary, himself. Mr Rees's unbounded enthusiasm at the coming of their new pastor to Sandfields had continued unabated despite the degree of puzzlement he was beginning to feel. Certainly he believed in a type of evangelical religion, but he was later to feel that he had been as ignorant of the doctrine of regeneration as Nicodemus, and his long studies in Socialism had led him to suppose that the coming of the kingdom of God could scarcely succeed by the rebirth of individuals. But under the new preaching he was now hearing, there came increasing doubts about the rightness of his position.

The crisis came on Sunday October 2, 1927, when the sermon was on the doubt of John the Baptist which had led him to send the message to Jesus, 'Art thou he that should come, or do we look for another?' (*Matt.* 11:2-5). Dr Lloyd-Jones argued that the meaning of Christ's reply to John's question — 'The blind receive their sight, and the lame walk, the lepers are cleansed, and the deaf hear, the dead are raised up and the poor have the gospel preached to them' — was proof that the Baptist's problem arose out of his wrong views of what Christ had come to do. John did not appreciate the true significance of what Christ was actually doing and he supposed that the Messiah would have made political deliverance from Rome one of his priorities. 'So great was the tyranny of his preconceived ideas,' said the preacher, 'that he even began to doubt what he had actually seen with his own eyes and what he had actually heard with his own ears.' As the sermon proceeded, E. T. Rees' whole system of thought finally collapsed and even from the pulpit the preacher could see from the look on his face what was happening. 'I shall always remember how you rushed to speak to me before I was down from the pulpit', Dr Lloyd-Jones was to comment twenty years later.

From that October Sunday in 1927, E. T. Rees' commitment to Christ made it impossible for him to speak for Socialism again and he left the Labour Party. Suddenly he had wider and more glorious horizons of thought and for the first time he could enter wholly into the changes which the last eight months had brought to the life of the church. Recalling the beginnings of this new era he was to say many years later:

> At the time of Dr Lloyd-Jones' coming to Sandfields there was an awful economic depression in the country and certainly in the Port Talbot area. It would be true to say that the majority of men were out of work. They were on the dole. I remember boys and girls in school who were affected by it all, in spite of the fact that their mothers sacrificed their breakfasts for them. I remember the efforts we made in soup kitchens, and the big dole queues when that iniquitous question was asked men, "Have you been genuinely seeking work?" There was no work to be obtained! That was the atmosphere, that was the environment. Yet this man dared to preach what would be called a simple gospel. God honoured his preaching and not only honoured his preaching but honoured his courage in re-organising the church activities. We believed in Sandfields, at that time, that to get a few pounds to meet the pressing debt, and to offset the poor collections, we should have in the church a dramatic society, a football team, and such like. Why, we even believed it was necessary to have temperance teaching in order that boys and girls might grow up to be sober. But this man believed that the preaching of the gospel was enough; 'these little side lines', as he would call them, were unnecessary. How well I remember him telling me one night, 'Look here, you can finish with that Band of Hope, don't waste your time with it!'

Speaking of the slow change in the life of the congregation, Dr Lloyd-Jones recorded:

> It took some time. I was there from February to July 1927 without a single conversion. The first conversion was in July and that was not a striking one. Then we went away on holiday. After we had come back E. T. Rees was converted on the first Sunday in October and that did seem to start something. It went on from there.

But Dr Lloyd-Jones knew that more was happening even in 1927 than was apparent, for his own wife had come into a state of concern and conviction. Having attended church and prayer meetings from childhood, Bethan Lloyd-Jones had always believed that she was a Christian. Not until she heard Martyn preach for the first time (on his second visit to Sandfields in December 1926) was she confronted, in his sermon on Zacchaeus, with an insistence that all men are equally in need of salvation from sin. The message shook her, even frightened her, and she almost resented the teaching which appeared to place her in the same condition as those who had no religion at all. In a sense she had always feared God; her life was upright, and yet she knew that she had no personal consciousness of the forgiveness of sins, no sense of inward joyful communion with Christ. In Mrs Lloyd-Jones' own words:

> I was for two years under Martyn's ministry before I really understood what the gospel was. I used to listen to him on Sunday morning and I used to feel, Well, if this is Christianity I don't really know anything about it. On Sunday night I used to pray that somebody would be converted; I thought you had to be a drunkard or a prostitute to be converted. I remember how I used to rejoice to see drunkards become Christians and envy them with all my heart, because there they were full of joy and free, and here I was in such a different condition.
>
> I recall sitting in the study at 57 Victoria Road and I was unhappy. I suppose it was conviction. I felt a burden of sin, and I shall always remember Martyn saying, as he looked through his books, 'Read this!' He gave me John Angell James' *The Anxious Enquirer Directed*. I have never forgotten what I read in that book. It showed me how wrong was the idea that my sin could be greater than the merit of the blood of Christ — his death was well able to clear all my sins away. There, at last, I found release and I was so happy.

* * *

For the first eight months of Dr Lloyd-Jones' ministry at Sand-fields he continued in the status of lay-pastor. His position was indeed unusual. According to the prevalent view in his denomination, anyone lacking regular ministerial training was liable to be singularly deficient in qualities necessary for a sustained pulpit ministry. Two or three years of theological training were judged to be necessities. The fact that Dr Lloyd-Jones was to be settled in what was virtually a mission-hall situation had helped the authorities to waive their usual rule. But it was almost immediately apparent to a number that Dr Lloyd-Jones' services would be required beyond Aberavon, that even at Sandfields he would be hindered if he were not ordained, and that, accordingly, his lay status should be altered without delay.

When the 1927 Association (*Sasiwn*) of South Wales met at Gilfach, Bargoed, on April 19, requests were received from the Forward Move-ment, the English Presbytery of West Glamorgan, and the London Presbytery, that Dr Lloyd-Jones should be ordained at once in view of the need at Sandfields. Procedure was complicated by the fact that the denomination had recently set up a Board for the examination of ministerial candidates as the feeling among the 'experts' in theo-logical training was that the judgment of presbyteries on the gifts of a preacher might not be enough. No sooner was Lloyd-Jones' name raised in the Association than one member, who was no supporter of the new arrangement, enquired sarcastically whether the candidate had been before the Board! He had not.

The Association proceeded to carry a proposal that Dr Lloyd-Jones should be ordained at the next Ordination Association. There was disquiet, however, in some quarters at the way the Southern Associa-tion had waived proper procedures. In August he was examined in a perfunctory manner with other candidates and the conclusion of the matter came in London in the last week of October 1927 when the Association met in the English capital for the first time hiring White-field's historic Chapel on Tottenham Court Road for the occasion. The day of his ordination, October 26, 1927 proved to be the same as that of the birth of their first child, Elizabeth.

16. On the beach with Elizabeth, c. 1934.

NINE

A Leader without a Party

The one thing to which Dr Lloyd-Jones conceived himself to be called in 1927 was the work of an evangelist in a local community. He desired nothing more. As a correspondent in the *Western Mail* correctly wrote of him during the week he began at Sandfields, 'He would naturally prefer to settle down to his work in peace and quiet.' This was to prove impossible, for he had scarcely settled in Aberavon before he was being asked to preach in other places. In one sense such a development was not unusual. The thirteen so-called 'free Sundays', stipulated in the terms of his call, was an arrangement common throughout the denomination. The purpose was to encourage ministers to preach away from their own pulpits for a number of Sundays every year with four Sundays remaining for holidays. But not only were there invitations to fill these vacant Sundays soon to hand for Dr Lloyd-Jones, there were also calls for him to preach at special mid-week services — often anniversaries — which were then so much a part of chapel life in Wales. Thus within twelve months of his induction he was often away from Aberavon preaching on two mid-week evenings (Tuesdays and Thursdays), frequently with afternoon services as well and before long this had become the pattern for most weeks, apart from his holiday period.

This is not to say that Martyn Lloyd-Jones was uniformly welcomed in all sections of Welsh Nonconformity. On this point he has recorded:

When I went to South Wales it was to a varied reception: the vast bulk of Welsh Calvinistic Methodists were delighted — not because of my beliefs but because I was, as they thought, boosting the ministry. Many in the English section of the Calvinistic Methodists, however, considered themselves intellectuals and they did not like me because they could recognise my views and my teaching. They were quite pleasant and polite but I felt they were antagonistic. The Baptists, as a whole, were most enthusiastic in my favour and received me with open arms. They were emotionalists. They all thought they were evangelical — actually they were not, they were often 'praising the gospel' without any theology or understanding — yet they were really very warm in their welcome of me. Now the Congregationalists were different again: they were doubtful of me. They also regarded themselves as intellectuals and philosophers and were suspicious and critical.

People used to tell me what their ministers would be saying to one another on their way out from services. At special services ministers all sat in 'the big seat' and I was often conscious of a strong wave of antagonism. I had to preach beyond them to the people. In those days, when I went to preach on a week-day in any district, all the ministers turned up; this is no longer the case, but at that time, before the Second World War, it was customary that ministers from the several Nonconformist denominations would support special services in any local chapel. They were afraid not to be there, as their members would be watching for them and saying, 'Where is our man?'

The differences between the Welsh and English-speaking sections of the denomination, noted above, require further comment. Of the 1,497 churches in the Calvinistic Methodist Connexion, 361 were 'English' — that is to say, congregations which did not employ Welsh as their first language, and these causes constituted separate presbyteries. Thus English-speaking Sandfields belonged to the Presbytery of West Glamorgan, while 'Carmel' (Aberavon) a Welsh chapel (where David Williams was minister) belonged to a different, Welsh-speaking presbytery. The English-speaking side was less traditional and reflected a good deal more of modern religious thought. 'The Welsh and the English sections', he later commented, 'were really entirely different. I did much more with the Welsh than with the English — much more! At mid-week services in the Welsh churches I would preach in Welsh in the afternoon and in English at night.'

Among the exceptions to this pattern was the English-speaking congregation of the Reverend Eliseus Howells, in a small mining community above Bridgend, which also belonged to the West Glamorgan Presbytery and where Dr Lloyd-Jones was early invited to preach after Howells had been to hear him. Speaking of that experience a few years later, Howells wrote:

> It is not strange that he won our unbounded admiration, but with him accepting a pulpit without the usual course of preparation, we felt that we should extend to him our utmost sympathy. Poor us! If we went to that first service expecting to sympathize with him, we came out pitying ourselves. He did not covet our admiration, nor was he in need of our pity. Rather, we thought not of what he had done but of what we were not.

Howells and Dr Lloyd-Jones soon became close friends. Brought up in the Rhondda and about eight years older than Lloyd-Jones, it was perhaps as well that Howells was not a close neighbour; for there was nothing he loved better than to talk away the hours with a fund of stories from earlier times. In a rather undisciplined kind of way, he had acquired both from books and from the older generation a considerable understanding of Calvinistic Methodist history.

Another minister who was notable in the warmth of his welcome to Dr Lloyd-Jones was W. E. Prytherch, whom Martyn had first heard at Llangeitho in 1913. Although he had retired from Trinity Chapel, Swansea, in 1919, Prytherch was still preaching after he turned eighty in 1926. In his earlier ministry Prytherch had spoken much of the judgment of God, but in middle life it was noticed how the emphasis changed, as he came to dwell much on the tenderness of divine love. ML-J rarely heard him without being moved to tears.

It was Prytherch who, in the early days of Dr Lloyd-Jones' ministry, encouraged him by exclaiming after one sermon, 'You are preaching the old truths but putting brand new suits on them!' One of the advantages of being asked to preach in a variety of places was the constructive criticism which he sometimes received. Sharing the work of preaching one week-day afternoon and evening with the Rev. Dr Cynddylan Jones at Llantrisant, he was given valuable advice by the older man who had listened to his afternoon sermon. Probably the date was Thursday, May 19, 1927, for his notes of a sermon on

Romans 3: 20 record that he preached from that text at Llantrisant on that day. As the two men sat at tea, between the services, Cynddylan Jones opened the conversation with, 'I have only one criticism to offer of your preaching,' and when Lloyd-Jones assured him that he would appreciate knowing what it was, his adviser proceeded: 'You demand too much of the people. You watch how I do it tonight. I have only one point, but I will make it in three different ways!'

This was wise advice which it took the younger man time to learn. Not long afterwards, his old friend Ianto Crydd, the shoemaker of Llangeitho, emphasised the same lesson after he had preached in the chapel of his childhood. Martyn, he declared, was expecting too much of his hearers. With one of his characteristic similes drawn from the way in which horses and cattle have to be fed in farmyard stables, he went on, 'You are putting the rack too high — it is wonderful hay but they cannot all reach it.' 'I remember lying awake in the chapel house that night and thinking I had probably failed', the preacher later recalled. 'I had preached a sermon not suited to a village chapel.' The greater the preaching, he came to believe, the easier it will be to understand it.

It is clear from Dr Lloyd-Jones' sermon notes that he preached in 54 places during his first twelve months in Wales. Such was the additional work of his first year in the ministry, and thereafter, for half-a-century, no year was to be so quiet!

By 1928 it was becoming evident that Dr Lloyd-Jones' ministry was going to polarise opinion both among ministers and churches. When he was asked to share services with the Rev. Tom Nefyn Williams at Shiloh Chapel, Aberystwyth, in February 1928, the contrast between the two men and their message was almost complete. In the words of one observer, the Rev. M. H. Jones, 'These are two remarkable men. One [Lloyd-Jones] is looking to the past and the other is looking to the future.' It was certainly not a description with which ML-J would have concurred. If Tom Nefyn Williams' unbelief was allowed to spread he knew that there would be *no* future for the church.

Dr Lloyd-Jones believed that the real opposition to evangelical and supernatural religion came from the pride which resents what is implied in Christ's teaching that men must be 'born again':

> By telling people that 'ye must be born again' you are simply telling
> them that as they are, they are '*all* wrong' and that nothing but

a divine, supernatural intervention from above can possibly save them and put them right. Come, let us be quite honest with ourselves and each other. Why is it that we do not like all this talk about 'conversion' and 'rebirth', why indeed is it scarcely ever mentioned in our chapels and churches these days? Why was it that a highly-educated, cultured gentleman, whom I know well, should the other day have said to a lady, who had undergone that great change of heart, that 'the word *conversion* was not a nice word and that he was surprised that a man like Dr Lloyd-Jones, who ought to know better, should allow himself to be carried away by fanaticism'?

A year later, in 1929, Dr Lloyd-Jones was asserting this still more strongly and widely. In one sermon, after tracing the spiritual decline of nineteenth-century Calvinistic Methodism, he continued:

> It is our own Nonconformist forefathers who are responsible for the churches becoming worldly institutions. Conversion and rebirth are never mentioned, they are embarrassing subjects which are dismissed when they are brought up; indeed one can almost say that the average church member is ashamed to speak about his relationship with God, but is proud of being made a Justice of the Peace! At these Presbyteries and District Meetings, votes of thanks and votes of congratulations are continually being passed on so-and-so for having been clever in some way or other — some examination passed, or office received, or other worldly honour, but I have never yet heard a vote of thanks being passed for a sinner converted, no acclamation when someone has gone from sin to saintliness. They never speak about that thing that makes a church a church — the power of God unto salvation.

It is scarcely surprising that as he preached in many parts of South Wales he was often conscious of that strong wave of antagonism from 'the big seat'! Lloyd-Jones was not unfeeling in the face of opposition. He did feel it. On one occasion, when a clerical attack on him took a particularly vicious form, he was much comforted by the assurance given by Paul to Timothy concerning faithful discipleship, 'all that will live godly in Christ Jesus shall suffer persecution' (*2 Tim.* 3:12).

Undoubtedly he was sometimes asked to preach simply because his name was expected to draw extra numbers. Once, preaching at a Presbyterian cause mid-week at Llantwit Major, he was shocked to be virtually told before the service by one of the church officers that he should 'do his stuff' — because the Baptists and Congregationalists had enjoyed good special services in the previous fortnight! At other times he was probably asked to speak at denominational occasions as a representative of evangelical opinion. Thus in 1929 and 1931 he was invited to give addresses at the Annual Conference of the Presbyterian Church of Wales. The published reports of these conferences reveal at once that the prevailing religious thought was very different from that of the preacher from Aberavon. Whereas in his addresses he quoted nothing but Scripture, apart from one reference to John Calvin, such names as A. M. Fairbairn (English Congregationalist and inspirer of the Welsh B.D. course), Albert Schweitzer and Stanley Jones (both liberal missionaries), and C. H. Dodd were commended by the other speakers. At the 1929 Conference, Professor Edwards of Bala quoted with approval the statement of H. Wheeler Robinson, 'The doctrine of verbal inspiration is not simply untenable; it is irrelevant.' Another speaker, criticising those who spoke of the failures of the modern church, quoted another liberal, Canon C. E. Raven, who was thankful that 'the church has shown during the last twenty years a power of adaptation to a new environment which can only be described as astonishing'.[1]

* * *

It was in the late 1920s that something happened after a Monday-night service at Bridgend which was to prove of considerable importance in the development of Dr Lloyd-Jones' ministry. The minister of the Calvinistic Methodist church in which this service was held was not at that date a supporter of the 'new' preaching at Aberavon, but its unusual emphases intrigued him. When the service was over the Bridgend minister greeted the visiting preacher with the remark, 'I cannot make up my mind what you are! I cannot decide whether you are a hyper-Calvinist or a Quaker.' When Dr Lloyd-Jones assured him that he was no hyper-Calvinist and enquired why he should make such a statement, he replied: 'Because you talk of

[1] *Report of the Thirty-Fourth Annual Conference*, p. 30. The same speaker commended the liberal A. S. Peake as 'one of the most enlightened and reverent students of the Bible'.

God's action and God's sovereignty like a hyper-Calvinist, and of spiritual experience like a Quaker, but the cross and the work of Christ have little place in your preaching.'

There was a shrewd element of truth in this observation. The keynotes of ML-J's evangelistic preaching were the helplessness of man in sin, and the necessity of rebirth through the intervention of God. He preached so strongly that spiritual change is sovereignly given, not dependent upon man's own efforts, that while his message gave hope to the convicted, it did not direct them with sufficient clarity to faith in Christ as the God-appointed means of relief. The result was that the note of appeal which closed many of his sermons was not full-orbed. It included such commands as, 'Pray for the rebirth, pray for it without ceasing, pray until you experience it', but in stressing human inability he did not give equal emphasis to man's responsibility to believe on Christ for justification, nor show with sufficient clarity how that justification flows from the acceptance of Christ's atoning death.

The criticism which he heard at Bridgend was thus a fruitful incentive to further thinking. In his own words, spoken at a later date: 'I was like Whitefield in my early preaching. First I preached *regeneration,* that all man's own efforts in morality and education are useless, and that we need power from outside ourselves. I assumed the atonement but did not distinctly preach it or justification by faith. This man set me thinking and I began to read more fully in theology.'

In particular, he concentrated upon the doctrines specified by his critic. At this point he was to receive help from the Congregational minister at Brynamman, the Rev. Vernon Lewis. Modern theology of an evangelical complexion was Lewis' special interest and he was quick to respond to the Lloyd-Jones' request for advice on reading, frequently calling at the Sandfields manse with further suggestions and books from his own library. High among his recommendations of authors on the atonement were the two English Congregationalists, P. T. Forsyth and R. W. Dale, and the Scots Presbyterian, James Denney, author of *The Death of Christ* (1903). It was Forsyth's *The Cruciality of the Cross* (1909) which proved of especial help at this stage in Lloyd-Jones' thinking. The weakness of these authors on the *full* inspiration of Scripture did not escape his notice, but that was not his subject of study, nor did he ever have difficulties in his commitment to all Scripture as the inerrant Word of God. His copy of Denney's book bears the date July 5, 1929.

* * *

Dr Lloyd-Jones' wider ministry soon confronted him with a problem. With invitations to preach coming from many and varied quarters it became clear that there were various groups hoping that they might attach him to their cause. The evangelicals with whom he did have a ready affinity were those who looked back to the Welsh Revival of 1904–05 as a time of true spiritual power and blessing. Yet, as in all revivals, the effects of that period of awakening had been mixed and in many places its fruits had not been consolidated within the traditional churches. Calvinistic Methodism — too often critical of spiritual babes and unsympathetic towards revival phenomena — suffered an exodus from its ranks and, in some parts of Wales, the Baptists and 'Plymouth' Brethren gained in number. Pentecostal groups, proclaiming what they considered to be the distinctive message of the Revival, also sprang into existence. They drew off men and women who were weary of the cold worship of many of the chapels.

Post-1904 Evangelicalism was thus fragmented in Wales and some of its leaders were men whose chief interests lay outside the more regular church and denominational life. One such man was the Rev. R. B. Jones of Porth who had been one of the most effective preachers at the time of the Revival of 1904. A Baptist, R. B. Jones had withdrawn from the regular life of that denomination on account of its toleration of Modernism, and he now presided over four independent churches, besides running his own 'Bible Institute' at Porth. He was also active in evangelistic projects (in which he failed to discern between the old gospel preaching of the Methodist Fathers and the new which had entered Wales through the Arminian influence of Charles G. Finney) and was an enthusiastic supporter of the holiness conventions held at Llandrindod Wells and elsewhere. The 'holiness message' of 'sanctification', received by an act of 'full surrender' to Christ, he preached as the great solution to the current religious malaise.

In the first year of Dr Lloyd-Jones' ministry R. B. Jones befriended him and urged him to unite his efforts with their own. 'You know you are like the Apostle Paul,' the Porth preacher told him, 'you are as one "born out of due time"; you belong with us, you are really one of the children of the revival, but you have come in over twenty years later . . .' It was through R. B. Jones' son and nephew, then students at Cardiff, that Dr Lloyd-Jones was first asked to speak to the Christian Union of that University College in October 1927. R. B. Jones' magazine *Yr Efengylydd (The Evangelist)* was to give regular commendation of Dr Lloyd-Jones' ministry and even carried a review from his pen in 1929. The minister of Sandfields, however, would never accept an invitation to speak at the Llandrindod Convention, and although he did speak, on occasions, for R. B. Jones at Porth, he knew that there was never any possibility that he could find a spiritual home in that ethos.

Along with much that was commendable in R. B. Jones there was also an erroneous conviction that his comparative isolation amidst Welsh religion was due solely to his stand for the Word of God and for experimental Christianity. There was certainly no questioning his commitment to Scripture but, like so many others of his generation, who lacked real theological understanding, R. B. Jones was prone to be swept from one idea to another. At one time he might preach that a great awakening was about to occur, and at another that the second advent of Christ was at hand. His teaching was an amalgam, a fact reflected in the absence of any clearly recognisable theological position in the teachings of his Bible Institute at Porth. Preaching tours in the United States, and the visits of American fundamentalist leaders to his Rhondda Monthly Bible Conferences, increased the mixture. Too uncritical of anything which went by the name of Fundamentalism, R. B. Jones was severe in his constant opposition to the Baptist Union and to the ministry in general. Frequently his preaching was denunciatory and Porth, instead of being a centre for a growing number of Christians, became a *cul-de-sac* for adherents to a declining cause — a cause which, to some extent, merited the negative and anti-intellectual image which it came to possess in South Wales.

As popular as 'holiness' meetings among Welsh evangelicals at this period, were the movements which existed to propagate the premillennial and dispensational views of unfulfilled prophecy. In many quarters, and almost universally among the Plymouth Brethren, the notes on prophecy in the Scofield Bible were unquestioningly accepted and proclaimed. Dr. Lloyd-Jones' introduction to the

Brethren occurred in December 1929 when he met Christians of that persuasion in Llanelli. They presented him with a Scofield Bible and encouraged him to note the importance of prophetic beliefs. Perhaps they were surprised that the young preacher was unenthusiastic. He had never encountered this view of unfulfilled prophecy before. The literature he was given was wholly new to him, and he might well have taken it up as so many other pastors had done.

Commenting in later years on what had kept him detached from associations with which it was often assumed that he would be identified, Dr Lloyd-Jones spoke of the two principles by means of which he had sought to determine his decisions: 'First, my understanding of the Scripture and, second, my reading of the Calvinistic Methodist revival of the eighteenth-century. These things governed me and when anything presented itself to me, if it did not fit into that framework, I had no difficulty over my duty. When I saw something which was so different from the high spirituality and the deep godliness of the Methodist Fathers I did not have a struggle over whether to follow it or not.' These convictions, both in his early ministry and throughout his life, were to keep him from many things commonly accepted in evangelical circles, and when people attributed his independence to individualism it made him the more eager that the lessons of church history might be more widely known.

As Lloyd-Jones surveyed the Welsh scene in the late 1920s he saw nothing to suggest that, whatever the difficulties, his work would not lie within Calvinistic Methodism. He preferred its church-centred structure, and its emphasis upon the regular and normal means of grace, to the individualism of the break-away groups with their delight in missions and conventions. His hope was that Welsh Presbyterianism could be brought back to its original position. He also thought highly of some of the older generation of ministers under whose ministry he had often profited, although, by this date, they were passing from the scene. Joseph Jenkins, the man under whom the Revival of 1904 began in his area, and who had befriended Lloyd-Jones in 1925, died in 1929. The final meeting of the two men was memorable. In the summer of 1929, when Jenkins was dying from a growth in the spine, Eliseus Howells called at Aberavon to report the seriousness of the old preacher's condition and to urge Martyn to travel to see him at Llandovery, which was some distance away.

Lloyd-Jones went and as he finally reached his destination he could hear groaning through an open window. Entering the house, Mrs Jenkins informed him that her husband was not really conscious but, as the visitor sat at his bedside, holding his hand, she asked her husband in the conversation which followed, 'Do you know who he is?' 'Of course I know!' replied the dying man, attempting to turn in his bed. 'Can you pull me back out of this river?' he asked Lloyd-Jones. 'I don't know that I can do that, Mr Jenkins.' 'I didn't know that this dear old river was so wide,' said Jenkins, 'but it's all right: I am going to Jesus Christ' — then, laying his hand upon his heart, 'I wish I felt it more here.' Like the old Methodists whom he resembled, Joseph Jenkins died well.

With men such as Jenkins and Prytherch (who died in 1931 in his eighty-sixth year) Dr Lloyd-Jones was truly at home and their passing only strengthened his resolve to work for the cause in which they had so long served. Yet, given his convictions, there was little possibility that he could become a 'denominational' man, or even a leader in those more evangelical circles of the Welsh section of the denomination where his wife's grandfather, Evan Phillips, had been so well known. Speaking of this, he commented: 'When I went to Aberavon, the Welsh Calvinistic Methodists thought I would drop into their mould and preach like they did. At first they were a little bit disappointed, they thought that I was going to become one of them, but I could not do it.'

Yet it was certainly not a feature of ML-J's temperament to want to act alone and one of the main encouragements of his early ministry was the quiet formation of a small band of like-minded brethren for mutual support and fellowship. A document still survives from the first of their meetings:

> Feeling the need of definite action and co-operation on the part of those who believe and preach the Evangelical truths of the Gospel, the following Brethren met together at Sandfields, Aberavon, on Tuesday, December 30, 1930, to consider means for promoting a Revival of Religion. The following matters were agreed upon:
>
> 1. That we pledge ourselves that in all our meetings together for fellowship, we shall frankly exchange with one another our thoughts and experiences, paying special attention to the confession of our faults and failures.

2. That we pledge ourselves to abstention from any practice which is not of faith, 'for whatsoever is not of faith is sin'.

3. That we pledge ourselves to wait upon God for one half-hour daily, in particular prayer for,

    (i) A revival of religion

    (ii) For one another.

4. That we accept and subscribe to the Brief Declaration of the Presbyterian Church of Wales, but feel that in addition the following matters be especially stressed and emphasised in our ministry.

    (a) That the call for decision, conversion and rebirth be pressed upon our congregations.

    (b) That all believers should have a full assurance of forgiveness and salvation.

    (c) That all believers be taught and instructed that it is the will of God that they be sanctified, that they receive the Holy Spirit, and that the fruit of the Spirit may be manifest in their lives. Gal. 5:22.

5. That the churches be cleansed from all worldly and doubtful means of maintaining the cause, such as Bazaars, Concerts, etc.

6. That we meet at Pencoed, Friday, April 10th, 1931.

The names of ten men were included in this statement, with that of Lloyd-Jones as 'convenor'. As a group it never gained public attention in the life of the denomination, but it was a centre of spiritual influence, and strengthened the resolve of those who came to share a common vision.

One of the men who benefited from this fraternal in the 1930s, when still a student for the ministry was I. B. Davies. Having gone into the pits at the age of thirteen, Davies had little secondary education and yet under the preaching at Sandfields he believed that God had called him to the gospel ministry. Broaching this conviction at length to Dr Lloyd-Jones, he was told to 'go home and study Greek', this being his pastor's way of testing the strength of his call. A year later as 'I. B.' was leaving a meeting at Sandfields, Dr Lloyd-Jones asked him what the book was which he saw sticking from his pocket. It was a Greek grammar which the young man had been assiduously studying for twelve months. After arranging to see him for a further conversation, ML-J thereafter gave him every possible encouragement in following his call to the ministry. In turn, the Rev. I. B. Davies was subsequently to gather numbers of young men around him, including his two sons, Wynford and Andrew, who would remain faithful preachers in the years to come.[2]

There can be no doubt that Dr Lloyd-Jones' increasing usefulness at this period was closely connected with the constant study which was a principal part of his daily living. Next to the Bible it was probably Jonathan Edwards' *Works* which provided the greatest stimulus to him at this date. While still in London he had asked a Welsh Presbyterian Minister for the name of books which would help him prepare for the ministry. One recommendation he received was *Protestant Thought Before Kant,* written by A. C. McGiffert. Although the book did not live up to his expectation, while reading it he came across the name of Jonathan Edwards for the first time. His interest aroused, Dr Lloyd-Jones relates:

> I then questioned my ministerial adviser on Edwards, but he knew nothing about him. After much searching I at length called at John Evans' bookshop in Cardiff in 1929, having time available as I waited for a train. There, down on my knees in my overcoat in a corner of the shop, I found the two-volume 1834 edition of Edwards which I bought for five shillings. I devoured these volumes and literally just read and read them. It is certainly true that they helped me more than anything else.

While authors such as Edwards were regular reading, certain large works, less directly related to preaching, he reserved for holiday reading. By the late 1920s he had come to organise his annual holidays so that the mornings were almost invariably spent with a major theological volume. One of Elizabeth's childhood memories is of herself in a bathing costume playing in and out of the pools on the beach, while her father sat, fully clothed in a dark grey suit, complete with shoes, socks and hat, leaning against a rock and reading Brunner's *The Divine Imperative.*

Another major work which he read about this period was *The Vision of God* by Kenneth E. Kirk, being the Bampton Lectures for 1928, delivered at Oxford where Kirk, nine years later, became

---

[2] A fiery evangelist, Mr Davies' most fruitful years were spent at the Forward Movement Hall in Neath (1949–62). He remained close to Dr Lloyd-Jones and preceded him to heaven by only a few years.

Bishop. 'These lectures', he commented later, 'had a great effect on me. Kirk dealt with the pursuit of God and the different methods by which men have sought God, but he did it historically and went right through — the medieval mystics, the later mystics and so on. I found that book absolutely seminal. It gave me a lot of background. It made me think. It helped me to understand the Scriptures and also see the dangers in such movements as monasticism and the anchorites. I regard *The Vision of God* as one of the greatest books which I ever read.' Thereafter he frequently took Bampton or Gifford lectures for his holiday reading. A year or so after Kirk it was Norman Powell Williams (Lady Margaret Professor of Divinity at Oxford) on *The Ideas of the Fall and of Original Sin.* 'From the standpoint of style that was the most brilliant book I ever read.'

The summer holidays for 1929 were to be remembered for the sheer enjoyment which he had in reading Luke Tyerman's two-volume *Life and Times of George Whitefield.* Part of that holiday was spent at an ancient farmhouse, St Mary Hill Court, in the Vale of Glamorgan. It was after the second Sunday at St Mary Hill Court that the peacefulness of the 1929 holiday was rudely interrupted. A bull in a field close to the farm had already disturbed Mrs Lloyd-Jones who enjoyed walking Elizabeth in her push chair while her husband was absorbed with Tyerman's account of George Whitefield. A crisis came after lunch one day, early in the second week, when as they looked on to the farmhouse yard from the kitchen window, they were amazed to see the bull lift the yard gate off its hinges and make triumphantly towards the house! Mrs Lloyd-Jones refused to stay one day longer and so it was agreed that she and Elizabeth should go on to London where Martyn would join them some days later. But St Mary Hill Court had other problems to raise and this time nocturnal ones. Scarcely was Dr Lloyd-Jones in bed with the light out, on the day of Bethan's departure, before he was arrested by a strange pattering on the linoleum around the bedroom. With a light on, the noise departed, only to return as soon as it went out. There was nothing for it but to pull the sheets tight about his head and to find an excuse to leave promptly the next morning. Bulls and farmyard livestock were one thing, facing mice quite another!

TEN

A Local Revival

Revival was a subject which did not occupy a separate place in Dr Lloyd-Jones' thinking and preaching, rather it was closely related to his whole understanding of the work of God in bringing men to salvation and to assurance. He saw revival as the extension to many of that same divine power which is present in the conversion of every individual. It is the same life, present wherever there is true Christianity, which in days of revival abounds and overflows. The same Holy Spirit as may be known by a single Christian is then 'outpoured' upon a multitude. So a time of revival does not witness results different in nature from those attending God's more normal work, but the multiplied instances of divine grace present at such a period reveal the glory of Christ to a degree, and upon a scale, which is extraordinary, exceptional and unparalleled. True zeal for revival is therefore nothing other than zeal for the glory of God in the conversion of many.

Dr Lloyd-Jones did not regard the view that a revival can be produced or 'worked-up' by human effort as a minor mistake. He traced that error to a false view of the meaning of conversion itself. No matter how great the effort and energy expended, man cannot induce one single true conversion. This emphasis was prominent from the outset of his ministry. To understand what conversion means is necessarily to deny that revivals can be produced by the activity of the church. The same sovereign and supernatural power which is essential to the saving of one individual is equally indispensable in the case of a multitude. Those who would 'rush' men into conversion and those who try to 'hasten' a revival have fallen into the same error:

> Pray for revival? Yes, go on, but do not try to create it, do not attempt to produce it, it is only given by Christ himself. The last church to be visited by a revival is the church trying to make it.

Revivals are 'special times' in the history of the church, 'made "special" not by the schemes and devices of men, but by the intervention of God'. The church, he preached, has her 'great days' and her 'ordinary days':

> There are not only the great experiences but also the ordinary, every-day experiences, and a church that is *always* praying for a continual revival is a church that has not understood her mission. The church is not meant always to be in a state of revival but is also to do ordinary, every-day work. But some remember this fact so well that they forget that the church is meant to have special occasions!

Dr Lloyd-Jones' early emphasis on the necessity of God's action, far from encouraging passivity, pointed men to the one source of true hope. And if conversion is God's work, then it is as possible for a hundred or a thousand simultaneously as it is for one. Yet Dr Lloyd-Jones would not have been in the ministry had he not also believed that God uses means to fulfil his purposes. Men singly or in multitudes are not brought to faith without hearing the Word of God. The Holy Spirit employs the truth in order to bring about conversion and he does so supremely by the agency of preaching. Thus Paul, speaking of his ministry, could assert, 'Our gospel came not unto you in word only, but also in power, and in the Holy Ghost and in much assurance' (*1 Thess.* 1:5). Upon which statement ML-J commented to his people at Sandfields:

> Paul knew while he was preaching to them that something was happening. He knew he was being used of God, he knew the Holy Ghost was driving his words deep into their hearts and souls, he was conscious of that power which changes men and women and which had changed him. So he says, that he had preached with 'much assurance'. Of course he did! He knew he was but the mouthpiece and the channel. God grant in his infinite mercy that it may be the same here tonight and that we all may experience

that power and the blessed, gracious influence of the Holy Ghost! There is no greater joy which any minister may ever have than that, to know for certain that it is not he himself, but Christ in him, who is doing the work.

Further, Dr Lloyd-Jones believed that the Scripture reveals the kind of preaching which is owned of God, and it was his persuasion upon this matter which was to render his own ministry so significantly different from that of many of his contemporaries. Much preaching, in his judgment, was controlled, not by Scripture, but by prevailing fashions of opinion and especially by the wishes of those in the pew. So-called 'intellectual preaching' was patently at variance with the Bible: 'As I read the Gospels,' he told his congregation as he began his second year in Aberavon, 'any man who gives the impression that "the mind of Christ" is open only to scholarship and learning is false to the very fundamentals of Christ's teaching. The words "absolute", "reality", "values", "cosmos", "Christology" and "Logos" are not the every-day words of our vocabulary, and yet, in reading contemporary literature and in listening to religious addresses in these days, these things seem to be vital and essential.'

Modern preaching, Dr Lloyd-Jones believed, had gone fundamentally wrong. He saw the main proof of that fact in the failure of the pulpit to recognise that the first work of the Holy Spirit is to *convict* of sin and to humble men in the presence of God. He knew that any preaching which soothes, comforts and pleases those who have never been brought to fear God, nor to seek his mercy, is not preaching which the Spirit of God will own. The truth is that he was going back to a principle once regarded as imperative for powerful evangelistic preaching, namely, that before men can be converted they must be convinced of sin. In 1883 C. H. Spurgeon declared:

> In the beginning, the preacher's business is not to convert men, but the very reverse. It is idle to attempt to heal those who are not wounded, to attempt to clothe those who have never been stripped, and to make those rich who have never realized their poverty. As long as the world stands, we shall need the Holy Ghost, not only as the Comforter, but also as the Convincer, who will 'reprove the world of sin, and of righteousness, and of judgment'.

It was this same principle, so largely forgotten even before Spurgeon's death in 1892, which reappeared at Sandfields, Aberavon. In ML-J's words in 1930: 'Present-day religion far too often soothes the conscience instead of awakening it; and produces a sense of self-satisfaction and eternal safety rather than a sense of unworthiness and the likelihood of eternal damnation.'

Among the varied features of Dr Lloyd-Jones' preaching nothing was to be more prominent than his insistence that, before the gospel can do good, men must be brought to understand the radical nature of sin. 'It is made perfectly clear in the pages of the New Testament that no man can be saved until, at some time or other, he has felt desperate about himself.' Accordingly, a large number of his sermons were preached with the specific intention of awakening spiritual concern. 'The way to obtain salvation is to seek it, and what makes one seek for it is that one realises one's need of it. That is, in reality, the great theme of the New Testament.' In an introduction to a sermon on John 8:32 he comments on the complaint that 'Present-day preaching does not save men, the churches are not getting converts':

> There is something even worse than that about the situation as I see it, and that is that present-day preaching does not even annoy men, but leaves them precisely where they were, without a ruffle and without the slightest disturbance . . . The church is regarded as a sort of dispensary where drugs and soothing mixtures are distributed and in which everyone should be eased and comforted. And the one theme of the church must be 'the love of God'. Anyone who happens to break these rules and who produces a disturbing effect upon members of his congregation is regarded as an objectionable person . . .

The Jews, he went on to preach in this same sermon, failed to receive Christ because they were unconvinced of sin, and all his unconverted hearers were in the same condition:

> Have you ever seen yourself as one so hopelessly involved in sin and so helpless face to face with life and the power of evil that nothing but Christ's death could save you? If not, then you are in the precise position of these Jews.

In another sermon from John's Gospel he reminded his hearers that the method of preaching which dealt first with sin was also followed by the Apostle Paul:

The great apostle finds it necessary not only to point out the glorious salvation in Christ Jesus, but also, before that, to bring to men conviction of sin, to point out to them the fallacy and the folly of their ways and their outlook. Many object to this and say that there is no purpose in it; indeed they go further and say that such preaching, which they call 'negative', is wrong and is contrary to the love displayed in the life of Christ . . . I say, with due reverence and consideration, unless we realise our deep and desperate need of it, the love of God is of no value to us and will make no difference to our lives. It thus behoves all of us, as we preach, not only to give our testimony as to the love of God towards us, but also to emphasise the equally great truth that all who have not felt a need of it are outside it.

This same teaching he applied with equal strength to what must be the church's vision of her work. Preaching near the end of 1928 from Nehemiah's words of distress at the state of Jerusalem, he urged that true prayer and spiritual work arise out of deep *feeling* for others: 'This is the beginning of all Christian work. Our time should be taken up in bringing conviction of sin to the sinner. The sinner must *feel* his own sin and the Christian must *feel* for the sin of others. We are called upon to *feel* the burden of sin around us, so to feel it that we drop on our knees and weep and pray.' A right understanding of sin and of the gospel will, he declared, certainly lead to prayer for the Holy Spirit:

> We say we are concerned for the sin of the town! How much prayer do we offer for the sin of the town? When we pass a drunkard it is not our business to say, 'What an awful man, what a beast!' No! judge not, but pray without ceasing. Christ came not to destroy — sin does that — but to save and release men from their sin. Will you as a church pray for the sinners of Aberavon and pray for God to save them through his Spirit? That is the meaning of a church . . . May God give us this power to pray for a visitation of his Spirit! God give power to all doing this in all places!

By 1929 conversions had become a regular feature of the life of the church at Aberavon. Church membership had steadily increased, from 146 (as the official figures stood in 1926) to 165 at the end of 1927, and then to 196 at the end of 1928. These figures, of course, included some Christians who had moved into the district and transferred their membership to Sandfields, but they do not show the considerable number who were already church members and yet were not converted until this period. The Robson family was one household which was profoundly influenced. Mrs Violet Robson was a leading figure in the church and a member of its Committee. Following one of the early Committee meetings soon after Dr Lloyd-Jones' arrival — the meeting at which he announced that there would be no more stage dramas in the hall — Mrs Robson said grimly to herself: 'You'll learn, young man, you'll learn!' 'But,' she said, telling the story years later, 'it was *I* who learnt.' Although already a Christian in 1927, her spiritual life was greatly changed in the years which followed. Her elder daughter, Peggy, who was already a church member (having entered *via* the candidates' class), after a great inward tussle, was to come to the realisation that she was not a Christian at all. By 1930 she knew that she had passed from death to life, and with a friend, Dorothy Lewis, who was another church member with an identical experience, she went to Dr Lloyd-Jones to ask what she should do. His reply was that they could bear testimony to their change of heart in an 'after-meeting' one Sunday evening and when this was done, their words encouraged a number of others to make the same confession. The result was that Dorothy Lewis, Peggy Robson, with her young sister, Marjorie, and forty others, were baptised by sprinkling on November 2, 1930.

By that date the number of those who were coming to a saving knowledge of Christ from outside the church was markedly increasing, some of them being among the forty-three whose baptism we have just noted. Church membership in 1930 was to increase by 88 of which number 70 were recorded as 'from the world'. With deductions made on account of 'deaths, transfers and expulsions', the nett increase in membership that year was 63 (from 248 to 311).

One of the forty-three of November 2 was a certain Harry Wood. In his youth Wood had played soccer for Cwmbran and Monmouthshire but by the late 1920s, when he was one of the many out of work, the sporting enjoyments of those care-free earlier years had gone. When, at length, he became a Christian, the old sportsman, who loved a picturesque turn of phrase, would relate his testimony in such words as these: 'I sought satisfaction in many ways. I had my problem, I was all wrong. I would go into the cricket match and there I would see the white splashes on the greensward. I would go in through the north gate with my problem, I sought satisfaction watching as they wielded the willow and there my problem would be forgotten, but as I went out through the south I picked it up again. Then I came into this church one Sunday evening, sat in the gallery, and heard the doctor preach. He preached to me and showed me the way whereby I could enter by the north gate, and go out through the south, with all my problems solved!'

Perhaps few who saw Harry Wood as he tramped the streets looking for work would have supposed that *all* his problems were solved. He had once been well employed as a colliery sawyer, but neither that work nor any other could now be found. Yet the one thing which now concerned him was his service to Christ, and when he was asked by the officials in the local Labour Exchange, 'Have you been genuinely seeking work?', he was so sensitive to the implications of that question that he walked all the way up to a colliery which was working part-time at Bryn, a village in the hills some miles above Port Talbot. There his enquiry to the under-manager was answered by the exclamation, 'Work? We haven't got work here!' Concerned at only having a verbal reply to report at the Labour Exchange, Harry Wood proceeded to the school where E. T. Rees was teaching, with a plea that the Church Secretary should obtain the under-manager's refusal in writing — a request which the Church Secretary gladly fulfilled later in the day.

The pastor of Sandfields had few more joyful conversations than those with Harry Wood and he was often surprised at the spiritual perception of one who, though well on in years, was such a young Christian. No one was more fully involved in the life of the church, and especially at the prayer meeting. After one especially memorable prayer meeting on the morning of a Good Friday, Dr Lloyd-Jones was surprised when Wood expressed his disappointment as he left. In response to his pastor's enquiry why he should feel like that on such an occasion, the older man replied that it had been his prayer that he should be allowed to go 'straight *home*' from just such a prayer meeting.

At the Monday night prayer meetings it was Dr Lloyd-Jones' practice to take no active part himself, save to give out an occasional hymn if it seemed appropriate in the course of the meeting. Otherwise the time was given wholly to prayer. Each week a different male member was asked — without prior notice — to commence the meeting with a reading from Scripture and with prayer. At a prayer meeting early in 1931 Harry Wood was called upon to open the meeting. He did so by reading Christ's High-Priestly prayer recorded in John 17, and then he prayed with such 'glorious unction' that Dr Lloyd-Jones felt that he had heard nothing like it. The man seemed to be more in heaven than upon earth. When he stopped, and went to take a seat in the front row, Dr Lloyd-Jones heard heavy breathing and, opening his eyes, had only just time to catch the beloved Harry Wood as he fell to the floor, dead. Although there was no more prayer in the church that night, for the pastor pronounced the benediction and asked the people to leave quietly, the departure of Harry Wood was one of the events which marked the beginning of an extraordinary spiritual stirring.[1] In the winter of 1930–31 the whole church seemed moved as by a consciousness of the presence of God and Dr Lloyd-Jones traced a quickening of his own spirit to this same period.

The year 1931 saw an addition of 135 to the membership of the church, of which 128 were 'from the world'. A number of the Sunday evening sermons of that year were to be remembered by those who were present as long as they lived. The text for the evening sermon on the first Sunday in March 1931, was Isaiah 55:8-9, 'For my thoughts are not your thoughts, neither are your ways my ways, saith the Lord.' At the close, fifteen people asked to be received into the membership of the church. On a similar evening, another twelve expressed their desire to be publicly identified with Christ and his people. One hot summer's evening, July 19, 1931, when the text was, 'For thus saith the Lord to the men of Judah and Jerusalem, Break up your fallow ground . . .', the message was to be particularly spoken of for years to come. The life of the natural man, the preacher declared, is like a farm in which the most important field is left waste, uncultivated, 'fallow'. Man neglects his soul and gives no thought to God and to eternity. He then proceeded to deal with the reasons for this neglect: first, ignorance of the fact that we have such a field; too many suppose that 'religion' is only for certain types of people. Second, laziness and thoughtlessness — objecting to the effort involved and desiring

[1] For Woods and other converts, see Bethan Lloyd-Jones: *Memories of Sandfields* (Edinburgh: Banner of Truth, 2008).

just to 'enjoy' life and pleasure. Third, 'Too busy in the other fields.'
The next head of the sermon was the command of God, 'Break it up!'
After emphasising that *man* has to do this, for 'he that cometh to God
must believe that he is, and that he is a rewarder of them that dili-
gently seek him' (*Heb.* 11:6), Dr Lloyd-Jones showed how the fallow
ground was to be broken. His brief sermon notes listed: 'Realise you
have it; Chapel-going; Prayer; Bible-reading; Meditation; Giving up
sins; Turning to God.' The sermon then concluded with reasons why
this command of God must be obeyed: because the 'fallow ground' is
the best part of the farm, the only part truly worth farming: 'Nothing
else yields a real crop. What does sin give us at the end? What have
we to show for it?' But the fallow ground is capable of yielding a crop
of love, joy, peace, longsuffering, gentleness, goodness, faith, meekness and temperance. And, finally, the crowded chapel heard on that
July Sunday evening, that the farm is only held on leasehold, a rent
day is soon coming. Our actions will be judged, and all who do not
break up the fallow ground and bear fruit unto righteousness will be
without excuse. In the silence of that crowded building every person
was called to immediate obedience to the divine command.[2]

Such is an outline of one of many such sermons preached at
this period for conviction and conversion. Without question it was
deeply disturbing to many who came to listen. Morgan Beddow, for
example, first came to Sandfields twice in 1928 and then decided that
he would listen no more to the man who 'put the breeze up him'. He
had never been distressed over spiritual things in all his life and he
did not intend to start. But, scarcely knowing why, Beddow was soon
back in Sandfields and the sermon he heard so awed him and led
him to the fear of God that he was never to be the same man again.
With assurance of salvation, he became a member in 1930 and men
marvelled at the change in his life.

---

[2] The command was always to faith and to repentance and not to an immediate
public profession of conversion. Far from encouraging anyone to stay to the after-
meeting and 'join the church', Dr Lloyd-Jones frequently gave warning against the
danger of a premature profession of Christ: 'There is a sense in which it is true to
say that the church is a very much more dangerous place than the world for the
unbeliever . . . The church has been far too anxious to put people into church-
membership . . . church-membership, unless it is based upon a true and definite
belief in and experience of Jesus Christ, the Son of God, can be exceedingly dangerous and can even be the cause of damning a soul.'

The guiding principle in Dr Lloyd-Jones' evangelistic preaching was that pride and ignorance are the chief reasons why men trust in themselves and will not turn to Christ. Men suppose that they know God and therefore confidently argue that in 'a moral universe of love it is not possible that only a few Christian people are to be saved', but the truth is, that they are at enmity against the God of whom they profess to speak:

> What accounts for the fact that so few ever speak of the judgment in these days is that they do not believe in God. They think that they do, but when you come to analyse their belief you find that it is but a projection of certain ideas which happen to please them. Their god is something which they created themselves, a being who is always prepared to oblige and excuse them. They do not worship him with awe and respect, indeed they do not worship him at all. They reveal that their so-called god is no god at all in their talk. For they are for ever saying that 'they simply cannot believe that God will punish the unrepentant sinner to all eternity'. *They* cannot believe that God will do so, therefore they draw the conclusion that God does not and will not. In other words, God does what they believe he ought to do or not do. What a false and blasphemous conception of God! How utterly untrue and unworthy! Such is the new paganism of today.

> The man who is concerned most of all about his public appearance before men is never much concerned about his private attitude before God. You have a great and a good name, bouquets are thrown to you during your life and wreaths innumerable will be placed upon your grave. You are proud of yourself and satisfied with yourself. Men and women think highly of you, you are praised as a 'good sort' and as a 'good fellow', for your good nature is proverbial. What a farce! What deceit! What if you were found out? What would they think of you if every act and every thought of yours were suddenly placed before them? What if they could but enter your heart and mind for just one day and find out what is taking place there? What if they knew your secret life as well as your public life? . . . As long as you are content to go on fooling others about yourself, you will never face yourself, and until you face yourself honestly you will never feel the need of Jesus Christ our Lord as your personal Saviour.

It should be said at this point Dr Lloyd-Jones believed that, while the truth ought to result in profound emotion, the cultivation of 'emotionalism' was thoroughly alien to true Christianity. Feeling *alone* he saw as not merely valueless, it was positively dangerous. 'Emotionalism is ever the most real, because the most subtle, enemy of evangelicalism.' True feeling must be the result of truth believed and understood, and he frequently gave warning against that type of service where attempts are made to induce emotion by 'working up' the meeting with music and choruses, or by the telling of moving stories. 'Tears are a poor criterion for faith, being carried away in a meeting by eloquence or singing or excitement is not the same as committing oneself to Christ.' To aim at emotion is the surest way to produce counterfeit Christians.

Thus his belief was that in a service where feeling could be restrained it ought to be restrained. The power of God was more likely to be known in a solemn stillness than amid noise and excitement. Silence and an expectant seriousness, born of a realisation of the nearness of God, were striking characteristics of the services at Sandfields. Audible interruptions, traditional in some branches of Welsh evangelicalism, were noticeable by their absence. This fact was not always appreciated by occasional visitors, and on one Sunday evening, after E. T. Rees had given the notices at the middle of a service, he recalls how Dr Lloyd-Jones directed him to go to speak to a man in the gallery. Before the first hymn had been concluded this stranger had made his presence known by a loud 'Amen!', and his interruptions were to continue until the Church Secretary finally reached him with the message he had been commissioned to deliver. 'Brother, I am sure you would like to see souls saved?' Mr Rees began. 'I would, Hallelujah!' was the exuberant response. 'Well,' said Mr Rees, 'shut up!' The silence which followed confirmed Dr Lloyd-Jones' opinion that the man's shouts had not been the irrepressible exclamations which may spontaneously occur when God stirs men's souls to their depths.

In the midst of the rising tide of blessing in 1931, one older Christian member, who could remember the beginning of the century, exclaimed, 'Why, this is revival! The power of the Spirit is greater here than in 1904.' What was occurring at Sandfields was certainly a repetition of what has been seen whenever there is a real spiritual awakening. In true revival, conviction of sin, sometimes amounting to agony of guilt, is widespread, and in the case of those who are finally brought to salvation no human endeavours can unloose them from their sense of bondage. A God-given persuasion of being lost and condemned can only be removed by 'the Spirit of adoption' who follows his first work of conviction with the assurance that sin is forgiven. The man who has truly felt his sin will not be prepared to stop short of a conscious persuasion of his salvation, and when he has that assurance the height of his jubilation may correspond to the depth from which he sees himself to have been delivered. Thus Dr Lloyd-Jones believed that, as in the days of the Acts of the Apostles, when a truly serious view of sin takes hold upon men, the ultimate result will be a glorious conception of the gospel. Believing this, he was not surprised that the vague, contemporary religion which professed to be Christian and yet said nothing to convict men of sin, should be equally silent upon the joy of true assurance.

Similarly, in a sermon on the words, 'Many of the Samaritans of that city believed on him for the saying of the woman, which testified, he told me all that ever I did' (*John* 4:39), he showed what happens when a person delivered from conviction of sin becomes a witness to others:

This sinful, forlorn, notorious character, who had fallen so low that she had even ceased to be a topic of conversation, was so desperate in her sin that no one was any longer shocked by what they might hear about it! Such was the one who called upon the townspeople to come out of the city to see Christ! Why! there is enough gospel in that fact alone to save the whole world if we could but see it . . . But if the messenger was strange, the message or the way in which she put it was even more remarkable. 'Come', she said, 'see a man, which told me all things that ever I did.' What an extraordinary message! 'Come see a man, not which told me all my good points, not one who praised me and told me what a good woman I was, but one who told me my faults, told me about my sins, revealed to me my own past life with all its horror.' Ah! that is the very secret of the gospel of Christ. Christ exposes our sins and weaknesses, but God be praised, he does not stop at that. Why was this woman shouting about the streets? Simply because Christ had not merely exposed them but had removed them . . .

Well, here were these men, listening to this woman. Seeing the change in the woman and hearing her story, they determine to try it for themselves. There is a danger of their sins also being exposed, but what does it matter as long as they get the happiness which she had! What does it matter though the whole world may know your past, and all the town laugh at you because of your penitential tears? What does it matter when you know that God has forgiven that past and you are filled with the joy of salvation and are thrilled with a new life? And off they go with the woman to see Christ.

There were many listeners in Sandfields who, in their new-found freedom, could assent entirely to these words. In the Monday prayer meetings earnest intercession had increasingly mingled with fervent praise. Assembled for prayer, the church came to know such a sense of liberty in the presence of God that there were nights when all sense of time seemed lost. Certainly the prayer meeting, once so poorly attended, could not now be contained within two hours on account of the numbers who were ready to pray and to engage in thanksgiving. One Monday night, about May 1931, the prayer meeting began as usual at 7.15 P.M. and was stopped by Dr Lloyd-Jones at 10 P.M. after forty-four had taken part in prayer! There were other occasions when the Wednesday Fellowship spontaneously turned into a time of praise. On one such evening, a man, new to spiritual things, rose to ask Dr Lloyd-Jones the question, 'What is a Christian?' The reply, as E. T. Rees remembers it, was this, 'To define a Christian would take all through the night, and all through tomorrow and all through the next night.' But, to the surprise of the whole gathering, a woman who was never known to speak at the Fellowship, and who was later to die of cancer at Bridgend, rose to declare: 'A Christian, Doctor, is the heir of salvation, the purchase of God, the born of his Spirit, the washed in his blood.' 'Thank you, Mrs B.', her pastor replied, and addressing the people continued, 'Those who can say — "I am the heir of salvation" — get up and thank God in just a few words!' A prayer meeting resulted in which more than forty were again to take part before the close.

One of the clearest memories of E. T. Rees from those days is of the eagerness with which the congregations gathered. On a Sunday evening the building would start to fill as much as an hour before the 6.30 hour of service, with sometimes not a seat remaining empty by 6 P.M. The Monday and Wednesday meetings had both to be removed to the church itself on account of the numbers attending.

Shop-keepers would arrive straight from their business without an evening meal. Night-shift workers, due to report for work at 8.30 P.M., would come in their working clothes, preferring to miss part of the meeting rather than the whole.

This new life witnessed at Sandfields required neither publicity nor organisation to carry news of it to others. The word spread in all manner of ways. Women spoke over their shopping of how their husbands now preferred prayer meetings to the cinema. At school, one afternoon, a teacher was told by a boy in her class, 'We *had* a dinner, today, Miss! We had gravy, potatoes, meat, and cabbage, and rice pudding' — they had rarely had such a meal at home before, and the reason followed: 'My father has been converted!' So the money this man had formerly spent on drink, when he got his pay on Fridays, now came home for his wife and children. Others saw a neighbour, who had been a well-known spirit-medium in Aberavon, abandon the only livelihood which she knew, for the gospel. Every Sunday evening she had been paid three guineas — quite a large sum in those days — for leading a spiritist meeting. Then one Sunday when she was ill, and unable to go out, her attention was attracted to the numbers who were passing her house on the way to Sandfields. The very sight of these people, and their evident anticipation, awakened a desire in her to attend a service herself. This she did, to be herself transformed and thereafter to live a consistent Christian life until her death. Included in the testimony which she subsequently gave to the messenger who had led her to Christ were these remarkable words:

> The moment I entered your chapel and sat down on a seat amongst the people, I was conscious of a supernatural power. I was conscious of the same sort of supernatural power as I was accustomed to in our spiritist meetings, but there was one big difference; I had a feeling that the power in your chapel was a *clean* power.

Some of the most unlikely characters were brought to Sandfields by friends. One such was Mark McCann, whom Mrs Lloyd-Jones still remembers from the night when he entered the chapel for the first time — 'A thin, tallish, raw-boned man, his grey hair well plastered down, a slightly embarrassed expression on his face and an incredible moustache!' As his Christian companion passed her pew he whispered, 'I've got one of the Devil's Generals here tonight, Mrs

Jones, pray for him to be converted.' McCann, of Scots and Irish parentage, was then probably in his early sixties. Once a miner, his living and his enjoyment had centred largely upon the fights in which he engaged at fairs. With his vicious temper, and considerable strength, it was only the providence of God which had restrained him from actually killing anyone. Once, when his dog had eaten the dinner intended for him to consume, he had cut off its head with a bread knife! McCann was one of those whose conversion was swift. On his first visit to the chapel he was arrested by the Spirit of God. The next Sunday evening he was there again and, to the surprise of his companion, when the service ended he indicated his intention to stay to the after-meeting. When the usual question was put at that meeting, amidst the solemn joy of many witnesses, Mark McCann stood to profess the name of Christ, 'And from that moment,' writes Mrs Lloyd-Jones, 'he showed himself to be a changed man, unfailingly faithful, truly born again — another, somewhat elderly, "babe" for the church to love and nurture.'

There were others who came, not as the result of Christian testimony, but simply because they heard about what was being preached in Sandfields. William Thomas, or 'Staffordshire Bill' as he was commonly known, was drinking in the Working Men's Club in Aberavon one Sunday afternoon. As usual, he was by himself, for even men who had few moral standards had long since learned to avoid his 'filthy language and general unpleasantness' whenever they could. In the words of Mrs Lloyd-Jones:

> There he was, drinking himself into his usual sodden condition, and as he afterwards confessed, feeling low, hopeless and depressed, trusting to the drink to drown those inward pangs and fears which sometimes disturbed him. There were several men in little groups of twos and threes in the Club room, drinking and talking, and suddenly he found himself listening, at first involuntarily but then anxiously, to a conversation between two men at the table next to his. He caught the words 'the Forward' and then something about the 'preacher', and then a complete sentence that was to change the whole of his life. 'Yes,' said the one man to the other, 'I was there last Sunday night and that preacher said nobody was hopeless — he said there was hope for everybody.' Of the rest of the conversation he heard nothing, but, arrested and now completely

sobered, he said to himself, 'If there's hope for everybody, there's hope for me. I'll go to that chapel myself and see what that man says.'

But William Thomas' intention was not easily fulfilled. That first Sunday he walked to the open gate of the railings that fenced the church, stood for some minutes, then, his nerve failing him, he turned and went home. Although throughout the wretched week that followed he waited for the next Sunday evening to arrive, somehow he reached the chapel only to hear singing. Faced with the realisation that he was late, 'with his heart in his boots and full of some nameless fear, he once more turned away and went home'. Now, though his misery was increased, he had no thought of attempting to drown his terrors of conviction in drink. The Spirit of God had already begun a work in his heart which would prevent him from going back to his old ways. The third Sunday evening he was again at the gate, 'wondering nervously what he should do next', when one of the congregation welcomed him with the words, 'Are you coming in, Bill? Come and sit with me.'

That same night 'Staffordshire Bill' passed from condemnation to life. 'He found,' Mrs Lloyd-Jones tells us,

> that he could understand the things that were being said, he believed the gospel and his heart was flooded with a great peace. Old things had passed away, all things had become new. The transformation in his face was remarkable, it had the radiance of a saint. As he walked out that night, lovingly shepherded by J. M., they passed me, and J. M. said, 'Mrs Jones, this is Staffordshire Bill.' I shall never forget the agonised look on his face, for he flinched as though he had been struck a sudden blow. 'Oh no, oh no,' he said, 'that's a bad old name for a bad old man; I am William Thomas now.'

The change in the man was apparent for all to see. He lived some three or four miles up the valley from Aberavon and in the years when he had employment he had carried on a door-to-door fish business. It was no uncommon sight in those days for people to see Staffordshire Bill's pony taking the fish-cart home, while the man himself, having fallen backward off the driver's seat as the cart went up the steep hill, lay drunk among the unsold fish! He was nearly seventy at the time of his conversion, the pony and cart gone, but, in the words of Mrs Lloyd-Jones, 'He thought nothing of those three or four steep uphill miles when once "the light of the knowledge of the glory of God in the face of Jesus Christ" had shined in his heart. He was at every meeting — twice on Sunday, Monday night prayer meeting, Wednesday night Church Fellowship and Saturday night Brotherhood — that old battered face transformed and radiant with an inner joy.'

* * *

The unusual nature of what was happening in Aberavon was common knowledge in South Wales in the early 1930s, though very little information appeared in print. Such secular papers as did report it scarcely saw more than what was externally observable, and yet that was surprising enough. C. Griffith-Jones wrote in the *News Chronicle* on 'A Physician of Souls':

> Seven years ago Martin Lloyd-Jones, M.D., M.R.C.P., was on the threshold of a brilliantly promising career in Harley Street. He renounced it to labour in one of the most difficult fields of Forward Movement evangelism in Wales. The Sandfields district of Aberavon is a dead end. Even when the sun shines, sandy wastes and dreary, crowded houses convey a sense of desolation, almost of hopelessness. What could a man denied work, disillusioned by social callousness, do here but live for a day, deteriorate, drift and die?
>
> Into this desperate little world came the young physician-minister, preaching, living the gospel of old-new hope. He shocked the locality out of its despair. This world had failed them; there was another world.
>
> Men listened amazed. Here was one who practised the gospel that he preached with such tremendous conviction. He had given up a great career — fame, money, leisure — to live and work among the poor and the hopeless.
>
> Christianity was not a mere fable, then, but a living modern fact!
>
> The little church filled. Under the previous pastor it had not been a dead letter by any means, but now it awakened to a galvanic new life.

Not only in Port Talbot, but all around the district, the word went forth that surprising things were happening at the 'mission hall' on the sand dunes. Curious, sceptical, doubting, hoping, believing, people flocked to the church.

It was no passing wonder. Today, years after the first revelation of new power, the congregations still overflow the church. Every meeting is a 'big meeting'.

More than 500 members, the faithful augmented by 'hard cases', sinners whom others considered, and who regarded themselves, as beyond redemption, irretrievably lost . . . No whist drives, bazaars or worldly side-shows, no dramas except the great drama of salvation.

A working-class (and unemployed) membership raising £1,000 a year for church work. Crowded prayer meetings, a crowded 'seiat' (church meeting) in mid-week, a crowded brotherhood meeting on Saturday, of all nights, when men discuss the problems of spiritual salvation and the pastor sums up the discussion.

Sandfields now shares the glad tidings with all Wales. The 'physician of souls', who shuns publicity, draws thousands to hear his message in all parts of the Principality. He will not stand for a Press photographer. But his name is a household word in Wales. An awe-inspiring new force has arisen in the life of Wales.

Interesting though such words may be to us, it was this kind of reporting which confirmed Dr Lloyd-Jones in his silence over the blessing they experienced in the church. He never referred to what they had seen in their midst as a 'revival'. Compared with the rain which the land needed, it was only a shower. Yet they had experienced a glimpse of the glory, and it left him more persuaded than ever that the supreme need of the church was to 'cease from man'. He had seen things of which he felt it was almost too sacred to speak. He preferred to suppress information rather than to risk anything which gave glory to man. So no one in Sandfields ever put pen to paper, and the figures recording the remarkable increase in church membership were never released.

ELEVEN

The Church Family

With so many newly-arrived members in Sandfields, differing so widely in age and often in background, it might be supposed that a certain degree of disunity was inevitable. Many had no previous experience of what was expected within a church; instead, they had to learn from the beginning. The members of the church Committee themselves were faced with a novel situation, for they had never seen such an enlargement of numbers before.

But the truth is that one of the chief features of Sandfields, noted by many outside visitors in the early 1930s, was the extraordinary degree of closeness and inter-dependence among the people. Although so many were new-born babes in the Christian life, far from feeling strange in their new position, they were instantly conscious of belonging to a family. The unity which they now knew was instinctive. And, for their part, the older Christians needed no directions on how to receive and help those for whom the gospel was so new. They had no greater interest than in the signs of grace and of growth which week by week were to be observed in the church.

The eagerness to be together which marked the young converts was indeed prominent throughout the entire membership. The Rev. R. J. Rees of the Forward Movement describes a visit he made to Sandfields one Sunday about the summer of 1931. Dr Lloyd-Jones was away, but that made no difference to the size of the morning congregation which filled the building to its utmost capacity. Rees wrote in *The Treasury* (March 1932):

The service was for me a breaking forth of God's glory, but I believe I rejoiced just as much on the Sunday afternoon to find myself seated in the midst of a Bible Class of some 80 in number. And what, think you, we discussed? Where did I find them? Nowhere else but in the midst of the Eighth Chapter of the Epistle to the Romans and there for the long but interesting, bright afternoon, I had to sit it out, the target of questions asked by young and older men arising from the dialectic of the Apostle concerning 'the mind of the flesh', the carnal mind, the new man, and the leading of the Spirit. It was a beautiful afternoon. The sands were near, but there they were — 80 strong — with me, not Dr Martin Lloyd-Jones.

Not long after this, Eliseus Howells was to make similar observations. Writing in *Y Goleuad* of the prayer and fellowship meetings at Sandfields, he said:

These meetings are noted for their length because hardly one of them ends in under two hours, and we have seen between 160 and 200 present in them on cold, stormy, winter evenings. The rejoicing that we commonly link with the feelings is hardly present, although a great measure of deep joy is present. Sometimes between fifteen and twenty take part, and it is easy to perceive that the atmosphere is too laden with the law for the wicked to live in it, and too abounding in grace for the legalist so much as to breathe in hypocrisy.

It was noteworthy that the composition of the Brotherhood meetings on Saturday nights was far from being as homogeneous as that of the other church meetings, for curiosity often brought visitors from other churches and from backgrounds alien to any kind of Christianity. Some who were not yet ready to venture into the chapel on Sundays might well put in their first appearance on a Saturday night to see what *Y dyn bach* ('the little man') had got to say. (The Welsh term has an element of affection in it not obvious in the English.) 'All sorts of men they were,' E. T. Rees has recalled, 'with all sorts of opinions. Roman Catholics were there as well as Protestants; sceptics as well as Christians; there were people who belonged to such bodies as the Apostolics and the Pentecostals sitting alongside one or two deep-dyed Calvinists. We were an odd mixture and sometimes things would get pretty hot! A man would say, "It's all right for you, Doctor, to talk about being a Christian, how can a man be a Christian on an empty belly?" Then you would have a clash between the man in the chair and the man on his feet.'

Not infrequently objections of that kind would be voiced by visitors who were convinced Socialists, persuaded that chapels stood for the interests of capitalism. But more than once, a man who came to the Brotherhood believing in political solutions was ultimately brought to confess that there was only one solution to life's problems, and that was to be found in the New Testament.

The Saturday night discussions were commonly hard-hitting and intensely serious. Next to the spiritual impact, the thing which so often struck E. T. Rees was the demands made upon the minds of those who came: 'I used to be amazed at the high educational standard attained in those debates which went on between 7.15 and about 9 p.m. It was comparable with University extension classes, which some of us had attended and some of us had conducted.' Anything of the nature of entertainment was entirely absent; on the contrary there was an element of severity about the leader which is not generally associated with church activities. On one occasion an individual was literally put out! The man rose to complain, 'I cannot believe in the deity of Christ.' After a moment's careful scrutiny of the speaker, with an instant and, as it proved, accurate assessment, Dr Lloyd-Jones, replied, 'You have said that more than once. Very well, you will say it no more here, you must go!' The man left, only to return subsequently in a different spirit and to take his place among believers. Dr Lloyd-Jones' penetrating assessments of those who spoke on Saturday or Wednesday nights were a regular feature of the meetings.

If love for the children of God is the mark of all who have 'passed from death unto life', as emphasised in the First Epistle of John, it is not surprising that there was an abounding love evident in Sandfields. We have already mentioned some of the converts, but the truth is that they were representative of many others, and in them all there shone a devotion to the messenger from whom they learned the truth. It was in profound affection that they all called him 'the Doctor'. Not E. T. Rees only, but a whole host of them counted it their privilege to serve alongside their pastor and to be with him whenever possible. Frequently after evening meetings or services Dr Lloyd-Jones would stay behind to talk with individuals, yet, no matter how late the hour, when he finished there would always be one or more of 'the men' waiting to accompany him back to his house. Often one of the inner band, of which E. T. Rees was the head, would offer to go with him on pastoral visitation. Mr Rees remembers one night when a case of peculiar difficulty kept them both out late at the home of one of the members after a mid-week meeting. Finally they left, hungry and tired, and not before Dr Lloyd-Jones had spoken sternly to the member of the household who was responsible for the trouble. Despite the late hour, E. T. set off as usual to the manse gate, before going to his own home. Deep in conversation as they walked, Martyn suddenly stopped on the bridge between Sandfields and his home and, looking back on the church silhouetted in the moonlight, he exclaimed, 'That's our church — a truly Corinthian church! Now for ham and eggs!'

The love of the men for their pastor took various forms. On one occasion in the early years at Sandfields, the foreman of the tin-plate factory, then on night-shift, enthusiastically agreed to wake the Doctor daily at 7 A.M. so that the two could have a six-mile walk on the moors before Lloyd-Jones' day began. But he was soon alarmed to find that these early-morning outings, far from benefiting his minister, brought him to confess that if he did not give them up he would have to abandon preaching! Another admirer of the outdoor life and would-be helper was a local army drill sergeant whose work gave him the use of some fine horses. Hearing of Dr Lloyd-Jones' love of horses, the sergeant arrived unexpectedly at the manse on horseback one day before breakfast, leading another fine stallion, with empty saddle, on a rein beside him. In this instance the Doctor was not to be enticed!

More normal occasions for one or more of the men to accompany Dr Lloyd-Jones were his twice-weekly preaching visits to various parts of South Wales. Even before the 1930s, the afternoons of Tuesdays and Thursdays each week were regularly employed for this purpose. He had no car and generally went by train, but sometimes when trains were not available he accepted the ready offers of transport from willing assistants who were ready to borrow a car from anywhere rather than leave the Doctor in difficulties. Morgan Beddow — whose first hearing of Dr Lloyd-Jones had put him to flight — was to become one of his travelling companions. In later years he was to recall how once he borrowed a car from Briton Ferry for this purpose. On another occasion, when the Doctor had missed the train to Llandeilo, it was a Fiat which a friend had recently purchased for £5, which was pressed into service. Despite the Doctor's misgivings at the appearance of the Fiat, it somehow held together as they sped over the Black Mountains at 'over forty miles per hour'. 'We looked', said Beddow, 'like a couple of race goers, I in my slouch cap and he in his old bowler (from his student days) which had become flattened in our rush.' Their destination was reached by 2.45 P.M. in time for the afternoon service!

One unusual incident during an outing which Beddow recalled concerned a clash between the Doctor and the Church Secretary of a chapel building which a smaller church had borrowed for the special occasion. When Dr Lloyd-Jones heard this Secretary telling his counterpart from the small church that they required £5 for the use of their building, he did not hide his anger, convinced that £1 would have been quite sufficient and that the smaller church which he had come to help was in need of funds. 'I will never come to your church again', he exclaimed. The Secretary, mortified and alarmed, stuttered, 'Oh, Doctor, don't say that. I was only having a bit of fun.' But his rebuker was in no mood for 'fun' and spoke his mind very plainly.

Much could be written on this bond between the pastor and his men, for it showed itself in so many ways. From George Jenkins, whose conversion had occurred on the same day as ML-J's birthday, he was to receive a birthday card on December 20 as long as this grateful Christian was alive. Another man, despite his good position as a docks pilot, had been a hopeless drunkard. After his conversion three photographs adorned his mantelpiece; one, taken during his pre-Christian days by a former friend, showed him leaning helplessly against a lamp-post; a second showed him sitting beside Lloyd-Jones on the seashore, where he had joined the Sunday-school outing one Whit Monday and been drawn into spiritual conversation for the first time; while a third showed him as a smart and clean-shaven figure whose life now centred in the church and the gospel. Each picture had its own one-word caption written beneath, 'Lost', 'Found', 'Saved'.

Sometimes a few words from these men would reveal the depth of their feelings. When, some years later, George Jenkins whose life was so radically changed lay dying in London, a former friend from Sandfields visited him. One of the old man's first enquiries was to ask for 'his beloved father in Christ' and, he added, 'I would rather see him, than Paul himself!'

The fellowship of the church was, however, a great deal more than the relationship between pastor and individuals. It was pre-eminently a family unity and, no matter what the background of the once broken elements of mankind which now filled the pews, all that was needed in order truly to 'belong' was a common attachment to Christ. While Acts 4:32 was not literally followed at every point, the resemblance between Sandfields and Jerusalem was indeed real: 'And the multitude of them that believed were of one heart and of one soul: neither said any of them that ought of the things which he possessed was his own; but they had all things common.'

There were many other ways in which the gospel had a practical out-working in the church family and in some of these Bethan Lloyd-Jones was involved. A Thursday afternoon 'Sisterhood' already existed at Sandfields in 1927, but when feminine converts were added to the church Mrs Lloyd-Jones began a small Bible class in the parlour at 57 Victoria Road. As the numbers of those wanting spiritual help grew, it had to be moved to the church. The class included such women as the converted spiritualist medium who, when asked by Bethan in the course of Bible study in 1 Samuel, what she thought of the action of the witch of Endor in relation to Saul and Samuel (*1 Sam.* 28), hung her head and confessed that she preferred never to think of such evil any more.

Such individuals as the former medium required the loving care of the whole church. Another young Christian in that category was Mark McCann, noted in the last chapter, whom Mrs Lloyd-Jones taught to read as she has described in her *Memories of Sandfields*.

The financial record of the congregation, in the midst of severe economic depression, bears its own testimony. For the four years 1930, 1931, 1932, 1933, the annual receipts from the freewill offerings of the members were £1,074, £1,069, £955, and £1,102 respectively. Within those years the debt on the property was cut from £1,750 to £615 (shortly to be cleared entirely) and the church indicated to the Forward Movement headquarters in 1932 that the Movement's annual grant of £90 was no longer required. The value of money at this date is indicated by the fact that, with the church's annual expenditure around £500–£600, the surplus was enough to build a new manse, install electric lighting and additional seating for more than 60 in the church, provide new heating apparatus in church hall and vestry, and to enlarge the church still further by the building of a large classroom adjacent to the main building and separated only by a sliding partition. The new classroom both served the Sunday school and enabled an overflow of people to be accommodated at Sunday night services.

While something of the spirit of the apostolic age was indeed present at Sandfields, it is also true that the faults which marked the early churches were not absent. Many of the converts had behind them the greater part of a lifetime spent in bad habits, many had minimal knowledge, and not a few upon their conversion found themselves wholly without any support or sympathy in their own families. One young Christian, returning joyfully from a Monday night prayer meeting, was greeted by his wife with the words, 'I would rather have you coming in drunk than coming in from a prayer meeting!' It is scarcely surprising if there were problems. Many had to struggle with difficulties and not always with success. As in the fast-growing churches of the New Testament, the situation required the corporate care of the whole membership one for another. Preaching on that theme from Galatians 6:1-5, 'Brethren, if a man be overtaken in a fault, ye which are spiritual, restore such an one in the spirit of meekness,' ML-J told his people:

> That is the rule of Paul. We are a family — one in Christ Jesus. If a brother falls the whole family suffers from the same and is dragged down by his fall. If a member of the church falls into the gutter the whole church falls with him. When a member goes down, this church goes down — we must all go down into the gutter after him and pick him up. You never know, one day you may be the one who falls into the gutter, and you will be glad that day if the church comes and pulls you out. It is no good turning your back on this fallen member, the world will only laugh at you, you may brazen it out, but the world will know. 'Restore such an one in the spirit of meekness; considering thyself, lest thou also be tempted', says Paul, 'For if a man think himself to be something, when he is nothing, he deceiveth himself'. That verse ought to be hanging on our walls, always before our eyes; not the usual nice little verses about the love of God, no, get a card printed with these words: 'For if a man think himself to be something, when he is nothing, he deceives himself'! If we read that every morning, what

a difference it would make to us and to the people working with us. It brings us back to the realisation that we are broken earthenware, saved by the grace of God.

As news of the fellowship that was known at Sandfields spread to Christians further afield an increasing number of letters arrived at the Lloyd-Jones' manse. Some were from believers who were unable to obtain counsel from their own pastors. They looked to Sandfields and joined in prayer for the spread of the power of true religion across the land. Morgan Beddow is sure that one week in the 1930s, when the Lloyd-Joneses were away from home and it was his duty to forward mail, he forwarded no fewer than ninety letters. Whether Dr Lloyd-Jones, without a secretary, answered them all, we cannot say, but it is clear from surviving correspondence that he did respond to this further demand on his time. The following undated reply to one regular correspondent near Swansea is characteristic:

Dear Mr Thomas,

I rejoiced to receive your kind letter this morning and to read all the good news you have to give. It is glorious to think that the life which we have received in Christ Jesus is Eternal Life, is it not? Though we have not heard from or of one another for some time, still the life goes on, and I rejoiced to find it in all its freshness in your words. Whatever may happen, whatever difficulties and obstacles may be in the way, still we know with St Paul that 'neither death, nor life, nor angels, nor principalities, nor powers, nor things present, nor things to come, nor height, nor depth, nor any other creature, shall be able to separate us from the love of God, which is in Christ Jesus our Lord'. That is the Christian confidence. Nay, also, we know that to the extent that we are faithful and loyal to that Lord, we shall never be separated from one another, but as fellow-believers, as joint-heirs, as brethren and sisters in the Lord, we shall go on together to all eternity. I thank God for you and for all who acknowledge Jesus Christ as their Saviour and their Lord. I thank you for the interest you take in me, and above all, I thank you for your prayers.

The question you ask me is difficult and yet I believe the answer is quite clear. It is difficult and galling for you to have to sit and listen to such doctrines from the pulpit and you naturally feel you should make some sort of a protest. My own view on the matter is that it would be inadvisable for you to make any public protest. It would lead to argument and disputation. But what I think you might do is to have a chat with such people 'in private'. And when you talk to them, do so in the spirit of meekness and prayer, and pray much before doing so. I would just tell them simply your experience of God in Christ and the difference he has made to you. Talk of the New Life, the New Nature, and the New Power that you have received, etc., etc. And having done all this, pray for him when you get home again, and go on doing so. Remember that such people are in darkness, and have not seen the Light and that 1 Corinthians 2:14 applies to them. Nothing but the Power of the Holy Spirit can ever bring them to a different state. Arguments never will.

Such is the way I deal with people of that type and I feel that it is the way indicated in the New Testament. I am always glad to hear from you and to be of any help that I can.

You will hear fairly soon of my being not very far from you, preaching.

May the Lord continue to bless you and yours.

Yours in his service
D. M. Lloyd-Jones

From the experience of these years Dr Lloyd-Jones was immovably confirmed in a truth which he had first seen in the New Testament. It was that evangelism is pre-eminently dependent upon the quality of the Christian life which is known and enjoyed in the church. The community around Sandfields was reached not by advertising or organised visitation, but by the manner of life of men and women whose very faces seemed to be new. No one in the congregation was offered courses on 'personal evangelism', nor told how to 'witness'. It was done in a whole variety of spontaneous and natural ways, differing according to the circumstances and temperaments of individuals. Some were not gifted at making public speeches. The soft-spoken, William Nobes, for example, who somehow on his meagre pension managed to keep his little bachelor room, would often be found sitting on a window-sill, outside the entrance to the market, 'chatting happily in his gentle, kindly manner to any and all who had time to stop and talk to him'. Despite his poverty in this world's goods, says Mrs Lloyd-Jones in her portrait of him, no one ever heard him grumble or complain. 'There's just four of us now,' was his contented answer to someone who asked him about family and relatives, 'my bed and my table, my Book and me!'

The converts witnessed, too, by death as well as by life. Even the most thoughtless in the community were sometimes arrested by what they heard or saw of the home-going of those who had confessed themselves pilgrims in this present world. Certainly the market was subdued and onlookers stood silent, the day when the body of William Nobes was carried from his few earthly possessions, through the town, and up to the cemetery on the mountain side. Few who saw the large crowd of church members, led by their minister, following the coffin, and not grudging one step of those long three miles, could have doubted that Nobes did indeed have a family!

'Staffordshire Bill' had just three years at Sandfields before people spoke of how the old man whom the church family had nursed as a spiritual babe departed this life. When Dr Lloyd-Jones and E. T. Rees arrived at his bedside it was clear from the high fever and the stertorous breathing that the end was not far off. William Thomas was dying from double pneumonia. As Mrs Lloyd-Jones heard the scene described later that day by her husband, from the moment of their arrival in the room:

> William Thomas was far away somewhere, but responded to a greeting and a prayer. He was obviously at perfect peace and all the evidences of the old sinful, violent life were smoothed out of a now child-like face. The minutes passed and became an hour, and more. Then suddenly the painful sound of the difficult breathing seemed to stop. The old man's face was transformed, alight, radiant. He sat up eagerly with upstretched arms and a beautiful smile on his face, as though welcoming his best of friends, and with that he was gone to that 'land of pure delight where saints immortal reign'.

TWELVE

_____

Enlarged Work

A lthough the period of awakening witnessed in 1931, with
large numbers of converts, was not repeated, there was no
decline either in spiritual interest or in numbers. *Yr Efengylydd* reported in December 1933, that at Sandfields 'it is necessary
to hold the week-night meetings in the chapel because the spacious
schoolroom is too small'. Three years later, the Editor of *The Treasury,*
the magazine of the Forward Movement, wrote of Sandfields in
April 1936: 'Every memory of this Church brings joy. Its ministry
is blessed of God in the building up of a great community rich in
numbers, experience and devotion. A further added testimony of this
is the announcement that the debt on all the buildings has now been
extinguished.'

By the early 1930s preaching visits to North Wales became a regular part of Dr Lloyd-Jones' ministry. In October 1931, *Yr Efengylydd*
subsequently reported that his 'lively and substantial ministry caused
a great stir' in parts of Anglesey. Four months later, in February 1932,
he preached for the first time in another area of North Wales, at
Rhos (Rhosllanerchrugog), near Wrexham, where he was often to be
in subsequent years. Although little more than a village, Rhos was a
place of vast Nonconformist chapels — buildings which had been
none too large for the memorable events which had accompanied
the 1904 Revival in that district. But times had changed, as one of
his first hearers at Rhos has recorded. John Powell-Parry was a miner,
converted as a young man of nineteen in 1904. In the years which

followed, Powell-Parry found little spiritual help in the local chapels and it was this which made the coming of Dr Lloyd-Jones into his neighbourhood all the more striking:

> It was something which I had not heard for a very long time when I heard the Doctor preaching. My impression was of a very humble man who spoke with conviction and holy boldness. The text of his first sermon in Rhos was Matthew 16:3, 'O ye hypocrites, ye can discern the face of the sky; but can ye not discern the signs of the times?' The people came from far and near to listen to him but the ministers were not sympathetic, Oh dear, no! There was a great change in Rhos compared with what it had been at the end of the nineteenth and the beginning of the twentieth century. It was different entirely. There was a turning from the Word of God and Modernism came in like a flood, especially after the First World War.
>
>   Dr Lloyd-Jones preached the Word and believed what he preached. I remember two ministers sitting right in the very back row of the chapel on the occasion of that first visit. The place was packed and they were there, looking to me like two critics or spies. Of course, the Doctor would not know them, but I knew them. They were rank Modernists. Today they have passed away and left nothing. Both their chapels are empty.

The same reporter spoke of how, subsequently, still larger crowds would gather whenever it was known that Martyn Lloyd-Jones was going to preach in that vicinity. 'One winter's day in February, in the midst of a heavy shower of melting snow, I remember people — many young men, young people — queuing five or six abreast for some distance to get into the chapel before the doors were opened.'[1]

An absence of sympathy towards ML-J from ministers was common throughout North Wales and yet it was not universal. One Calvinistic Methodist minister, J. J. Morgan of Mold, sent the itinerating preacher the following assessment of his preaching:

> I have been weighing your preaching in the balance of 'The Treasury'. Of course, you will remember that these are not the balances of heaven so that you must not rejoice on the one hand nor

---

[1] The words of John Powell-Parry were taken down by the author in conversation in the early 1970s. Mr Parry died in June 1978.

grieve on the other whatever weight the scales record. 1. Freedom from the aim of entertaining: 95%. Some of the dramatic situations elaborated. 2. Freedom from the aim of soothing: 100%. 3. Freedom from the exhibition of one's own cleverness: 99%. 4. Freedom from detracting mannerisms: 95%. A tendency to pick the cheek (unconsciously) with the right-hand finger and thumb sometimes. A slight screwing of the face in making palpable hits. The screw mustn't grow. 5. Audibility: 100%. 6. Length: 100% Monday; 99% Wednesday. 7. Freedom from uncouth expressions: 99%. 8. Simplicity: 99%, 're-action' and 'negatived' would try the simple souls of the audience. 9. Pointedness: 100%. 10. Fervour: 100%. 11. Spirituality. I will not presume to put that in the balances. This will help you to keep in mind that there is such a place as Mold.

The extent of the spiritual need in North Wales led Dr Lloyd-Jones to be in the North, often as frequently as once a month, normally taking engagements in the week when he was not due to be in his own pulpit the following Sunday. One typical letter sent to him from Ruthin, North Wales, spoke of daily prayer for his ministry and of 'a number of people here willing to go anywhere within a radius of 50 miles' to hear him preach again. Eliseus Howells wrote in *Y Goleuad* (Feb. 1, 1933):

> Dr Lloyd-Jones' primary difficulty is entering the chapel where he is to preach for, like his Master, the crowds press on him. We know of some of the poor of the valleys keeping back some 'dole' money for weeks in order that they might travel to listen to him and throw their mite into the treasury. Yes, returning to empty, bare homes with a song in their hearts.
>
> We have seen people standing in the rain outside chapels for two hours in the hope that some word would come to them in his shouts and we heard that one crowd asked permission to break the window so that they could hear him, promising to pay for the damage done.

A letter to the preacher from Cardiff tells it own story:

Monday 22/10/34

Dear Mr Jones,

Many thanks for your masterly exposition of last night. It was a sermon I shall remember for all time. May God prosper your ministry — is the fervent prayer of

Yours in Him,

Gratitude

P. S. I am unemployed and put my last few coppers in the plate last evening, and not having the heart to pass the plate tonight, I decided to put this in instead; my gratitude is none the less sincere however.

In 1931 and 1932 he visited the Calvinistic Methodist training college at Trevecca. Of the first of these occasions, *Yr Efengylydd* reported, 'He encouraged the students there to resort to prayer together and to read the Word.' On his second visit, when *Y Goleuad* referred to him as 'the evangelist Dr Martin Lloyd-Jones', he urged more preaching upon holiness, speaking from the words, 'He must increase, but I must decrease' (*John* 3:30). Thereafter invitations to address ministerial students and ministers multiplied. In 1933 he gave a series of addresses at the Calvinistic Methodist College at Bala, North Wales, on themes related to the pulpit and the pastoral office. From his own few pencil notes which survive, it is evident that many of the points which he urged upon ministers at a later date were already uppermost in his mind at the age of thirty-three. 'A preacher', he began, 'is a man who has a distinct call to his work. He is not looking for something to say; he is a witness who testifies. He is not always talking about himself and his own experience, but preaching the truth.' He then proceeded to develop the significance of this principle. Preaching is not an end in itself. It must not ignore the people, yet it must not be ruled by the people. 'But it must follow Paul's method; truth and the Faith are committed to us to be applied to different people in different ways.' There must be a plan to a sermon and, in content, the sermon needs to include 'teaching, conviction and appeal'. Doctrine must precede moral duties, 'the right way is to make the ethical *inevitable*'.

In another address on 'The Minister as Pastor' he covered the organisation of church life, also dangers to avoid in accepting new members, together with such things as personal work and visitation. He warned that visiting is not to be undertaken as a duty in order to quieten one's conscience. 'The secret of all church work', he urged, 'is to realise our calling and our terrible responsibility (*2 Cor.* 5; *1 Cor.* 3)'. Speaking further on 'The Minister as a Man', he began:

This matter is difficult and may seem uninteresting but it is vitally important. The ruling idea ought to be that the pastor is a shepherd, *not* a pet lamb. He must be alert to the danger of trying to be nice and popular and chatty. The minister is to be always and everywhere 'the man of God' and not merely when he is in chapel or taking a service. It is our duty to remember our calling. The minister should always move amongst the people as one who has been with God. His chief object should be to please God rather than to please men. What is needed is not the spirit but the Holy Spirit. What the minister thinks of himself is of vital importance. He can only win his place and have respect by a holy life.

* * *

It was from about this date that people began to think of Dr Lloyd-Jones less exclusively in terms of his being 'an evangelist' and this change had a connexion with his first visit to North America in the summer of 1932. The public events of that visit, which included nine Sundays at the United Presbyterian Church on Sherbourne Street, Toronto, and five memorable days as an unknown visitor, supplying the place of an incapacitated speaker at the Chautauqua Institution, had their significance. But the long-term effect of his crossing the Atlantic, as far as his future ministry was concerned, came from the many hours he spent alone. His Toronto hosts had arranged that, with Bethan and Elizabeth, he would stay at 74 St George's, directly opposite Knox Seminary, a leading Presbyterian theological school. On hearing that Knox possessed a fine library, and intending to follow his usual practice of giving his mornings to study, ML-J was scarcely settled in Toronto before he obtained permission to use its facilities. In the event he never got beyond the shelves reserved for new acquisitions, for there he found several volumes of the works of Benjamin B. Warfield which were then being published in a definitive edition by Oxford University Press. He revelled in these volumes, he was later to say, like Cortez when he first saw the Pacific. As in the older Reformed authors, here was theology anchored in Scripture, but with an exegetical precision more evident than in the older authors, and combined with a devotion which raised the whole above the level of scholarship alone. 'Such was Warfield's own knowledge and experience of the truth, and of God in Christ through the Holy Spirit,' Dr Lloyd-Jones was to write in a review, 'that more than most writers he gives a profound impression of the glory and wonder of the great salvation we enjoy.' Once back in Britain, he was soon to become, in his own phrase, 'a proud possessor of the original ten volumes'.

We have already noted the usefulness of such writers as James Denney and P. T. Forsyth to Dr Lloyd-Jones, yet, partly because of the deficiency in their doctrine of Scripture and also because of weakness in other areas of doctrine, the impression which they made upon him was neither so profound nor so influential as that which he now received through Warfield. To Warfield more than to anyone else he was to attribute a development in his thought and ministry which occurred at this period. Hitherto ML-J's reputation was built very largely on his evangelistic preaching. Intellectual though he was by aptitude and training prior to this date, he showed no great interest in distinctly doctrinal teaching or in the defence of the Faith against modern error. No one would have described him as a 'theologian' or 'teacher'; there were even occasions in his early preaching when he decried the niceties of doctrinal correctness. The Gospels and the Book of Acts were his first love and, while he rejected the claim of liberals that our Faith must come from these sources rather than from the Pauline Epistles, the Pauline element in his thinking and teaching was as yet comparatively weak compared with what it was to become. Warfield gave him new insight into the necessity for doctrinal teaching. While not ceasing to be an evangelist, he was now brought to the strong conviction that more was required.

Certainly this development was not due to Warfield's influence alone. There were other factors at work in Lloyd-Jones' life which were pointing in the same direction. The many young converts at Sandfields needed to be established in the Faith. Further, because of his leadership as a preacher, ministers were increasingly looking to him for counsel on a number of contemporary religious issues, and evangelical students in the Welsh University Colleges — particularly those at Cardiff and Swansea — were asking for his help in the defence of the truth from the attacks of unbelieving scholarship. It was the presence of these demands upon him which made the 'discovery' in the library of Knox Seminary of far-reaching significance. In the years to come the words which he wrote of Warfield could well have been written of his own ministry: 'He not only asserted the Reformed faith; he at the same time demonstrated its superiority over all other systems or partial systems.'[2]

This development in his thinking led him to oppose the teaching of Karl Barth (1886–1968) whose eminence as a theologian had become world-wide. Against liberalism, Barth called not only for a recognition of the supernatural, but also for a restoration of 'the Reformed Faith' itself. Once more, the names of Calvin and other reformers were heard with respect in Barthian circles, and Presbyterians, in particular, on both sides of the Atlantic came to view Barth with admiration. The Swiss theologian's belief in a universal salvation, and his wish to construct a theology which did not rest upon an infallible Bible, were scarcely noticed. In British Universities and elsewhere voices were raised acclaiming Barth as a restorer of 'orthodoxy' and — in contrast with the Westminster divines of the seventeenth century — as a 'true interpreter' of John Calvin.

Lloyd-Jones was drawn into reading Barth, and subsequently Emil Brunner, another Swiss theologian, in order to help students whose lecturers had come under the new spell. He did not find its study to be of any personal profit, but it had the effect of making him a resolute opponent of what he regarded as a serious deviation from the Reformed Faith. Accordingly, when asked to speak at ministerial gatherings, there were times when, to the surprise of his hearers not yet accustomed to think of him in a theological role, he chose to demonstrate why Barthianism was not orthodox Christianity.

While Dr Lloyd-Jones' growing influence among ministers might have been anticipated by observers of the religious scene, there was at this time little to indicate a similar development of his influence among students. Much of his ministry seemed to be carried on as though he was oblivious to all age distinctions. Certainly there was no 'youth work' at Sandfields, and the larger gatherings popular among evangelical students — the Keswick Convention, for instance —

---

[2] Review of *Biblical and Theological Studies*, B. B. Warfield, *Inter-Varsity Magazine*, Summer, 1952, pp. 27-28. For his estimate of Warfield as a theologian see also his Introduction to *Biblical Foundations*, a collection of Warfield's writings published by Tyndale Press, 1958. The entire OUP set of Warfield was reprinted by Baker in 1981.

were places where his voice was never heard. Furthermore, unlike so many of his evangelical contemporaries he did not hold the view that the various inter-denominational youth movements represented the most hopeful field of labour: indeed his doctrine of the church left him with little sympathy for that attitude. Consequently, although, he spoke occasionally for the Christian Union of evangelical students at Cardiff University College, he had no connection with the wider 'Inter-Varsity Fellowship of Evangelical Unions' (IVF, later UCCF) which had been formed in 1928.

One of the few inter-denominational societies with which Sandfields came to be connected in the early thirties was the China Inland Mission. As spiritual concern deepened in the congregation, so did commitment to foreign missionary endeavour which was faithful to Scripture, and in 1934, for the first time, a member of Sandfields — Peggy Robson — was accepted as a candidate for the CIM. That same year, on May 8, Dr Lloyd-Jones spoke for the first time at the Annual Meeting of the CIM, held in Westminster Central Hall, London. CIM had close links with the Inter-Varsity Fellowship and several of the youthful leaders of IVF, including the honorary secretary, Dr Douglas Johnson, were present that evening. Johnson, who had qualified at the Medical School of King's College Hospital in the late twenties, had known of Lloyd-Jones' reputation at Bart's. He also recalled having seen him, on one occasion, crossing the Square at Bart's, when the thought occurred to him that Lord Horder's assistant looked 'too streamlined and severe' to be a physician! When Lloyd-Jones left London for Wales in 1927 Douglas Johnson and other evangelical Christians in the medical schools were left wondering what was the nature of the cause of the change of profession and his going to Port Talbot as a preacher. After all, Lloyd-Jones had not been known as a Christian at Bart's, he had no ties with the Evangelical Union in that hospital, and his closeness to the agnostic Horder was common knowledge. Some evangelicals in the student world were thus left to question whether the Welshman's unexpected entrance into the ministry was only motivated by the same 'Social Gospel' concerns which were then so prevalent in Nonconformity. These doubts as to his orthodoxy can be better understood when it is realised that adherence to the Evangelical Faith was extremely weak in all university and academic circles. The Student Christian

Movement — from which the Evangelical Union was a breakaway — had shared in the departure from the Faith, its General Secretary affirming in the 1920s that 'the doctrine of the verbal inspiration of the Bible is as dead as Queen Anne'.[3]

Not without reason, therefore, Douglas Johnson and friends with him were not prepared to listen to the China Inland Mission's new speaker uncritically in May 1934. Dr Lloyd-Jones's text was Romans 1:14, and before he had finished the doubts of any critical hearer were swept away. When the IVF Executive Committee met shortly after, the question of how Dr Lloyd-Jones could be secured for the Annual Conference of 1935 was high on the agenda. The discussion was not far advanced before the Welsh Representative declared that he was not hopeful that any invitation which they might give would be accepted, and he went on to explain that Dr Lloyd-Jones was a 'high-churchman' in the Presbyterian sense. Only with some difficulty had he been persuaded to agree to speak at the Swansea Evangelical Union which began in 1930. After further deliberation it was at length resolved that Dr Douglas Johnson himself should make a personal visit to Wales to put before Dr Lloyd-Jones the IVF's need of his help. The result of that visit was ML-J's subsequent agreement to come to Swanwick for the Conference scheduled for Tuesday April 9 to Monday April 15, 1935, though with the provisos that he would only give one address — the subject he did not specify.

From the standpoint of IVF the 1935 Conference was a great success. Besides well-known figures such as Bishop J. Taylor Smith, who was Conference Chaplain, there were several new IVF speakers from various countries, including Dr Robert P. Wilder from the United States, and missionaries home on furlough. A report of the Conference in the *Inter-Varsity Magazine* spoke of splendid scenery, 'very happy fellowship', sports, 'a delightful lantern lecture', and commented briefly on some of the speakers, excluding Dr Lloyd-Jones. Perhaps the writer detected a different note in the visitor from Wales and had not yet made up his mind what he thought of it.

For his part, however, ML-J was far from satisfied with his first IVF Conference. It confirmed his earlier impression that he was out of his element in English evangelicalism. In his view, the Conference, while

---

[3] Douglas Johnson, *Contending for the Faith, a History of the Evangelical Movement in the Universities and Colleges* (Nottingham: IVP, 1979), p. 131.

strongly emphasising evangelism and missionary endeavour, lacked seriousness. Speakers and hearers alike, Dr Lloyd-Jones felt, had little interest in the kind of literature which meant so much to him. Their sense of church history seemed to be practically non-existent. Theology of any kind was viewed with suspicion, and the degree of concern for an intellectual understanding of the Christian Faith was almost childish in its proportions. Despite his personal liking for Douglas Johnson, which deepened with this second meeting, Lloyd-Jones went back to Aberavon persuaded that his own ministry lay elsewhere.

Uppermost in his assessment of the contemporary situation was his conviction that national religious trends could only be changed by an outpouring of the Holy Spirit in true revival. As he read his Bible, and turned afresh to such men as Jonathan Edwards and George Whitefield, he knew that there was nothing in the past which could not be repeated. The church needed to be called back to her true work of prayer and preaching and, given existing religious conditions, he saw more hope of that occurring in Wales than in England. In England the evangelicals, in their preoccupation with evangelism, were failing to see that the real problem lay within the church herself.

There were also particular reasons why, in 1935, the longing for a great awakening was much upon Dr Lloyd-Jones' spirit. Several times that year he knew marked evidences of God's presence and blessing. Others felt the same. On January 1, 1935, preaching on the Ten Lepers (*Luke* 17:11-19) at a broadcast civic service in Cardiff, held in Wood Street Congregational Church, there was a general sense that something unusual was happening. One Cardiff newspaper, commenting on the spirit of the 2,000 who packed the building, asked the question: 'Are we on the eve of another religious revival in South Wales? Not only ministers, but laymen as well, state with conviction that there is a new spiritual stir among the people.' The same paper described Dr Lloyd-Jones, whose sermon was carried by the radio to thousands of Welsh homes, as 'the new John Elias'. Unlike the usual radio sermon it was not read from a script!

In many parts of Wales during the same year Dr Lloyd-Jones was to see similar intense attention given to the Word of God. After he had preached at the Tabernacle Chapel, Haverfordwest, the *Western Telegraph* reported, 'The building — capable of holding more than

17. The day of the Cardiff Broadcast Service, Jan. 1, 1935.

a thousand people — was crowded out an hour before the service commenced.' 'The service', continued the same reporter, 'shows that the alleged "coldness and indifference of the times" is greatly exaggerated, and that when there is a man with a message the people are ready to respond.'

The most memorable service of 1935, however, was to occur in the South Wales Welsh Presbyterian *Sasiwn* held in Llangeitho because it was the bicentenary of the conversion of Daniel Rowland. The *Western Mail*, August 16, under a heading 'Amazing Scenes at Llangeitho', gave their reporter's eye-witness account. Two days before the services planned for August 15, people 'from all parts of Wales poured into this little village throughout the night and during the greater part of the day. Many of them slept in the open air.' The meetings planned were arranged to take place in both the old Llangeitho church and in a great marquee erected on ground used in the open-air services of two hundred years before, the former able to hold no more than 800, and the latter an estimated 6,000. Lloyd-Jones was announced as speaking in the church but when thousands assembled there to hear him there was such confusion that the service had to be moved to the marquee. Even here, 'hundreds' had to stand outside while the preacher spoke for nearly an hour from Acts 2:38, 'Then Peter said unto them, Repent, and be baptised every one of you in the name of Jesus Christ for the remission of sins, and ye shall receive the gift of the Holy Ghost.'

The sermon, carefully and fully prepared (his notes filled thirty sides of small writing-pad size), while not dealing with the subject of revival, presented the truths which had heralded all the great awakenings from Pentecost onwards — man in sin, face to face with God, and the certainty of death and eternity, together with true repentance and faith in Christ as the only means of deliverance. In the opinion of the *Western Mail* it was 'one of the most remarkable services that has been seen in West Wales since the revival of 1904'.

James Evans, another newspaper correspondent, gives this impression of ML-J's appearance:

I found he was not unlike the mental picture of him that I had been carrying about with me. His outward appearance gave no suggestion of the pulpit. His clothes were in every respect those of the ordinary citizen. I must confess that I fully expected to see the 'collar'. But no! A man of medium stature, his white hands were rather fat and short-fingered. As for his head and features, however, there was nothing fat about those. His pale, thoughtful face, his forehead high and wide, his black shiny hair, keen eyes, and thin lips often brought to mind the features of the late Sir John Morris Jones. His gestures, like the inflexion of his voice, were perfectly natural. There was no attempt at that peculiar intonation known as the Welsh *hwyl*.

His abiding seriousness was frequently noted and so also were his eyes. Some hearers felt they were being scrutinized by gaze; his own people at Sandfields said that there was often a quality in his eyes which tempered the near severity of his look: 'He is seldom seen to smile, but everyone speaks of the subtle laughter that dwells at the back of his eyes.'

Many reasons for the influence of his preaching were offered by the press. The *Herald of Wales* affirmed, 'It is not the oratory of Dr Lloyd-Jones which draws the crowds', meaning by 'oratory' that he did not use the dramatic and emotional techniques popularised by nineteenth-century Welsh preachers. Nor did his pulpit language follow the traditional. 'One of the attractions of the Doctor's preaching is that his language is entirely his own. Not an out-worn phrase. Not a platitude. Not an age-old expression. It may be that his freedom from the language of the pulpit is one secret of his drawing force.'

It was almost universally accepted by the commentators that the note of authority was the most arresting feature of Dr Lloyd-Jones' preaching. 'The secret of his power is the note of certainty that pervades his preaching.' 'There is evidently no diminution in the extraordinary drawing power of Dr Jones, due largely to his intense earnestness and the definite message which he so confidently proclaims.' 'A dominant personality, intensity of conviction, clarity of thought and directness of speech, with an entire absence of striving after oratorical effect, portray this modern Puritan.'

This is not to say that those who assessed his preaching were agreed as to the nature of the influence. One vivid but spiritually unsympathetic account comes from the pen of the novelist, Rhys Davies, in a chapter on 'The South Wales Workers' in his book, *My Wales* (London, 1937):

> That a preacher with a romantic mantle can still draw a crowd was proved to me, nevertheless, one week-day evening in the Rhondda. Dr Martin Lloyd-Jones was to give a sermon in one of the largest chapels. Still a young man and possessing first-rate pulpit gifts, Dr Lloyd-Jones first attracted celebrity by abandoning his prosperous Harley Street medical practice and going down to Wales as a full-time missionary in a poor Glamorganshire district. The romantic heart of Wales was touched: it was won when chapels all over the country invited him to prove his oratorical gifts in their pulpits. He looks like a less emaciated James Maxton: intense, vibrant, and unwavering.
>
> The doors of the chapel where he preached were opened two hours before the service began. I have never seen a building so unhygienically packed. The ground floor seethed in slow, awful movements of wedged humanity. The enormous gallery, which ran all round the building, steamed with bodies that were piled up to the walls in a warmth that was stifling. Not a window was open, for winter was outside. At last, with the utmost difficulty a man climbed to a sill and opened a window six inches. A minute

afterwards a woman sitting under the window climbed up and shut it again. Little ventilation could come through the open doorways and passages; they were tightly wedged with people, who also dripped over the staircases and filled each aisle. A pie could have been cooked nicely in the warmth.

Dr Lloyd-Jones picked his way up the steps of the pulpit, also crowded with late-comers. He wore an overcoat, which he astonishingly kept on until he began his sermon twenty minutes later. Outside were special coaches and buses which had brought people from up and down the valley. The hymn-singing shook the building; it rose to a deafening demand, it sank to a sweet plaint infinitely gentle.

The over-melodramatic technique of the old-time preachers was not used by Dr Lloyd-Jones. The opening of his sermon had almost an intellectual primness; his sincerity had a cold ruthlessness, very attractive, at least to me . . . The key-word of the sermon was Surrender. Surrender to God. Not a word about the evils outside the chapel, the raw bitter life concentrated in the broken valley. Why should there be! Surrender to God was the palliation: it was enough to announce it, perhaps. Dr Lloyd-Jones' fine violin-like voice was exquisite enough in its entreating. And there was one thrilling moment when, by use of that magic which all the great preachers of Wales possess, he called on the name of God with tremendous passion and, opening wide his arms, he seemed like a great black bat swooping down over the congregation.

At the close of the sermon an invitation was issued. Would any members of the congregation who felt the need of further guidance, or who wanted to give themselves anew to God, remain behind? There was a closing hymn, magnificently sung. The difficult exit began. I was one of the last to leave. Feeling dingy after the wicked air of the chapel, I went through some breathing exercises and then tottered across a square to a public refreshment house.

Such comment neither deterred nor excited Dr Lloyd-Jones. He was well aware of the mixed character of his congregations and the blind admiration of some of his hearers concerned him more than the flippancies of a Rhys Davies. Though few seemed to realise the fact, it was his close assessment of the Welsh character and temperament which vitally influenced his preaching. Nationality, he was to argue a few years later in three broadcast addresses for the Welsh BBC on

'Religion and National Characteristics', does affect a man's approach to religion. Although spiritual rebirth is God's sovereign gift, it does not erase natural or national characteristics. After expounding this truth he went on to analyse the difference between the Welsh and the English. The basic point of difference, he believed, was that the English character is more simple and integrated than the Welsh. The Englishman's tendency is to function as a whole — feeling, mind and will operating together. The Welshman, on the other hand, has a character which is capable of operating on 'a number of different levels which are not organically connected together'. The level of feeling and imagination lies nearest to the surface in the Welshman, yet it is a complete mistake, he argued, to say that the Welshman is *basically* emotional. Merely to move the Welshman emotionally is to accomplish nothing, because much stronger in its final influence in his make-up is his mind which does not necessarily move in accordance with his feelings: 'It is very easy to make a Welshman cry, but it needs an earthquake to make him change his mind . . . In this respect the Welshman's character is truly deceptive, because the Welshman's feelings constitute merely a thin layer on the surface, and underneath is the thick, strong layer — the most important and the strongest in the Welshman's character — namely, the mind. That which characterises the mind is its love of reason and of definitions. It must have everything plainly and clearly and orderly. It follows the argument to its furthermost point and it demands consistency.'

Believing this analysis to be correct, Dr Lloyd-Jones viewed the tendency of Welsh preaching to entertain the emotions as a dangerous mistake. He concurred with the judgment that the danger in Wales had been to produce 'a race of actor preachers, and that their pulpit eloquence merely pleased the ear but had no permanent effect on the heart and conscience of men and women.' In contrast, he argued:

> The chief need of Wales is great theological and doctrinal preaching which will emphasise the sovereignty of God, the ugliness of sin, the uncertainty of life, the judgment and eternity, the glory of the person of the Lord Jesus Christ, and the all-sufficiency of his saving work for us on the cross, the resurrection and the blessed hope we have.
>
> These are the only truths which will produce great preaching and which will prove a foundation to sweeping eloquence . . . To

reach the Welshman's will, nothing will suffice but the strength and might of God, as it is in Christ's gospel. But this gospel at the same time is large enough to answer all the questions of the mind and reason, to quench the thirst for wholeness in the realm of the mind and also to move us to the depths of our being.

Abundant spiritual confirmation of this judgment existed in the hundreds of individual lives across Wales changed by the grace of God through the recovery of this preaching. It was in the industrialised South of Wales — amidst the coal-mines, narrow terraced houses and factories and smoky valleys — that the influence of his preaching was so far-reaching. One observer of the period, with no sympathies for Calvinistic Methodism, and who became a Professor of Law at the University of Liverpool, was of the opinion that two men were foremost in keeping South Wales from Communism in the 1930s. One was Aneurin Bevan, who held back the politically-minded; the other was Martyn Lloyd-Jones who kept such large numbers of chapel-goers to the Christian Faith.

18. En route to New York, with his mother (second from left), 1937.

THIRTEEN

Leaving Aberavon

C alls on Dr Lloyd-Jones from beyond the Principality of Wales began in the 1930s. His broadcast service from Cardiff on January 1, 1935, was noted by the *Sunday Companion* (London) which printed a summary of the sermon. On November 28, 1935, *The Christian,* one of the best-known of British evangelical weeklies, gave a page of comment to the 'Preacher-Physician: Dr Martin Lloyd-Jones,' along with an announcement that he was to preach at the Albert Hall, London, on December 3, 1935 in a witness to the Bible arranged by the Bible Testimony Fellowship. When that night came one of ML-J's hearers was the seventy-two-year-old veteran preacher, Dr Campbell Morgan. After visits to Britain from the United States in the 1920s, Morgan had finally returned in 1932 and, despite his age, resumed at Westminster Chapel as a helper of its minister, Dr Hubert L. Simpson, whose health was failing. After Simpson retired in 1934, Morgan had continued alone in the pulpit which he had made famous at the beginning of the century.

In the course of his message that night, ML-J told the gathering that 'the real cause of the present state of the church of God on earth is to be found in the church's voluntary departure from belief in the Bible as the fully inspired Word of God and from stressing the great evangelical doctrines'.[1] What Morgan thought of what he heard was clear enough two days later when a letter from him arrived

-----

[1] *Proclaiming Eternal Verities,* 1936, pp. 25-26. A booklet containing the addresses given.

at the Aberavon manse urging the Aberavon pastor to come to fill the pulpit of Westminster Chapel for the last Sunday of that same month. Despite the shortness of the notice, Lloyd-Jones accepted, being mindful of the debt which he owed to Westminster Chapel for the ministry he had received in Dr Hutton's days and, as it happened, free to take a break from his own pulpit on that day. Thus on December 29, 1935, he stood for the first time in Westminster Chapel's large circular pulpit and gained a new view of the building which he had first entered twenty years before.

The morning sermon was on John 6:66-68, 'Will ye also go away?' In the evening he preached on 'The Narrowness of the Gospel' from Matthew 7:13, 14, 'Enter ye in at the strait gate . . .' Both sermons were heart-searching and evangelistic, though not in the usual sense of that term. Even relatively evangelical congregations were not used to being asked, 'Are you ready for the judgment? Have you a personal conviction of sin, and a personal knowledge of God?'

Other congregations in England followed Morgan's lead with more invitations to him. One which he accepted came from Spurgeon's Tabernacle, now vacant after the pastorate of H. Tydeman Chilvers who had worked to restore the congregation to the spiritual condition from which it had fallen earlier in the century. The *Baptist Times* reported that he preached from Hebrews 6:11, 12, on how the Hebrews were reproached for their neglect of doctrine.

The enquiries whether the preacher would consider a call which followed received no encouragement. It was more than the question of baptism by immersion which restrained ML-J. The convictions with which he had left the IVF Conference at Swanwick just twelve months before were still with him. At the same time a concern for the wider situation in the British Isles was being awakened in him and he was finding that English hearers were not all as uncomprehending of his convictions as Welsh newspapers thought. 'I doubt if the English people are capable of appreciating his preaching as we do in Wales', *Yr Efengylydd* assured its readers.

More signs that this thesis was faulty were soon to occur both in the United States and in England. In May 1937 ML-J accepted an invitation to make a second visit to North America, this time alone as Bethan had to remain at home following the birth of a second daughter, Ann, who completed the family circle. His principal engagement during three weeks in the States was at Columbus, Ohio, where the Department of Evangelism in the Presbyterian Church in the USA had invited him to speak at a conference on Evangelism, immediately prior to their denomination's 149th General Assembly. Four sessions in all were allocated to him, two being 'Seminars' related to Evangelism which had the general title, 'The Present Situation'. At the first of these he dealt with 'Investigation and Analysis' and at the second, 'How to Deal with it'.

The Presbyterian for June 3, 1937, reported: 'Dr Martin Lloyd-Jones set a fine keynote in his pre-Assembly ministry, and its effect was felt.' The same paper, however, also indicated that there was some division in the response of his hearers: 'Dr Lloyd-Jones fulfilled the old-time test John Wesley set for effective gospel preaching. He won followers and provoked enmity, but this time the enmity was on the part of noted theological indifferentists and religious Liberals. Dr Lloyd-Jones laid down Christian truth and called to repentance on lines that were so forthright and particular, that some of his audience felt uneasy.'

At the time Dr Lloyd-Jones wondered whether this unease was not shared by some of the leaders themselves. Strong doctrinal preaching and experimental Calvinism were by no means common even among conservative Presbyterians. A number of the other speakers at the Conference certainly belonged to a different spiritual tradition.

In later years ML-J came to think that perhaps the most significant incident of this visit was the hot June night in Philadelphia when Campbell Morgan, just arrived from England, was again in the congregation and may then have made up his mind to seek the young preacher as his associate. Although not anticipating such a possibility, when an invitation arrived, Dr Lloyd-Jones agreed to take a second Sunday at Westminster Chapel on June 27, 1937. He was aware of the difference between his and Morgan's theological standpoint. Three years earlier he had written to his mother: 'As for Westminster I feel that it is extremely unlikely that I shall ever visit there while Campbell Morgan is alive or has anything to do with the place.'

While not seeking a call elsewhere, ML-J was becoming aware that the demands being made on him could not be long sustained. An additional demand had developed entirely unexpectedly. We have already noted how, when a number of his friends first heard of his conviction that he was called to preach, they had urged him to continue in medicine and to be a lay-preacher. Speaking once at Sandfields on the peril of compromise, he had referred to this advice as an instance in his own experience: 'Before I came here, the Devil said to me, Why don't you go on practising medicine and preach on Sundays? I listened to him and I tried it; but I did not go far before I found what a hopeless failure it was. When God calls a man to preach, he calls him to preach and nothing else.'

He was convinced that he had to say farewell to medicine. Had he needed any help in carrying out this decision it was provided by members of the Welsh medical fraternity. At the time of his arrival at Sandfields the local branch of the British Medical Association at Swansea held a special meeting to decide what to do about him, the common opinion being that he only intended to preach until he was well enough known to set up either in a general or consultant practice. Speaking of this meeting (of which he heard from one who was present and who later became a good friend), Dr Lloyd-Jones recalled, 'They solemnly decided to have nothing whatever to do with me, and they carried it out!'

His contacts, medical or social, with fellow doctors in the Port Talbot area were to be non-existent until, one tea-time, a knock at the Lloyd-Joneses' door announced Dr David Rees, along with a consultant from Swansea. He had come to ask ML-J if he would see his brother who was seriously ill. They went at once to the home of Illtyd Rees and even as they drove in the car, and spoke of his symptoms, ML-J recognized that the man was suffering from Hodgkin's disease (Lymphadenoma) and a particular type of it called the Pell-Epstein type. It was a condition which ML-J had studied repeatedly in the course of research. An examination confirmed his diagnosis and the two surprised medicals were now ready to ask advice on possible treatment. Horder, Dr Lloyd-Jones told them, could treat these cases and obtain some temporary relief, but such was the pattern of the disease that ultimately it was bound to lead to death. Illtyd Rees was sent to London and his subsequent history was exactly as the minister of Sandfields had predicted.

This incident became the talk of the town and it gave ML-J a new relationship with men from whom he had formerly been alienated. A few days later the leading doctor of Port Talbot — a man with an

Oxford M.D. who had previously passed Dr Lloyd-Jones in the street without so much as looking at him — arrived at the manse door and announced himself by saying, 'My name is Phillips.' 'I recognise you, Dr Phillips', replied Lloyd-Jones who had answered the door himself. 'Will you come in?' 'If I were half a man,' the visitor at once responded, 'I would drop on my knees in front of you and beg your pardon for the way we have treated you!'

This revolution in the local medical attitude, good though it was, led others to appeal to Dr Lloyd-Jones for medical advice. Previously he had on occasions given advice, without fee, if a patient's doctor had consented to his being consulted, but now, with almost all the local doctors only too glad to consent, calls for his help multiplied. Dr Phillips himself became a considerable culprit in this respect, for he let it be known that the only opinion outside London which he recognised was that of Dr Lloyd-Jones!

To a limited extent Dr Lloyd-Jones was thus compelled to re-enter medicine when cases were referred to him for help which he felt responsible to accept. When these cases were outside the church he might take a fee, which invariably went to the Sandfields funds, and these amounts became an important factor in finally paying off the debt on the building. However, on one occasion a prosperous individual, who had benefited from medical consultation at the Sandfields manse, pulled out his wallet to settle 'his account' as he was leaving; but when he heard that any fee offered went 'to the church' he promptly replaced his wallet and searched his trouser pockets for any loose coins to be found there!

It was during this same period that the question of mental illness forced itself upon Dr Lloyd-Jones' attention in a new way. In medical thought it was by this date almost universally accepted that any powerful and distressing 'conviction of sin' was a form of neurosis requiring psychiatric treatment. The kind of 'symptoms' which appeared in a number of cases of conversion recorded in the Acts of the Apostles, or indeed in such men as 'Staffordshire Bill' in Sandfields, would commonly have been regarded as types of mental illness. Indeed, there were those at Bart's who had not disguised their belief that Dr Lloyd-Jones himself was suffering from 'a 'mental complaint' when he gave up his medical career.

From the medical standpoint Dr Lloyd-Jones was, of course,

familiar with true mental disease and its distressing symptoms. Nor did he underestimate the importance of psychiatric help in many instances. But at this date he began to meet with individuals who were being treated as 'mental' cases, and yet, he had reason to believe, were only in spiritual trouble. In their case nothing except spiritual remedies could help them as was confirmed to him by more than one case.

These experiences confirmed Dr Lloyd-Jones in a principle which he regarded as crucial in counselling. He saw that just as it is disastrous to attempt to treat a case of real physical or mental illness with spiritual remedies, so it is equally wrong to treat a *spiritual* case with what may be of benefit to those who are genuinely mentally ill. Yet as symptoms in the two classes can be very similar, how can one discern to which class a distressed person, in need of help, belongs? His conclusion was that where, in a regenerate person, distress arises out of a sense of sin and an absence of assurance — in other words, where the condition has spiritual causes — then the person will respond to such truths and promises of Scripture as are suited for their need. Such response may not be immediate and total, but it will be recognisable to the careful pastor. On the other hand, where this use of Scripture is of no avail in removing the distress of persons of whom there is reason to believe that they are Christians, then the likelihood is that medical psychiatric assistance should be sought.

It was in Aberavon, with its comparatively poor working-class population, that demands on his medical skill were most frequent, and this was one factor which made him conscious that he was now working 'at the edge of his strength'. For the first time he was having trouble with his voice. The large chapels of those days generally had no microphones and sometimes there was the even greater demand made upon him by occasional preaching in the open air. For no apparent reason there were now times when his voice failed and twice at Aberavon during this period he had to sit down in the pulpit without being able to complete his sermon. The cause, as he subsequently came to see, was that his voice production was wrong. He spoke far too much 'from the throat'. As long as he had the physical and nervous energy of youth to carry him through, this mistake was neither serious nor obvious, but with the lessening of that energy the problem had become manifest and for some years, until his practice changed, it gave him real concern.

A conviction that his work at Sandfields was nearly done came to him almost as unaccountably as the awareness with which he had been led there ten years before. 'It was', he would later say, 'as if a shutter had come down', and far from being an experience he welcomed, 'I was really quite upset about it.'

It was in these circumstances that Dr Lloyd-Jones in the autumn of 1937 received a pressing request to preach for Marylebone Presbyterian Church, London, who were without a minister. Situated in George Street, off Edgware Road, with institutional buildings 'among the finest in London', the Marylebone church was one of the most influential Presbyterian congregations in England. Besides not a few emigré Scots, including Jane Stoddart who had just retired after fifty years' editorial work with the *British Weekly*, the church had recently had the support of such prominent figures as the American Ambassador and his wife. After an early evangelical tradition, the congregation — as so often in English Presbyterianism — had become accustomed to a more nondescript message, and when the previous minister had accepted a call to Australia in 1937 there were some who saw the possibility of a change. A few years earlier the Moderator of the General Assembly of the English Presbyterians, in a discussion as to why the denomination made such small appeal to the masses, asked the question, 'Is it that we have not discovered the best method of preaching the gospel? Is the preaching of Presbyterian ministers in England for the most part too academic in character?' (*British Weekly*, May 5, 1932).

It was because he also felt the force of such questions that J. Chalmers Lyon, the Interim Moderator at Marylebone for the vacancy, took the unusual step of turning to Welsh Presbyterianism and, in his letter of invitation to Dr Lloyd-Jones, he confessed that he was unable to get his name out of his mind.

The result was that the first Sunday of 1938 found Dr Lloyd-Jones in the pulpit of Marylebone Presbyterian Church where he preached in the morning from the story of the widow and the cruse of oil (*2 Kings* 4:1-7) as illustrating the secret, supernatural nature of the Christian life. In the evening, from the miracle of the raising to life of the son of the widow of Nain (*Luke* 7:11-16), he preached one of his characteristic evangelistic sermons. Only the power of Christ, he told his hearers, could halt the funeral procession which made its way out of Nain, and only the same power can change the world's hopelessness as it stands in the presence of failure, sin and death.[2] The Marylebone congregation heard nothing of the prose or poetry which visiting preachers too often brought to the pulpit. They do not seem to have missed it.

The *British Weekly* of the first week in February 1938 announced:

> At a largely attended meeting of the Marylebone Church on Thursday evening it was decided to invite the Rev Dr Martyn Lloyd-Jones, of Port Talbot, to succeed the Rev. J. Golder Burns as minister. The call was unanimous and enthusiastic.

At the time of the press announcement on February 3, 1938, Dr Lloyd-Jones was inclined to view the call to Marylebone as the guidance of God. Although London was not a preaching sphere which naturally appealed to him, the Marylebone pulpit offered an important opportunity. In London there would be no question of his medical counsel being needed as had been the case in Wales, neither would he have the many preaching engagements which had become so much part of his Welsh ministry. For the moment he said nothing, nor did he yet need to reach a decision; for the call to London had first to be approved and passed on to him by the Presbytery of London North (of which Marylebone Church was a part) and it was not due to meet until April 12, 1938.

Before that date, however, other developments had occurred. The National Free Church Council Assembly, one of the most important annual events in English Nonconformity, took place during the last week of March. With 800 delegates, the venue was Richmond Hill Church, Bournemouth, and Dr Lloyd-Jones had been invited to speak on the Wednesday evening, March 30. When Dr John Short subsequently gave a lengthy account of the Assembly in the *British Weekly* it was to the meeting of that evening that he drew particular attention under a sub-heading, 'Voice from South Wales'. He wrote:

> The Rev. Dr Martyn Lloyd-Jones, who gave up a fine career in order to become a Methodist minister, informed us that he was

---

[2] Outlines of these sermons were taken down by a reporter of the *Christian Herald* and published, in reverse order, on March 17 and October 27, 1938.

to preach a sermon and not deliver an address. It was an inspiring experience, fresh, arresting, challenging, moving. This man is a born preacher and is destined to become a great force in the religious life of our land. He is orthodox in his theology and thoroughly convincing in his mode of presentation of his message . . .

Taking as his text Acts 9:32-35, he applied the miracle as a parable to our present situation . . . The vast congregation was gripped and held from start to finish. If the National Council is thinking of adding to the number of its evangelists, it ought to do its utmost to secure the services of Dr Martyn Lloyd-Jones. He is the modern Moody for whom we are waiting.

The week after Bournemouth, on April 6, 1938, Dr Lloyd-Jones was asked to meet with six brethren, appointed by the South Wales Association of his denomination, who were anxious to confer with him prior to his reaching any decision on the call to Marylebone Church. The President of the Association chaired the meeting which met in the vestry of the Forward Movement Hall, Neath, and, after speaking of their 'sadness and sorrow', 'beseeched him in the name of the Connexion not to leave us'. After the other members of the deputation from the Association had spoken to the same effect, Dr Lloyd-Jones explained the reasons which were compelling him to consider the call to Marylebone. As later reported back to the Association by the six deputies these reasons included:

(a) He felt that he had completed the work he had been called to do in Sandfields.

(b) He felt that he could not labour in another church in Wales and also do all the travelling and preaching that he had been doing lately.

He stated further that he had no desire to leave the Calvinistic Methodist Connexion, which was dear to him, but his present heavy duties had become a physical burden and he did not see how he could fulfil his ministry satisfactorily if he continued.[3]

In response, the deputation pressed upon him the possibility of a post of wider influence within the denomination, without the responsibilities of a pastoral charge. They foresaw 'within two years'

[3] Printed (in Welsh) as part of the deputation's report, Appendix VI, in the published *Agenda of the Quarterly Association of the Presbyterian Church of Wales to be held at Salem, Llandeilo,* June 14-16, 1938.

an opportunity for him to become directly involved in the education of men for the ministry. What they had in view was that the principalship of the denomination's college at Aberystwyth was about to fall vacant with the retirement of the Rev. Harris Hughes. If, as they thought probable, Principal D. M. Phillips was transferred to that position from the denomination's other college at Bala, then Phillips' present work would be ideally suited to Dr Lloyd-Jones' gifts; for it was at the Bala College that all students for the ministry did a year's course in pastoralia.

While Dr Lloyd-Jones was faced with this unexpected development, another consideration arose which was to prove decisive to him. It precluded one of the possibilities at once. When the Presbytery of London North met on April 12, as no mutual eligibility for ministerial interchange existed between English and Welsh Presbyterianism, they would only authorise the call on condition that the candidate applied for transfer to the ministry of the English Presbyterian Church — a step which would include an examination as to his ministerial competence! ML-J declined the call.

Meanwhile, during this same month of April 1938, yet other possibilities arose. Dr Lloyd-Jones received a letter of enquiry from the Free Church Council concerning his availability. The Council had not needed the published remarks of Dr Short to prompt them to recognise the good which the Welshman might do by preaching at inter-denominational services under their auspices in different parts of the country. Also, as we have earlier noted, there was another party deeply interested in Dr Lloyd-Jones' future. Campbell Morgan had been on the verge of approaching him when, to his consternation, Marylebone forestalled him! He had not forgotten Lloyd-Jones and confidential conversation with other leaders in Congregationalism notably with his old friend Dr J. D. Jones. The latter, recently retired from his famous pastorate at Richmond Hill Church, Bournemouth, had confirmed his growing conviction that the Calvinistic Methodist from Aberavon was the best man both to hold the congregation of the denomination's citadel in London and also, from Westminster, to exercise future leadership within English Nonconformity.

Concerned with the outcome of the matters under discussion, Campbell Morgan had asked Lloyd-Jones to keep him informed, and accordingly, when the latter phoned on April 27 and gave the news that he had declined Marylebone, the older man was delighted. But also hearing at the same time of the other possibilities Morgan did not immediately reveal his mind. Instead he wrote the next day:

> I want to thank you very much for phoning me up yesterday. It was good of you to let me know your decision, and I greatly rejoice in it, and believe you have been guided aright.
>
> I am tremendously interested, moreover, in what you have told me about Bala.
>
> Now I do not know how far you have committed yourself to the Free Church Council after July, but I am wondering whether you could postpone anything definite until you hear from me again. I have an idea in my mind that I should like to talk to you about; but before doing so, need a little time. Please write me.

Joy at Sandfields over their pastor's decision not to proceed with the Marylebone call was short-lived. Uncertain of the outcome of the various considerations now before him, Dr Lloyd-Jones could not escape the conviction that he was nearing a point of exhaustion and that, irrespective of his future work, a real break was urgently needed. On Sunday May 1, 1938, the church family at Sandfields was stunned to hear their pastor announce his resignation as from the end of July. Not without the usual inaccuracies the press at once gave headlines to the 'Aberavon Pastor Sensation'. His 'ill-health' was over-emphasised in some papers, in one case under the heading 'A Long Rest Necessary': 'He informed a church meeting at Aberavon of his decision to retire from the ministry . . . An astonished diaconate asked Dr Lloyd-Jones to reconsider his decision.' There was, of course, no question of 'retirement' from the ministry. The statement of another paper was much closer to reality:

> He said that he was resigning because he was grossly over-worked, and he was a tired man and had the desire for a complete change and rest before he undertook the further work which his denomination had for him in the future.

Meanwhile, the same weekend as this news was announced at Aberavon, another letter was in the post from Campbell Morgan. Hearing in reply to his first letter of April 28 that Lloyd-Jones was not committed in the immediate future, Morgan lost no time to seize an opportunity. In the letter which arrived the morning after his resignation, he asked Lloyd-Jones to come and share the Westminster pulpit with him for six months, 'I believe that you would find here a real opportunity for the work for which you are so marvellously fitted, namely, that of preaching.'

The invitation appealed to Lloyd-Jones as a temporary arrangement. It meant no more than that for him because his thoughts were principally on the anticipated opening in his own denomination at Bala. After further discussion he wrote to Dr Campbell Morgan confirming his acceptance of the interim arrangement and also urging that any announcement of his coming to Westminster should be kept in low key.

* * *

Shortly before the time came for Dr Lloyd-Jones to leave Aberavon, one English national newspaper carried the kind of lengthy article which the minister of Sandfields had always sought to avoid. The reporter had no access to Dr Lloyd-Jones himself but by means of a number of enquiries in Aberavon he was able to record some facts under the heading, 'The Harley Street Doctor who became a "Modern Saint."' He rightly discerned that the almost unique relationship between Dr Lloyd-Jones and many of the people of the town was based primarily upon a conviction about ML-J's personal life:

> For eleven years now Dr Martyn Lloyd-Jones has been a minister in Aberavon, and around him has grown a living legend of sainthood.
>
> I came through dull streets to learn something of this legend — the legend which you will never learn from the 'beloved doctor' himself. Hundreds of humble dwellers in Aberavon, church members or not, regard Martyn Lloyd-Jones, the man to whom all men are brothers as a matter of course, with a reverent gratitude that holds a touch of awe.
>
> There are a thousand splendid deeds of Aberavon's doctor-saint over the past eleven years that will never perhaps be told, yet, in their cumulative influence, they seem to sweeten this little town even as the strong winds from the Severn sweeten and cleanse it. He has spent, they say, a small fortune in giving practical help to people in need of money, has helped them to clear off arrears of rent and even to buy their homes. His constant question at meetings of his church committee is: 'Now, who is there in *real* want?'

Here in Aberavon they pray he will come back to them. When I asked why he had decided to leave Aberavon and the little wind-swept church, a friend told me: 'I do not know. I only know that he has decided nothing in his life — not the slightest thing — except after many hours of prayer.'

At the end of July 1938 came the final packing at 28 Victoria Road, the new manse built by the church a short time earlier in Aberavon. It was far from easy and still less was the parting which followed. Sandfields had long become much more than a place of gathering for various activities. It was a spiritual home; a place where, for many, the 'family' life was a true taste of coming glory. Whatever their future ministry would be, Martyn and Bethan sensed that they could scarcely experience again the closeness of the spiritual ties forged since those first memorable visits in 1926. It was, in part, because of all that Sandfields meant to them that fifteen years were to pass before he was to preach there again.

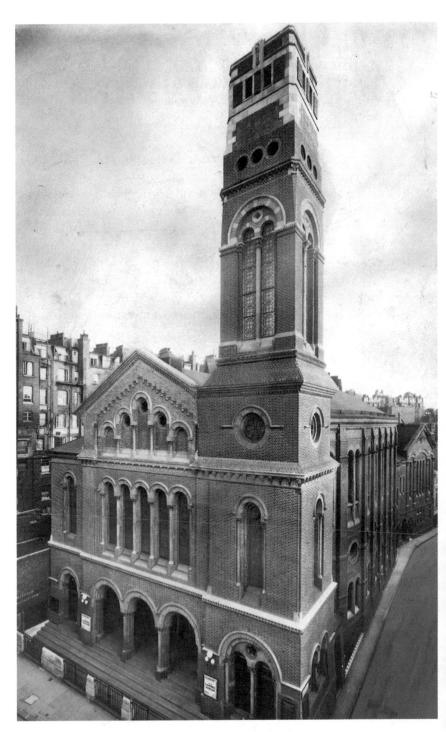

19. Westminster Chapel.

FOURTEEN

England and War

The sight of Westminster Chapel looming ahead as one rounds the bend of one of the city's narrow streets — its tower rising above the surrounding roofs of apartment blocks, shops and houses — has hastened the steps of many generations of worshippers. Yet it may be doubted whether the external appearance of the building alone ever really contributed to that sense of attraction. Probably most people pass by — as Martyn Lloyd-Jones on his milk deliveries in 1915 — without its making any impression. The truth is that the Congregationalists who between 1863 and 1865 took down their former building and rebuilt, never had enough room on their site at the corner of Buckingham Gate and Castle Lane to give their Victorian 'cathedral' the setting which it needed. Even two centuries earlier when the original Westminster Hospital had stood on that same corner, those historic streets and lanes were already crowded with buildings. The new church of 1865 was inevitably hemmed in.

Campbell Morgan had set his mark on the building in more ways than one. Such was the enthusiastic reception of his first settlement in 1904 that he had even succeeded in obtaining the removal of the old pulpit — used by such figures as C. H. Spurgeon — and had replaced it by a large circular rostrum which was an ideal pulpit. But in a more important sense Campbell Morgan had influenced Westminster Chapel and not least since his return in 1932. Three ministers had served the church in the period since he had first occupied that pastorate (1904–17); they were, J. H. Jowett, John A. Hutton, and

Hubert L. Simpson. While all three were to varying degrees evangelical, none of them had distinctly upheld the full inspiration of all Scripture. As a result, Westminster Chapel, along with the general trend in Nonconformity, had become a congregation in which the Bible was less vitally believed and followed. Left to themselves, there would have been nothing to stop the majority in the congregation from calling any preacher who impressed them, irrespective of his position on Scripture. It was precisely on this subject that Campbell Morgan's own belief had stiffened. A quarter-century of religious decline in Britain had caused him to see spiritual conditions which he had not dreamed of when he had gone to his first pastoral charge in Staffordshire in the far-off summer of 1889. The change, he was convinced, was connected with the popular error that Christianity could prosper amidst a variety of 'theories' on the inspiration of Scripture. Accordingly, when the offer of leadership at Westminster came to him again it was not so much his own future ministry which concerned him — for that must necessarily be short — but rather the need to ensure that the pulpit and church, by firm adherence to Scripture, would be committed to biblical Christianity.

Morgan rightly sensed the providence of God which had brought him back to Westminster was in order to settle the church's direction for years to come, and it is probable that even when Lloyd-Jones joined him as a 'pulpit supply' in September 1938 he was already convinced this was the man for whom he was preparing the way.

By 1938, with very few exceptions, the Free Church pulpits of central London were committed to views widely different from those of the newcomer to Westminster Chapel. That year, in fact, saw changes in several London pulpits. At nearby Westminster Central Hall, Dinsdale T. Young ended his evangelical ministry of fifty years. Dr A. D. Belden also concluded a ministry at Whitefield's Chapel, where he had preached a very different message from that of the eighteenth-century evangelist whose biography he had attempted to write.

The 1930s had brought a new generation of preachers to London, the last of whom, R. F. V. Scott at St. Columba's Church of Scotland, Pont Street, and W. E. Sangster at Westminster Central Hall, arrived almost simultaneously with Lloyd-Jones. Prominent pace-setters among these new men were Donald Soper at the Methodist Kingsway Hall, and Leslie D. Weatherhead who, although a Methodist, was now minister of the historic Congregational cause, the City Temple. Unlike men of an older generation, who while rejecting the full inspiration of the Scriptures yet thought it the part of wisdom to say nothing on that subject from the pulpit, Soper and Weatherhead were ready to speak plainly of the 'errors' of the Bible and to decry making the Bible the starting point for religious belief. People needed deliverance, they declared, from the narrowness of the old doctrines if Christianity was to progress in modern times. As though to illustrate in practical terms what this 'deliverance' would mean for the churches, the City Temple led the way in appointing a woman assistant minister in 1938.

The church-life into which the Lloyd-Joneses came at Westminster Chapel requires some comment. Although in principle ruled by the church-meeting (according to Congregational church polity), the long-established custom gave the minister almost sole power of the church as long as he remained in office. In part this was due to Victorian conceptions of ministerial autocracy, which lingered far into the twentieth century, and large congregations where the church meeting was necessarily ineffective as a means of control and leadership.

For Dr Lloyd-Jones the first twelve months back in London brought much which he could not have anticipated. In contrast with Sandfields, church life at Westminster was different to a startling degree. Few church members lived near the church and no sense of community existed between the congregation and the local population. By the use of deaconesses, and other workers, attempts had been made to reach the neighbourhood, and the poor in particular, but this outreach seems to have contributed very little to the strength of the church. In an effort to overcome the problems associated with large downtown churches, Morgan, in his early period, had introduced 'the Institute'. Under the umbrella of the Institute, many and varied meetings were organized, ranging from Sunday School and Bible classes to missionary gatherings and recreational interests. For Morgan the centre-piece of the Institute was 'the Friday Evening Bible School' which he conducted weekly at 7.30 P.M. This Friday night was so much Morgan's brain-child that even after Lloyd-Jones became co-pastor in 1939 the older man continued it entirely by himself.

Though the Institute was still continued in the late 1930s — the Friday night meeting being strongly attended — Campbell Morgan had come to doubt its value, and he was subsequently to tell his colleague that if he had his time over again he would never have started it. When Lloyd-Jones asked, 'Why?' the older man replied, 'Well, it produced a church within a church.' This was indeed true. Whereas the Sunday congregation usually filled the ground-floor and the first gallery — perhaps 1,500 — the number of members attending church meetings were only a fraction of that congregation. Many people came to Westminster Chapel who had no actual church commitment.

Certainly the Lloyd-Joneses, after their experience at Aberavon, felt that there was little sense of unity in Westminster Chapel and little close spiritual fellowship among the people. Too much attention was given to organisations at the expense of spiritual life, the most striking omission of all from the weekly activities of the church being a prayer meeting. Those who only knew Dr Lloyd-Jones at Westminster in later years could scarcely imagine him as chairman at a display of 'the gymnastic classes' but with such things he was to be occasionally involved in his first year at Westminster. Branches of the Girl Covenanters and the Boys' Brigade, also to be found at the Chapel, looked to him for aid, assuming that he — as everyone else — regarded their existence as vital.

Dr Lloyd-Jones had only been a month at Westminster Chapel when Morgan moved the proposal that he should share a joint pastoral charge on a permanent basis. This invitation was renewed and carried unanimously at a church meeting on December 8 (the day before Morgan entered his seventy-sixth year). ML-J did not accept and that because of a controversy that was going on in Wales over his future. The South Wales Association had continued to press for an appointment for ML-J within Wales and various possibilities were aired or proposed both within the Association and also in the public press. Could he not be a 'general missioner', or the next Superintendent of the Forward Movement, or even Principal of the Bala College if the existing Principal moved to the Aberystwyth College? None of these possibilities materialized and the South Wales Association eventually settled on pressing for his being given a teaching post at Bala. But this ran into an ultimate problem, the denomination was ruled by two Associations, the Southern and the Northern, between which there was a long-standing rivalry. When the Northern Association met at Chester in April 1939 it became very clear that its leadership had no intention of supporting any call to ML-J for a Bala post. Although they did not care for it to be debated in public, the principal cause of their opposition was doctrinal. For ML-J the outcome of the Chester Association was the guidance he needed and on April 23, 1939 Campbell Morgan announced to the congregation that Lloyd-Jones had accepted the call to join him as associate pastor. The Rev. William Jones of Cardiff understood this development correctly when he wrote in the correspondence columns of one of the South Wales newspapers: '"Man proposes, God disposes." Neither a chair at Bala College, nor the superintendency of the Forward Movement would suit this preacher of the Word; he would be a caged bird in either office. The removal of Dr Jones from Wales to England is no loss to the church universally. Methodism and Congregationalism count for nothing save in the councils of sectarians.'

There was another development in Dr Lloyd-Jones' first year in England which also came as a surprise. He had supposed that mid-week religious services were less usual in England than in Wales and that consequently invitations to such services would be far less frequent. His surmise was soon proved wrong. Through unofficial reports of his sermons, his name was becoming well known in England, and after the Bournemouth Assembly of March 1938 the leaders of the Free Church Council recommended him for inter-denominational services in different parts of the country. He was soon preaching quite as much as he had done in Wales, and for the first time in the cities of the North, in Newcastle-upon-Tyne in October 1938, and in Glasgow and Edinburgh the following month. In the Spring of 1939 he was back in Edinburgh for a week's united mission in the city's largest auditorium, the Usher Hall. One paper reported, 'Nothing weightier or more impressive, spiritually as well as intellectually, had been heard in Edinburgh for a long time.'

In London itself Dr Lloyd-Jones was now faced in a new way with his relationship to the inter-denominational evangelical movements, at the head of which was the Inter-Varsity Fellowship. Although still troubled at the poverty of doctrinal understanding within English evangelicalism, he came to see that, given IVF's adherence to

Scripture as the Word of God, he owed it support. In this he was aided by the persistence of Dr Douglas Johnson, its General Secretary. He also noted that, since the Swanwick Conference of 1935 when he had last spoken for the IVF, the work had strengthened its international links, particularly with Scotland and Holland. Such Free Church of Scotland figures as Dr Donald Maclean, first known to Lloyd-Jones through the pages of the *Evangelical Quarterly*,[1] were now speaking for Inter-Varsity and contributing the same kind of deepening influence as was also coming from the new ties with the Calvinist Student Movement of Holland. Dr Lloyd-Jones began to believe that he would not be a lone voice in IVF and that there was a possibility of broader, God-centred convictions. This belief was confirmed at the International Conference of Evangelical Students, convened by IVF at Cambridge from June 27 to July 3, 1939 when he gave three addresses, one of which became a booklet, *Christ Our Sanctification,* to be circulated for many years to come. What was involved, he demonstrated, was not only the meaning of sanctification but the whole definition of what it means to be a Christian:

> You cannot receive Christ as your justification only, and then, later, decide to refuse or to accept him as your sanctification. He is one and indivisible, and if you receive him at all, at once he is made unto you 'wisdom and righteousness and sanctification and redemption'. You cannot receive him as your Saviour only, and later decide to accept or refuse him as your Lord; for the Saviour is the Lord who by his death has bought us and therefore owns us. Sanctification is nowhere taught or offered in the New Testament as some additional experience possible to the believer. It is represented rather as something which is already within the believer, something which he must realise more and more and in which he must grow increasingly.[2]

[1] Maclean, appointed Professor of Church History at the Free Church of Scotland College, Edinburgh, in 1920; he, and J. R. MacKay, were joint editors of the *Evangelical Quarterly* from its inception in 1929. Lloyd-Jones wrote the Foreword to G. N. M. Collins, *Donald Maclean,* (Edinburgh: Lindsay, 1944).

[2] *Christ Our Sanctification* (London: IVF, 1948), p. 12. When this ceased to be published it was rumoured that this was his own wish, on account of his subsequent change of view. This he denied, saying there was only one Scripture reference he had quoted (*Acts* 19:20) which he had come to understand differently. See *D. Martyn Lloyd-Jones, The Fight of Faith 1939–1981*, pp. 383-3. It remained on sale in the

Although Dr Lloyd-Jones' co-pastorate had been announced in April 1939, no suitable date for an Induction service offered itself before the long summer break which he spent in Wales. The induction date was therefore fixed for September 4. On August 31, however, the radio warned of the imminent possibility of war and announced immediate plans for the evacuation of children from London and other major cities. Taking the precaution of leaving the family — Bethan, Elizabeth and Ann (born in 1937) — in South Wales, ML-J went back alone to London for Sunday, September 3, expecting to preach at Westminster in the evening. At eleven o'clock that same morning Campbell Morgan was scarcely in the pulpit before he was handed a note with the information that war with Germany had been declared; soon after, when an air-raid siren sounded, he stopped the service. The evening service and the Induction, planned for the following evening, were cancelled.

For ML-J, as for countless others, life was suddenly crowded with uncertainties. One of the first things to do was to cancel the plans which he and Bethan had been making to purchase a house of their own in London. There were discussions with Dr Morgan whether or not to announce services for 11 A.M. and 6 P.M. on Sunday 10. They decided to go ahead as usual. For the time being the Lloyd-Joneses had been staying in the old family house at 12 Vincent Square. Here there was urgent practical work to be done to prepare for war-time conditions. 'We have spent most of the time today', Martyn wrote to Bethan, 'in putting "sticking paper" on the windows to save them from blast, breakages and splinters. Sticky and very tiring work!' The houses in the Square overlooked a garden in which an air-raid shelter — actually a trench — had already been dug. 'About my quarters,' he wrote Bethan on September 5, 'quite seriously I am of the opinion that these shelters are safer than anywhere else, because there is no risk of fire, or explosions or collapsing buildings — no pieces of glass, splinters, etc. The time given as warning is more than sufficient . . . You need not worry about my not going into the trenches. I shall do so invariably.'

London was in a state of confusion and unreality. The air-raid sirens, heard since Sunday morning, were not 'false alarms', they were simply trial runs for the 'Air Raid Precautions' (ARP). A

Westminster Chapel Bookroom in 1959.

million-and-a-half people had left Britain's cities, urged by the government which, privately, feared as many as one million casualties
from aerial bombing in the first two months of the war. Gas masks
were issued to all although, as Dr Lloyd-Jones found when he called
at the City Hall in Charing Cross Road, there were none yet available
for children aged two to five: 'They are being made. When available
I will send one on', he reported to Bethan.

The next time the thirty-nine-year-old co-pastor entered the
pulpit, on Sunday evening, September 10, there was only one text
from which he could preach, 'For here we have no continuing city,
but we seek one to come' (*Heb.* 13:14). He saw that the war would
soon test the spiritual position of all church-goers. The new situation was therefore a call to self-examination. As usual, the message
was preached to himself first. He wrote to Bethan: 'This is a real test
of our beliefs and of our faith. Without a doubt, we have — all of
us — been slack for various reasons, and the first call upon us is to
repentance.' His text for Sunday, September 17, he told Bethan, was
Acts 16:25, 'And at midnight Paul and Silas prayed, and sang praises
unto God: and the prisoners heard them.' 'I preached on Paul and
Silas singing in the prison — the contrast between the two Christians
and the other prisoners. I was given freedom in preaching, and I felt
that there was unction on the message.'[3]

In the same letter, Dr Lloyd-Jones also told his wife something of
the direction which his thoughts were taking on the future course of
his pulpit ministry: 'I feel that there is a tremendous opportunity for
preaching. At the moment what is wanted is the comforting note to
help people over the shock. But, following that, the need will be for
the prophetic note to awaken the people.'

The comforting note was still prominent as he took up a series
for the five Sunday mornings in October. A 'general theodicy' — a
justification of the ways of God — was how he described to Bethan
the theme of the series. The first of these sermons was intended to
deal with the tendency of people to complain about their unan-
swered prayers. 'Many ask', he said in his introduction, 'why it is that
God did not hearken unto the prayers that have been offered since

---

[3] Reprinted in *The Christian in an Age of Terror, Sermons for a time of War* (Chich-
ester: New Wine Press, 2007), a book containing ML-J's sermons in the period
1939–47, with one sermon from Jan. 1950.

the crisis of September, 1938?' Having further stated the question, he took his answer from his text, 1 Timothy 2:8, 'I will therefore that men pray everywhere, lifting up holy hands, without wrath and doubting.' 'There is nothing which is so utterly contrary to the whole teaching of the Bible as the assumption that anyone, and at any time, without any conditions whatsoever, may approach God in prayer . . . Man, by sin, has forfeited his right to approach God, and, indeed, were he left to himself he never would approach God.'

From a further two texts from the New Testament, and two from the Old, he developed the theme, 'Why Does God Allow War?' He argued that not only were wrong answers being given to the question but that the whole approach to the subject was commonly wrong. The church was unprepared to face the unexpected because:

Precise thinking, and definition, and dogma have been at a serious discount. The whole emphasis has been placed upon religion as a power which can do things for us and which can make us happy. The emotional and feeling side of religion has been over-emphasized at the expense of the intellectual. Far too often people have thought of the Christian religion merely as something which gives a constant series of miraculous deliverances from all sorts and kinds of ills. The slogans of which we have heard so much testify to this. The phrases most frequently used have been 'Try religion' or 'Try prayer', and the impression has often been given that we have but to ask God for whatever we may chance to need and we shall be satisfied . . . We have been so intent upon ourselves and our moods and feelings and inward states, that when we are confronted by an external problem that nevertheless affects us profoundly, we do not know how to think or where to begin.

War, said the preacher, was not to be viewed as the interruption of personal convenience and of the enjoyments of life. Something far more serious was involved. War is divine judgment upon the very lives which men pursue; it is permitted 'in order that men may see through it, more clearly than they have ever done before, what sin really is' and thus be led back to God.

The advent of war, he argued again, ought not to have been a surprise:

Under the blessing of peace since the last war, men and women, in constantly increasing numbers, have forsaken God and religion and have settled down to a life which is essentially materialistic and sinful. Thinking that the last war was indeed 'the war to end war', with a false sense of security, buttressed also by insurance schemes and various other provisions to safeguard themselves against the possible dangers that still remained, men and women in this and in every other country gave themselves to a life of pleasure-seeking, accompanied by spiritual and mental indolence. This became evident not only in the decline in religion, but still more markedly in the appalling decline in morals; and indeed, finally, even in a decline in a political and social sense. It led to the decadence on which the rulers of Germany banked, and on which they based their calculations. Then came a crisis in September, 1938. Men and women crowded to places of worship and prayed for peace. Afterwards they assembled to thank God for peace. But was it because they had decided to use peace for the one and only true purpose, namely, to 'live a quiet and peaceable life in all godliness and honesty'? Was it in order that they might walk 'in the fear of the Lord and in the comfort of the Holy Ghost'? The facts speak for themselves. Thus I ask the questions: Had we a right to peace? Do we deserve peace? Were we justified in asking God to preserve peace and to grant peace? What if war has come because we were not fit for peace, because we did not deserve peace; because we by our disobedience and godlessness and sinfulness had so utterly abused the blessings of peace? Have we a right to expect God to preserve a state of peace merely to allow men and women to continue a life that is an insult to his holy Name?

These five sermons from October, 1939 were immediately published.[4] Some who heard him were young people who did not survive the war. Carl Johan Bruhn was a young Dane who with his British bride, Anne, was driving over forty miles to sit under Dr Lloyd-Jones' preaching when war broke out. Although not yet qualified in medicine, it was only after Dr Lloyd-Jones' strong advice that he desisted

---

[4] *Why Does God Allow War? A General Justification of the Ways of God* (London: Hodder and Stoughton, 1939).

from offering to serve for the Red Cross in Finland's terrible struggle against Russia. When Dr Lloyd-Jones preached from Romans 8:28 (the last of his series on 'Why Does God Allow War') it was Carl Bruhn who came to the vestry to ask for the exact Scripture references which he had quoted at the conclusion of the sermon and especially where he could find the words, 'My grace is sufficient for thee.' The next year, there was no detaining Bruhn — now qualified — from the struggle in Europe. He offered and was accepted for service with the Resistance Forces in his own country, now overrun. Taken by the RAF to be dropped by parachute into Denmark in December, 1941, weather conditions proved too bad for the jump. A second run was made on December 28; about midnight, with his plane over its correct position, Bruhn said farewell to the flight crew and leaped into the night. His parachute never opened.

His widow, Anne Bruhn, remained a life-long supporter of Dr Lloyd-Jones' ministry and would write: 'He so exalted the Lord Christ, and never obtruded himself, that he created a real thirst in me for the living God — but never left me with a feeling of self-satisfaction, neither so deflated as to be near despair.'

* * *

In the winter of 1939–40 Germany continued to show no interest in an onslaught on western Europe. It seemed possible that once Poland was conquered, the Reich would offer terms which France and Britain might accept. Certainly France, which had 106 Divisions on the Maginot Line confronted by only 23 German Divisions, was not about to launch any offensive to save Poland. 'I feel tolerably certain that the war will not last a year', wrote ML-J, anticipating by many weeks 'a general feeling' which was to be widespread in Westminster the following month. With London so quiet it was difficult to believe anything else.

It was scarcely surprising that with the expectation of an early, intensive attack from Germany proving false, there was a general bewilderment over the real state of affairs. After a brief visit to see the family in Wales on September 15, Martyn wrote to Bethan, 'I don't think I ever felt so miserable at leaving you.' On his return journey to London he had observed the movement of evacuees back to the cities which was already occurring: 'There were dozens of women and children on the train yesterday, some very little children like Ann. I understand them perfectly, but still feel that they are very unwise.'

The confusion in the national position was matched by a large element of uncertainty in Dr Lloyd-Jones' own mind. For one thing, given his qualifications, there seemed to be a real possibility that he might be called upon for medical duties in the national interest. On September 4 he was expecting 'something might come to me here from the BMA regarding medical services'. On this subject he wrote to Bethan on September 18:

> It seems that everything is in great confusion in the world of doctors. The consultants are all out in the base hospitals — with nothing to do! The agreement they made was that they would leave their private practices at once and be paid £800 per annum in these hospitals. All this was in expectation of terrible air-raids on London beginning immediately. In view of this, it is no wonder that people like Douglas Johnson and myself have heard nothing from the BMA.

Dr Douglas Johnson we have already noticed briefly. Although only thirty-five years of age Johnson had already led the IVF as its General Secretary for fifteen years (since 1934 in a full-time capacity). At the persistent urging of Professor Rendle Short — one of the movement's first presidents — he had relinquished his hopes of serving as a medical missionary in Southern Rhodesia in order to give his life to a calling which was to be far more international than he could then have realized.

With the advent of war these two ex-medicals, only five years apart in age, were brought more closely together. It was not simply that ML-J, who was elected annual president of the IVF in April 1939, now had an official advisory role in the student work, but rather that the two men had a natural affinity — despite the nationality differ-ence ('DJ is so *English*', quipped an American, 'that he even carries his gloves to church on Sunday!'). Both were omnivorous readers and born conversationalists. The exchange of views over books was to form part of their life-long friendship. In the autumn of 1939 they would meet over tea at the large table in the basement dining room at Vincent Square, when Mrs Lloyd-Jones Sr. was the hostess.

With the IVF's simple office at 39 Bedford Square closed and helpers scattered (some as chaplains in the Forces), the continuance of the work needed firm leadership, and the commitment of ML-J gave needed strength.

Some weeks were to pass before it was clear that ML-J and Johnson would not be called up for military service. By that time Dr Lloyd-Jones' mind was concentrating on the unexpected problem to be faced at Westminster Chapel. Although the congregation in the years immediately preceding the Second World War was not as large as that which Morgan had known in earlier days, it was well able to support two ministers. On Sunday morning, September 3, the numbers had been much as usual but thereafter, with the evacuation and petrol rationing, there was bound to be a change. The autumn evenings were already bringing a shortening of daylight hours, and, as the long, high windows of the chapel could not be 'blacked out' to comply with the restrictions now imposed on buildings used at night, the future of Sunday and Friday evening services was in doubt. A Friday evening Bible School was held for the last time on September 15, with about 500 present, and thereafter it was switched to 2.30 P.M. on Saturdays. Similarly, a final Sunday evening service was held at 6 P.M. on September 17 and thereafter an afternoon service was appointed for 2.30 P.M.

The probability of difficult days ahead at the chapel was rightly foreseen by Dr Morgan. The older minister had no pension and at seventy-five still depended for income on the work of preaching which he loved. Westminster, where he lived at St Ermin's Hotel two blocks from the chapel, was the centre of his life. But in the early days of the war Morgan did not see how his ministry could continue. In a letter to his wife Martyn reported:

> Blackie[5] phoned today to say that CM is very depressed, feeling that he ought to go — that there is no need for him at Westminster now. But then they have nothing to live on. I had told him on Saturday, that I would go if the church could not support both. What he tells Blackie about that is that it is he who

[5] Margery Blackie, a distinguished physician and general practitioner, was a member at Westminster Chapel and a close friend of the Morgans. For Morgan see, *A Man of the Word, G. Campbell Morgan,* Jill Morgan (London: Pickering and Inglis, 1951).

ought to go and leave the younger man in charge. But you will see his difficulty. I cannot allow him to suffer, and I am determined, should it be necessary, that I will go for the time being. But perhaps we shall find congregations better than we think, and the problem may not arise.

On the third Sunday of the war the loose collections came to £35. 'Quite good,' ML-J commented, 'and yet, in view of the expenses on the place, not nearly enough.' At an emergency meeting of the deacons on October 1, four senior men were appointed to review the entire financial position. The Chapel had only £48 left in its 'reserve fund' and the treasurer had had to borrow £100 from another fund in order to meet expenses to the end of September. Martyn wrote to Bethan the next day: 'I shall be very glad when the position at Westminster is made clear one way or another . . . I understand that there would be very strong opposition to my leaving. We must exercise patience and live from day to day.' At the next deacons' meeting, on October 22, it was reported that when Dr Lloyd-Jones was invited to become joint minister the estimated receipts for the six weeks following were £4,227, whereas now the receipts in the first six weeks of war were £2,686 — a decrease of £1,541. In the words of the Deacons' Minutes, 'The problem was how to decrease our expenditure to the extent of £1,541.' It was decided that, except for terminating one of the Chapel cleaners, all other staff could be retained provided salaries were cut. Thus Dr Morgan's salary was reduced by £300 to £800, Dr Lloyd-Jones' by £200 to £500 and those of Mr A. E. Marsh (Church Secretary) and Sister Dora (Deaconess) were halved to the figure of £150.

Dr Lloyd-Jones was perfectly satisfied. Reporting the meeting to Bethan, he said, 'In view of this, I will, of course, go on, and we shall have to consider various possibilities for you three.' The family, as we shall note later, was to return from Wales in December.

The problems of autumn 1939 were to prove small indeed compared with what was to follow. During this initial period of the 'phoney war' the reasons for Hitler's inactivity in the West were not rightly understood. Repeating newspaper reports, Martyn wrote to Bethan that autumn: 'Many are prophesying that there will not be any air-raids. It seems that London's defences are beyond our comprehension.'

The illusion was soon to be dispelled. In April, 1940 with the East secured behind him, Hitler launched his forces into Norway and Denmark. A month later it was France's turn. The last British troops were out of Dunkirk on June 3 and the Germans entered Paris on June 14. Upon the fall of France, Hitler expected Britain's surrender as a natural consequence and then a 'thousand-year Reich'. But Britain, in which the only fully-equipped division of troops was Canadian, stood fast. 'The Battle of Britain' for the control of the air over south-east England began in August and, although not won by the Germans, they were still able on September 7, 1940 to begin day and night bombing on London in earnest. At that same date across the English Channel forty German divisions were ready to invade on a front extending from Folkestone to Bognor, an action which they postponed on September 17.

The era of mere ARP practices and of 'false-alarms' already seemed to lie in the distant past. On Wednesday, September 25, Dr Morgan wrote in his diary: 'Went to look at church after incendiary bomb hit it last night. A sad sight.'

Since 1938 the two colleagues at Westminster had been alternating every month in the services which they took, one man taking the morning service for four or five weeks and the other the second service. In October 1940 it was ML-J's turn to take the morning service. But some, and probably Morgan himself, clearly felt that it was too dangerous to continue services at Westminster. The damage from the incendiary bomb on September 25 had not been serious, yet it was enough to lead Morgan to change the venue for morning worship on September 29 to the Livingstone Hall, the headquarters of the London Missionary Society in nearby Victoria. At Westminster Chapel there were no air-raid shelters at hand for the congregation when alarms occurred during services, neither could anything adequate be provided upon the premises. After two Sunday mornings in October in the Chapel all services were transferred to Livingstone Hall.

As though a witness to the uncertainties of this dark hour, for the next three months the long-kept Vestry Register at Westminster Chapel, in which the preacher noted his text every Sunday, lay unused and no record of what either man preached has survived. Something of what was being discussed by the two preachers in private, however, is known. Morgan, had moments when he feared that the end of the work at Westminster was near. Humanly speaking that was a real possibility, with the old congregation scattered and the very survival of the building in serious doubt. For fifty-seven nights in succession, an average of two hundred German bombers were over London every night. Churchill later wrote, 'At this time we saw no end but the demolition of the whole Metropolis.' Before the end of October, 1940 the Bishop of London was to state that in his diocese alone 32 churches had been destroyed, and 47 seriously damaged. What hope had Westminster Chapel, standing as it did so close to Buckingham Palace and other primary targets for German bombing? Morgan and Lloyd-Jones usually met weekly and the old veteran did not hide his dismay over the situation into which his friend had been brought. It was not so much that Morgan was concerned for himself. 'Although I confess it is not easy,' he wrote, 'I am constantly hearing in my own soul the words: "In nothing be anxious, but in everything by prayer and supplication with thanksgiving, let your requests be made known unto God."' But he did fear that Lloyd-Jones might be left without work and without a pastorate. Already his colleague was facing numbers considerably less than those to which he had been accustomed on Sundays in Wales. Recalling the effect of the war on the size of the congregation, ML-J was to say in later years: 'Almost immediately our congregation went down to about 300 as most people who could get out of London did so . . . Finally only 100 to 200 were left of Campbell Morgan's great congregation.'

In October 1940 Dr Morgan temporarily left all the work to his colleague by cancelling his own afternoon services. He wanted there to be no question of his friend leaving, so long as there was any congregation at all. No one could have been more magnanimous. 'Dr Morgan', Lloyd-Jones was to say, 'was a very kind and very generous man.'

In the deacons' meetings held in October, 1940 something of the strain behind the scenes was revealed. In a meeting on October 13 there was some comment on the different practice of the two ministers with regard to air-raids. The records note: 'It was pointed out that at present Dr Morgan closes the service at once [if warning sounds] whereas Dr Lloyd-Jones continues at any rate until the more imminent danger.' After discussion, the general but not unanimous opinion was that 'the service should be closed when warning was given'.

A church meeting on November 10, 1940 revealed there were a number who did not approve the move to Livingstone Hall. A senior member of the church, Mr J. B. Gotts, wanted to know, 'Why are we having services at Livingstone Hall? Would it be possible for Dr Lloyd-Jones to amplify the statement he recently made from the pulpit at Westminster regarding the holding of services in Livingstone Hall?' Perhaps as a result of this discussion the Vestry Register for the first Sunday of 1941 contains the note, 'Returned to Church' although not until the next Sunday was the more than three months' silence broken and a record of the preachers' texts resumed. Possibly because of the sickness of his colleague, Lloyd-Jones preached at both services throughout January 1941. For January 12 his text for one service, as recorded in the Vestry Register, was Habakkuk 3:17, 18, 'Although the fig tree shall not blossom, neither shall fruit be in the vines; the labour of the olive shall fail, and the fields shall yield no meat; the flock shall be cut off from the fold, and there shall be no herd in the stalls: Yet I will rejoice in the Lord, I will joy in the God of my salvation.'

It was a text singularly appropriate for the ministers as well as for the people. Lloyd-Jones presided at a deacons' meeting on January 26, 1941, Morgan being 'absent with a chill'. The Church Treasurer, Mr J. Ryley,[6] was also absent but he sent in a statement which was read by his friend, Mr A. W. Caiger. Despite all economies and cuts in salaries already agreed, he reported that the year 1940 had ended with an overdraft of £150.6s.0d. Further, the weekly offerings through the winter had been averaging little more than £10 and the position was worsening! Reading Ryley's statement, Caiger said: 'I think we should begin by telling our Ministers that we see no prospect of paying them their present stipends after the end of March, possibly February. How to keep the Church going at all is a problem.'

While granting the reality of the difficulties, it cannot be said that the diaconate at this date appear as men with strong spiritual priorities. Concern was expressed that the Bible School should be restarted in order that the funds which were being lost from that source might be made up. Finally, it was agreed to continue the ministers' allocations until the end of March when the position would be reviewed. At the next recorded meeting of the diaconate on April 6, 1941, Messrs

[6] A member since 1905, he died in 1943, when he was succeeded by Caiger.

Ryley and Caiger proposed that henceforth both ministers' salaries be terminated and that they both be paid simply on a supply basis of £10 a service — thus reducing weekly expenditure upon the ministry to £20 per week, or £30 when Dr Morgan resumed his Bible School on May 2. It was also proposed that money be saved by ending the tradition of inviting a visiting preacher in the summer period (John Hutton had preached for four weeks in August, 1940). Instead the two ministers should alternately take double duties during the holiday months. Such were the extremities to which the deacons now believed themselves to be driven and they unanimously adopted the above proposals.

The spiritual deficiency in the diaconate reflected the long-standing weakness of the whole congregation. The large pre-war attendance had disguised the extent to which lower standards prevailed. There was a definite liberal element in the membership and particularly in that of the 'Institute'. Speaking of his reception at the Chapel, Dr Lloyd-Jones once said: 'They were very kind to me but I felt a great lack of spiritual understanding and spiritual fellowship. There was no prayer meeting at all and no spiritual meeting.' With Dr Morgan's ready acquiescence, ML-J introduced a Monday evening 'Fellowship' meeting in the autumn of 1939 with the intention of encouraging spiritual conversation and discussion. With the advent of serious bombing this meeting had to be abandoned for the time being.

From that date onwards the destruction of London continued. By March 1941 a number of London's most historic churches had been damaged in the bombing, some irreparably. They included St Andrew, Holborn where George Whitefield once preached; Austin Friars, a Reformed church of immigrants from the reign of Edward VI; St Magnus-the-Martyr, the burial place of Miles Coverdale the Bible translator; John Newton's St Mary Woolnoth and St Andrew-by-the-Wardrobe, scene of the ministry of William Romaine. Among more modern buildings, St Columba's (Pont Street), Spurgeon's Tabernacle and the City Temple shared in the devastation. An observer, writing on 'London Churches in the Blitz' in the *British Weekly* for April 24, 1941, reported: 'The first building visited, The City Temple, was the completest ruin I ever saw . . . Among the rubbish where I stood were pieces of a tablet commemorating the founding of the church in 1640 by Thomas Goodwin, the Puritan.' At the Congregational

Union Assembly the following month, it was reported of the denomination that 'no fewer than 260 churches have been damaged more or less seriously.' At one of their weekly conversations in St Ermin's Hotel, Morgan, reflecting on what was happening, exclaimed to his colleague, 'I have brought you here, and this is what I have brought you to! We are almost certain to be bombed completely to the ground.'

Severe difficulties continued throughout 1941. On October 8 Morgan could write, 'London is going through a tremendous ordeal. I have not been in bed for six weeks. Down in the lounge we do get some sleep during the night at intervals, and so we are keeping up . . . The Chapel has been hit three times.' Without fire-watchers, sometimes fire-fighters, constantly on the premises it would undoubtedly have been burned out. One of these men at this time was Geoffrey T. Thomas, a member of the church who lived in Chelsea. But he recalls being more awe-struck by some of ML-J's preaching than by the bombing. On one hot Sunday evening in the late summer of 1940 one memorable sermon ended with a call to repentance, based upon the 'woes' pronounced upon Chorazin and Bethsaida and the words 'for if the mighty works which were done in you had been done in Tyre and Sidon, they would have repented long ago in sackcloth and ashes' (*Matt.* 11:21).

Despite the fire-fighters, the congregation had to return for a time to Livingstone Hall. The financial situation improved. On October 26, 1941, a letter from Mr Ryley, who was unwell, was read to the diaconate once more emphasizing the seriousness of the position and proposing that the ministers should appeal for higher giving. One of the ministers, at least, is unlikely to have acceded. Dr Lloyd-Jones was never known to appeal for money in the churches which he served.

No records exist of how many who attended Westminster Chapel lost their lives in the blitz. One unusual case, however, has been recalled by Mrs Lloyd-Jones. From the first days of the war, two sisters, the Misses Spain, were among the most faithful attenders at all services. 'They always sat together in the middle block, near the front — hardly elderly, late middle-age perhaps — always pleasant and courteous, but we knew very little about their background, except that their father had been a business man, and that both he and their mother were dead.' One Sunday they were present as usual though the church was then meeting in the Livingstone Hall. Dr Lloyd-Jones was preaching that day on 'the wedding garment' and on the danger of being found without 'the wedding garment'. Mrs Lloyd-Jones continues:

> At the end of the service, the elder Miss Spain came to speak to him. She had come to thank the Doctor for the sermon — a thing she had not done before — and during the conversation she told him that they had one other sister in an important government post down on the South Coast. Apart from this, they had no family, near or far. Drawn to talk because of Martyn's interest, she told him that this third sister was feeling lonely and was coming up to London that very evening to stay for a few days with them. As she was leaving, she turned back and half shyly said: 'Doctor, I am so glad I have on that wedding garment, thank you', then went out to join her sister.

That night a bomb fell on their house and all three sisters were killed outright. The members of Westminster Chapel were their family at the burial.

FIFTEEN

Inside the Family

From the time of the Lloyd-Joneses' arrival in London in 1938 they had lived at 12 Vincent Square until it was clear that they were meant to stay in England. Then, as already noted, on the eve of buying their own house, war had been declared. The first months of the war brought the longest separation of Martyn from Bethan to occur during their years of marriage.

From the end of August 1939 Mrs Lloyd-Jones, Elizabeth and Ann stayed with a family of friends in Llanelli. The house was large enough for them to live separately and to look after themselves independently. In Bethan's later words: 'It was kind enough of our hosts to give us house-room, without adding another family to their load of domestic work. So, I "did for us" to the last detail.' (The lack of such freedom for most evacuee mothers and children was a factor in the decision which soon brought them back to the cities.) Martyn had only one major concern about the household arrangement at Llanelli and it was one which was to amuse them in later years. Hitherto, as in most middle-class families, their home had never been run without a maid. Even while staying in Vincent Square, Theresa, their Welsh maid, had been with them. Suddenly the Second World War ended this household pattern forever. 'What worried Martyn', his wife tells us, 'was that I was not used to it. In those incredibly far away days, I had never been without some domestic help with household chores, and he thought that the cleaning and working and washing and care of the girls would find me wilting! Actually, of course, it was nothing but a gentle introduction to the change that the war was going to make in ordinary domestic life and living. It never worried me.'

The letters from ML-J at Vincent Square to Llanelli reveal how troubled he was at Bethan having to do such things as lighting fires in the morning. Expressing his objections, he reluctantly admits in a letter of September 16, 1939, 'I have thought and thought again, but I cannot see any better arrangement than the present one.' 'Don't kill yourself with work, and get enough sleep', is a characteristic exhortation. On another occasion, after a visit to the family, he expressed his pleasure that, despite so much to do, Bethan had been able to speak at a local 'Sisterhood' meeting. His reasoning, however, made her smile:

> If I did not remember to say a word about your talk in the Sisterhood yesterday, I did remember to pray for you in the train. I'm sure you were doing the right thing and I'm sure you would greatly help the women. But quite apart from that, even, I want you to do this, if only to use your mind. That is one of the things that grieves me when I think of you with so much to do that you do not have time to read.

Their financial situation at this time also gave him added concern lest Bethan's necessary economies should be too stringent. Although he shares with her the likely difficulties ahead at Westminster — 'Gotts told me that the collections are down £1,500 [i.e. per annum] on an average!' — he is insistent: 'There is no need for you to cut back on expense at all. Take care to prepare and to eat proper meals . . . Don't worry about the cost of Elizabeth's books, she has got to have them.' In later years when he so often helped struggling pastors with gifts for their families, they little realized that he and Mrs Lloyd-Jones had known what it was to experience that same problem.

Dr Lloyd-Jones' capacity for sympathy with others is an aspect of his character which often appears in his letters to Bethan. It comes out in comments on many people, from Campbell Morgan and Bethan's parents, to their former maid, Theresa, who had become seriously ill: 'I am truly sorry for Theresa, I have thought much about her and remembered her in prayer all day.' In an address to fellow doctors he once said, 'I seriously question whether anyone has a right to be practising clinical medicine who has no real concern for persons and for people.'

It was not ML-J's habit to speak of what he was doing and the church officers at Westminster Chapel may well have supposed that, in the troubled autumn of 1939, he was dividing his time between London at the weekends, and Llanelli mid-week. That was not the case. Mid-week preaching engagements — which he had once supposed might ease on his leaving Wales — continued to take him to many places. Certainly Llanelli was where he wished to be, but calls to preach were not to be refused on account of war or his family, and so visits to South Wales could only be occasional. Letters, however, were constant, and while his week-day engagements away from Westminster Chapel were similar, he never failed to tell Bethan what they were:

> I had a somewhat busy day yesterday, as I had to prepare two new addresses — one for the ministers, who belong to the London Baptist Association, with whom I am to be on Tuesday morning, and the other for Rheinallt's induction meeting.[1] I felt that the two addresses had to be quite different. I shall address the ministers on the ministry today, but Rheinallt on the unchangeable nature of the ministry.

Concerning another week he writes:

> I am preaching in a Mission with the Congregationalists in the Old Kent Road on Monday afternoon and, of course, there is the Fellowship on Monday night. Then on Wednesday I am due to preach in Richmond Hill, Bournemouth for Dr John Short, who followed Dr J. D. Jones, preaching afternoon and evening. I shall have to stay there overnight, I'm afraid. That is all I am doing this week . . .

While the war caused a few mid-week meetings to be cancelled, even so, in the period September–November, 1939, his engagements away from Westminster included visits to such places as Worthing, Whitchurch, Carmarthen, Brighton, Croydon, Fulham, Cambridge, Nuneaton, Aldershot, Manchester, Holywell, Rhyl, Cardiff and Haslemere. The visit to the last-named proved to be of particular significance. Haslemere is a small country town high in the Weald of Surrey. Gerald Golden, a surgeon who lived there, had invited Dr Lloyd-Jones to preach in a local cinema on two consecutive evenings towards the end of October. By this date, as ML-J had been

---

[1] Rheinallt Nantlais Williams, later to be the Principal of the Theological College at Aberystwyth.

travelling in quiet areas of Southern England, the idea had already occurred to him of their renting a house near enough to London for him to be able to travel into Westminster by train. Both Worthing and Brighton were tempting; he did not know how vulnerable both coastal resorts were soon to become in their situation on the English Channel. Haslemere, however, deep in the country and half-way between the South Coast and London, had not occurred to him prior to his visit. By early November 1939 he was still considering housing possibilities in various places in Surrey and Sussex, though now of the opinion that 'Haslemere is the best idea.' Meanwhile the Goldens were looking in their neighbourhood, and on November 9, 'almost too excited to write', Martyn passes on to Bethan a letter from Dorothy Golden which describes a 'find' which she and her husband could recommend. It was a new semi-detached house available on a rental. In Mrs Golden's words, 'clean and marvellously healthy, with a lovely view at the back, and the living rooms get all the sun'. Dr Lloyd-Jones speedily went to see it, and after letters and phone calls to Bethan they decided to take it. The disadvantage was its smallness, it would not be large enough to take all their furniture and his books which were still in storage in Cardiff. But on the situation he shared Dorothy Golden's enthusiasm: 'It is very beautiful,' he wrote to Bethan, 'standing about 500-600 feet above sea level. Pine trees all over the place and lovely walks . . . It is a hundred times better than Brighton.' It could be leased for the duration of the war and at a rental of only £150 per year, 'whereas rates and rent for one year at Kensington would have been £210'. The house was taken and because it had no name or number ML-J had to find a name quickly for its identification in the legal agreement awaiting signature. 'The Haven' was his choice and it was to be their home for the four years from December 1939 to November 1943.

Before we leave the period when Bethan, Elizabeth and Ann were at Llanelli, there remains one thing more to be said about the letters between husband and wife. There is an argument which recurs in their letters (the only argument, as Philip Henry used to say, permitted between a husband and wife), namely, who loved the other the most. Bethan's side of the 'argument' has not survived, but it would not have been easy for her to be the winner. Dr Lloyd-Jones was always indignant about the view he sometimes heard in evangelical circles that any two Christians should be able to marry one another. On the contrary, he believed that couples needed both to 'fall in love' and to stay in love. The following gives a glimpse of the happiness of his relationship to 'the dearest girl in the world':

> I see time passing terribly slowly, and the absence of your company is overpowering. There are dozens of things that arise from what I notice, or from what I am thinking or reading, that I would like to talk about with you. But you are not here . . . I was thinking much about you on my travels yesterday. I was passing through Harrow and that brought back innumerable memories of the days when I used to make my way down to see you, and of our trips out to Rickmansworth, etc. I remember the inner excitement as we approached Harrow station and as I thought about you. But that was not to be compared with what I felt yesterday as I thought about you. With every passing year I realize more and more that I am the luckiest man in all the world . . . No lover ever longed for his beloved as much as your poor husband longs for you.

At the end of November 1939 he was due to preach in Cardiff (not far from Llanelli) and he was anxious to make arrangements to meet Bethan there, although the next week they were all to remove together to the new home in Haslemere. The following letter is so characteristic that it is given in full:

12 Vincent Square
November 27, 1939

My dear Bethan,

A word in a very great hurry, to give you 'instructions' for tomorrow. I was glad to have your letter this morning and to know that you had really enjoyed yourselves Saturday and yesterday.

We had amazingly good congregations yesterday, considering the weather. I preached a new sermon on Acts 3 — the point being: 'expecting to receive something of them' — wrong attitude to the church and her gospel.

Vin[2] returned last night having found everything all right in Hereford. I have been at it all day doing this and that — talking to Douglas Johnson, preparing a manuscript for Marsh[3] for the

---

[2] Vin, his brother, Vincent.

[3] Arthur E. Marsh, the Church Secretary. Prior to 1907, when he went to Princeton Theological Seminary, he had been a secretary to Campbell Morgan, but

Westminster Record, and so on. Of course the Fellowship is at 6.30. Now, about tomorrow. Here are the 'instructions': You'll arrive probably on Platform 2. If you find, on asking! — that my train is *not* yet in, walk down the steps to the subway and walk up the steps to Platform 3 — the one on which I shall arrive. If you are told that the train is going to be late, go and sit by the fire in the waiting-room. When the train arrives stand on the platform, *between* the two stairs that lead to the subway. I shall make for that point. If I am in first, I shall stand between the two stairways leading to the subway, on Platform 2. So, have a look there first. We cannot miss each other. There is no danger of our missing each other — if you were in a haystack I'd find you. My only anxiety is that someone else will be trying to get hold of you too! Remember that Cardiff is a very cold place. Put plenty of warm clothes on and eat plenty of breakfast. How to wait till tomorrow I don't know?

Till then all my love to you my dear love, and to the two girls and my affectionate regards to all there.

Ever yours, Martyn.

Although it might hardly seem so from his itinerary, Dr Lloyd-Jones was still at this date struggling with the health problems which were noted at the conclusion of his ministry at Aberavon. He had not yet been able to throw off the general feeling of exhaustion which he came to experience in his late thirties and this had given him sufficient concern to put himself under his old chief, Lord Horder, in 1939. ML-J's own experience in treating ministers and clergy when he was practising medicine had led him to consider them all 'a pack of neurotics'. Given the state of his own health, he had to revise that view and to confess, 'There are tensions in the ministry — the very nature of the work tends to produce them.'

Not naturally inclined to exercise, Dr Lloyd-Jones made a special effort at this period. There were frequent references to it in his letters to Bethan while she was still at Llanelli. 'The post is here at about 8.10 every morning, so I read your letter before going out for my walk every day.' 'I walked for 45 minutes before breakfast this morning.' 'Nowadays I am walking for 40 minutes before breakfast,

---

the following year Morgan had called him back to be his assistant. He was to remain for more than half a century, appearing to the last in the same impeccable Edwardian dress which he had worn six years before the First World War.

and again in the afternoon for the same length of time. It must surely be beneficial.'

When the family was together again under one roof there was still need of occasional letters to Bethan. With war-time conditions too uncertain to be able to depend upon the railway on Sunday mornings, and not possessing a car, ML-J usually went up to London from Haslemere on Saturday evenings. Sometimes, depending on the location of his mid-week engagements, he was not home again until the following Thursday. Wherever he was he rang Bethan every day and often sent a short letter. From these letters it is clear that his health was a continuing concern to them both.

In a note to his wife from Vincent Square at the conclusion of Sunday, February 11, 1940, Martyn reported: 'The catarrh was quite bad as I preached and, after some 30 minutes, I felt that my voice was going. This meant that I could do no more than give a synopsis of the two last points. CM had not noticed that anything was wrong.' The following night he travelled overnight by train for engagements at Newcastle.

Two weeks later, after the Sunday morning service at the Chapel, he wrote:

> Just a word to let you know that I feel much better today. I decided in the train last night that my 'gout' was the trouble, after all, and having made the right diagnosis, I began to get better. I am now quite sure that I never had the influenza at all!
>
> I got through the service with no difficulty at all — Vincent says he never heard so much resonance in my voice. It was quite a good service, too, and yet I feel that this is the weakest of the four sermons.
>
> I am now off to Paddington Chapel . . .[4]

Apart from his general run-down condition it was his voice which was giving him the greatest problem at this time. The trouble was the result of a long-established bad habit, for, instead of the use of correct voice production in public speaking, he had depended on the

[4] That is, to take an evening service. While sharing the Sunday services at Westminster with Dr Morgan, he frequently took another service elsewhere in London. At Sunday lunch-time, and in the afternoon, he took the opportunity to meet various members of the congregation. An evening service at the Chapel was restored on April 6, 1941.

physical energy of youth. As that energy came to fail him he faced persistent problems. There were several references to it in the letters of 1939 to Bethan. 'I don't feel tired, but I had to be careful with my voice last night.' 'I'm sure you were thinking of me in the services yesterday. Well, I got through both without losing my voice, but I had to be very careful.'

His deliverance from the misuse of his voice in preaching owed much to a lady by the name of Miss Hicks who had helped many other public speakers, including Lloyd George. Bethan Lloyd-Jones speaks of her 'genius in voice production', and writes the following about her visits to Haslemere:

> Miss Hicks deserves notice. She was of the same general shape and outline as Queen Victoria, with equal authoritative determination and gimlet eye. I cannot remember how Martyn got in touch with her. She came and stayed at a small hotel and spent two or three hours every day correcting Martyn's faulty voice production — giving him various exercises, etc. She was to be remembered with gratitude for she certainly knew her job. To the very end if he had any throat trouble or if he were tired, I would hear him go through the exercises and the trouble would soon be gone.

With regard to the measures needed for the recovery of ML-J's health in 1940, there was some difference of opinion among his medical advisers. In Horder's view he was still doing far too much and many of his commitments needed cancelling. But in a letter to Bethan from Vincent Square on April 1, 1940, Martyn reported another opinion:

> As for myself, as I told you on the phone, I have been feeling very tired all day. I did not sleep too well last night for some reason. The sermon on Matthew 11:28-30, went very well. I don't think I have ever been wiser or more sensible in my preaching, as far as the use of my voice goes — no, never before. I do believe that I have mastered the principles in this matter.

While his voice thus improved, his general health still gave concern. He reported to Bethan that a doctor had assured him it was simply due to over-exertion, but he had not recommended a cancellation of mid-week engagements. 'As you know,' he wrote, 'I agree entirely with this.' Bethan was not so sure.

ML-J certainly did not want his health discussed at deacons' meetings. 'He persuaded us all', says Bethan, 'that to do only one service on Sunday was enough of a rest. But, of course, it never came to that — well, hardly ever.'

His own health in 1940 was over-shadowed early in that year by the more serious illness of his friend, Douglas Johnson, who, after prolonged overwork, suffered a coronary occlusion. In the course of a letter to Mrs Johnson of January 19, 1940, ML-J wrote:

I am so glad to hear that he is somewhat better.

I feel I must tell you that every time I pray for him (and I do so twice daily) I have a very definite and unmistakable consciousness of the fact of his complete and entire recovery.

That kind of thing, as he will know, is not common with me. I report it because it is so very definite.

Unable to meet, the two men corresponded as well as speaking on the phone. In a letter to DJ on May 8, 1940, ML-J writes: 'It is good to hear of your continued progress. I am also improving daily — with Miss Hicks still in attendance!'

ML-J's slow improvement he attributed — for the present, at least — to the greater opportunities for physical exercise afforded by the situation at Haslemere. Besides afternoon walks with his girls when school was over, the garden of the newly-built house which they were renting was in need of attention. It consisted merely of rough earth, with much builder's rubble still lying about. And there was another reason, in addition to his health, for addressing himself to the garden. Gerald Golden recalls: 'This was a time of great national stress, and everyone was deeply committed to helping the war effort in some way or other. In a small country town the most obvious way for many was food production, and the vegetable garden was a "must". Martyn was not slow to accept the challenge, though his competence in this direction was limited. I remember his laboriously planting out cabbage plants, but they did not prosper. I don't think he ever had much satisfaction from his garden labours. Though he took the work seriously he always looked ill at ease and gently amused.'

In the early summer of 1941 Bethan was ill with pneumonia and for convalescence she went, with Ann, to her parents who had evacuated from Harrow to the peace of Newcastle Emlyn in West Wales.

Martyn and Elizabeth remained at Haslemere and from a letter to Bethan of June 18 it is evident that gardening was still in full swing:

> I'm glad you had a better journey than I did and that you arrived safely. I hope above all things that you are having the same wonderful weather as we are — it is marvellous, if anything too hot.
>
> I have earthed the potatoes, all but two rows. I have also given the peas some kind of support — with some string running from one to another. I believe that will be enough to hold them until I can get some better stakes. The cabbage and lettuce have taken well. I am afraid that one of the marrow plants has died. I give them water every night. The carrots and beetroot are looking very well, and there are flowers on the broad beans. So you see that I am fairly diligent! I go to the garden every night at about 6.15 for a couple of hours.
>
> Oh, yes, Mr Oberheim lent me a spanner and I was able to correct the fault in the two hot taps. You can see that, between one thing and another, you have a really useful husband!
>
> The days pass very slowly, but if you come back strong, well, I am willing to wait in patience.
>
> You know that I am preaching in the More Street Baptist Church tomorrow evening at 7 o'clock. I mean to go up [to London] with the 2 o'clock train to meet Sangster and to have tea with him.[5] Tell Ann I greatly miss the 'little gardener'.

According to ML-J's later memories, his achievements at gardening came to a head one Good Friday (probably in 1942). While he was up at Westminster preaching on that particular day Bethan accepted the offer of a load of manure which was dumped in the road at the front of the house. It had all to be removed to the back, by wheelbarrow, and over rough ground as there was no pathway around the house. The result of this 'splendid' Saturday exercise was that, after preaching at Westminster on the Sunday, he had to spend three days in bed to recover! Amusing though the incident was, it led him to reach the final conclusion that he was not meant for physical exercise. He would later say that it took him a number of years to recognize this. By way of explanation he distinguished sharply between nervous and physical energy. In his opinion, he possessed much of the former

---

[5] W. E. Sangster (1900–60) became the Methodist minister of Westminster Central Hall, close to Westminster Chapel, in 1939.

and little of the latter. 'Any physical exertion always exhausts me.' The after-effect of physical labour was to lower his blood pressure and, thus, far from being a stimulus, it was actually debilitating. Referring later to his 'more exercise' period he said: 'I had to stop. I couldn't do my work if I didn't. I have no physical energy at all, if I expend it I cannot read or think.' But in situations demanding 'nervous energy' (such as public speaking), he could say, 'I have seen physically strong men almost fainting when I was fine.'

This was one of the few personal things about which ML-J did speak in ministers' meetings. He was convinced that 'great damage' could be done to some men by the theory that a vigorous athletic life is always the best way to promote health. He regarded all such generalizations as wrong:

> I am an opponent of universal set rules for all. Nothing is more important than that a man should get to know himself. I include in that that he should get to know himself physically as well as temperamentally and in other respects. I say this because there are those who would prescribe a programme for a preacher and minister; they tell him when to get up in the morning, what to do before breakfast, and what to do later and so on. They do not hesitate to draw up systems and programmes and to advocate these, and indeed almost to suggest that, if a man does not follow such a programme, he is a sinner and a failure. I have always been an opponent of such ideas and for this reason, that we are all different, and that you cannot lay down a programme of this nature for everybody.
>
> We live in the body, and our bodies differ from case to case. We also have different temperaments and natures, so you cannot lay down universal rules . . . Some of us are slow starters in the morning; others wake up fresh and brimful of energy in the morning, like a dog on the leash, waiting to go to work. We do not determine this; it is something constitutional. It depends on many factors, partly, if not chiefly, on blood pressure and such matters as your nervous constitution, the balance of your ductless glands, etc. All these factors come in. I argue therefore that our first business is to get to know ourselves. Get to know how you, with your particular constitution, work. Get to know when you are at your best and how to handle yourself.[6]

[6] *Preaching and Preachers,* pp. 167-8.

These words came from personal experience as well as from medical knowledge. It was in large measure his better understanding of himself which led to the improvement in his health in these years. He passed out of a tendency to depression (which he regarded as common in the early-forties age group) and, in Bethan's words, 'steadily regained his old tireless elasticity'. Those who only saw him so amazingly active at a later period would have found it hard to believe that he had ever passed through such a problem with respect to his health.

* * *

The war had brought a change to the family routine on Sundays. When they had first moved to England, and were staying at Vincent Square near Westminster Chapel, they were all in church, with Ann being introduced to public worship from her infancy as Elizabeth had been. There was a crèche for babies and infants but ML-J expected children to be present with their parents for a whole service just as soon as they could be quiet. Of course, there were occasional mishaps, as the Lloyd-Joneses themselves experienced. Once when Elizabeth was very small, on observing her father bow his head to pray as he led the service, she exclaimed audibly, 'He has gone sleepy byes!'

With the move to Haslemere, it was virtually impossible for Bethan and the children to be at Westminster on Sundays and so the local Congregational church became their place of worship until November 1943. Another Sunday event which these new circumstances ended was the afternoon walk. While still at Vincent Square either Bethan or Martyn would take the girls on a short walk to St James' Park. Ann was still a toddler. When the duty was in Bethan's hands it usually ended with the weary infant being carried home and both mother and child exhausted. But the conclusion was different when her father was in charge. On hearing the plea to be carried he would respond cheerfully, 'Oh, I *am* sorry, are you tired? All right you shall carry my umbrella then.' This never failed both to bring him back fresh and Ann happy, trailing the umbrella behind her. 'He was devoted to the girls,' writes Bethan, 'and however busy and hard pressed he was would always have time for them. He would also, it seemed, be as defensive as he dared, on their behalf, when mother was "laying down the law"!'

Speaking of her husband's view of the Lord's Day, as it affects the family, Mrs Lloyd-Jones has also written:

> Martyn regarded Sunday as a gift to Christians from the Lord — for one day in seven they were released from 'the daily round and common task' and could give every waking minute to the things of God and of the spirit. Therefore he believed that chores should be cut down to the minimum but one ought not to be like the orthodox Jew who gets his neighbours to come in and light the fire on a Sabbath morning. Such legalistic Sabbatarianism is born of the spirit of fear. Be reasonable — leave all that can be left till Monday. Don't spend your Sunday afternoons writing letters. If you have no church duties, spend it reading the Bible and books helpful to the spiritual life.
>
> He was never strict or rigid with the children. They came to Church (where they soon learnt to sit still) and Sunday School, and then, as long as they did not play noisy games to disturb other people, they could do what they liked. It was left to me to suggest that dolls were suitable, as they were their children, and had to be washed and dressed — and taken to Sunday School! M's dictum always was: 'Don't expect Christian behaviour from non-Christians [e.g. the children before conversion], you are being cruel in taking from them innocent natural things they can enjoy, before they know anything of spiritual joys — it leaves them with nothing, and that is unkind.' All he asked was that Sunday should be seen to be 'different', by our example.

On the practical level, two areas of life affected by the austerities of war-time were those of food and clothing. These were the years of queues and scarcities, of ration cards and clothing coupons. With respect to clothing ML-J was unconcerned for it was a subject about which, in his wife's words, 'he had no interest'. That is not to say he was indifferent to the question of what he wore, on the contrary he believed that a minister of the gospel should always dress appropriately to his office, not in terms of a clerical collar (which he never wore) but in general appearance. He was invariably dressed in dark grey, with ties to match and a stiff white collar. Such things as coloured shirts or socks he never owned. The one item of his dress which tended to draw attention was his heavy dark overcoat, not on account of its appearance, but rather because of its use which frequently mystified people. Whenever he was preaching, regardless of the weather, the overcoat and, often, a raincoat, would be with him. After perspiring freely in the pulpit he would invariably don the overcoat before leaving the pulpit and might add the raincoat as he left the building! Westminster Chapel provided the one variation in this procedure, for he could there go straight from the pulpit to the warmth of the electric fire which would be on in the vestry awaiting his return. In later years, when on visits to the States, there was another exception which could be still more bewildering to an onlooker. If the weather was overpoweringly hot he might leave a service with his coat over his arm and *then* put it on as he went into the hotel or wherever his hosts were taking him to lunch or supper. Having been caught once by the coolness of the air-conditioning common in public buildings, he never suffered from it again!

On the question of alcohol, his wife writes:

> He would never say that to take an alcoholic drink was a sin, though he would expect Christians to abstain from indulging because its *misuse* in these days has become a national sin and a very real moral problem. In other words, abstain for the good of the 'weaker brother'. In addition to this he would often say, you never know that you may not yourself *be* the weaker brother. We never kept alcoholic drinks in the house, nor offered them to anyone.

What had been true of ML-J's experience in his childhood was to remain true all his days, 'Our family life', he could say, 'was extremely happy.' Home was his highest earthly blessing and to miss it — *hiraeth* — was the worst of all natural afflictions. On that level nothing ever exceeded the pain he had known in having to leave home for school in Tregaron at the age of eleven, and later years only deepened his conviction about the rightness of that feeling. Few who knew him only as a public figure would anticipate the side of his character which the following narrative reveals:

> I shall never forget myself travelling in a train back from Plymouth to London once. We arrived at Newton Abbot and a woman with two small girls came into the compartment where I was sitting. It was obvious that the children were returning to a boarding school

after the holidays. After placing the girls in their seats the mother got out and stood on the platform until the train started. As the carriage began to move slowly away the smaller of the two little girls kept on looking after her mother longingly with tears filling her eyes. And then the elder sister told her sharply — and she was as near to tears herself — 'Don't look at her you fool!' I am not ashamed to say that I lifted the book which I was reading to hide my face and I cried with the little girls. I was back in my lodgings at Tregaron once again, and it took me a great deal of time to recompose myself. I believe that I shall never totally recover from this until I reach the country where we shall meet never to part anymore.[7]

When Dr Lloyd-Jones' preaching engagements often took him away from Bethan and home he would usually ring her at night and, if his absence was for more than 48 hours, often write to her as well. Typical of the newsy letters which he wrote on these occasions is one from Hertford College, Oxford, on February 4, 1941, while he was taking part in a mission to the University:

I was disappointed that I failed to phone last night. I was kept in Jesus College till 9.50. I got on to the phone as soon as I got back, but was told '2 hours delay'. I put the call in tonight before leaving for the meeting so hope to get through about 10.00 — we'll see. I sent the telegram to let you know I was all right.

The meeting in St Mary's on Sunday night went very well. I had not a moment of trouble with the acoustics, and I felt that the congregation listened well. The text was Luke 12:54-57, the place was full.

I dined with the dons in 'Jesus' before the meeting with some 20 of the boys. The discussion was exceptionally good, and I believe that the Chaplain received great benefit.

I went to listen to Prof. O. C. Quick lecturing at 10.00 this morning. He was very good, but, to tell the truth, I felt that I had dealt with the matter in a much deeper way in the Brotherhood at Sandfields!

Today I am due to have lunch with Dr and Mrs Micklem in Mansfield. I am to be in Ena's old college[8] at tea-time and speaking tonight at 8.15 in the Sheldonian Theatre.

[7] 'Reminiscences of his early life'.
[8] 'St Hugh's, where his sister-in-law Ena had attended.

There is nothing special on Thursday but meetings in different colleges. On Friday I am due to have breakfast with William Riddle's son — a second edition of his father. Then I will go with him to a lecture given by C. S. Lewis (author of the book on *The Problem of Pain*) and I am to have lunch with Lewis,[9] dinner that night with John Marsh, the chaplain at Mansfield, speaking to the medicals at tea-time and a meeting at Christ Church at 9.15 P.M.

It is very cold here. Ann's hot water bottle has been a blessing and I have had an extra rug on the bed. The snow has cleared and today is a better day.

That's my news, and I feel all right. I hope it's not too cold with you — mind you keep warm. I hope to phone tonight.

* * *

For summer holidays in war-time the conditions naturally curtailed travel. It made little difference for Martyn and Bethan as they had no higher preference than Wales which was easily reached by train. The first stop each year was usually at Sunnyside, Bethan's parents' home at Newcastle Emlyn where they could enjoy quiet and restful days. As usual on vacation, ML-J would read in the mornings. His main authors continued to be B. B. Warfield, J. C. Ryle and Charles Hodge but he was also at this date appreciating the Anglican, E. A. Litton and enjoying Henry W. Clark's *History of English Non-conformity* ('I was reading a lot of history at that time'). 'We spent many afternoons', writes Bethan, 'visiting Martyn's relatives in the farms all around. Martyn loved the farming "ambience" (for want of a better word) and was never bored. We would go here and there for a day or two when mother had company.'

From Newcastle Emlyn they would commonly move on to Aberystwyth and to the home of Professor Morris Jones, 'Jasper House', which was lent to them on many occasions. Sometimes as

---

[9] Lewis is said to have valued ML-J's appreciation and encouragement when the early edition of his *Pilgrim's Regress* was not selling well. Vincent Lloyd-Jones and Lewis knew each other well, being contemporaries at Oxford. ML-J met the author again, and they had a long conversation, when they were on the same boat to Ireland in 1953. On that later occasion, to the question, 'When are you going to write another book?', Lewis replied, 'When I understand the meaning of prayer'. Lewis' associations were not with evangelicals.

in earlier years there were also August visits to Nantstalwyn sheep farm in mid-Wales, near the source of the Towy river. Speaking of times at Jasper House, Bethan Lloyd-Jones writes: 'The girls loved Aberystwyth. Our Sundays there were typical of Martyn when he was not preaching — 10 A.M. Welsh service. 11 A.M., slope out with the last hymn and go to the English. 2.00 P.M., about a mile up the hill out from Aberystwyth, a Welsh service. Home for tea. Evening, 6:00 or 6:30, wherever there was a preacher he was anxious to hear. He loved it all. He loved to hear preaching — he did not often have the chance.'

Wales never failed to refresh ML-J even though soon there were some things he would begin to miss. No words of his can give a better impression of the mark which his childhood among Welsh farms had left upon him than the following, spoken many years later, with which we conclude this chapter:

> For me, there is no animal that beats a horse for grace and pomp. If someone should ask me, 'What sound would you like to hear again?' I should ask to hear the sound of a Shire stallion of about eighteen hands in height, newly shod for a show, walking accompanied by a man along a hard street and breaking, now and again, into a half trot and then walking orderly, regularly and graciously. Let the psychologists make what they like of the fact, but that sound had the same effect on me as listening to the music of Mozart. The thought of it still gives me a thrill, but unfortunately I have not heard the sound for years. If someone else were to ask me, 'What would you like to see?' I should answer at once, 'To see a number of hackneys in harness competing for a prize in one of the main shows.' Who can describe the dignity of these beautiful creatures with their heads and tails in the air, raising their four feet high and then striking the front ones forward? If seeing something of the sort is not undeniable proof of the being of God, then one must be a blind sinner.[10]

---

[10] 'Reminiscences of his early life'.

20. ML-J in the 1940s.

SIXTEEN

The Emerging Leader

From the outset of Dr Lloyd-Jones' permanent settlement in London in September, 1939 it is clear that a number of his ministerial peers expected him to take a leading role in his new church connexions. This was not only true of the Congregational Union but of all the Free Churches. Almost immediately he was called upon by the London Baptist Association, as earlier noted; the London Presbyterians already knew him and Methodist churches and missions throughout the country now extended preaching invitations. All these denominations commonly worked together through the Free Church Federal Council and the Secretary of the Council, the Rev. S. W. Hughes, was one of Dr Lloyd-Jones' warmest supporters. In the suburbs of London and throughout England and Wales many local Free Church Councils, linked to the National Council, convened special mid-week services.[1] It was in part due to Hughes and other leaders of the National Council that Dr Lloyd-Jones very rapidly had calls to preach on such occasions in many places.

Dr Lloyd-Jones was early introduced also to the private London meetings of the Council leaders. Referring to this he wrote to Bethan on October 9, 1939:

> I was in a meeting with the Free Church Council this morning in S. W. Hughes's Council Chamber. There were about 40 present

[1] In 1914 there had been 1,000 local Free Church Councils. By 1956 there were only 400 as the ecumenical movement and the British Council of Churches gradually diminished their importance.

— all of them leaders such as Sidney Berry, Dr Garvie, Dr Scott Lidgett, James Reid, Belden, Weatherhead, Sangster, etc. etc. It was almost exclusively a political discussion and a great deal of misunderstanding and disagreement. Some wanting peace immediately and others wanting to get rid of Hitlerism. Interesting enough. I never said one word — neither did Reid, Sangster and many others.

Tomorrow morning I have to meet the London Congregational Union in Whitefield's Tabernacle, in order to be received! A purely formal occasion, it seems.

W. E. Sangster asked ML-J to share in their May 24, 1941 commemoration of the date associated with the conversion of John Wesley. Leslie Weatherhead was to preach an afternoon sermon. The *British Weekly* summarised what he had to say on that occasion:

> Dr Lloyd-Jones saw the need today of preaching that led to conversion, an opinion evoking marked approval from the audience. Methodists must think more carefully over the discrimination between the 'once born' and the 'twice born'. Attendance at worship or even official service did not necessarily mean that 'something had come to a man that had an inward reality and power in his life'. Decision may not mean conversion. The tragedy of the pulpit was that ministers were not preaching a 'converting gospel'.

The younger generation of Free Church ministers (and a number of the older) were certainly not in favour of any return to the old message. Weatherhead and Soper were united in the conviction that it was 'stern' views of God which were the supreme reason for the alienation of the people from Christianity and they were ready to blame 'bibliolatry' for the existence of such 'wrong' ideas of God. When, a little earlier, H. Tydeman Chilvers, the retired pastor of Spurgeon's Tabernacle (and a man who appreciated Spurgeon's doctrinal emphases) wrote in the *British Weekly* on 'The Revival of Calvinism', a shocked elder statesman of Congregationalism, Dr A. E. Garvie, responded, 'A return to Calvinism would be reaction not progress . . . Are we to cast away the gains of the progressive theology of the last half century?'

Other senior Free Churchmen, however, were far less confident that the Christian scene revealed 'progress'. J. Ernest Rattenbury, the retired Methodist minister of Kingsway Hall, and author of *The*

Conversion of the Wesleys (1938), would frequently come to Westminster Chapel and let it be known that 'Dr Lloyd-Jones is the only man who preaches to my conscience.' Another senior Methodist, Dr Henry Bett, told ML-J, 'I would like you to know that a large number of us in Methodism are thanking God that you are in London to counteract the film stars of Methodism!' (an allusion to Weatherhead and Soper).

While confessing that he did not want 'the extreme Calvinistic dogmas', Dr J. D. Jones encouraged ML-J and wrote on one occasion, 'We should be all the better for some of the Calvinistic iron in our blood . . . For the past fifty years we have allowed the gospel of the greatness of God to fall into the background.' It was Jones — 'the unmitred Bishop of Congregationalism' — along with some other leaders of the Free Church Federal Council who thought to prepare the new minister at Westminster Chapel for leadership in the days to come.

J. D. Jones had retired from Richmond Hill Congregational Church, Bournemouth in 1938 to Brynbanon, a beautiful house in the Welsh hills near Bala, from whence he kept in close touch with Nonconformist affairs. In 1941 at the age of seventy-six he suffered something like a seizure. When, after a final visit to London in February, 1942, it was apparent that he might not recover, he sent a message to ML-J, through Dr Vernon Lewis, expressing a great desire to see him. Faced with the urgency of this unexpected request, Dr Lloyd-Jones made the journey to Bala where the former 'Archbishop of Nonconformity' pleaded with him to recognize his duty and to lead the Free Churches in the years ahead. He was the man destined for it! Mindful of what he already knew of conditions in the English Free Churches, Lloyd-Jones protested that he could not do it because he was an evangelical. 'Oh, just give them some political sops occasionally,' JD retorted, 'and they will follow you.' From church affairs the conversation at length turned to more personal things as Dr Lloyd-Jones recalls that evening at Brynbanon:

> It was for me a crucial night. I will never forget it. He asked me point blank whether he was going to get well and although he had been a very strong man I had to say, honestly, 'I am afraid not.' He began to weep and said, 'It's all right. I really don't want to leave this' — pointing out of the window to the beautiful scenery

— 'but it's all right, I believe what I've been trying to preach', placing his hand upon his heart. When I went to bed I could not sleep because I was faced with this question. 'What if somebody said to you what you have told him, that you have got to die quite soon? Where would you stand? How would you feel?' This was the subject which kept me awake and confirmed me in my decision that I could not do what he was asking me. I also had to face death ultimately; I had to render an account unto God.

J. D. Jones died on April 19, 1942 and ML-J was often to look back on that last meeting as one of the most significant events in his life.[2] With his congregation so depleted by war-time conditions, there was force in the dying man's plea that he should pursue the wider leadership. But the seriousness of death, as he saw it afresh that night, far superseded all questions of earthly positions and he knew with certainty that the compromise proposed to him was impossible. He could not lead the Free Churches, nor did it much concern him, for of what worth was it in comparison with the issues of eternity?

Such decisions as the above which, on the face of it, appeared to limit his larger usefulness were a necessary ingredient in what was to be his true calling. Preaching 'as a dying man to dying men' is not a commitment arrived at in the pulpit. It requires an inner life in the preacher and a readiness for costly renunciations.

By 1942 Dr Lloyd-Jones' leadership as an evangelical preacher was being seen in Scotland where his acceptance was entirely unrelated to any denominational status. In March 1941 he had accepted an invitation from Dr Donald Maclean, Professor of Church History at the Free Church of Scotland College, Edinburgh, to speak on 'The Tragedy of Modern Man'. It was ML-J's first engagement under Free Church of Scotland auspices. On successive afternoons the Presbytery Hall of the College was packed to capacity, with others sitting in adjacent rooms and corridors for as far as his voice could be expected to carry. In addition to Free Church of Scotland men there were also some from the Church of Scotland whose theological hall (New College) stands close by on the Mound. Each morning *The Scotsman* gave a synopsis of the addresses on Romans 1:8-22, and they were

---

[2] Arthur Porritt in *J. D. Jones of Bournemouth* (1942), p. 150, simply notes that 'Dr Martyn Lloyd-Jones of Westminster Chapel journeyed specially to Brynbanon, on Mrs Jones's appeal, to break the news to him that he could not get better.'

to become his second book.[3] In the opinion of Professor Alexander Ross: 'No one who has heard Dr Lloyd-Jones speak will doubt for a moment that in preaching he has found his real life-work, and no one who has listened to him will fail to recognize that in him God has given to his church a singularly gifted preacher with an authentic message, indeed, with *the* message which the modern world most desperately needs.' Professor Donald MacLean reported to American readers, 'In the religious world of Britain today Dr Lloyd-Jones occupies quite a unique place.'[4]

There were to be long-term consequences from this visit. As the words of Ross indicate, Free Church of Scotland men were mightily encouraged, while for ML-J himself the experience opened a large, new circle of friendships. Hitherto he had met a few of the denomination's leaders — including one of their much-esteemed elders, Professor Duncan McCallum Blair, formerly Professor of Anatomy in King's College, London, and by now Regius Professor of Anatomy in Glasgow — but at this time he came to know others well in this 'week of rich fellowship in the great city of John Knox'. Outstanding for ML-J were the times spent daily with Principal John MacLeod after lunch in his study at the Free Church College. Lloyd-Jones was enthralled with the aged preacher's knowledge and love of the great periods of revival when experimental religion characterized the Scottish church. He was later to speak of John MacLeod as 'one of the godliest men' he had ever met. MacLeod's book, *Scottish Theology: in Relation to Church History since the Reformation* remains the best in its field. Close ties with the Free Church of Scotland were to endure for the remainder of Dr Lloyd-Jones' life.

It was in the following year, shortly after the death of J. D. Jones, that the extent of the Welsh preacher's acceptance in Scotland received its fullest confirmation in a 'Bible Witness Rally' held in the great St Andrew's Hall, Glasgow, on Tuesday, May 5, 1942. While the newspapers gave one account of the meeting, Dr Lloyd-Jones was to remember it as an occasion when he was unusually conscious of the special help of God. Glasgow's veteran religious reporter, Alexander Gammie, wrote in the *Evening Citizen* for May 9:

---

[3] *The Plight of Man and the Power of God* (London: Hodder and Stoughton, 1942). The striking thing about its 96 pages is its almost exclusive use of Scripture.

[4] *Calvin Forum*, April 1941, p. 98.

In all my experience of religious gatherings in Glasgow I have seen nothing more remarkable than the Bible Witness Rally held this week.

On Tuesday evening the longest queues in the city were not at cinemas or other places of entertainment, but all round St Andrew's Hall were queues of people eager to secure admission to this great Rally. After the hall had been packed in every corner it was estimated that over 1,000 people had to be turned away. Nor was it wholly, or even largely, a crowd of 'greybeards hoary'. The proportion of younger people impressed every observer.

What was the purpose which attracted such a throng? Its aim was defined as being 'to proclaim belief that the Bible is the Word of God, and to recall the nation to the prayerful reading and study of it'. It was not only one of the largest gatherings of the kind ever seen in Glasgow, but it was one of the most mixed. Never, perhaps, had there assembled under one roof at one time so many representatives of so many different creeds. The atmosphere was not ecclesiastical but evangelical. Almost every branch of the Church was represented, along with the Salvation Army, the Christian Brethren, and the many undenominational and independent missions and agencies in which Glasgow is so prolific. It raised the question as to what might not be accomplished were it possible to marshal for action all these evangelical forces in the city.

The speaking was worthy of so great an occasion. Professor D. M. Blair, as chairman, struck the right keynote. Professor Daniel Lamont, in speaking on the Authority of the Bible, was at once academic and evangelical, as is his wont, with that inflexion of tones in his voice which made him known as the silver-tongued Moderator. Professor A. Rendle Short of Bristol, eminent surgeon as he is, made ruthless and skilful use of his knife in dealing with some aspects of modern science. And with a rare intimacy of knowledge, he revealed some aspects of the Bible.

Then came the Rev. Dr D. Martyn Lloyd-Jones, the former Harley St. physician, who is now colleague-minister with Dr Campbell Morgan in Westminster Chapel, London, and he brought the meeting to a triumphant and impressive climax. To him had been allotted the task of speaking on 'The Bible and Today', and right nobly did he use the opportunity. His address was as gripping and powerful as it was popular in appeal. As an oratorical *tour de force* it would have roused a political audience to tumultuous enthusiasm.

He held his hearers in thrall as he made point after point, and altogether the impression he produced was profound.

Just as Scottish response to Dr Lloyd-Jones showed that he was to be much more than a denominational statesman, so did the theological leadership which he was now giving in the Inter-Varsity Fellowship in England. Elected president in 1939, the war-time conditions gave reason for him to be retained as president, it was hoped, for the duration of the war. In the event, he held it for three years, finally insisting in 1942 that he should not be regarded as a 'serial president'. Douglas Johnson speaks of the 'outstanding' presidential addresses which he gave in these years at the students' annual Easter Conferences. In the years 1941–42 these five-day conferences were held in Trinity College, Cambridge. In 1941 the presidential address was on 'Christian Leadership'. The next year it was virtually an evangelistic sermon, with the raising of Jairus' daughter as its theme. On both these occasions the students were surprised to see present the Master of Trinity, G. M. Trevelyan, in cap and gown, accompanied in 1942 by another Trinity man, Professor G. D. Broad, the eminent Cambridge philosopher. After the address on the raising of Jairus' daughter Trevelyan made his way to the speaker and, removing his cap, said with considerable emotion, 'Sir, it has been given to you to speak with great power.' Broad, less impressed, was later to tell a student, 'If the Master hears that man much more he is going to be converted.'

Much other speaking for ML-J both in these IVF conferences and in those of the Theological Students' Fellowship was now inevitable. The latter was a younger branch of the IVF and at this period its annual conference was often at the same venue and overlapping with the general conference. The theme for the 1940 TSF Conference was 'Soundness and its Limits'; with ML-J down to speak on 'The Biblical Doctrine of the Fall'. In the 1941 general conference he shared the leadership of four informal sessions with Duncan Blair when the topics for discussion included 'What *is* "Preaching the Word"?' and 'How Should We Combat the Spirit of the Age?' The title for the 1942 Conference at Trinity was 'The Word of God to Rebellious Man', and in another discussion session led by Lloyd-Jones the title put down on the programme was, 'How Shall We Confront the New Secularism?' It is noteworthy that the influence of medical men was strong in all these conferences; the 'chiefs', Blair and Rendle Short, were there in 1940–41, and Blair again in 1942. Douglas Johnson, holding his usual place in the background, was also always present. The 'informal meetings' or 'discussions' were invariably led by the medical men, introducing the students to the Socratic method of questioning to which they had become accustomed in student days. In handling this form of instruction and debate ML-J was the only minister who could match the two 'chiefs'. There was no experience in the normal ministerial training which resembled the grilling which a medical professor's students were put through on ward rounds and sometimes it was the other conference speakers (as well as the students) who were shaken by the interrogation involved in this method.

The effect of Dr Lloyd-Jones' leadership in the IVF was quite as important in private as it was in public. Not only in the Fellowship's Advisory Committee (made up of senior evangelical leaders) but in almost constant contact with Douglas Johnson, there was much discussion which would bear fruit through the years in the lives of thousands. No General Secretary ever led a work from such an unobserved position as Johnson and only his closest friends knew what he was doing. 'He is', wrote ML-J in a letter to Philip Hughes (March 2, 1942), 'in many ways, the most important person in evangelical circles these days.'[5] The two men were ideally complementary to one another, one a public spokesman and leader, the other a born administrator and organizer behind the scenes: ML-J strong in general principles and insight, DJ careful and exact in matters of detail. ML-J often saved DJ much time — in his judgments of issues and of people — 'his Welsh intuition was deadly accurate', while the General Secretary saved his friend's time in a whole variety of ways from note-taking, proof-reading and book-hunting to reports on contacts and situations important to the evangelical cause. In a sense it resembled a medical partnership. Each talked in terms which the other understood including the 'My Dear Dr Lloyd-Jones' and 'My Dear Dr Johnson' with which their letters to each other generally began.

---

[5] For other high assessments of the influence of Douglas Johnson see, Geraint Fielder, *Lord of the Years: Sixty Years of Student Witness: The Story of the Inter-Varsity Fellowship, Universities and Colleges Christian Fellowship, 1928–1988* (IVP, 1988), pp. 62-63; and Christopher Catherwood, ed., *Martyn Lloyd-Jones: Chosen by God* (Crowborough: Highland Books, 1986), p. 65.

One of the most important examples of the work of the two doctors was the private conference at Kingham Hill School, near Oxford, in which they shared with others to plan for the future. Held from 7-10 July, 1941, the host was the Rev. G. T. Manley (Vicar of St Luke's, Hampstead) and others present included F. F. Bruce (lecturer in classics at Leeds University), Donald Maclean, W. J. Martin (Rankin Lecturer in Semitic Languages, Liverpool University), Alan Stibbs (Vice-Principal of Oak Hill Theological College, at this time evacuated to Kingham) and J. Stafford Wright (Principal of the BCMS College, Bristol).

The stated objective of this Conference was the revival of evangelical theology, a need underlined during the previous twenty years by the almost complete absence of good commentaries and doctrinal works from evangelical authors. All present were sympathetic with this objective although there were some differences with respect to priorities. Manley was disturbed 'that so few conservative evangelicals had recently been appointed as Bishops, Headmasters or members of the staffs of the Theological Colleges'. Maclean saw the need for more doctrinal precision within their own ranks and advocated that future endeavours for biblical theology should be linked with an acceptance of the Reformed Confessions (e.g. the Thirty-nine Articles and the Westminster Confession). To Lloyd-Jones was given the task of delivering the first of the main addresses and, proceeding on the principle that correct diagnosis should precede any proposal of cures, he spoke on 'The Causes of Present Weakness'.

Other addresses at Kingham Hill dealt largely with particular proposals for future action. These included plans for more literature, the establishment of a Centre for Biblical Research, Summer Vacation Schools for Study, and the organization of funds to assist students. During discussion it was noted that many promising evangelical scholars were lost to the cause through the influence of University supervisors who were liberals or advanced modernists. Would it not then be possible, asked a younger member of the Conference, to set up a new interdenominational theological college, with a wholly conservative staff? This, in turn, could go on to develop a postgraduate department, taking higher degrees either in the University city where it was established, or an external Ph.D. of London University.

This latter proposal alarmed several of the senior men. The

mainline denominations would simply ignore such a college and it would lead to a new denomination just as Westminster Theological Seminary in Philadelphia had recently led to a new denomination. The alternative was to give extra-curricular help to evangelical theological students and to encourage them to attain to standards of scholarship that would bring about a revolutionary change in the theological departments of universities. Urging this viewpoint, W. J. Martin of Liverpool University explained: 'None of the experts or leading figures paid much or any attention to work from the average theological college or lesser academic centres. Hence, it is essential that the work of evangelicals should be good enough for their work to compare with that of the best authorities and to get included in the right journals and larger publications. If we wish to challenge or modify the work of those in university chairs, then they must be met at their own standards.'

In the midst of enthusiastic support for the proposal to raise up evangelical specialists in biblical studies, Dr Lloyd-Jones intervened before the end of the Conference. He feared that they were aiming to supply a corrective which would bring new dangers. He was not against teams of evangelicals facing problems at the highest levels. By God's grace, and given a right call, steps should be taken by some in this direction at the close of the war. But if the end result was the creation of 'specialists' something would be seriously wrong. Having himself worked 'at university levels' in the research department of St Bartholomew's Hospital, he fully appreciated and endorsed Dr Martin's plea for standards. But in his experience, he went on to say, there was danger in ultra-specialization. As expertise increases over an ever-narrowing field, the perspective which sees the proportions in the whole case is easily lost sight of. 'General physicians' and 'general practitioners' were what the church chiefly needed. Let specialists do their work, but if the end result was that elements of Old and New Testament theology were not co-ordinated into the whole of truly systematic biblical theology, there would be no true benefit. Later developments, as we shall see, proved the rightness of this judgment.

At Kingham Hill, Lloyd-Jones was among men highly competent in their own fields and, in some instances, his seniors in years. In the unpublished reports it is, however, his contributions which stand out both in their spiritual insight and in their grasp of general principles.

They help us to understand the significance of his unrecorded and on-going contribution to the organization which was doing more than any other to shape the thinking of coming generations of university students.

The many-sidedness of his leadership in IVF is also noteworthy. His part at Kingham was distinctly theological, along with lessons analysed from church history. Yet in much of the time which he gave to the student world at this period he was doing the work of an evangelist and he was in repeated demand to take a leading part in university missions.

We have already mentioned the Oxford mission of 1941. In February, 1943 he took a main part in a mission to the same University organized by the evangelical union (OICCU), when his first engagement was to speak to about 30 medical students in Balliol College. His main mission addresses were sermons from Jeremiah 6:14-16. The Rev. E. Noel T. Sandford, a student at that period, remembers how several conversions were recorded in the term before the Mission and 'at least ten' while it was taking place. Dr Lloyd-Jones, he recalls, 'would come to the lectern, take a very small Bible out of his pocket, read out the verse he had chosen, probably close the book again, and then launch into a closely argued and entirely coherent address without a note to guide him. He would speak for upwards of half an hour, though it never seemed long.'

ML-J's preaching at Oxford demonstrated his conviction that while specialists had some part to play in the defence of the Faith, the Faith itself advances in the world as it is proclaimed in its own terms, without concessions to what hearers might want or expect. He had no special apologetics designed for undergraduates — a fact which sometimes surprised both students and fellow-missioners.[6]

All kinds of evangelistic enterprises sought ML-J's support. His was the first name announced in connection with a five-month campaign planned in Glasgow in 1943–44. 'The full list of speakers is not yet complete,' reported the Glasgow press, 'but an invitation to take part has been accepted by Dr Martyn Lloyd-Jones who has become one of the most powerful evangelical forces of our time.' Similarly, when English evangelical leaders met at the Bonnington Hotel, London, about the same date, 'to consider the launching of a

---

[6] See *Preaching and Preachers*, pp. 129-30.

nation-wide campaign' it was Dr Lloyd-Jones who was asked to give the main address.

We shall note later ML-J's reasons for being critical of the prevalent type of organized evangelism. But he was glad to accept these invitations and he used the opportunity to urge Christians to recognize that they were in danger of missing the *first* need of the hour. At the inaugural Glasgow meeting in the St Andrew's Hall on October 4, 1943, instead of giving a ringing call for more evangelistic action, he spoke on the words, 'This kind can come forth by nothing but by prayer and fasting' (*Mark* 9:29):

> Before we rush into activities let us make certain that we know the nature of the problem that confronts us . . . Is this Evangelistic Campaign going to be enough? You will probably get results, but I say, if you stop at that, you will fail . . . Go on with your campaign, but do not stop at that. 'This kind can come forth by nothing but prayer and fasting.' In other words it seems to me that the call to every one of us is not to help in general with this great organized campaign; it is to consecrate and dedicate ourselves specifically to the task of praying for that spiritual revival which God alone can send. The trouble with us, I am afraid, is that we have not sufficiently diagnosed the situation. We are still confident in our methods. It seems to me there is no hope until we shall have so realised the nature of the problem that we are driven to our knees, to wait upon God.

At the Bonnington Hotel Conference in London he elaborated his reservations still further:

> Whereas we are all agreed about the fundamental truths of the gospel, the vital question is, What is the particular emphasis that is needed today? For myself I have no hesitation at all in answering that question. The sooner we realize that the evangelism of fifty to eighty years ago is no longer adequate to meet the present conditions the better it will be. Yet we still cling to those methods, and we act upon certain assumptions which we are not entitled to act upon. The fundamental position with which we are confronted is that there is almost a complete ignoring and forgetfulness of God . . .
>
> I am one of those who still believe that the key to the present situation is the individual local church. It is possible for a revival, if

we are waiting and praying for it, to start at any moment. Before we think about planning and organizing in order to reach the outsider, let us concentrate upon our own churches. Are our own churches alive? Are our people real Christians? Are they such that in their contacts with others they are likely to win them for Christ and to awaken in their hearts a desire for spiritual things? That would be my own word to you today; that instead of spreading outward, we should concentrate inward and deepen and deepen and deepen our own spiritual life, until men here and there get to the place where God can use them as leaders of the great awakening which will spread through the churches and through the land.[7]

---

[7] 'Notes' of this address were printed in the *Christian Herald,* Feb. 11, 1943.

LONDON BIBLE COLLEGE

19 Marylebone Road, N.W. 1

From the Principal—
REV. ERNEST F. KEVAN. M.TH.
Private Telephone : WELbeck 9011

WELbeck 5850

EFK/JW

20th January, 1948.

The Rev. Dr. D. Martyn Lloyd-Jones,
39 Mount Park Crescent,
Ealing, W.5.

My dear Dr. Lloyd-Jones,

There are just one or two things upon which I wanted to
write to you. The first is to say how exceedingly sorry I
am that on the occasion of your visit to the L.I.F.C.U. Conference
on Saturday 7th February I have to be away speaking at two
meetings at Southend-on-Sea. I fear that this means I shall
not be able to see you at all; I do trust the occasion may
be one of blessing, but I felt I wanted to express to you my
real regret about my absence on the day of your visit.

I trust you will forgive my constant importunity, but our
men equally with myself are insistent that we do wish you to
pay us a visit as a College. I realise that Monday mornings
are not the best time for you after your heavy day on the
Sunday. At the end of every term, however, on the last two
days we have special visitors to deal with topics which are
somewhat outside the ordinary run of the curriculum. The
last two days of this term are Thursday and Friday 11th and 12th
March. Do you think you could come on Thursday 11th March
at 11.30 a.m. to give the men a talk on the subject "The Place
of Theology in Pastoral Preaching"? You would have a whole
hour for this, and then nothing would please our men more than
to have the opportunity of your presence with them at the
College lunch immediately following. If this particular day
is not convenient to you then as an alternative there is a
session on Friday 12th March at 9.30. I do hope you will be
able to come on one or other of these dates.

It was a joy to be in Westminster Chapel on Sunday and I
received blessing in the worship.

With my kindest regards in which Mrs. Kevan joins me.

Yours most sincerely,

Ernest F. Kevan
Principal.

*21. A letter from Ernest Kevan, Principal of London Bible College, to ML-J
inviting him to address the students on 'The Place of Theology in Pastoral
Preaching', Jan 20, 1948.*

SEVENTEEN

New Agencies

D r Lloyd-Jones' early period at Westminster Chapel saw the establishment of three new agencies in London which were to have widespread influence. In all three he was closely involved, and two were to remain under his leadership until the end of his life.

The most improbable of these new institutions was the Evangelical Library. Although the name and site in London were only determined in 1943, the beginnings of this work may be dated to the conversion of a certain Geoffrey Williams forty years earlier. On a stormy day in 1903, 'at the request of a school girl', seventeen-year-old Williams went to a service at Galeed Chapel, Brighton, a Strict Baptist congregation of Gospel Standard persuasion. There, through J. K. Popham's ministry, Williams was directed to some of the classics of Christian literature, and especially to the works of Puritan authors. Inspired by a love for the 'free-grace' teaching in such books, he began to collect their works, yet without seeing any connection between them and his desire to be useful in the cause of Christ. By the 1920s he was lending some of his books to Christian friends and, seeing the help which they proved to be, he felt an 'irresistible urge' to provide 'a widespread loan library fitted to enable people everywhere to borrow books true to Scripture, calculated to bring sinners to the foot of the cross and to establish Christians in our most holy faith'.

Borrowers slowly increased and by hunting in many quarters Geoffrey Williams' books multiplied. Old second-hand volumes of spiritual worth were then comparatively plentiful, as well as little valued. Convinced of their long-term importance, Williams became like Joseph in Egypt, laying up stores for famine years which were ahead. By 1928 the library had outgrown his house and garage at Beddington, Surrey, and had to be moved to a small building in Wordsworth Road, Beddington. It amounted to some 20,000 volumes, 'specializing in the more rare works of the Puritans and the Scottish covenanting authors as well as in the great eighteenth-century revivals'.

To Geoffrey Williams' disappointment the 1930s saw little or no increase in the readers and borrowers of his books, in part because of the inaccessible location twelve miles south of London. His concern was that the library should be 'a living force', not a curiosity for occasional visitors, and yet humanly speaking there was no prospect that it would be anything other than a museum. With this concern on his mind and in his prayers, he called one day in 1938 at John Phillips' chemist's shop in Great Portland Street, London, to make a small purchase. The owner, who served him, happened to be a member of Charing Cross Calvinistic Methodist Chapel and the two men soon found that they had things in common. In the words of Williams: 'I was attracted by his Welsh accent and getting into conversation I opened my heart to him in regard to the difficulty I faced. He at once exclaimed, "Why you must meet Dr Martyn Lloyd-Jones. His interest will be aroused and he will suggest a way out. I will tell him about your project."'

Williams came to view the day when he visited Phillips' shop as a turning point in his life. Hitherto almost all his Christian contacts had been among the Strict Baptists and for him the minister of Westminster Chapel was a figure 'out of the unknown'. Phillips fulfilled his word and, not long after, Dr Lloyd-Jones with his friend Eliseus Howells made a visit to Beddington. His opinion was expressed to Williams in a letter of January 4, 1939:

> The collection is remarkable and indeed unique. For anyone who is at all interested in true Protestantism, and especially in its revival in the eighteenth century, the Beddington Free Grace Library is a sheer delight.
>
> I have but one criticism to offer, and that is with regard to the location of the Library. It should be somewhere in the heart of London within easy reach and access.

These words encouraged Williams to look for ways for an early removal of the library to a central London location. In this, at ML-J's instigation, he was helped by Douglas Johnson who raised a little 'working money' and advised the calling of a provisional committee. For this purpose four men met on December 15, 1942, with an agenda which read: 'Consideration of the Library to Christendom (and especially to the Evangelical School of thought) and what can be done to: (a) Secure it, free of all claims, for the Church of God (b) Centralize it (c) Finance the running of it as an active organization.'

However, the relocation of the library, now with 25,000 books weighing 15 tons, posed no small problem. The money needed was not available and the committee had no means of awakening public interest. Williams came to the conclusion that nothing would be accomplished until Dr Lloyd-Jones threw in his weight but the latter held back from personal involvement for two reasons: a disinclination towards involvement in a committee, and his caution over identification with a ministry which might not be compatible with his own. Certainly he admired Williams' choice of books and he meant what he had said in 1939 about making the library known. But to be 'President' of the library, as others now wanted him to be, would identify him more closely and there were aspects of Williams' restricted Strict Baptist background which worried him. The older man — 15 years his senior — clearly needed coaching and guidance at many points. There would be an on-going work of shepherding needed. But the potential of the library prevailed and he committed himself to what was to prove a life work. He was in the chair at two meetings of an enlarged committee held in his vestry at Westminster Chapel, on June 15 and 28, 1943, when a trust deed was settled, and the name 'The Evangelical Library' unanimously agreed. A statement recorded their 'utter dependence on the Holy Spirit for the success of the undertaking'. It was further agreed that the Library be housed at 55 Gloucester Road, Kensington, at a rent of £70 per annum.

With all difficulties — including the second blitz which London suffered in 1944 — finally overcome, the Gloucester Road premises were opened with a public meeting on January 15, 1945. After an address by ML-J, a reporter for *The Times* agreed that there was promise of a work of 'far-reaching importance' (Feb. 4, 1945). The *British Weekly* (Jan. 25, 1945) announced the opening under the heading, 'Discovering a Library', and supported the sentiment of the chairman's address: 'It was no ordinary enterprise, a statement with which his hearers agreed, for on entering they had found books in several rooms, with passages and landings also lined with books, books everywhere, indeed . . . Great institutions, when vitalized by the experience and sagacity of some devoted individual, have had such an origin as this Evangelical Library.'

Dr Lloyd-Jones' hope that he would be able to help Geoffrey Williams — the honorary librarian — as well as the library itself was fully realized. Far from being resistant to counsel in those areas where his limitations had troubled the younger man, Williams became increasingly appreciative and was to write in the 1970s:

It is impossible to exaggerate the profound effects of Dr Lloyd-Jones' influence upon my thinking and indeed my very life . . . He taught me to eschew the extreme elements of the thinking in the body of Christians in which I was cradled from my conversion, and yet left me tenaciously adhering to the vital basic teaching for which that body is distinguished.

The second new agency which came into existence in the early years of the war was the group of ministers who were later to be known as 'the Westminster Fellowship' or 'Fraternal'. This seems to have begun in 1941 as a quarterly Tuesday-morning meeting at Westminster Chapel intended for pastors and men in positions of Christian leadership. It was a private meeting, prompted by ML-J's ministerial contacts, some of whom knew of the similar gathering which ML-J had led at Aberavon. One of early members of this fraternal was the Rev. Alan Stibbs (Vice Principal of Oak Hill College). Stibbs also led an IVF study group and when it ran into difficulties over the doctrine of original sin, he asked ML-J if he would read two addresses which had been given at his group. One of these followed the more superficial view current among evangelicals and the other given by Philip Edgcumbe Hughes (a London curate) argued for a more biblical and reformed position. In addition, Stibbs asked ML-J to speak and lead a discussion on the subject at their next meeting, January 27, 1942.

Philip Hughes had wanted to meet Lloyd-Jones since first hearing him at the Albert Hall in 1935, when 'the intense firmness of his features and the earnest eloquence with which he spoke' had arrested him. From January, 1942 the two became life-long friends. To a letter from Hughes, Lloyd-Jones replied on February 3, 1942:

> I had never heard of your name until I received your paper from Mr Alan Stibbs . . . The character of your exposition appealed to me tremendously. For years I have bemoaned the fact that as evangelicals we lack scholars and writers. I have been looking out for men constantly . . . A number of us, including Rev. Alan Stibbs have started a new fellowship of evangelical ministers and clergy. I have suggested that all of you who meet with Mr Stibbs be invited. The next meeting is on March 10, at 10.30 A.M. If you come to that we shall have a long talk afterwards.

In this way Hughes and others from the IVF study group came to join the Westminster group of which Stibbs became the Secretary. In October, 1942 the men met at the new hours of 1.30 to 4.15 P.M. and for many years this remained the established time for the quarterly fraternal. In form the meetings differed from what they became in later years. The afternoon was divided into two, with a fifteen-minute break in between. In the first session opportunity was given for everyone present (upwards of a dozen men) to speak from personal experience of recent blessings or difficulties in their work — a procedure which led someone to dub the fraternal 'the Confession' (a name which stuck for a few years). The smallness of the numbers attending required a room rather than a hall for the venue and the only one suitable on the premises of Westminster Chapel was the downstairs 'parlour'.

Dr Lloyd-Jones did not envisage the gathering as a place for listening to addresses. He wanted it to be a 'fellowship'. The experimental and practical issues were to be prominent, and at the same time he sought that men should learn, through discussion, how basic biblical theology points to the solution of almost all problems in the life of the church.

The deliberate restriction of the Westminster Fellowship to ministers did not mean that ML-J was slow to give time to laymen who were in positions of Christian leadership. One such man who came to have a close relationship with him at this time was A. J. Vereker who was prominent in the inter-denominational evangelical organizations. He was secretary of a joint committee of the four major youth organizations, made up from two or three representatives of the Inter-Varsity Fellowship, the Children's Special Service Mission and Scripture Union, the Crusaders, and the Girl Crusaders.

Vereker introduced Dr Lloyd-Jones to the work of the Crusaders' Union and it was at a conference of leaders of that organization, meeting at Sion College, that ML-J gave his first major comment on modern evangelism in February, 1942. It was as clearly different from prevailing evangelical views as his address on 'Sanctification' had been at Cambridge in 1939. By way of introduction he indicated that there were two positions to be avoided — first, that of men whose belief is 'perfectly orthodox' yet whose work is utterly barren and, secondly, that of those who seem to get 'phenomenal results' without concerning themselves over-much how they are obtained: 'They take a campaign, or preach a sermon and, as a result, there are numbers of decisions for Christ, or what are called "conversions": but they are not permanent; they are merely of a temporary or passing nature.' He then went on to lay down 'five foundation principles':

1. The supreme object of this work is to glorify God. The first object of preaching the gospel is not to save souls. Nothing else, however good in itself, or however noble, must be allowed to usurp that first place.

2. The only power that can really do this work is that of the Holy Spirit . . .

3. The one and only medium through which the Holy Spirit works is the Word of God . . . The medium which is used by the Holy Spirit is the truth.

4. The true urge to evangelization must come from apprehending these principles and, therefore, of a zeal for the honour and glory of God, and a love for the souls of men.

5. There is a constant danger of error, and of heresy, even amongst the most sincere, and also the danger of a false zeal and the employment of unscriptural methods.

These principles constituted the first half of his address. The second half consisted of an application of the principles to the contemporary evangelistic scene. It was published by the Crusaders' Union with the title *The Presentation of the Gospel* and subsequently reprinted by both CSSM and IVF.

Vereker and Lloyd-Jones continued to be in regular contact. In

November 1943, he wrote as secretary of the Joint Committee to ML-J, asking him to speak to them and commenting: 'We think it would do us good if we were to hear some frank criticism of the work of these Societies from one who has not grown up amongst us, but at the same time is interested in us — and you are the man.'

Vereker also played a main part in the third new agency with which ML-J came to be connected. From about 1933 Vereker had repeatedly urged the idea of a college in London which would give biblical instruction to Christian workers. Slowly various parties became interested. Among the Anglicans were the Revs. W. H. Aldis (home director of the China Inland Mission and chairman of the Keswick Convention) and H. A. Evan Hopkins. The Christian Brethren were represented by Montague Goodman and J. W. Laing. Campbell Morgan threw in his weight and — need it be said — so did Douglas Johnson. Some progress was made, only to be stopped by the advent of war. But unwilling to let matters rest, in the latter part of 1941 and when the blitz was at its worst, Johnson and Vereker, joined only by H. A. Evan Hopkins, met again. At the Drift Bridge Hotel, Tattenham Corner, 'they talked and prayed, and there they resolved to resume the self-imposed labours which had been laid down in 1939'. Johnson and Vereker were unwilling to let the college matter rest. They both lived at Epsom Downs, often travelled in and out of London together, and shared the same air-raid shelter. In these circumstances, Johnson says. 'We used to draft letters to the tune of the guns and the crash of the bombs in the distance and sometimes near.'

Neither man had any doubt as to who should be principal of the new evangelical college, plans for which were well in hand by 1942. 'Almost from the beginning,' writes the historian of the London Bible College, 'it had been hoped that Dr D. Martyn Lloyd-Jones would serve as Principal of the proposed college'. In the early summer of 1942 the invitation was put to him. He declined but he gave crucial help in the next formative years as Vice-Chairman of the College Council. It was ML-J who proposed for the new faculty the name of Ernest F. Kevan, born in 1903 and serving in the Metropolitan Association of Strict Baptist Churches. Kevan had been pastor of Zion Baptist Church, New Cross, in South London since 1934.[1] The Association

[1] See Paul E. Brown, *Ernest Kevan, Leader in Twentieth Century British*

to which the New Cross Church belonged was a traditionally Calvinistic grouping, although now mixed with influences from a broader evangelicalism. But the Strict Baptists, as a whole, retained enough Calvinistic doctrine to prevent their being popular in the main current of evangelical life, nor did they have many preachers from other denominations in their pulpits. They regarded Dr Lloyd-Jones, however, with equanimity and in the war years he became a welcome preacher at annual chapel anniversaries and other special occasions. It was in this way that he had first met Ernest Kevan and discovered his love for Puritan authors.

Kevan joined the Westminster Fellowship, and was added to the Evangelical Library Committee in June 1943. When he was asked during the same summer to consider the post of part-time tutor at the new college, he no doubt knew who was behind the proposal. Following discussion with ML-J, Kevan accepted the part-time post and, with others, subsequently commenced to supervise correspondence courses and to give evening lectures. By the time the college was settled at 19 Marylebone Road, London in 1946, with sixteen full-time students, Kevan was the principal — a role in which he was to continue until his death at the age of 62 in 1965.

While the three evangelical institutions outlined above possessed no formal connection with one another, the involvement of the same personnel secured cordial relationships and mutual support. The overlap in the leadership in the Westminster Fellowship, the Evangelical Library and the London Bible College added significantly to the strength of their early years. No one except ML-J and Johnson was initially involved in all three. That these three agencies should have become established in central London simultaneously was undesigned and how much each was to mean to the others later years would show. Slowly ML-J was coming to occupy a position of influence at the centre of an evangelicalism about which he had considerable misgivings but he was fitted both to bring and to hold men together. The degree of harmony in the evangelical leadership is a marked feature of this period and he contributed largely to it.

These new agencies also brought ML-J into contact with a larger circle of men, and two particularly should be mentioned. The Rev. E. J. Poole-Connor, born in 1872, was reared in the Calvinistic

Evangelicalism (Edinburgh: Banner of Truth, 2012).

Independent tradition, and became a pastor in the Baptist Union. After finding himself increasingly isolated, he left the Union and served Talbot Tabernacle, London. Dismayed by the few connections between independent evangelical congregations and by the decline of biblical Christianity in England, he had initiated 'The Fellowship of Undenominational and Unattached Churches and Missions' in 1922, subsequently the Fellowship of Independent Evangelical Churches (FIEC). Still a man of energy and enthusiasm at the age of seventy — he was the principal 'carpenter' in the provision of book shelves in the Evangelical Library — between him and Lloyd-Jones there came a deepening bond of mutual esteem and affection.

A second close and enduring friendship dating from this period was that between Dr Lloyd-Jones and Fred Mitchell. Mitchell came to London in January 1943 to succeed W. H. Aldis as Home Director of the China Inland Mission. Previously a chemist and Methodist lay-preacher in his native Yorkshire, it was the first time that a man who had not served overseas was called to this influential position. At meetings of the Council of the London Bible College ML-J came to admire Mitchell. Although representing, as they did, two different branches of Methodism — Calvinistic and Wesleyan Arminian — the two men were drawn to each other. ML-J liked Mitchell's north-country personality and would later say: 'Fred Mitchell came into evangelical circles at the right time, as a breath of fresh air.' Both men had similar temperaments, combining a gentle graciousness with firmness; and both belonged to that school of spirituality which believes that men of God should be God-fearing men.

After hearing a lecture by ML-J in October 1943 Mitchell wrote to thank him and to say, 'I only wish I were near enough to be a member with you there!' Prayer for Westminster Chapel became a regular part of his life and through their friendship ML-J was to be drawn more fully into the work of the China Inland Mission, speaking repeatedly at their public meetings, to their missionaries on furlough at the headquarters in the London suburb of Newington Green, and becoming a member of the CIM Council in October 1945. Given Lloyd-Jones' aversion to committees as thieves of time, his frequent presence at the CIM headquarters (until 1959) is a testimony both of his attachment to Fred Mitchell and to that missionary agency. Mitchell died in a plane crash over India in 1953.

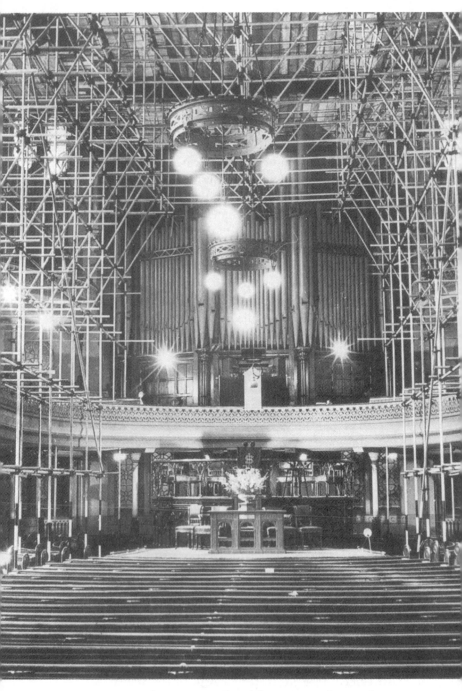

22. *Interior of Westminster Chapel during repair for war damage.*

EIGHTEEN

Westminster Chapel, 1943–45

On a July Sunday in 1943 Dr Campbell Morgan announced his resignation from the pastoral charge at Westminster. He was in his eightieth year and the fact was that the man who had once preached twelve times a week now found the burden of one regular sermon every Sunday too much for his failing powers. Twice before Morgan had offered his resignation only to be met by the appeal of ML-J and the church officers that he should continue. But in 1943 it was clear that his public work — first begun at Westminster in 1904 — was done. His letters to his family indicate that the decision was made easier by the certainty of his colleague's loyalty to the Word of God. 'Preaching is not what it used to be', he wrote to one of his sons a year earlier. 'I have now just to work my way through my notes and not trust to the inspiration of the moment for anything . . . However, I mean to keep on as long as I can and am able. I am greatly comforted and helped by my colleague . . . He is a remarkable preacher and a delightful personality.' To another correspondent Morgan says of his successor, 'I cannot tell you with what pleasure I listen to him . . . It is mighty preaching, most appropriate for these days.'[1]

On the last Sunday in August, when Dr Morgan entered the pulpit of the church he loved for the last time as its minister, he brought nearly twenty-four years of service to Westminster to a close as he

---

[1] Jill Morgan, *A Man of the Word,* p. 318.

preached from the words of Deuteronomy 1:6, 'Ye have dwelt long enough in this mount.'

The transition from the joint ministry at Westminster to that of ML-J continuing alone was not, in fact, as smooth as the appearance might suggest. There were influential members of the congregation from pre-war years who were by no means enamoured with the prospect of hearing nothing but Dr Lloyd-Jones. Hitherto they had tended to suffer the new preaching while expressing their undisguised preference for Dr Morgan. Some members even chose to attend only when the older man was preaching, and one of these, mistaking the arrangements for a particular Sunday, was overheard at Sunday lunch in the Grosvenor Hotel to say with indignation, 'I went to Westminster to hear Dr Morgan but it was that Calvinist.' The same attitude was represented in the diaconate itself. One of its most forceful men even took exception to ML-J's customary benediction that the presence of the triune God might abide throughout the remainder of this 'our short, uncertain earthly life and pilgrimage and' — 'and before we are carried out dead to the mortuary' he would interject under his breath. Others lacked his animus yet remained uncommitted. The biographer of Dr Margery Blackie, for example, tells us, 'When Margery first knew Dr Lloyd-Jones, and listened to his sermons, she did not take kindly to him . . . She was even somewhat prejudiced against him.'

Another member of Westminster, Mrs Norah Rowe, throws some light on this. She had joined the Chapel as a young woman about 1927, and also the 'Institute' 'which was quite liberal in its teaching'. 'Congregationalism', she recalled, 'was, of course, very modernistic.' She owed her conversion to Campbell Morgan's preaching on a summer visit, yet, though the pulpit was stronger after his second settlement in 1932, there was a major spiritual weakness in the congregation. Mrs Rowe became a missionary with the China Inland Mission and remembers how shocked two of her colleagues were at the 'atmosphere' when they were asked to speak at the 'Institute' in 1938. When Dr Morgan resigned in 1943 it was her belief that, behind the scenes, 'the liberal element tried to get Dr Lloyd-Jones out'.

I never spoke to ML-J on this point but a document from the time seems to confirm it. Although Morgan's letter of resignation was dated July 18 he had actually given that resignation verbally to the deacons on May 30. The deacons then proceeded to meet — alone! — on June 16, after which they wrote to ML-J 'to ascertain', in the words of their letter of June 17, 'your views as to the position arising from Dr Morgan's resignation, as it affects your Ministerial office as Dr Morgan's colleague'. The same letter expressed their 'intention to hold another session as soon as we have further information as is required from Dr Morgan and yourself'. The implication seemed to be that as it had been a collegiate ministry ML-J's appointment might terminate along with that of Campbell Morgan. No record survives, but we can assume that ML-J dealt firmly with this ploy.

Commenting on this period, Mrs Lloyd-Jones has written:

> There were those who did not want him, he was far too evangelical for them — he even made them 'feel like sinners!' I know I just watched and waited, and saw how, in nearly every case, he — or his gospel — won them and many who had been less than inviting became his firmest friends.

One of the latter was Margery Blackie. Yet unsupportive men remained on the diaconate for some years to come and by the time that they were finally gone the custom of paying ML-J a comparatively poor salary had become so habitual that it was never properly adjusted. Dr Morgan's pre-war salary at Westminster had been £1,100. The deacons determined on a figure of £800 for ML-J from October 1, 1943, and ten years were to pass before this was increased by £300.[2]

One of the first men at Westminster with whom ML-J came to have a close affinity was Mr A. G. Secrett, a builder in Ealing, who joined the church from a Strict Baptist background in the dark months of 1941. He was to become, in later years, one of ML-J's most trusted deacons. How much the understanding support of this one individual meant to ML-J is revealed in a letter he wrote to Secrett on April 19, 1943:

---

[2] As recorded earlier, the deacons took the desperate measure in 1941 of reducing both ministers' stipends to £10 for each service taken. How long this arrangement continued is not recorded in the Westminster Chapel archives, nor do details appear of any change after 1953. One American preacher who visited Britain in the late 1940s somehow heard the unpublicized figure which ML-J received as his salary and immediately deduced that he could not possibly be the outstanding preacher that he was reputed to be!

I have told you before of what you have meant to me as regards my ministry at Westminster. You can never know what it means to have someone who is in such sympathy with the message and from every standpoint. Coming as I did from a warm-hearted community where I was surrounded by men and women whose main and supreme interest in life was the gospel and who delighted in discussing it, and the problems which it raises, more than anything else, I felt terribly lonely at Westminster for the whole of the first year. Indeed I could scarcely believe that it was actually possible for a church to be so spiritually cold.

According to the report of one London newspaper at the time of Dr Morgan's resignation, while the two ministers had shared the preaching since 1938, Lloyd-Jones was already undertaking the pastoral and administrative work. The sole responsibility for all future services now meant a considerable addition to his workload. If his health and voice had not much improved since 1940 it would have been impossible both to lead Westminster single-handed and to maintain his itinerant ministry throughout the British Isles.

For many it was in that latter role that Lloyd-Jones was now best known. 'Wherever he goes,' reported the *British Weekly* of November 18, 1943, 'in England or Scotland, but especially beyond the Tweed, he is recognized as a powerful evangelist.'

From October 3, 1943, his first Sunday back home after a family holiday in Wales, ML-J seems to have established a pattern for his two services which he would continue. One sermon would usually be more directly evangelistic and the other designed primarily as instruction for those already Christians. It was a reflection of his priorities that the evangelistic emphasis was pursued in the morning congregations, which were larger at this date than the number attending the second service in the afternoon. Thus for the morning of October 3 he took 1 Corinthians 2:2 which he introduced with the words, 'There is no more perfect statement to be found anywhere of the function of the ministry and of the church than in these words.' In the afternoon of the same day, for the smaller congregation meeting at 3.30 P.M., he began his first extended expository series, giving the first of what were to be 25 sermons on the Second Epistle of Peter.[3] As the idea of a series by him was new to the congregation he considered

---

[3] *Expository Sermons on 2 Peter* (Edinburgh: Banner of Truth, 1983).

some explanation to be necessary: 'I propose', he told the people, 'to consider the message of this epistle in a series of consecutive studies. While, therefore, there will be of necessity a connection between them, each one will be a separate sermon and message and complete in and of itself.'

On the day before this first Sunday as sole minister, ML-J had written to his mother who was now spending much of her time in Wales. The letter was written from Haslemere where the Lloyd-Joneses had recently given notice of their intention to terminate the lease on the house they were renting:

> Somehow or other we have been extremely busy ever since we returned. The black-out material has arrived and I helped Bethan to cut it out. It took a long time.
>
> And of course I have more preparation work to do for West-minster now. We four are all well here. There was great excitement because the house was advertised as 'for sale'. Several came to view it on Tuesday and Wednesday.

The explanation regarding the house is that with the heavy bombing apparently over in London, and the war moving slowly towards the victory of the Allies, Dr Lloyd-Jones had decided to move back to the capital and end the incessant train journeys to Haslemere. Mr Secrett, from his knowledge as a builder, had been able to guide them to a suitable house available on a rental in West London. To this new home, 2 Colebrooke Avenue, Ealing, the family moved in November, 1943. The remainder of their possessions (which had been stored in Cardiff since 1938) were at last brought up to London with the material for the black out of the windows which the war-time conditions required.

If the new work-load was not a burden to Dr Lloyd-Jones, other factors certainly pressed him hard. One was the problem of establishing a true church fellowship in the congregation at Westminster. Traditionally it had been regarded by many as a preaching centre where people were strangers to one another. The total absence of a church prayer meeting, as already mentioned, was indication enough that a strong spiritual bond was missing from amongst the people. Compared with Sandfields the weakness was unmistakable. And not unrelated was the fact that there were few in the regular membership who understood the distinctive nature of his preaching although, as already seen, some understood it sufficiently to dislike it.

In five sermons on Acts 2:42, preached on Sunday mornings in October and November, 1943, Lloyd-Jones set before the people what he believed to be the biblical pattern for the life of the church. The place of prayer was fundamental. A writer in the *British Weekly* commented on this series at some length under the eye-catching but misleading heading, 'Free Church Minister Discusses Liturgy':

> What truth was there, the preacher asked, in the fathers' description of the prayer meeting as a thermometer and as the 'power-house of the church'? The apostolic church was undoubtedly a praying church. Could there be anything sadder than the decline of the prayer meeting during the past 25–30 years. Prayer kept the first community fervent in spirit and hot in its evangelism. Church history showed a close relation between prayer meetings and revival.

With Campbell Morgan's ready agreement, Dr Lloyd-Jones had started a church prayer meeting in 1942. When the longer light of summer permitted an evening service at 6 P.M., the prayer meeting preceded the service at 5.15 P.M.; otherwise it was held at 10.15 on Sunday mornings prior to public worship at 11 A.M. While present at these meetings ML-J took no vocal part apart from a brief concluding prayer; he always asked some other man to commence with a short reading of Scripture and prayer. Open prayer and intercession followed with a succession of men and women praying in turn.

For over six months after his sole pastorate commenced Dr Lloyd-Jones left Campbell Morgan's long-standing 'Bible School' in abeyance. Then, instead of resuming that meeting, traditionally convened on a Friday evening, he re-established in its place the 'Fellowship and Discussion' which had met on Monday evenings in 1939–40. That he gave preference to this type of meeting over a more formal service, was an indication of his conviction that every church must have a meeting in which there can be general participation. This Friday evening meeting was to continue unchanged until 1952 and we shall return to it later.

* * *

Equally significant, perhaps, with regard to the work at Westminster was what Dr Lloyd-Jones refrained from doing with regard to any re-organization of congregational life as people began to drift back to London. The Sunday School was resumed in 1943 but otherwise all the pre-war institutions such as the Women's League, the Institute (with activities ranging from table tennis and gymnastics to an annual *Eisteddfod* of singing and elocution), the Boys Brigade, the Girl Crusaders, and even the Church Choir, were to disappear permanently. There was to be no separate youth organization (an informal gathering of younger people on Sunday afternoons hardly meriting such a designation). Nothing was said about the omissions but they were noted and particularly so by some of the 'old guard' who were long accustomed to regard such things as essentials for numerical success. In a building capable of holding 2,000, and with an actual regular congregation at this date perhaps less than a quarter of that figure, people might be forgiven for a certain preoccupation with numbers. Some of Dr Lloyd-Jones' friends were themselves not without doubts whether the primitive simplicity of church life in Calvinistic Methodism could succeed in London. Dr Johnson later confessed, 'when I saw that he was (without choir, musical entertainment and any external aids) set to *preach* the Chapel full, I wondered if he could — with his away preaching in the week — sustain the load'.

Those who knew Dr Lloyd-Jones only in the pulpit were often surprised on their first meeting with him in private. He was eminently approachable and the first impression which Christians had was not of his gifts but of his spirituality. Geoffrey T. Thomas, recalling the pastoral help which he often received from ML-J, has written:

There was nothing forbidding and no hint of condescension in the great preacher. One felt in his presence that he was a man who obeyed his oft-quoted injunction 'Take time to be holy.' Thus his bearing was one of benign calmness and kindly gravity and on one occasion on calling at his house at Ealing I thought he had come straight from the presence of God. Indeed at my very first interview with him as a pastor I felt, as he showed me to the bus on the way home, a sense of calm by being in his presence. This was in 1944. Some 15 years later, when writing an article on the bicentenary of the birth of Wilberforce, I was interested to note his words after an interview with the saintly John Newton, 'I felt in Mr Newton's presence a great sense of calm.'

By 1943–44 the number of men and women from the Armed Forces present at Westminster had markedly increased. Sometimes it was only after they moved on that ML-J heard of what being present had meant to them. A soldier with the Dutch Free Army wrote to say how eighteen months before, when he began to attend Westminster Chapel 'as a Christian' he had learned that he had never been one at all. A time of conviction and hopelessness had followed before the truth had set him free.

Among a number of service men and women from the United States who attended was Mary-Carson Kuschke who belonged to a unit of the American Women's Army Corps. Her subsequent letters home were to contain many references to Westminster Chapel:

Jan. 12 [1944] Received Arthur's letter about Dr Lloyd-Jones so went to his church last Sunday.[4] He preached an excellent sermon, I talked with him afterwards, and he knows all about Dr Machen and Westminster Seminary and he heartily approves. Delighted to have me, hopes I will come often, etc. The people seem very friendly, and altogether it's a delightful situation.

Jan. 18 Last Sunday I went to hear Dr Lloyd-Jones again and heard another very good sermon. He's giving a series on the Epistle to the Hebrews. Dr Campbell Morgan came in during the first hymn and went out during the last hymn. He's a nice-looking old man with snow white hair and a vandyke beard, and he's very feeble. It seems he was still preaching until about four or five months ago.

April 19 Dr Lloyd-Jones has started a Friday night discussion group, which I attended last week and enjoyed a great deal. They couldn't have picked a worse night for me, as Friday is the night we all stay in and scrub the billets for Saturday morning inspection. But the meeting starts at 6.30 and lasts only a little over an hour, so if I skip supper and go straight from the office I can make it on time and still be back to do my share of the work. The meeting opens with a hymn, scripture reading and prayer, and then Dr Lloyd-Jones calls for a question. Anyone may pose any question he

---

[4] Her brother, the Rev. Arthur Kuschke, who would serve as librarian at Westminster Theological Seminary, Philadelphia, through many years.

wishes (on Christian faith or practice) and from there on it's open discussion, with Dr Lloyd-Jones acting as 'parliamentarian'. There were about seventy-five people there last week.

April 30 Went to the Friday night discussion group again this week. They were considering the problem of what should be done to increase church attendance — although I don't know why, as Westminster Chapel is usually quite well filled. In the course of the evening I ventured a few opinions on the strength of which several people came over and shook my hand — and two sisters named Hewitt invited me out to their home with some of the young people for one day next week.

Unknown to the people of London at the time of the D-Day landings of the Allied Forces in France in June 1944, they were themselves about to face a new and final peril. On June 12, 1944, the first pilotless planes (the V1) were launched by the Germans on London from bases in north-west France. Although these 'flying bombs', each carrying a ton of explosives, were soon disdainfully called 'doodle-bugs' on account of their flying slowly and low, they caused 10,000 casualties within their first week of operation. In addition to the actual danger the psychological factor was considerable in a population which thought it had seen the end of heavy bombing. Thousands heard the menacing sound of their flight — 'A terrific noise like an express train with a curious hidden undertone' — never knowing when the noise was about to cut out and the rocket descend. On the night of June 15 fifty of these flying bombs exploded in the London area.

To all appearances the morning service at Westminster on June 18, 1944 was going to be much the same as any other wartime service. But at 11.20 A.M., when Dr Lloyd-Jones had not long begun the long prayer, the unmistakable rumbling of a V1 could be heard approaching. 'I went on praying', he said afterwards, 'until the noise was so great that I could not hear myself speak.' Many who were present that day have unforgettable memories of what followed. Derrick Fenne, based in London with 21st Army Group and shortly to join the troops already in France, has written:

> The engine cut out almost overhead and after the silence, when the Dr faltered — a tremendous bang! The chapel structure cracked audibly under the effect of the blast and bits of ceiling and dust fell from the roof.

It had actually landed only a few hundred yards away on the Guards Chapel at Wellington Barracks where a service commenced at 10.30 and was still in progress. Over sixty people, many of them serving officers, were killed and 300 were injured. A nurse from the Westminster Hospital had intended being at the Guards Chapel but was late getting off duty on account of the number of casualties from the previous night's air-raid. As Westminster Chapel was slightly nearer Molly Pickard stopped there and was one of the congregation at 11.20 A.M. She recalls:

> As the impact of the doodle-bug was heard, the entire congregation rose to its feet. After the most brief pause the Dr continued his prayer, as though nothing had happened, and we all sat down again. It was only after he had finished talking to God that anything regarding the incident was said to the congregation.[5]

The Chapel received small damage but a few weeks later, when the congregation arrived on Sunday July 9, it was to discover that the building had suffered the worst damage of the war. 'Arriving at the Chapel,' writes Derrick Fenne, 'I found the building damaged and debris lying everywhere. A bomb had fallen on the flats opposite the Chapel in Castle Street. A notice outside indicated that the service would be held in Livingstone Hall.' The bomb had blown half the roof off and shattered all the windows on the side of the building nearest to Buckingham Palace, moving the wall itself an inch and a half out of position. Some main joists in the roof were also damaged but remarkably the interior of the building was undamaged.

In terms of aerial attack this was one of the most dangerous periods of the war for all who lived in London and from that aspect the move from Haslemere in November, 1943 had certainly been premature. Elizabeth and Ann slept nightly in the Morrison shelter in the living room at Colebrooke Avenue, joined by their parents when warnings sounded.

By July 31, 1944, flying bombs had killed 4,735 people, and about 17,000 houses were totally destroyed. In the weeks that followed the

---

[5] At the National Club, to which a number of army officers belonged, one high-ranking officer said to Major Human over lunch on that same Sunday: 'Were you at Westminster Chapel today? I have seen many things in the trenches in France but I have never seen anything more remarkable than the way that man went on with his prayer as though nothing had happened.'

bases from which the V1s had been launched were overrun by the Allies. The family's return to London in September coincided with the commencement of the last and most irresistible of the German weapons, the V2. This new rocket was fired from the greater range of 200 miles and reached a height of fifty miles before dropping at a speed of about 4,000 miles an hour without warning on its target area. The potential of this missile was not at first commonly realized. Martyn wrote of them to his mother on September 18: 'Nobody seems to take them very seriously here and most people think they are coming from Holland so they shall soon come to an end.'

Dr Lloyd-Jones had hoped that Westminster Chapel could be sufficiently repaired to be in use again by the end of July. He had strong feelings on the merits and deficiencies of particular buildings and disliked the Livingstone Hall but they were still meeting there in September.

As Mary-Carson Kuschke told her parents:

Sept. 19 In the morning M went with me to hear Dr Lloyd-Jones who preached an excellent sermon on a verse which I can't quote exactly, but you know it — to the effect that sufferings of this present time are not worthy to be compared with the glory that lies ahead. After the service we were talking briefly with Dr Campbell Morgan.

Sept 24 Cycled in the rain to my church, which is still meeting in a borrowed hall. Dr Lloyd-Jones preached on Romans 5:3-5, a continuation of last week's message. He said that we should glory in tribulation, not in and of itself, but because tribulation transforms our doctrine into *experience,* our *faith* into *assured knowledge.* Wish you could hear him sometime.

One of these services at the Livingstone Hall at this period so impressed one visitor that he wrote of the experience nearly twenty years later in a Glasgow newspaper. Tom Allan first heard Lloyd-Jones in Glasgow in 1938 when, he says, his interest in religion was 'immature, speculative and second-hand'. Although he was to forget the preacher's face — which he saw only at a distance — he never forgot the text and burden of the sermon. After speaking of that first hearing of ML-J, Allan continues:

Six years later, in 1944, I was stationed in London with the RAF. My religion — in so far as it had ever been a personal thing —

had long since gone by the board. I needed help, and I needed it badly. I remember going one Sunday morning to the Caxton Hall in Westminster — where Martyn Lloyd-Jones's congregation was worshipping. They had been bombed out of their own church a few weeks before.

I wanted to hear Lloyd-Jones, for in my pursuit of some kind of peace in the midst of breakdown, I had listened to so many other voices. There was a thin congregation. A small man in a collar and tie walked almost apologetically to the platform and called the people to worship. I remember thinking that Lloyd-Jones must be ill and that his place was being taken by one of his office-bearers. This illusion was not dispelled during the first part of the service, though I was impressed by the quiet reverence of the man's prayers and his reading of the Bible.

Ultimately he announced his text and began his sermon in the same quiet voice. Then a curious thing happened. For the next 40 minutes I became completely unconscious of everything except the word that this man was speaking — not his *words* mark you, but something behind them and in them and through them. I didn't realize it then, but I had been in the presence of the mystery of preaching, when a man is lost in the message he proclaims.

The essence of Lloyd-Jones's message to our time is vivid and unmistakable — the only hope for man in this world or in the world to come is to abandon his illusions and come as a helpless child to God.

Mary-Carson Kuschke was still in London as the year 1944 drew to the end. In October she wrote home of the Saturday evening she had spent with the Lloyd-Jones family in Ealing: 'I enjoyed them *thoroughly*. There are two daughters, Elizabeth, aged 17, and Ann, about six or seven. Ann and I held a lengthy discussion on the works of Beatrix Potter. Elizabeth expects to enter Oxford next year — is extremely bright and very nice.' Her pleasure was the greater on Christmas Day when, with others, she was again a guest at the Ealing home:

Their dining-room was nicely decorated for the season and we had a fine dinner of *goose* — with all the trimmings — followed by two hot Christmas puddings. They put 'prizes' in their puddings, as we do in wedding cakes, and I drew a duck and a thrupenny bit, which I shall bring home with me as souvenirs of the occasion. I took along my two-pound box of chocolates and they were all delighted — said it was the best they had eaten since pre-war days. After dinner we talked a while, listened to the King's speech, and then started to play games. We played all sorts of games, some old, some new, and everybody played — from seven year old Ann to her grandmother and everybody in-between. We all laughed uproariously and had a marvellous time.

After supper we sang, around the piano. Carols first and then Welsh hymn tunes. I wish our hymn books at home had more of the Welsh music in them — it's really beautiful.

I had an over-night pass, as we all knew it would be too late for me to get back to town, and was staying with Mr and Mrs Davies. We left at about midnight. It was about a fifteen minutes walk to their home, and a beautiful night. Moon shining through a light fog, heavy frost on the trees and shrubbery, coating every twig — as we have so often seen it in the Poconos. Had an early breakfast with them the next morning, and got back into town in time to report for duty. And so ended the story of my Christmas — a very happy one, thanks to some very fine people.

* * *

Dr Lloyd-Jones' work in the opening months of 1945 followed its normal course. His mid-week itinerant preaching included visits to Wales in January, Yorkshire in February and Somerset and Wiltshire in March. There were the usual public meetings in London (in support of evangelical agencies or suburban churches), committee meetings of the Evangelical Library and the Free Church Council, and Westminster Fraternals in January and March.

Dominating all other interests in the public mind was the approaching end to the war in Europe with the Allied Forces now poised to enter Germany itself. The prospects for the post-war world were already being widely discussed in the press and on the radio. While against what is normally understood as 'topical preaching', ML-J believed in making full use of current moods to drive home the teaching of Scripture. In October and November, 1944 he had preached nine sermons from Ephesians on 'God's Plan for World

Unity' and when the BBC in Wales asked him to give a further series of radio addresses he took for his subject 'Religion Today and Tomorrow'. The third and last of these was recorded on February 23, 1945. It did not supply the customary comfort given by religious broadcasters:

> All our fears for the future of the church and religion, our feeling of hopelessness as we see the world falling deeper into sin and vanity, our inclination towards multiplying arrangements, committees and movements, stem from the same thing, namely our lack of faith in the workings of the Holy Spirit.[6]

If the church in Wales would go back to the lessons of the eighteenth century, then, he believed, she would see that the first step to recovery is not to bring down the standard of church membership, but to raise it up.

On March 13, 1945 in the course of a letter to Philip Hughes in South Africa, ML-J wrote:

> I can say quite honestly that I have never enjoyed preaching as much. The word and its message grips me more and more and the joy of preparation has never been so great. I am conscious also of freedom in speaking and of authority. And yet I feel that these are but days of sowing. I long for revival comparable to that of the 18th century. More and more am I convinced that there, and there alone, lies our hope. I believe that the people at the back of the 'Faith for the Times Campaign' are beginning to see that now. But they so enjoy organising activities and meetings!
>
> I have given three talks in Welsh recently on the wireless on 'Religion Today and Tomorrow' and in them I have been at pains to stress the need for revival. I enjoyed analysing and trying to answer the current issues that characterise the present phase — Barthianism, ecumenicity, sacerdotalism, Religion and Life weeks, factory meetings etc. etc.
>
> Oh! how I long to know exactly what Paul means in 1 Corinthians 2:1-5, and to experience it in my ministry. I have become tired of all else and when I read of Whitefield I feel that I have never really preached in my life.

---

[6] 'Religion Today and Tomorrow', ML-J, *Knowing the Times* (Edinburgh: Banner of Truth, 1989), p. 30.

In April 1945 the one question in every mind was when the war in Europe would end. British armies were into Germany in the north, American further south, and Russian in the east. On Tuesday, May 1 at 3.30 P.M., Hitler killed himself in the bunker of the Chancellery in Berlin. A further week was to pass before London went jubilant with the news of Germany's unconditional surrender and celebrated 'Victory Day in Europe' on May 8. That same day King George VI wrote in his diary, 'We look back with thankfulness to God that our tribulation is over', and Parliament laid aside its business to 'attend at the Church of St Margaret, Westminster, to give humble and reverent thanks to Almighty God for our deliverance'.

When the thanksgiving service was held the next morning in Westminster Chapel one figure particularly was missed. Campbell Morgan, who first preached in that building in the far-off summer of 1902 and who had been with the church through the worst of two World Wars, would be there no more. Jill Morgan wrote of her father-in-law's passing in their nearby apartment at St Ermins:

> Winter yielded to Spring, and VE Day came on the eighth day of May. The moon shone down upon the scars of London, but the terror of pilotless planes and rocket bombs was over. The weary, the aged, and the young could sleep unmolested and waken to see flowers appearing in the ruins. Another chapter in history was closed. The man lying on the couch in St Ermins was waiting. Through the window the tower of Westminster Chapel could be seen standing against the sky. The work would go on; the Word would be proclaimed to the generations to come.

Morgan died on May 16, 1945 and for many who assembled for a memorial service at Westminster Chapel on May 28 his passing was akin to the passing of a whole era. The men, and the one woman, who shared that service with Dr Lloyd-Jones — W. H. Aldis, John A. Hutton, Mildred Cable, Charles Brown, Sidney M. Berry and S. W. Hughes — were people whose work was done in the Evangelicalism which had survived for fifty years after its influence was strongest in the Victorian era. They were themselves older representatives of a tradition which was passing and of which Morgan was, in a sense, the last great preacher.

23. Thirty-nine Mount Park Crescent, Ealing, to which the family moved from Colebrooke Avenue in July 1945, was to remain their home to 1965.

24. Ann facing her father's fast bowling.

NINETEEN

Guidance Confirmed

It might seem obvious that Dr Lloyd-Jones, once called to London, would remain there for the rest of his pastoral ministry. At the end of World War II he had seen Westminster Chapel through seven of its most difficult years and was now aged forty-five. But it was far from obvious to the preacher himself that his work there was to continue and in later life he was to say that had he been offered the Superintendency of the Forward Movement of the Welsh Presbyterian Church in 1947 (as many anticipated he would be) he believed he would have taken it. The truth is that he was not consciously settled in a life work at Westminster Chapel in 1945. To the factors which contributed to his uncertainty we must now turn.

Though not at the top of his concerns, there was in the first place the influence of his enduring attachment to Wales. To his old friend, E. T. Rees of Aberavon, he could write in 1943, 'Your letter filled me with a great *hiraeth* for those great days at Sandfields.' At other times he would speak of the cloud of homesickness which he felt on returning to Westminster after summer holidays in Wales and of how he would console the Chapel organist, Mr E. Emlyn Davies, who suffered from the same problems. 'I knew exactly what he felt,' ML-J was to say on Davies' death in 1951, 'and he was one of the few people who could sympathise with me when I felt the same.' Dr Lloyd-Jones also knew how his friends in Wales had not been entirely enthusiastic about his becoming pastor at Westminster in 1943 following the associate ministry with Morgan. As one of them had written from

Ton Pentre, Glamorgan: 'I had always hoped that you would some day return to your native land and to the *Hen Gorff*[1] where your presence is very much needed.'

A broader consideration against the permanency of this settlement in London was that the climate of opinion amongst the leadership of the Free Churches in England — the churches for which J. D. Jones and others hoped he would be a powerful spokesman — was alien to him. He still spoke alongside men whose theology was far different from his own, but the difference was unmistakable and he knew that it was not going to be reduced. Nor was it merely over one or two subjects. Beginning with a different standpoint, his thinking never seemed to be in agreement with his peers in their plans for the future of Nonconformity. All except ML-J, for example, believed that priority should be given to finding a new unity between churches. But in the opinion of the minister of Westminster Chapel:

> Spiritual power is not something which belongs to the world of mathematics, and so if we united all the denominations and added all the powers which each has together, even that would not create spiritual life. The burial of many bodies in the same cemetery does not lead to resurrection. Life is more important than unity.[2]

At the annual meetings of the Congregational Union in May 1944 ML-J was asked to give an address on evangelism — a practical subject upon which he could, perhaps, be expected to speak for the denomination. Instead of simply giving a plea for more evangelism, however, Dr Lloyd-Jones offered reasons for the existing ineffectiveness. As reported by *The Christian World*, he said:

> The churches had lost their evangelistic power because the authority of the Bible had been undermined and because some fifty years ago Nonconformity had become too politically minded. He discussed the right and wrong motives for evangelism. The crux of the whole matter was the message to be delivered: we had stressed the social aspect for the past fifty years, and men had increasingly turned their backs on us. It was not the wooing note which was needed but the note of judgment. We must convict men of sin and make

---

[1] *Hen Gorff* — literally 'the old body', a colloquial and affectionate way of referring to the Calvinistic Methodist Connexion.

[2] 'Religion Today and Tomorrow', 1945. *Knowing the Times*, p. 24.

them feel that they were under the condemnation of God. There were many in the Assembly who did not agree with Dr Lloyd-Jones' diagnosis of the position and who could not accept all his theology.[3]

A division between him and the English Free Church leadership was only a matter of time. This did not concern him nearly as much as the likelihood of disagreement with fellow evangelicals. What he had said to evangelicals on evangelism in 1943 and at other times had not been heeded by the majority and the hope of reaching an increasingly irreligious society by means of 'campaigns' remained a main feature of the evangelicalism of the post-war years. ML-J was, of course, closer to the type of evangelism which believed in sin and conversion than he was to the broader denominational type which thought more of winning people 'back to the churches'. Yet co-operation with the popular evangelism was a difficulty for him. After helping at an evangelistic meeting of this kind, he wrote of his unease to Philip Hughes, on April 17, 1946: 'Much time was spent in singing choruses. There is a levity and carnality which I simply cannot reconcile with the New Testament ... The general state of the people in London and in the country is one of apathy and deadness ... Nothing but an unusual manifestation of God's power through the Holy Spirit can possibly meet the present need. I pray daily for revival and try to exhort my people to do the same.'

It was clear to ML-J that, if he stayed in England, the problem of trying to help evangelical agencies while maintaining a conscientious adherence to what he believed would remain a problem. This was part of the reason why he declined the principalship of the London Bible College in 1942. The broader evangelical ethos which the College was intended to represent was not his own and he knew that acceptance of the post 'would only lead to trouble'.

More pressing than all these concerns was the state of Westminster Chapel itself. He had experienced one major readjustment in the unexpected situation brought about by the war and now he was faced with another. The war had broken up the 1939 congregation; since then numbers had increased to about 500, yet not for the most part by Londoners. From 1945 the many uniformed figures in the pews

[3] *Christian World*, May 18, 1944.

were scattered by demobilisation and soon became a thing of the past. 'People began to return to London,' ML-J said of this time, 'but we lost the vast majority of our membership; the pre-war remnant that remained was middle-aged and elderly.'

Virtually a new congregation was in need of being built up. This was a problem which went much deeper than a question of numbers. Some who had joined the church in recent years were beginning to share their minister's vision for what a church should be, but this was not the case with the majority of the pre-war remnant who still looked back to the 'great years' when the building was crowded. They could see no difference between a successful preaching centre where people did not know one another and a spiritual, united fellowship. At the same time, this low view of the local church was often coupled to a strong denominational attachment, as ML-J found when he proposed the withdrawal of the congregation from the Congregational Union at a church meeting in 1947. The vocal protest from this party within the membership was one of the factors which led him not to press his initial resolution for disaffiliation from the Union at that date. There had been no election of deacons throughout the War years, and resistance to his proposal was strongly represented in the diaconate.

These were reasons why, in the period immediately following the war, ML-J was not convinced that he was intended to stay at Westminster. It was a question with which he had to struggle, for, while an invitation to lead the Forward Movement in Wales never came, there were enquiries from churches in Canada, the United States and Scotland concerning his availability to receive a call. The outcome, as we know, was his persuasion that he was intended to remain in a situation which he would not have chosen for himself. When, in later years, younger ministers would hear him exhort them to see difficulties and challenges as God-given opportunities, they little knew the extent to which he was speaking from experience.

I turn now to the manner in which ML-J faced the work of rebuilding. It is worth noting that he did nothing to uproot church officers who had clearly little sympathy with his ministry. He wanted to win them to the truth. His conviction was that everything depended upon God using his Word as it was preached week by week. He was also persuaded that too often Christians had no grasp of truth as *a system* because of the type of preaching to which they had been chiefly accustomed. 'The great trouble of our time is the lack of theological preaching', he told the students at Spurgeon's College when he spoke there in January 1948. While preaching 'should be essentially exposition', with the text and context governing the form of the sermon, 'theology will safeguard a correct exposition; it will save us from becoming fanciful'. Before concluding that address he anticipated the question likely to be put to him, 'Will people listen to this kind of preaching?' To which he replied:

> They have more or less given up listening to the other kind! The low level of the life of the church today is due to the lack of doctrinal preaching. This is a question never to be asked: we have the commission of God to preach, not a call to satisfy the popular palate. 'Preach the Word'. Our one concern should be to preach the truth.

But while the pew is not to control the pulpit, the preacher is always to consider the state and capacity of his hearers and ML-J at this period was only gradually introducing them to consecutive expository preaching. His early series were usually no more than four sermons long. Gradually the length increased. His series of sermons on 2 Peter, which began in October 1946, were continued until the end of March 1947, and on Sunday evenings, from October 27, 1946, he began a series of six evangelistic sermons on John 3, to be followed by another six on Isaiah 35:1-8. Many sermons at this date, however, were not in a consecutive series at all.

It would appear that there was a marked evidence of the Holy Spirit's work in the congregation in the second half of the year 1946. In his letter to Philip Hughes of April 17, 1946, from which we have already quoted, ML-J could speak of 'seeing occasional conversions'. At the end of that year, however, in his annual letter to members, dated January 1, 1947, he wrote: 'The steady increase in the size of the congregation both morning and evening has been noticeable . . . above all else we rejoice in the fact that God has been pleased to bless the preaching of the word to the conversion of many souls.' Even so, the numbers attending in 1946 were insufficient to fill the ground floor of the auditorium, with the two galleries above entirely empty. Numbers grew during a morning series of sermons on Philippians beginning in October 1947 (37 sermons to July 1948), and in May 1948 it became necessary to re-open the lower gallery. The fact that this re-opening occurred for the evening services some weeks *before* the morning ones may indicate that the evangelistic preaching — now during the second service — was slightly ahead in drawing in visitors and outsiders.

Alongside the work of the pulpit Dr Lloyd-Jones pursued his conviction that changes were needed if the congregation was to be more than a collection of individuals. He gave new emphasis to the meetings for church members, slowly increasing their number, and whereas they had once been short, formal meetings, he introduced the practice of having a missionary speaker to give an address after matters of church business were concluded. At an informal 'At Home', preceding the first church meeting after the summer vacation, he and Mrs Lloyd-Jones sought to meet everyone personally, and on January 1 of each year he wrote a letter exclusively for members in which he spoke more personally of the work at the Chapel. In this annual letter, from which I have already quoted, the corporate nature of the fellowship in which they shared was often underlined.

In the establishment of a closer unity ML-J gave great importance to the Friday meeting 'For Fellowship and Discussion' of which we have already spoken. More needs to be said, however, of this meeting and of the part which it came to play in strengthening a common vision within the congregation.

Some two hundred people were attending the Friday discussion by the autumn of 1947 and, in many cases, they were to become spiritual leaders either in the congregation or in other places in the years ahead. Anyone was free to propose a question of a practical and spiritual nature. ML-J wanted questions arising out of the personal circumstances and problems which Christians encounter in their lives; the merely theoretical was not allowed. His objective was to bring people to apply the teaching of Scripture and to see that 'it is failure to understand doctrine that causes failure in practice'. So, if a question was accepted as the subject for the evening, he made no attempt to answer it himself immediately. Rather he aimed to stimulate a discussion in which the people themselves would think their way to the relevant biblical principles and to their correct application.

The questions raised were such as these: How do we know the will of God? How do we distinguish between an intellectual assent to Scripture and true faith? Should a Christian covet experience or power? Has God a plan for our lives? Does physical tiredness or bodily illness excuse sin and failure? How do we deal with a person who has suffered a calamity in their life? What is the least knowledge we can expect in a new convert?

Once a question had been accepted, the discussion might often start with ML-J asking for Scripture references appropriate to the subject. If a speaker thought that one or two texts proved that the right answer to the question was perfectly simple he might well suffer an interrogation from ML-J which would leave him convicted that his assurance was premature. The strength of this interrogation might depend upon ML-J's assessment of the self-confidence of the person concerned, his intention being to deepen the level of thought and to bring other speakers to their feet. A new and nervous contributor would never get the rough treatment which tended to be reserved for some of the over-confident young men in whom the chairman had a special interest. John Waite (a future college principal) recalls how he and Fred Catherwood (a future son-in-law of ML-J and a future Member of the European Parliament) were 'often shot down in flames'! Sometimes a critical cross-questioning was only to test the strength of a speaker's convictions (with whom ML-J actually agreed); or he would temporarily allow speakers to pursue a wrong track so that ultimately the whole gathering could understand more clearly the reason why it was wrong. Frequently the main question could not be answered until other preliminary questions were also dealt with and so one theme might extend over several weeks. Even so, there were conclusions (towards which ML-J had been steering and directing the discussion) reached every week. It was in the latter part of the evening that he usually said more; at times he would engage in a debate with one or two individuals who were not willing to be carried to the conclusion to which they suspected they were being led. His final summing up was generally impressive and heart-searching.

* * *

From 1946, when Elizabeth Lloyd-Jones became an undergraduate at Oxford, her father would generally write to her weekly during term time. News of home affairs were left to Mrs Lloyd-Jones. The main impression given by these letters is of the close relationship between father and daughter. With counsel and encouragement there was occasional correction, as when Elizabeth had told him of the view which was being adopted by her and others in the Oxford Inter-Collegiate Christian Union on attendance at their colleges' chapels. They were critical of the chapel services, especially of the hymns sung. Her father replied:

> Your attitude is not one that I can commend . . . Your duty is to show that your views and beliefs lead to a higher and finer type of Christian life and living. Then that will lead others to speak to you and to enquire as to your secret. To start a division on odd points and to raise difficulties especially in a matter like that of hymns seems to me to be the worst possible approach. It gives the impression that you are intolerant and that you regard yourselves as heresy hunters. Your duty it seems to me is to attend the services. If you find you cannot sing a hymn, just refrain from doing so.

While there is much parental affection evident in his letters, he writes to her more as a Christian than as a teenage daughter and he frequently shares with her some of his concerns about the work at the Chapel. 'The problem of Westminster as a church', he says in one letter, 'is that people simply do not know one another and it is difficult to see how they can. It is the old question of a church or a preaching station or an evangelical centre. I feel that the only ultimate solution is to have a prayer meeting on a week night. That will test and sift people. But again one hesitates to call upon good and faithful people to travel such distances on another night and also in view of fares and the present cost of living. However, I am thinking much about it.' There is news of the Friday night meetings, and virtually every letter contained full outlines of both his Sunday sermons. On January 20, 1948 he wrote to her:

> My report from Westminster this time is I fear not a good one. The damp muggy weather last week made me feel utterly dull and I fear that that must have revealed itself in my various activities. The Friday night meeting I felt was dull, largely due to me.

In the letters of 1948 he mentions the increase in numbers and the re-opening of the gallery in May. One of the visitors who happened to be in church on the Sunday morning the gallery was brought back into use was H. W. K. Mowll, the Archbishop of Sydney, who preached to the Queen in an evening service that same day in Westminster Abbey.

What ML-J looked for in the Sunday evening services especially is clear enough from other letters where he writes: 'It was a night of much conviction.' 'It was solemn and I think all felt a powerful service.' 'All seemed to be conscious of a spirit of deep conviction.' On yet another occasion, after an outline of an evangelistic sermon from Luke 12:13-15, he said:

> Several came to see me at the end. It was certainly a night of much convicting power and I felt I was being used. But oh! how far short do we fall of Paul's description of the Christian! If only we knew more about and meditated more upon the glory that awaits us.

From time to time his letters referred to individuals he had seen who were 'under conviction' or, he believed, 'definitely converted'. Looking back on 1948, he wrote in his annual letter to members of Westminster Chapel:

> We thank God for the fact that during the year many have been brought to a saving knowledge of the Lord Jesus Christ. My own experience is that I am increasingly conscious of being surrounded and supported by a truly spiritual fellowship . . . As to the future I feel more and more that we have been called and set by God to witness together here in the heart of London, and to 'earnestly contend for the faith which was once delivered unto the saints'.

This was a decided change in his feelings of ten years earlier. The uncertainty over remaining at Westminster had been taken from him.

In 1949 the *British Weekly* ran a series on 'Giants of the Pulpit' from which ML-J's name was conspicuously absent. What was overlooked by Englishmen was not, however, missed by an Indian, Mark Sunder-Rao, Assistant Editor of the *Guardian* of Madras. This writer, being temporarily employed by the *British Weekly* while on a visit to Britain, produced an article entitled 'An Indian Hears a Great Preacher in London' (Sept. 15, 1949). He began by saying how he had been visiting various churches in a kind of pilgrimage in order to find the kind of church which had been responsible for the gospel ever reaching his own land. At Westminster Chapel, and in the ministry

of Dr Lloyd-Jones, he declared, he had found that real source of foreign missions.

The physical appearance of ML-J in the pulpit, this Indian
journalist wrote, reminded him of what was once said of William
Wilberforce, who was a man of small stature yet 'as he spoke the
shrivelled shrimp swelled to the proportions of a colossus'. Sunder-
Rao continued:

> But what impressed me, in the end, was not the personal aspect
> of the famous preacher, though that made no uncertain impact.
> It was that as the preacher unfolded the theme he seemed to have
> been possessed, or to be discreet, perhaps, motivated, by One
> greater than himself, in whom he lived, moved and had his being.
> All great preaching becomes a sacrament, nay, a miracle, when in
> and through it, it holds forth the indications and intimations of
> the presence of God.
>
> It was small wonder, then, that the chapel was filled to capacity,
> unlike a church I went into a few weeks before. Here one did not
> see a few old women and tottering men only, but a goodly fellow-
> ship of persons of all ages with a generous sprinkling (I had almost
> said *sparkling!*) of the youth.
>
> And why? Here one touches the significant point. Because in this
> typically Nonconformist chapel one realised at once the meaning
> of the 16th century reformation and the 18th century revival: that
> where the gospel is preached within the congregation and taken
> out to the uttermost parts of the world, there the church is. Impor-
> tant as they are, liturgy and church order are yet secondary; the
> primary thing, and one which renders a community dynamic and
> mobile, is the gospel: the fact of the reality of God, his concern for
> our lives, his love from which nothing in this world or the next can
> alienate us, his sufficiency. These were the points in the sermon of
> Dr Martyn Lloyd-Jones.

This foreign journalist was like Barnabas who, guided to Antioch,
'when he came, and had seen the grace of God, was glad' (*Acts*
11:23). He rightly traced the works going on at Westminster Chapel
to the same explanation. Lloyd-Jones knew it and uncertainty over
remaining at Westminster had been taken from him.

────────────

TWENTY

Wales and the Summer of 1949

In 1947 when the Rev. Richard J. Rees, after 54 years in the ministry, concluded his work as the leader of the Forward Movement
of the Welsh Presbyterian Church, many had wanted ML-J to
succeed him. As already mentioned, this did not happen; he was not
offered the post and for the same reason that his possible appointment to the Bala College had been blocked in 1938. The leaders of
the denomination did not want a man in a position of authority
who was so out of step with their thinking. This in no way lessened
ML-J's commitment to preaching far and wide in Wales, and it ever
remained the family's favourite place for holidays in the mid-summer.

The controlling principles by which ML-J lived were not Welsh,
but in a thousand secondary things he was Welsh through and
through and proud to be so. While he condemned 'carnal nationalism', and regarded any idea that nationality continues in heaven
as 'dangerous speculation',[1] he also rejected the idea that because a
person is a Christian he should lose his national identity, or change
his temperament, or leave the culture into which he was born. 'Greek
and barbarian, male and female', do not cease to be what they are
by nature when they are made one in Christ. Just as the variations
between individuals are not removed by regeneration, so the differences between national groupings and national characteristics remain
among believers.

[1] 'Nationalism, Tradition and Language', a Discussion between Dr Gaius Davies
and ML-J, in the *Evangelical Magazine of Wales,* Aug-Sept, 1969.

Welsh was the language in which Martyn almost always spoke and wrote to Bethan. He read Welsh newspapers and listened to Welsh radio. He deplored the Welshman who deliberately tried to lose his accent, regarding it as the attitude of a serf (*cymhleth y taeog*) wanting to please his English masters.

Perhaps it is in his letters to his mother, written to her in London when he is on holiday in Wales, that the depth of his interest in his native background comes out. These letters are often so full of things Welsh — relatives, farms, agricultural shows and so on — that it scarcely seems possible that he ever lived anywhere but in a rural locality.

In accepting preaching engagements I doubt if he gave any priority to the Principality, but it is remarkable how often he was there for that purpose. In 1948, for example, apart from holidays, commitments took him to various parts of Wales in no less than seven months of the year. A number of these engagements would frequently be far away from the large centres of population to be found in the South. The spiritual state of the countryside profoundly disturbed him. While taking one weekend off from Westminster in April 1948 he could not resist offering to preach on the Sunday afternoon in the hills above Newcastle Emlyn where they were staying. 'The congregation consisted of 15 people,' he wrote to his mother, 'most of whom did not know me.' Later in 1948 he had a commitment in Newcastle Emlyn, at Bethel Calvinistic Methodist Chapel which had formerly been a strong and lively congregation. After this visit to Bethel he wrote to Elizabeth (at Oxford) on November 3:

> Never have I felt so much that the people down there are in a state of almost heathen darkness. They listened well but gave the impression that what they were hearing was altogether new. I preached in Welsh on the Tuesday night and the Wednesday afternoon and then in English on Wednesday night . . . I see no hope whatsoever for Bethel and for the whole district apart from a revival. A new minister would scarcely make any appreciable difference. It is really a most sad state of affairs. I feel increasingly, and said so in one of my sermons, that the real trouble is inside the church. The vast majority of the people are not Christian at all and do not know what it means. The work must start with them.

Roger Weil, who was a member of Westminster Chapel, recalls seeing a side of his minister's character in a new light when he happened to visit the Lloyd-Joneses during one of their summer holidays in Aberystwyth. They spoke together in the course of an evening on the state of the Welsh churches, past and present, and this was followed by family prayer which, as usual, closed the day. The English visitor writes:

> I will always remember the deep note of sadness in that part of his prayer when he interceded for Wales, that God who had so signally blessed her in days gone by would revive his work there once more. It was that tone of sadness that stuck in my mind at the time — I did not realise how it grieved his heart. I suppose it was memorable, too, because while on our knees there together we were privileged to glimpse him on a more personal level than ever we could in the services at the Chapel. It was not so much the words but something more like a *groan* in how he said what he did.

Evangelical witness in Wales had been so largely amongst the churches of Calvinistic Methodism (the Welsh Presbyterian Church) that when these churches were overtaken by liberalism and worldliness the cause of the gospel went down in many parts of the land. The last revival of 1904 had put a break on that descent and people involved in the '04 Revival were, in subsequent years, those who kept prayer and fellowship meetings going in their chapels even where liberalism might be found in the pulpits. While ML-J was ready to admit some serious deficiencies had accompanied the work of 1904 he would also say, 'I tremble to think what the churches would have been like without the *plant y diwygiad*' (children of the revival). By the middle of this century, however, such people were becoming few in number and the general condition of the country was well described by ML-J's brother-in-law in the words, 'The old religious background of our people is disappearing and a pagan generation is springing up.'

* * *

The summer of 1949 in Wales was to prove one of the most remarkable in Dr Lloyd-Jones' life. Originally it was not his intention to be in Wales at all over the summer period, for he was committed to spending July and August in the United States. But before concluding at Westminster prior to this North American visit he was suffering from persistent catarrh and other symptoms of over-work. When he consulted his old chief, Lord Horder, he was firmly told to cancel the trans-Atlantic trip and that it was high time he took a proper holiday. ML-J was himself sufficiently concerned about his condition to accept the advice.

Thus, when another year's ministry — his eleventh — at Westminster Chapel ended in June 1949 he went with Bethan down to Sunnyside, Newcastle Emlyn. Here in his beloved Cardiganshire he was free of engagements other than some which came unexpectedly in that quiet country town. Writing to his mother on July 8, he notes: 'I had to preach here morning and evening on Sunday as Nantlais Williams failed to turn up. I was none the worse for it.'

25. Sunnyside (on left), Newcastle Emlyn, Wales.

At this time in Newcastle Emlyn, Dr Lloyd-Jones was going through a personal struggle of which he very rarely spoke. He was suffering from depression which he attributed to his low physical condition. With the depression, however, there came a temptation in the form of a 'fiery dart' of doubt. The doubt did not concern his faith or his ministry but it had to do with a person whose regard for him had long been of great support to his whole life. The temptation was to question the reality of this friend's regard. This suspicion was entirely without foundation and he did not give way to it, yet the power of the temptation put him into an agony of spirit: 'There are times', he would later say, 'when the enemy concentrates on individual Christians, on Christian churches . . . when the devil makes a broadside attack upon you and would sweep you off your feet.' This awareness that the onslaught was from the devil did not, however, bring comfort, for the temptation had brought with it a discovery about himself. The attack had come at a point where it could have success: it was an appeal to his pride, 'not my pride in the ministry but my carnal pride'.[2] More than thirty years later he could only speak of it with pain: 'It was a terrible thing, it was the thing that revealed to me ultimately the pride of the human heart. I knew I was a sinner without any hope at all, but I never realised the depth of the pride of the human heart. Eventually I saw it was nothing but pride. Carnal, devilish pride. And I was humbled to the ground.'

On July 13, Bethan returned to London while he proceeded to a Nursing Home near Bristol where he had booked a place some weeks earlier for the treatment of his catarrh. This institution was run by Dr A. B. Todd, a highly individualistic physician of whose judgment he had a high opinion. Here he spent nearly two weeks largely on his own in a private room. For the first few days the inner tempest continued. Besides his usual reading of Scripture he had with him some of the writings of A. W. Pink which he had often found helpful, but now nothing seemed to give him any spiritual comfort. Then one morning he awoke soon after 6 A.M. in 'a complete agony of soul' and even feeling a sense of evil in the room. As he started dressing, his eye caught the word 'glory' in a sermon of Pink's which lay open beside his bed.[3] Instantly, 'like a blaze of light', he knew the very glory of

---

[2] 'That sin of all sins, which runs through all ages, and through all the race of mankind, is pride . . . Now Satan, that knows this full well, labours with might and main to provoke all men to this sin; it was his own sin, the very sin that made him of a blessed angel a cursed devil.' Isaac Ambrose, 'War with Devils,' p. 62, in *Complete Works,* 1674.

[3] ML-J read A. W. Pink's monthly *Studies in the Scriptures* from about 1942 until it concluded with the author's death ten years later. In 1945 he advised Paul Tucker, a student for the ministry, 'Don't waste time reading Barth and Brunner. You will get nothing from them to aid you with preaching. Read Pink.' But he would also say that

God surrounding him. Every doubt and fear was silenced. The love of God was 'shed abroad' in his heart. The nearness of heaven and his own title to it became overwhelming certainties and, at once, he was brought into a state of ecstasy and joy which remained with him for several days.

Lloyd-Jones never wrote of this experience, and he was very reticent to refer to it.[4] He believed that the experience was the work of the Holy Spirit testifying to his sonship (*Rom.* 8:16). In the similar experiences of others (to which he referred on a number of subsequent occasions) it is observable that two features, in particular, paralleled his own. First, there was the sense of light and glory. In the words of William Guthrie: 'It is a glorious divine manifestation of God unto the soul . . . It is a thing better felt than spoke of. It is no audible voice, but it is a ray of glory filling the soul with God, as He is life, light, love and liberty, corresponding to that audible voice, "O man, greatly beloved" (*Dan.* 9:23).' Another Puritan, Thomas Goodwin, writes: 'There is light that cometh and over-powereth a man's soul and assureth him that God is his, and he is God's.'[5] Secondly, there was the suddenness and the unexpectedness with which the assurance came. Speaking of such an occasion, Robert Bruce could say, 'I leapt no sooner on my horse but the gates of heaven were cast open to me', while John Flavel and Christmas Evans were alone in the course of journeys when they similarly met suddenly with God.[6]

When he resumed his holiday with Bethan, together with Elizabeth and Ann, in the last week of July they were making their first of many visits to the farmhouse of Mr and Mrs Ellis Davies at Pant-y-Neuadd, Parc, near Bala. From there ML-J wrote a postcard to A. G. Secrett on July 29:

> We had an excellent journey. You will be glad to know that I am feeling really better and I am sure that from now on I shall continue to gain strength.

Pink, and especially his early writings, should be read with discrimination. In connexion with reforming churches he said, 'If I had behaved as Pink did, I would have achieved nothing. I could see that the only hope was to let the weight of the truth convince people. So I had to be very patient and take the long-term look at things.'

[4] See footnote on p. 430.

[5] See ML-J, *Romans, Exposition of Chapter 8:5-17, The Sons of God* (Edinburgh: Banner of Truth, 1974), pp. 341-2.

[6] *Ibid.,* p. 315.

We are staying right in the mountains. I had not realised that this farm was so situated. It is delightful to wake up to the sound of the running brook . . .

A note from Bethan to the Secretts some days later, gives a rather different view of her husband's health:

I thought I should have written you many letters before this, but somehow or other it is the most difficult thing to *get at* and I cannot think why! I think that up here it has been because Martyn was so *low* that he has not been doing any reading at all and I have spent all my time pottering about with him. He has been pathetically content to do nothing but *laze* up till now, but now we are beginning to walk the hills and are enjoying it more and more.

It was on this visit to Pant-y-Neuadd that Dr Lloyd-Jones had another experience akin to that described above. The Davies' farm-house was busy with visitors and he had retired early one Saturday evening. Alone in their bedroom, he was reading the Welsh hymns of William Williams in the Calvinistic Methodist hymn book when he was again given such a consciousness of the presence and love of God as seemed to exceed all that he had ever known before. It was a foretaste of glory.

While the remembrance of the experiences of God which he had at Dr Todd's Nursing Home, and, again, at Pant-y-Neuadd, were to remain with him all his life, the times of joy were followed by further conflict. He was apprehensive over returning to London in September after the longer than usual break and, in the first days back, he felt utterly unable to preach. Various attempts to prepare a sermon for Sunday morning, September 11 all ended in failure, and so it continued until the preceding day when there was scarcely time left for preparation. In his own words: 'That Saturday afternoon in my study I felt I couldn't preach but the word came into my mind from Titus 1:2, "God who cannot lie", and I'll never forget it. I was absolutely overwhelmed, in tears, and I was given the sermon there and then.'

The sermon notes which he took into the pulpit the next morning bear their own witness to the abnormality of that week-end. Instead of the more usual four sides of notes, written in ink with heads and sub-heads, he had one scrap of paper (torn from an agenda of a London Bible College Committee meeting), with pencil notes hurriedly set down on the unused side. Only a few introductory words were written in full. They read:

> Good to start with something great and fundamental. Always danger of becoming immersed and lost in details . . . Paul generally makes things plain at the beginning of every letter. Our whole basis and position rest on the fact of God and his great purposes. It is the only ground of confidence. The great thing is the 'hope of eternal life, which God, that cannot lie, promised before the world began'. Whatever may be happening to us and whatever our feeling, this is certain. But how can we be sure of it? Answer here . . .

These words thus led into his four heads:

> *The fact* — God cannot lie. Incapable of it. *The explanation of fact* — His character, immutable, just, holy, antithesis of all that is false and deceptive. *Proof of the fact* — Bible and history, especially the sending of his Son and his work. *Comfort of the fact* — 'promised before the world began . . . in due times manifested'. Certain things delayed. The promises — 'I will never leave thee nor forsake'; 'When thou passest through the waters'; 'Let not your heart be troubled.'

It may appear strange that the darkness in which Dr Lloyd-Jones struggled could persist even after the very conscious nearness of God which he had known on those two remarkable occasions. And the conflict was to go on until late in the year, though never with the same force after Sunday, September 11, when he was enabled to speak with much power and liberty. But to Dr Lloyd-Jones it was the marked contrast in the nature of his experience at this time which pointed to the real meaning of what was happening to him: 'In my opinion God wanted to do something new to me so he gave the devil liberty to attack like he did with Job. That was a real Satanic attack and the devil would get me right down but then God would lift me up. So the two went together. That is most important.'

No small part of Dr Lloyd-Jones' ministry in the years ahead was to help Christians to know their enemy and how to resist him. His emphasis in this regard became akin to Martin Luther's. The knowledge which he had gained from experience was to illuminate many passages of Scripture, first for himself and then for others. In expounding Ephesians 6:10-21, he would later say: 'There is nothing which is quite so disastrous as not to accept in its fulness the biblical teaching concerning the devil. I am certain that one of the main causes of the ill state of the church today is the fact that the devil is being forgotten. All is attributed to us; we have all become so psychological in our attitude and thinking. We are ignorant of this great objective fact, the being, the existence of the devil, the adversary, the accuser, and his "fiery darts".'

The experiences of 1949 deepened his conviction both about his own superficiality as well as the superficiality of much evangelical religion. All that he allowed himself to say about himself was: 'I was brought to the end of myself in a way that had never happened before. I really saw the depths of sin and that man's ultimate problem is his pride.' He concurred entirely with the words of Sibbes, 'After conversion we need bruising by reason of the remainder of pride in our nature, and to let us see that we live by mercy.' The hallmark of a true experience of God, he would constantly preach, 'is a sense of awe, and accompanying it, a sense of unworthiness'.

In personal conversation ML-J once spoke to me of the experiences of 1949 constituting 'a real turning point when I got my true balance. I had been becoming too intellectual, too doctrinal and theological, because when I came to London I suddenly found I was the teacher, the theologian, and it tended to make me lose my balance, although that had started in Sandfields by reading Warfield.'

It would be a mistake to make too much of the words 'turning point'. There was no change in the content of Dr Lloyd-Jones' ministry after this time. No one observed any significant alteration in his preaching after that date. The address of truth to the mind remained primary, 'let me beseech you, never put the love of God and doctrine as opposites'. Far from putting 'experience' in the place of faith in the Word of God, some of the strongest warnings against that danger came in the autumn of 1949 when he resumed preaching from 1 John. But he was himself conscious of an increasing element of the experimental in his ministry, a stronger emphasis on the love of God, and on the need for preaching which changes hearts and lives as well as minds. Fellowship with God is *more* than orthodoxy. Love to

God — a love that wholly possesses us — is *the* supreme need. After preaching on October 9, 1949, on the love of God in the giving of his Son, he said:

> My beloved friends, I do not know what your feeling is at this moment, I will tell you what mine is. I cannot understand the hardness of my own heart. How could any of us look at all this, and believe it, and not be lost in love to God? How can we contemplate these things and not be utterly broken down? How can we do anything but love one another as we contemplate such amazing love? How can we look at these things and not feel that we owe everything to him and that our whole lives must be given to express our gratitude, our praise and our thanksgiving?

Dr Lloyd-Jones came to look back on 1949 as a year when he had been guided by God with unusual clarity. He had been humbled and strengthened for the long years ahead. He had learned more of what it means to enjoy the love of God. He would help others to know that such dealings of God are not uncommon with those called to serve him. In the words of Isaac Ambrose, three hundred years earlier: 'Sometimes when Satan is most busy, the Lord steps in with his own testimony, and stops the lion's mouth that he can say no more.'

TWENTY-ONE

———————

A Rising Tide of Youth

Lloyd-Jones' work among students had been slowly mounting in the post-war years, both at home and overseas: he spoke for the Inter-Varsity Fellowship a number of times at Oxford, and London students (especially from the great teaching hospitals) were attending his ministry. He also took a leading part in conferences of the new International Fellowship of Evangelical Students (IFES). But there came now a marked enlargement of usefulness among a rising generation of young men. It was strange, on the face of it, that until the summer of 1949 he had very little connexion with student work in Wales itself. Thirty-five students went from Cardiff to the annual IVF Conference at Swanwick in 1947, but he had spoken for none of the Evangelical Christian Unions in Wales. This was partly because he had no desire to see the IVF become a stronger organization in Wales. He would later say, 'I opposed the setting up of an IVF Conference in Wales, I opposed it for years.' He wanted work in Wales to remain centred in the churches, not in movements, and the evangelistic teaching in IVF circles was commonly Arminian. 'We have been too ready to allow the English tradition to influence us', was his comment.

The nature of the IVF work in Wales bears this out. Through the 1940s the major emphasis was on student-led campaigns of the type then usual in English evangelicalism. Such campaigns were held in the Rhondda Valley, in Carmarthen, Llanelli and even in ML-J's former church at Sandfields, Aberavon. As some of the young student leaders came into touch with ML-J they noted a difference in his outlook. In the words of Gwyn Walters, the first IVF travelling secretary in Wales,

> We understood that he had some antipathy to evangelistic campaigns — without quite understanding on what grounds. Dr Martyn was warm toward us, and expressed interest in what was happening in the Welsh Christian Unions, but we didn't discuss the campaigns. His encouragement of us as students, however, was significant, especially the exhortation to ground ourselves in the Scriptures and in the foundational doctrines of the faith, and to depend not on ourselves but on the Spirit of God.

A first change in ML-J's practice came when he shared with Gwyn Walters in a mission in the Evangelical Union of Bangor University College, North Wales, January 23–26, 1949. The customary appeals for immediate public profession of Christ were missing, but an unusual sense of conviction of sin was present in crowded meetings, and numbers came to speak with him. He recalled: 'All sorts of men came to see me. They did not know where they stood or what they believed, and they included theological students.'

Some of the Bangor students now started a new magazine, *Y Cylchgrawn Efengylaidd* (*The Evangelical Magazine*), and from a concern to reach fellow countrymen, they hired a tent at the National Eisteddfod held in August 1949 at Dolgellau. ML-J supported this endeavour by speaking for them during that event. More significantly, after resuming his ministry at Westminster in September he returned to Wales for a first Welsh IVF Conference, held from September 19 to 21, 1949. Some sixty Welsh students assembled at Pantyfedwen hostel in the seaside village of Borth, outside Aberystwyth, for this three-day Conference where the three main addresses were given by ML-J on 'The Biblical Doctrine of Man'.

Wynford Davies, the student chairman of the conference, remembered how ML-J first 'demolished' wrong views of man and of the biblical teaching, and then gave 'a very strong and powerful biblical exposition of the whole doctrine'. He further commented on how, although there had been marked growth in the Evangelical Unions, with many conversions since 1945, such teaching was very new to many who were present:

> By and large there was no doctrinal understanding of the whole way of salvation and of God's grace as we understand it, especially

from a Reformed perspective. I remember at the end of the first day, when he had been dealing very much with the opposite views, several of the new converts, especially the girls, were not too sure of this. But then the second day, when he moved on and began positively to expound the Scripture, many people came to me and said what a tremendous feast it had been and how they had really begun to see in a completely new way. And what amazed me about the Doctor was that, though the conference was so small, he spoke with such conviction and passion as he would have done, I guess, at Westminster Chapel on an ordinary Sunday. His mind never seemed to tire. It was a remarkable conference. At the end I took the Doctor to the station to see him off. He said how much he had enjoyed it and added, 'I hope that you will keep these conferences moving in this direction especially for the benefit of the theological students.' He went on to say how in the English scene there had always been an aversion to doctrinal study.

This conference, and what was to follow, shaped Inter-Varsity thought in Wales for the next decade. Meanwhile, in England, there was a change of still wider significance. To trace the precise means by which it took place would be to deny its real nature. As every true work of God, the origins were quiet and mysterious. A hunger for a more biblical and doctrinal Christianity was occurring in a number of places simultaneously and in more than one country. In so far as any one instrumentality was involved, it was the prayers of Christian people, many of whom died before they ever saw the tide turn. Some of these people belonged to the few small British denominations which remained orthodox, yet it is clear that the resurgence of Calvinistic belief owed little to these denominations as such. The change was first in evidence among university students, and in this no one was more closely involved than ML-J. In the words of Dr Oliver Barclay of the Inter-Varsity Fellowship, 'He had enormous influence. He taught a whole generation of Christian Union students to love doctrine and to be bold in declaring it.'

Undergraduates at Oxford were early involved and were among the first of a younger generation of men in England who were to understand the theological reasons why ML-J's preaching was not in the mainstream of contemporary evangelicalism. One of the leaders among this group was Raymond Johnston of Queen's College who returned to Oxford from the IVF Annual Swanwick Conference of

1947 enthusing about the addresses he had heard from ML-J. The next year Johnston and another student, Bernard Gee, were to cycle across France to be present at the IFES Conference at Lausanne.

James I. Packer was a friend of Johnston's who had become a Christian soon after he had won a place at Corpus Christi in 1944. He first heard ML-J speak at the Theological Students Fellowship Conference at St Hugh's College, Oxford, in December 1946. Of that first meeting he has written:

> He struck me as grim and austere, but vastly impressive, with his magisterial mind and intense seriousness. I intercepted him, I remember, and asked him a question — I can't recall it for sure, though I know I thought it rather intelligent, but he was very short with me. His answer — worth noting, it was so typical, even if the question is gone beyond recall was this: 'Yes, that's to keep us humble.'

In what order these Oxford students began to read the Puritans cannot now be precisely determined. In Jim Packer's case his interest was awakened through the pages of an old set of John Owen which had been donated to the OICCU Library. Elizabeth Lloyd-Jones was at Oxford during this period and ML-J recalls the day when she introduced Bernard Gee to him when he called and stayed for tea at their home in Ealing. As they sat down to tea, ML-J says:

> I put him to sit at the table facing my bookcase — bottom row, John Owen, next row, Richard Baxter, and so on. I could see him looking at all this. In the end I said, 'Are you interested in these books?' He replied, 'What are they?' I said, 'They are Puritan authors.' 'What are they? I have never heard of them.' So I talked to him for quite a long time and opened the books and told him about them.

Before the end of 1947, Packer has recorded, Elizabeth Lloyd-Jones, he, and others 'belonged to a group who used to eat cheap food together in British Restaurants[1] and talked about revival; also about Calvin, Owen, the Welsh evangelical heritage and the Puritans.' Raymond Johnston seems to have been the first to put pen to paper and to give notice that a new note was soon to be heard in evangelical literature. The IVF magazine for the summer term

[1] Cafés provided by the government to supply cheap food. Food rationing continued in the immediate post-war years.

of 1948 carried an article by him entitled 'John Owen: A Puritan Vice-Chancellor'.

Both Johnston and Packer exchanged Oxford for London in 1948 and became regular attenders at Westminster Chapel. Packer, tutoring at Oak Hill College, could only be present on Sunday evenings, about which he writes:

> I was able to hear Dr Lloyd-Jones preach his way through Matthew 11. I had never heard such preaching and was electrified. I can remember at least the thrust of most of the messages still . . . All that I know about preaching I can honestly say — indeed, have often said — I learned from the Doctor by example that winter.[2]

Johnston and Packer were able to remain in London for only a year but not before a significant step had been taken. They both went to ML-J's vestry one Sunday to propose to him the holding of a 'Puritan Conference'. His response was enthusiastic; it could be hosted at the Chapel and some of the church ladies would help with the catering. An announcement appeared in the June 1950 issue of the IVF magazine, the *Christian Graduate*. The September issue of the same magazine carried an article by J. I. Packer on 'The Doctrinal Puritans and their Work'. He contrasted the Puritans' thorough treatment of Christian experience with 'an endemic subjectivity in much modern teaching on the Christian life'. The article concluded with a low-keyed postscript drawing attention to a conference to be held at Westminster Chapel, December 19–20, 1950, under the general title, 'The distinctive theological contribution of the English Puritans'.

The only speaker announced for the Puritan Conference was 'the Rev. Dr D. Martyn Lloyd-Jones'. The remaining speakers for the six sessions, spread over two days, were either students or recent graduates. The plan, to be followed for many years to come, was for each session to be opened by a speaker dealing with a Puritan author or with some aspect of Puritan teaching, followed by an approximately equal period of discussion. As well as making a large contribution (in terms of prepared addresses) at the first conference, Jim Packer became responsible for its arrangements in conjunction with ML-J who was to chair all the sessions. Recalling the small beginning of 1950, Packer has written:

[2] Letter to the author, May 21, 1981.

I simply wanted to share what my own reading had taught me, and was quite happy with the 20 or so folk who came on that first occasion. The Doctor, however, with whom as conference organiser I was now conversing for the first time, made no secret of his belief that what we were doing was of great potential importance for the church: which struck me, for really I had never thought of it that way.

At this first Conference ML-J spoke on 'Puritan Preaching'. The younger men taking part did so with all the enthusiasm of those who were possessed with a great discovery. They had no more idea of the encouragement they were bringing to the chairman than they had of the fact that the second day of the Conference marked his fiftieth birthday. He was not interested in seeing numbers. His concern was to reach men who would be future pastors and teachers of others. Accordingly when two young ladies attended the sessions of this third conference he was not wholly approving. 'They don't come to study the Puritans,' he said to Packer, 'they're only here for the men! I know one of them; she's a member of my church.' 'Well, Doctor,' the Conference organiser replied, 'as a matter of fact, I'm going to marry her' (Kit Mullett had accepted his proposal the night before). 'Without batting an eyelid,' Packer recalls, 'he said, "Well then, you see I was right about one of them; now what about the other?"' The humour intended in this repartee was probably only visible in his eyes.

At this date ML-J was giving much time to the strengthening of doctrinal commitment within the IVF. As well as continuing to speak at student and Theological Students Fellowship conferences, for four years he chaired a Summer School of the Graduates Fellowship, which met at Tyndale House, Cambridge. These Summer Schools brought together some of the ablest men and speakers, including Cornelius Van Til from Westminster Seminary in 1950 when the subject for a five-day conference was, 'Recent Theological Trends in the Light of Holy Scripture'. Marcus L. Loane (a future Archbishop of Sydney) who was present, says of ML-J, 'His mind was as sharp as a gimlet and he managed every session with very clear and acute thinking.'

In the following years the subjects at the Cambridge Summer Schools were, 'Justification by Faith' (1951), 'The Principles and Practice of Biblical Interpretation' (1952), and 'The Plan of Salvation' (1953). The last of these subjects (which ML-J had not chosen) was bound to lead to controversy, not least because one address by John Murray of Westminster Seminary was on definite (as opposed to universal) redemption. The subject was a bombshell to many and it seems there was no senior man present who was prepared to support John Murray on the extent of the atonement except ML-J. This he did with such effect that one speaker from the other side protested with some heat, 'I am not going to be ruled by your logic.' ML-J recalled that Jim Packer was present but silent in this exchange, perhaps not yet convinced of the error of Richard Baxter's belief in a universal atonement. That was not to remain the younger man's position as ML-J later remembered:

> I will never forget one morning when the Puritan Conference was due to start. Packer came rushing up to me and said, 'I am now a complete Calvinist, Doctor!' He had finished with Baxter and turned to Owen.[3] At first I alone was contending for limited atonement.

Meanwhile an awakening to the doctrines of grace was proceeding in Wales. For two more consecutive years after the first IVF Conference there in 1949, 'Dr Martyn' — as he was affectionately known in Wales — remained the main speaker. In 1950 the second conference, held in the Easter vacation at Cilgwyn Conference Centre, Newcastle Emlyn, the subject given to him was 'The Doctrine of the Holy Spirit'. In these addresses he carried forward what he had given the students the previous year on man's state in sin. For a number present the knowledge that conversion begins, not with man's decision to repent and believe, but with the power of God in the imparting of a new nature, was a shock. Some questioned whether they were converted at all. Others were upset and disturbed. One future minister's wife, Eluned Rees, came close to breaking off her engagement to John B. E. Thomas (a student at the Theological College in Aberystwyth), when she discovered that he believed this teaching. She was one of the many to whom ML-J gave help in private. Wynford Davies recalls the conference as 'a time of real assurance' when many who had believed in Christ came

---

[3] That is, on this point of doctrine. Packer's thesis on Baxter for his doctoral degree at Oxford, presented in 1954, has been reprinted, 'almost exactly as submitted', *The Redemption & Restoration of Man in the Thought of Richard Baxter* (Vancouver: Regent College Publishing, 2003).

to see how their conversion was due to the effectual work of the Spirit of God.

The third IVF Welsh Conference met in July 1951 at Pantyfedwen, Borth, and 'The Sovereignty of God' was the subject of ML-J's three addresses. The first address was almost wholly taken up with the definition of divine sovereignty and with reasons why an understanding of the doctrine is so important. The sovereignty of God means that all that exists and happens does so because he wills it. Sovereignty is not to be considered as an attribute of God — in the sense of being a quality which exists in God (such as omnipotence and omniscience). He acts sovereignly because of who and what he is, *God is God*. To assert divine sovereignty is to assert the supremacy of God.

By way of introduction, he then proceeded to the question, 'Why do we hear so little of this doctrine today? Why are sermons or articles on the subject so rare?' He believed that there were two main reasons:

First: *All* doctrine is at a discount today, both outside and inside the church. This doctrine particularly is disliked because of its implications to man. In his pride he has no wish to hear that God 'sitteth upon the circle of the earth, and the inhabitants thereof are as grasshoppers' (*Isa.* 40:22). Therefore, men represent this truth as unfair and unjust.

Second: Human philosophy militates against this doctrine. Men start with their own ideas and thoughts and do not like the sovereignty of God. But the truth is that only as God graciously reveals himself can he be known: 'Canst thou by searching find out God?' (*Job* 11:7); 'The world by wisdom knew not God' (*1 Cor.* 1:21). Philosophy is the greatest enemy of Christian truth.

He then proceeded to ask further, 'Why is divine sovereignty heard so little even among *evangelicals?'* The answer, he believed, was that in their anxiety to present salvation in terms of the person and work of Christ, evangelicals had become unbalanced and tended to forget God the Father. There was a danger of 'Jesusology'. The worship of God as three Persons must always be remembered. In particular, the emphasis, 'I believe in God the Father almighty, Maker of heaven and earth', needed to be restored — not simply God the Saviour, but before that, God the Creator. He pointed out that modern hymns and choruses had encouraged the tendency which he criticized, a tendency which had reached a point at which evangelicals would rather have talks on 'Personal Work' than on the character of God.

In his second address ML-J proceeded to a lengthy exposition of the testimony of Scripture concerning divine sovereignty. All these addresses, it should be said, can hardly have been less than an hour's duration in their delivery. He started with the sovereignty of God in creation. In his self-sufficiency and self-existence God created all things because he chose to do so; nothing existed to persuade him to do so. He was unaided and unadvised. Nothing in nature happens outside the control of God. ML-J then went on to divine sovereignty in the fall and sin of man, with all the world's resultant disorder, disharmony, strife and bloodshed. 'Why God allowed the Fall and entry of sin to the world, why he permitted angels of light to rebel, I do not know. I do not understand. The mind of God is so great and eternal that I cannot understand (even if there were no sin in me, which there is). But by permitting it, and then doing what he has done, the manifestation of his sovereignty is the greater.'

There followed an extended treatment of many passages in Old and New Testament history — all showing that 'the Lord reigneth' (*Psa.* 93), and that he acts against all mighty powers which oppose him, manifesting his sovereignty both in the appointment of all times and seasons as well as in the details of individual lives. The beginning and the end are all determined by God. After showing from the books of Esther, Isaiah, Judges and Psalms that what is called 'secular' history is controlled by God — even sin and the Devil himself — he began, in a general way, to deal with the sovereignty of God in the new creation, beginning with Abel, Abraham, and Jacob, and proceeding to the manner of the gospel's first coming to Europe (*Acts* 16).

With his time more than exhausted, he broke off from this marshalling of scriptural evidence, and pointed to the same lesson in the history of the post-New Testament church, and in her revivals at times when God had permitted her life to become almost dead. 'God lets the church become moribund. The sceptics and scoffers say, "Where is your God?" Then revival comes. I defy you to say that it is anything but the sovereignty of God. In the last century men worshipped preachers, so God withdrew them and you get the position we have today.'

In the light of such truth, he concluded, it is not only sad but sinful for the Christian to feel despondent. 'This is the victory that overcometh the world, even our faith' (*1 John* 5:5).

On the afternoon of the last day, the whole conference went in two crowded coaches to Llangeitho, the scene of the ministry of Daniel Rowland. Here ML-J led all the young people in a tour of places connected with Rowland: first to the old parish church, scene of Rowland's ministry before his ejection from the Church of England and where his Bible was still to be found; then to the natural amphitheatre where the great open-air communion services were held; and finally to the Calvinistic Methodist Chapel, where Rowland had continued his ministry (and where ML-J himself had attended as a boy). Here everyone sat down and heard ML-J give an impromptu address on the beginning of the eighteenth-century revival in Wales and on Rowland's subsequent fifty years of ministry in Llangeitho. The setting and the message of Llangeitho's history, following as they did upon the expositions already given at Borth, made the afternoon one of the most memorable events of a lifetime for numbers there. In Geraint Fielder's words, 'A lot of young minds and hearts were opened that day to the value and meaning of church history.'

Dr Lloyd-Jones' third address followed that evening. As he came to the question, How do people become citizens of the kingdom of God?, he warned against approaching it in a spirit of dispute. The question can only be approached aright in a higher spirit. He then proceeded to the truth that every part of salvation is all of grace and that the sovereign work of God in salvation is in order to the manifestation of his own glory. In the first instance, he affirmed, the whole plan of salvation demonstrates the sovereignty of God. Why is the sin of Adam imputed to all his descendants? Why was Adam made the representative of the whole human race? 'I answer, God so decided. It was all in the will of God. Why had Christ to die? It was because it was the Father's will. Why is the righteousness of God imputed to all believers? The only reason is that God decreed that it should be so. There is nothing in the world, nor in man, which dictated this. God alone is the reason.'

Divine sovereignty as it concerns individuals shows that salvation is altogether of grace. The sovereign will of God has chosen certain

26. *The IVF Welsh Conference at Borth, 1951.*

people to salvation. This is not a truth, he stressed, for unbelievers but for those who are already believers. He then put to them a series of verses 'to study later', namely, Acts 13:48 ('as many as were ordained to eternal life believed'); Romans 11:5, 6; 1 Corinthians 1:26-29; Ephesians 1:3-5; 2 Thessalonians 2:13; 2 Timothy 1:9; 1 Peter 1:2; Romans 8:28, 29 and 9:1-24; and Matthew 11:25, 26.

The meaning of these verses, he argued, is confirmed by other negative statements: no man can save himself, he must be reborn (*John* 3:3); no man can come to Christ 'except the Father draw him' (*John* 6:44 and *Matt.* 16:17); no carnal mind can be 'subject to the law of God' (*Rom.* 8:7); no natural man can 'receive the things of the Spirit of God' (*1 Cor.* 2:14), etc. Such negatives complement the affirmatives.

He proceeded to deal with possible objections. 'Does the Scripture not say, *"Whosoever* believeth in him shall be saved"? and "Him that cometh unto me . . ."' The whole question, he replied, is this: 'What is it that makes a man believe? What makes a man come to Christ? What determines the "whosoever"?'

> The argument is foolish and fatuous that says, 'A believes and is, *therefore,* chosen of God', and 'B does not believe and is, therefore, not chosen'. Why does A choose to believe? What makes him believe? What makes B not believe? Here are two brothers, they hear the same sermon, the same preacher, in the same chapel, and yet they hear with such different effect. If it is not God who makes the difference, you must say that it is man's constitution, which means that they were born that way. You have thus handed yourself over to the psychologists. They say that some people are made religious and some are not. What can be more unfair than that? No, the difference is the result of his sovereign will.

In his final words he returned again to the manner in which this doctrine affects the believer's life and assurance. Repeating Romans 9:20, he insisted on the necessity of humility: 'There are certain questions which we should not ask. To ask them is unbelief and an insult to God. No doctrine so glorifies God and so humbles man as this. Boasting is excluded. We were lost and would be still but for this. Only divine sovereignty makes salvation certain.'

These addresses had a profound effect and some had few hours' sleep in the night which followed. Geraint Morgan says:

On the last evening of the conference I came under a tremendous conviction of sin, and joining the queue to see Dr Martyn, I reached him at just after midnight. In that conference I yielded gladly my Arminian views and came to rejoice in the doctrines of sovereign grace. That conference gave me an anchor.

Derek Swann, also a student for the ministry, writes:

When Dr Lloyd-Jones spoke on the sovereignty of God, many of us came to the doctrines of grace for the first time, myself included. I accepted everything in the first two talks and had eventually to accept them in the third. I remember it was early in the morning in conversation with Gwyn Walters that the truth of election dawned on me. I was so overcome with the wonder of it all that I had to fight back the tears. For many of us since, election has been an affair of the heart as well as the head.[4]

Gwilym Roberts, yet another future minister of the gospel who was present, and shortly to be the IVF's Welsh travelling secretary, says of the addresses on divine sovereignty:

I cannot express in writing what a tremendous impact these addresses made on the vast majority of those present at the Welsh IVF Conference in 1951. It changed our thinking about God (and, therefore, about man, salvation, evangelism and so on!). We were *prepared* for such things as the Graham Harringay meetings, etc. We saw where they fell short of the scriptural pattern because the Doctor had grounded us so firmly in the truth of God's sovereignty and all its implications.

* * *

Although Douglas Johnson believed that the 1951 series at Borth was the best he ever heard him give at any student conference, Lloyd-Jones was emphatic to the student leaders, as the conference ended, that he would not be coming the following year. The year 1951 was his last IVF conference in Wales. Wynford Davies recalls him saying: 'I think you are fairly launched. The time has come now that you can move ahead on your own.' This decision has the same explanation as

[4] *Excuse Me, Mr Davies — Hallelujah! Evangelical Student Witness in Wales 1923–1983* (Bridgend: Evangelical Press of Wales and IVF, 1983), p. 157.

his decision to stop leading the Tyndale House summer conferences after 1953. He was conscious of the extent of his influence in the IVF work. A new theological perspective had dawned and, where it would all lead he did not know, but an attachment to his person could all too easily become unhealthy. He often remarked on the injurious consequences of the cult following of some of the great nineteenth-century preachers. He believed passionately that the elevation of men — whoever they be — is a snare and ultimately injurious to spiritual prosperity. It was a practical application of his Calvinism which led him to want to stand aside. The opinion of a later critic that ML-J had 'a great need to be *in control*' was wide of the mark.[5] He was happy to see young men such as Jim Packer, Raymond Johnston and others come to the fore in the doctrinal recovery.

His approach to the developing situation was also one which sought, as far as possible, to avoid controversy. When Raymond Johnston wrote to him of difficulties he was encountering in the Graduates Fellowship of the IVF, particularly over the Keswick view of sanctification, ML-J replied:

> I feel that Mr Packer and yourself are doing most important work which may well have a great influence in the future. But you must both learn to 'walk circumspectly'. I mean by this that there is a danger of their dismissing your teaching because of the manner in which it is presented. We must be patient and teach these people in a constructive manner. I write as one who has found it very difficult himself to learn this lesson, but as the years pass I have come to see more and more that the difficulty on the other side is really due to ignorance.[6]

This ignorance over the real meaning of Calvinistic belief was not surprising. It was the result of long years in which pulpits, even in the Calvinistic Methodist denomination, had been silent on the subject and when publishers had virtually set aside all literature in that tradition. The label 'Calvinist' (or its variant 'Reformed') had no clear meaning attached to it and was often used in a pejorative sense. ML-J seldom used either term himself, nor was he interested

---

[5] *Engaging with Martyn Lloyd-Jones: The Life and Legacy of the 'Doctor'*, eds. Andrew Atherstone and David Ceri Jones (Nottingham: IVP, 2011), p. 26.

[6] D. *Martyn Lloyd-Jones, Letters 1919-1981*, (Edinburgh: Banner of Truth, 1994), p. 130.

to see any revival of their use. Further, he was opposed to making the theology which he believed to be true Calvinism a requirement for fellowship among Christians. For an 'orthodoxy' which prided itself on its exclusiveness he had not the slightest sympathy. He knew that a Christian, dependent upon the death of Christ alone for salvation and trusting the Word of God, may have a very limited understanding of how God's grace came to him: 'What an impudence it is', he says in one place, 'for any of us to expel or withdraw from a fellow sinner saved by the same grace because we believe that his deductions about how grace works are defective as compared with our own deductions.'

That statement, however, he rejected when used as an excuse for not seeking a better understanding of Scripture, and he forcefully answers the question, 'If we are not saved by our understanding of these matters, why bother with them?' 'We "bother" to use the term because the Scripture has a great deal to say on the subject. I know of nothing that is so strengthening to faith, nothing which so builds up my assurance, nothing which gives me such certainty about the blessed hope for which I am destined, as the understanding of Christian doctrine, the understanding of the way, yes, the mechanism of salvation.'[7]

A restoration of the standpoint which is called Calvinistic was a fundamental because it was biblical; because it shows how the gospel begins not with man and his happiness but with God and his glory. 'In our churches we have lost this sense of the importance of the glory of God, even in those claiming to be evangelical. But the Bible is concerned for the glory of God and then, after that, for the good of man.' For this reason it meant much to ML-J when in 1949 the publishers James Clarke and Co. listened to his plea for a re-issue of Calvin's *Institutes of the Christian Religion,* and used his copy of the Beveridge edition for their photoprinting. A few years earlier Dr Lloyd-Jones had summarized Calvin's belief, and his own, in these words:

> Calvin's main feature is that he bases everything on the Bible . . .
> he does not wish for any philosophy apart from that which eman-
> ates from the Scripture. It is in the *Institutes* that one gets biblical

---

[7] *God the Holy Spirit, Great Doctrines of the Bible,* vol. 2 (Wheaton: Crossway, 1997), p. 58. His late-night discussion of the subject with Bethan, p. 62, is an interesting piece of autobiography.

theology for the first time, rather than dogmatic theology . . . For him the great central and all-important truth was the sovereignty of God and God's glory. We must start here and everything else issues from here. It was God, of his own free will and according to his infinite wisdom, who created the world. But sin entered and if it were not for God's grace, there would be no hope for the world.

Man is a fallen creature, with his mind in a state of enmity towards God. He is totally unable to save himself and to reunite himself with God. Everyone would be lost if God had not elected some for salvation and that unconditionally. It is only through Christ's death that it is possible for these people to be saved, and they would not see or accept that salvation if God through his irresistible grace in the Holy Spirit had not opened their eyes and persuaded them (not forced them) to accept the offer. And even after that, it is God who sustains them and keeps them from falling. Their salvation, therefore, is sure because it depends, not on them and their ability, but on God's grace. The church is a collection of the elect.[8]

This faith which put God first was, he believed, 'the iron rations of the soul'. It enables men and women to stand alone, to be ready to die for the truth of God if need be. He would continue to need that faith in the days ahead.

---

[8] *Knowing the Times*, p. 35.

TWENTY-TWO

Sundays in the 1950s

There was such a degree of similarity about the work at West-minster Chapel that any strictly chronological description of successive years is unnecessary. I intend rather, in this chapter, to give some account of what it meant to be there on Sundays in the 1950s.

The keenness with which 11 A.M., the hour of public worship, was awaited each Sunday will ever remain in the memories of those who were there. In a day in which church-going was no longer fashion-able, a certain sense of expectation could be found in the very streets approaching the Chapel as hundreds converged from all directions. A minority came by car, some on foot and others by bus to Victoria Street. Most travelled from various parts of London by the under-ground which they left either at Victoria Station or, more usually, at St James' Park where a general exodus from the tube brought a temporary congestion to the two-hundred yards of pavement in Petty France, the road which leads to the Chapel.

A comparatively small number of people met for prayer at the Chapel at 10.15 A.M. Dr Lloyd-Jones himself usually arrived around 10.30 and spent the time remaining before the service in his vestry. He would seldom have more than five minutes on his own. Deacons, and others closer to him, generally took advantage of speaking with him at this time before many others later in the day would seek to do the same. In an emergency he might see a member of the congre-gation about some pressing problem at this hour but not normally.

One invariable caller at the vestry door was the organist. He had received the hymns from ML-J by phone the previous day, but there was now a final check on the tunes. Bethan Lloyd-Jones would also call briefly shortly before the service. At no more than five minutes to the hour of service the deacon on duty at the vestry door would see if the minister was ready and then all the deacons would crowd into the comparatively small room. The purpose of this meeting was for a short prayer but if anything urgent required attention there could also be some short conversation. There was always one particular feature present in the atmosphere in the vestry immediately before services, namely, the remarkable absence of any sense of tension. When a new-comer joined that circle it was the sense of calmness, emanating from the minister which he was most likely to observe first.

Behind the vestry wall, in the church itself, it was different as stewards hurried or pointed people to vacant seats, the front seats on the ground floor always being the last to start filling up. In the pew rack before him a worshipper would find a Bible, a hymn book *(Congregational Praise[1])* and a brief card. The card gave the times of service and other regular meetings and indicated Dr Lloyd-Jones' willingness to speak with anyone at the conclusion of services. These arrangements varied so little that the same cards lasted many months. There were no printed service sheets — in part for the very good reason that hymns and sermons were never finalized before the preceding day.

For visitors two things, particularly, were usually striking about the gathering congregation. The first was its diversity and cosmopolitan character. There were parents and children, young people and students (whose appearance denoted many different countries of origin), professional people and others whose appearance gave no hint of their occupation. While the percentage of older people was probably lower than in a normal city congregation, the ratio of men to women was definitely higher. In a sense there were two congregations present, the actual church members, and probably a larger number — including the sizeable student body — who for one reason or another never joined the church. A considerable proportion consequently did not know one another, and there would have

[1] First published in 1951, it was a considerable improvement on the *Congregational Hymnary* of 1916; a number of older hymns were restored and a selection from the Metrical Psalter included.

been many surprises if they had. These were days when strangers did not commonly greet one another in church, and often one could only wonder at the identity of neighbours. Perhaps that middle-aged single lady, for instance, was a hairdresser, a member of hotel staff, a keeper of the Queen's linen at Buckingham Palace, a missionary on furlough, a hospital sister, a buyer at one of the large department stores or even a land-owner in town for the day. Of all the professions the medical was probably the most largely represented. Its personnel ranged from student nurses to a few of London's top surgeons and physicians, with a large group of medical students from Bart's, Guy's, the London and other famous teaching hospitals.

But to conclude from this diversity that the congregation lacked all homogeneity and was only a mass of individuals would be entirely wrong. Along with the diversity there was a second feature equally observable. It was the unity of spirit and purpose, already mentioned, which was becoming apparent even as people approached the building. While the numbers were impressive, much more so was the evident spirit of eager anticipation which gave unity to the whole gathered assembly. Yet this animation bore no resemblance to the bustle and excitement of people awaiting a concert performance. The spirit was subdued as the organist began a quiet voluntary some ten minutes before 11 A.M. There was, therefore, no sudden hush as the deacons first emerged from behind the rostrum to take their places in the congregation and Dr Lloyd-Jones, having climbed the stairs at the back of the rostrum, crossed the six or seven paces to the pulpit desk where he would immediately slide the large and heavy pulpit Bible from its central position to the left in order to give himself room to lean his forearms on the desk as he bowed his head momentarily in prayer. In black gown (without hood) he looked small and slight in the large auditorium. A note from the organ then brought the whole congregation to its feet for the unannounced singing of the doxology, 'Praise God from whom all blessings flow'. This was immediately followed by the minister's opening words, 'Let us pray', as the people resumed their seats. It was a short prayer, addressed to God the Father, usually begun with thanksgiving and always concluded with the repetition of the Lord's Prayer. It led naturally into the first hymn — a burst of song which late-comers could readily hear as they neared the building. Undoubtedly ML-J had his own favourite opening hymns, none more so than Isaac Watts',

> How pleased and blest was I
> To hear the people cry
> Come, let us seek our God today!

The opening hymns were strong in their objective statements about God. To avoid a too-frequent use of any great hymn he kept a careful record of each Sunday's hymn numbers, minutely written on a sheet of paper which he could see at a glance. To the choice of hymns he always gave much care and they were chosen with reference to the unity of the service as a whole. The theme of the first hymn was one of praise, or very occasionally, of invocation (James Montgomery's, 'Command Thy blessing from above, O God, on all assembled here', being another favourite). There was nothing in the way of a leader of the singing. In so far as anyone led he did, not by voice (for his singing of the bass part could be heard only over the loudspeaker relaying the service to the vestibules and the rear halls) but by example. During all worship his whole being was a study of concentration; he never used times of singing as an opportunity to look round the congregation or to look at notes. Unlike one or two of his predecessors, if there were celebrities in the congregation he neither knew nor cared. He was there to worship God and did not raise his eyes from his hymn book. The idea that the minister should smile benignly at the people, or make them 'feel welcome' with some words of social greeting, was foreign to his whole conception of the grandeur of Christian worship. If the church were the minister's home and the people *his* guests, then, he argued, it would be permissible to say, 'Good morning friends; nice to see you, how good of you to come', but he regarded that whole approach as wrong: 'It is not our service; the people do not come there to see us or please us . . . They, and we, are there to worship God, and to meet with God. A minister in a church is not like a man inviting people into his home; he is not in charge here. He is just a servant himself.'[2]

The first hymn was followed by the reading of Scripture, usually from only one passage which was announced clearly and repeated. He read (always himself) at moderate speed, in ordinary tones and with nothing resembling an affected elocution. But inflection of voice always drew sufficient attention to the sense of the words.

[2] *Preaching and Preachers*, p. 263.

The second morning singing was invariably part of a metrical psalm and as there are only sixteen contained in *Congregational Praise* most of them were used more frequently than many hymns. From such words as,

> The Lord doth reign, and clothed is he
> With majesty most bright (*Psa.* 93:1)

or,

> How lovely is thy dwelling-place (*Psa.* 84:1)

the congregation moved on into what many regarded as the high point of the early part of the service, the main prayer. While only one voice was heard, it was unmistakably clear that Dr Lloyd-Jones was praying on the understanding that true public prayer is corporate prayer. He used no singular pronouns, but always the plural, 'We come into thy holy presence and *we* come, O Lord, to worship Thee.' Yet there was not a phrase nor a sentence which each Christian could not regard as his own. The worshipper often forgot the large congregation around him as prayer thus became an individual as well as a corporate dealing with God. In ML-J's actual petitions there was often the blending of two seemingly diverse elements. There was both consciousness of sin *and* a thankfulness for what God is. Not one, or the other, but both. If the minister appeared to speak boldly with God it was clear that the most discouraged Christian in the congregation, or even one who was no Christian at all, might do the same, provided he came in the same way:

> We come in the name of thy dear Son. We recognize we have nothing else to plead, we have nothing which we can present before thee . . . O God, we see how poor and sinful and vile we all have become as the result of man's original disobedience and sin and fall, and our own misdeeds and transgressions. We have sinned against thee. We have followed our own wills, been proud of ourselves, of what we are, not even recognizing that what we are was the result of thy gracious gifts to us . . . So we come and we plead only the name and the blood of thy dear Son, and we do thank thee that in him we know that we have this access.

It was not unknown for self-satisfied listeners to meet with conviction when hearing such prayer, while those who came with heavy and burdened spirits were often wonderfully uplifted. Not infrequently

Christians spoke of being so conscious of God's help to them personally during the prayer that they could have been content to go home
at its conclusion.

One reason that Dr Lloyd-Jones was against liturgies in prayer was
that he believed that true prayer is *given* by God and, therefore, one
must always be free to be led by him at the actual moment of praying.
In the words of A. M. Toplady (often sung at the Chapel) God is the
'Inspirer and hearer of prayer'. ML-J did not prepare prayers (though
he sought to prepare himself) and no two prayers were ever identical in thought and expression, notwithstanding general similarities.[3]
In length the main prayer was around ten minutes. We never heard
it commended for 'eloquence' or criticized either for verging on
preaching or for being too long. It was prayer which left the impression that there is such a thing as first-hand communion with God.

Dr Lloyd-Jones' language in prayer was natural and unadorned.
Although he had such large command of both Scripture and hym-
nology, he did not regard quotation as appropriate in prayer. If
occasionally a quotation was introduced, it was used as a plea to God
or as a profession of trust in him. He might, for instance, when confessing the magnitude of our needs, repeat with much feeling the
words of Oswald Allen,

> When all things seem against us
> To drive us to despair,
> We know one gate is open,
> One ear will hear our prayer.[4]

As much as half of the long prayer was generally taken up with
intercession, in which there was usually a similar pattern in the order
of the petitions and a greater identity of phraseology than at other
times. 'The aged and infirm', those on 'beds of pain' and other groups
were represented by the same terms week by week. Yet in the matter
of intercession Dr Lloyd-Jones also believed in the possibility of the
direct guidance of the Holy Spirit. One remarkable example of this

[3] 'You cannot pray to order . . . I have found nothing more important than to
learn how to get oneself into that frame and condition in which one can pray.'
Preaching and Preachers, p. 170.
[4] From the hymn 'Today Thy mercy calls us', No. 684 in the revised edition of
The Church Hymnary (the hymn-book to which ML-J was accustomed in Wales, and
used by Presbyterian churches throughout the British Empire).

concerned a Welshman who, having professed Christ, had later ruined his life and family. He ended up destitute in London, deserted by the woman who had taken the place of his wife, until finally a Sunday came when he solemnly decided to end his life by throwing himself into the Thames from Westminster Bridge. Such was his feeling of utter hopelessness. But when he arrived at the bridge the striking of 'Big Ben' suddenly reminded him that it was the hour of public worship and there and then he decided to go and hear Dr Lloyd-Jones again before he ended his life. Six minutes' walk took him to the Chapel which he reached as ML-J was leading the congregation in prayer. The very first words which he heard as he walked up the stairs and was about to enter the gallery were, 'God have mercy upon the backslider.' It was not a customary petition in that prayer. The man was restored in that very service and lived a consistent Christian life for a number of years before a triumphant death.

One testimony to Dr Lloyd-Jones' pulpit prayer comes from Emmi Müller, a German, who as a young Christian came to study at the London Bible College in the early 1950s. With the Second World War still a vivid memory, Müller was to encounter much prejudice and coldness even from fellow Christians. Still feeling very much a foreigner and an outsider, she came to Westminster Chapel and has described how it became a spiritual home:

> In the beginning there was of course the language problem. For someone not yet fluent in English the sermons as well as the prayers were rather long. But this very difficulty made me all the more aware of the spiritual atmosphere in the services. The spirit of worship and prayer, the eagerness on the part of the congregation to listen, to receive God's message through his servant were a great blessing. I was very much aware of the Lord's presence in the services. What in the beginning was trying, in the long run proved to be a special blessing to me personally, namely the pastoral prayer, which lasted longer than in most churches. As a foreigner the Doctor's pastoral prayer in particular made me feel included and truly part of the congregation because it usually embraced more than just Westminster Chapel and Britain.

The main prayer was followed by the only pause in the service. First the Church Secretary, Arthur E. Marsh, still in the frock coat and Edwardian dress of his pre-1914 years at Westminster, mounted the rostrum and, after clearing his throat, as he had done for fifty years, gave the barest minimum of announcements.[5] Notices of any special kind, or invitation to the communion (which followed the main service twice a month — once in the morning and once in the evening) would be given by the minister himself. The collection was then taken up by deacons and brought forward to the communion table, Dr Lloyd-Jones employing these few minutes to glance over his sermon notes. After a brief offertory prayer, when the deacons who had brought the plates forward stood at the communion table on the lower rostrum, the third hymn followed, its theme looking forward to the sermon either by invocation of the aid of God or by the relation of its subject matter to the subject about to be introduced. At close on thirty-five minutes after the commencement of the service Dr Lloyd-Jones would begin to preach. No title was announced beforehand and the opening sentence had liturgical uniformity, 'The words to which I should like to draw your attention this morning are to be found in . . .' and there followed a clear and emphatic announcement of the text upon which he intended to preach.

Through the Sunday mornings of the 1950s Dr Lloyd-Jones preached in consecutive series. The only exceptions to this procedure were the holiday periods when a number of regular hearers were likely to be away. On Sunday morning, June 4, 1950 he preached the last of a series on 1 John.[6] A short series of six sermons on Habakkuk then followed and was concluded by the time of his summer break. On October 1, 1950 he began the Sermon on the Mount (*Matt.* 5-7) and this was to continue, apart from the breaks mentioned above, until April 6, 1952. The next passage for exposition was John 17 (May 4, 1952 – July 19, 1953). Eleven sermons on Psalm 73 occupied the autumn Sunday mornings of 1953, and these were followed by a series on Spiritual Depression begun on January 10, 1954 and concluded on July 18, 1954. After the usual summer break, he preached on the first verse of Ephesians chapter one on October 10, 1954. A further 260 sermons on Ephesians were to follow until this major Sunday morning

---

[5] A. E. Marsh was 'Secretary of Westminster Chapel' from 1907 to 1961, dying at an unstated age the following year (*WR*, Dec., 1962, p. 183).

[6] There were 67 sermons in this series. Numbers were not announced and although the sermons were consecutive it was important to ML-J that each one should be complete in itself. Published as *Life in Christ* (Wheaton, IL.: Crossway, 2002).

expository series of his ministry finally concluded on July 1, 1962. He was prepared to interrupt a series for special circumstances, as on the deaths of King George VI and of Fred Mitchell. He preached funeral sermons for both these men and they were both published.[7]

In the 1950s ML-J was virtually alone in England in engaging in what he meant by 'expository preaching'. For preaching to qualify for that designation it was not enough, in his view, that the content be biblical; addresses which concentrated upon word-studies, or which gave running commentary and analyses of whole chapters, might be termed 'biblical', but that is not the same as exposition. To expound is not simply to give the correct grammatical sense of a verse or passage, it is rather to set out the principles or doctrines which the words are intended to convey. True expository preaching is, therefore, *doctrinal* preaching, it is preaching which addresses specific truths from God to man. The expository preacher is not one who 'shares his studies' with others, he is an ambassador and a messenger, authoritatively delivering the Word of God to men. Such preaching presents a text, then, with that text in sight throughout, there is deduction, argument and appeal, the whole making up a message which bears the authority of Scripture itself.

His preaching demanded thought on the part of the hearer, yet it was not preaching from which the more intelligent present could gain the most. He pitched the level of his argument and paced its development in a way which many children present could generally follow. While some critics thought him guilty of repetition, he regarded repetition as essential to good preaching. He knew it was not enough merely to state a truth, one needed to 'walk around in it'. As with all great preaching the message was both profound and simple.

To say this, however, is to leave unsaid the most important part of what he was in the pulpit. In his view, one could possess the natural ability and the understanding of the truth necessary to follow the expository method, and yet still never be a preacher at all. The Holy Spirit must be active in true preaching, active not only in owning the truth as it is heard but active in anointing the preacher himself. Only

[7] For George VI, *Honour to Whom Honour* (The Bookroom of Westminster Chapel, 1952); for Mitchell, in abbreviated form, under the title 'Faith's Reaction' in *The Millions, Journal of the China Inland Mission, Overseas Missionary Fellowship,* July–August 1953.

then is his heart as well as his mind rightly engaged and the result is speech attended by liveliness, by unction and by an extemporaneous element.

As with prayer, this element cannot be produced to order. It has nothing to do with the emotion affected by an actor for effect (a preacher of that type is 'an abominable imposter'). But it is the Holy Spirit so taking hold of the man with the truth of the message, and with love for God and man, that the messenger himself is lost in sympathy with his message and with his hearers: 'Preaching is theology coming through a man who is on fire. A true understanding and experience of the truth must lead to this.'[8] The only right condition for preaching, he believed, was to 'be so absorbed in what you are doing and in the realisation of the presence of God, and in the glory and the greatness of the truth that you are preaching, that you forget yourself completely'.[9]

There have been periods in history when the anointing of the Spirit upon the preacher has tended to be identified with such things as tones of voice, mannerisms, gestures or even mere volume of sound. Dr Lloyd-Jones was careful to warn against a confusion between pulpit style and powerful preaching. He knew that liveliness in preaching will not always take the same form; all he stipulated was that the expression of passion in the pulpit should be natural to the individual. In his own case he always began a sermon quietly and calmly, in the tones of an ordinary conversation. The voice usually rose gradually and quickened as the subject was opened until — as the message gripped speaker and hearer alike — his animation added its own expression and emphasis to the message. There was movement and gesture in such harmony with what was being said that the hearer was scarcely conscious that the two things were not the same. The preacher and the truth became one.

Dr Lloyd-Jones repudiated the deliberate use of oratory as a means to condition or persuade people. At the same time, he knew that no subject was more worthy of true oratory than the Word of God and he believed that the truth needed to be presented in a form which could attract the interest of the non-Christian. Preachers *are* responsible for making people listen. Some who heard him undoubtedly

[8] *Preaching and Preachers*, p. 97.
[9] *Ibid.,* p. 264.

went away impressed only with the outward, and reporters for the religious press were often of this kind. 'For real drama', wrote one religious columnist, 'nobody can beat the Rev. Martyn Lloyd-Jones at Westminster Chapel, Buckingham Gate. Old fashioned Calvinistic preaching at its best.' Others, however, went away moved by the message and not with the way in which it had been delivered. God had used the preacher and they felt like Emmi Müller, already quoted above, who said, 'Time and again coming home from church I went straight to my room, locked my door and went on my knees and prayed.'

The length of the morning sermon was around forty minutes, sometimes less and occasionally more. It was followed immediately by a short prayer and then the final hymn. This hymn he chose with special care, for it had to provide the congregation's response to the message, whether a response of penitence, of trust or of triumphant praise. It came as an 'Amen' to the whole service. The benediction was nearly always introduced with the words of Jude 24, 25, 'Now unto him that is able to keep you from falling . . .' and concluded, 'be with you throughout the remainder of this our short, uncertain, earthly life and pilgrimage, and forevermore.'

A few things more need to be said about these services. The first is the silence which prevailed in the large congregation. The stillness generally deepened as the service proceeded, being undisturbed during the taking up of the collection and even, to a large extent, when the service was over. There were certain arrangements designed to encourage quietness. For the first part of the service ushers always stood at the doors and no one was allowed to enter while prayer or the reading of Scripture was in progress. A crèche was provided for babies and infants. From about the age of three, children were usually in the church for the whole service (usually without colouring books or other things to 'occupy' them), but if they could not be quiet the parent and child were expected to remove speedily to a rear hall where the service could be heard by relay. Any failure to depart could earn an intimidating look from the pulpit! Remarkably, many young children were in the congregation throughout and they grew up believing that public worship was for them as well as for adults. By the age of ten it was not uncommon for some of them to be taking down notes on the sermon. That practice would have been encouraged by parents rather than ML-J. He did not recommend it although numbers of all ages did take notes.

Dr Lloyd-Jones led public worship with an almost total lack of asides and informal comments. Hymns were announced, and calls to prayer were given, in precisely the same language week by week. As we have seen, even the flying bomb that nearly ended the service abruptly in 1944 received virtually no notice from the preacher. Similarly, if some civic dignitary was paying a visit to the Chapel it made no difference to the service. Practically the only occasions when he was provoked to comment during a service were when things occurred which he regarded as intrusions into the true spirit of worship. Thus he might, at times, if he thought a hymn was being wrongly sung, actually stop the people between the verses and warn them that they were singing the tune more than the words. He would not tolerate, for instance, an exuberant and hearty singing of such words as 'False and full of sin I am' in Charles Wesley's, 'Jesus, Lover of my soul'. Neither would he tolerate gloomy and dragging singing.

He did not like audible responses, or words of approval, during a sermon, and if enthusiastic visitors were present, unaware of this fact, they were liable to be informed. On one occasion the sermon had scarcely begun when vociferous 'Amens' were to be heard from a group close to the front of the congregation. When this happened more than once a number of regular attenders were beginning to surmise what the possible outcome would be when the preacher chose his own method. He had gained a temporary silence as he was speaking on man's fallen and ruined condition and, seizing the opportunity, he looked hard at the interrupters and exclaimed, 'I notice that there are no "Amens" now.' There were no more!

There were other times (these generally in an evening service) when he would add a word before the final hymn, or even while the congregation was standing awaiting the benediction after the final hymn. In such moments he might assure any in spiritual trouble that he was very willing to speak with them, or he might add a final plea to the unconverted to go to Christ without delay.[10]

---

[10] Sometimes members of the congregation, unable to wait to see ML-J after the service, would scribble a brief message to be passed to him. A Norwegian visitor once conveyed greetings from a mutual friend in Oslo in this way and added, 'Personally I will say I have been in heaven under this service.'

Some, reading the above account of a service at Westminster Chapel, might suppose that while it fitted with church life of the 1950s its whole concept is remote from the present day. Such thinking is a mistake, for the truth is that this form of service was far from being representative in that particular time. At that date the older views of divine worship were already being widely displaced. Edwin King, who first went to Westminster Chapel in 1946, writes: 'I had become accustomed to the propaganda for change. The emphasis was very much upon let us be bright and breezy, and above all don't let the service last too long, especially the sermon.'

The contrast between Westminster Chapel and the then prevailing church life is clear enough in various newspaper accounts of that decade.

Under the title, 'A stern preacher — but they flock to hear him', Norman Phelps wrote three columns on Dr Martyn Lloyd-Jones in the *Liverpool Daily Post* for June 8, 1954. They included the following:

These big London churches have a continuous tidal wave of floating listeners — visitors from the provinces and the suburbs, strangers dropping in for one service and then perhaps, never seen again, sermon tasters with no steady religious roots — but here I was impressed with the number of families present. They came in — father, mother, daughter, son, and I think, engaged couples on the family perimeter — to their own special seats in that obviously accustomed manner which many of us believed had died with the Victorians.

There was, so far as I could see, no choir, but the congregation did not appear to need one. Philip Doddridge's opening hymn, 'Awake, my soul, stretch every nerve and press with vigour on', set the key to the preacher's soldierly sermon on the loins girt about with truth, the breastplate of righteousness, the helmet of salvation, and the shield of faith. Words flowed in a fluent stream from the preacher's clipped, almost harsh voice as he compared the cults which offered a spurious perfection with Christianity, which was an eternal fight against principalities and powers, and the rulers of darkness.

'As soon as a man becomes a Christian', he cried, 'the powers of evil are immediately deployed against him with suggestions, innuendos, subtle temptations. They are always battling for his soul.'

Only a small minority, I suppose, now believe in the existence of that Satan, but Lloyd-Jones, pointing with upraised hand an invisible sword, putting on with gestures the helmet, the breastplate, the girdle, and the shield, made us conscious of the immense, menacing presence of the dark, unresting forces of evil. We felt they were right there just outside the sanctuary walls in Victoria Street, in all the streets of London and of the world.

Similar observations occur in a *British Weekly* article for March 21, 1957, written by Derek Walker and entitled, 'Westminster Chapel Has a Great Tradition'.

Westminster Chapel is a church which thrives without making any visible effort to achieve success — or so it would seem at first sight. It is well filled every Sunday, morning and evening, although its activities are not widely advertised, and although the form of service makes no concessions to modern tastes . . . It may be that in this very absence of any trace of 'modernity' we have the clue to the well-filled pews in Westminster Chapel. This kind of service, centred on the long, expository sermon, makes an appeal to a certain group within Nonconformity — the conservative evangelicals. These are the people who are drawn to Westminster every Sunday, and their numbers are added to by young people who have been influenced through the London Inter-Faculty Christian Union.

Looking at a typical Sunday morning congregation in Westminster Chapel, it is tempting to reflect that this is what a service in Cromwellian England might have looked like . . . There are only slightly more women than men, and the middle age-groups are well represented. About 16 per cent of the congregation are young people in their late teens and early twenties.

In the mornings, people in their fifties and over make up about 18 per cent of the attendance, but the proportion falls to nearer 10 per cent in the evenings. So, between two-thirds and three-quarters of the congregation are in the 25 to 50 age group.

All powerful preaching has been accused of producing only a temporary emotional effect upon hearers. That temporary effects do follow such preaching in the case of some is not to be denied. Christ himself teaches us to expect it. But in others the effect is far from being a temporary emotion. Two instances of this from the 1950s will illustrate how the lives of Christians were affected by this preaching.

On Saturday, November 28, 1953, Ralph M. Hettrick arrived in London on a first visit from the United States. Recalling the event, nearly thirty years later, he wrote:

I had been given a three-month sabbatical as pastor of a church in central Washington State, and through a series of providential happenings was led overseas by ship to Southampton and then to London.

I had had part-ownership interest in a Bible Book Store in Washington and was familiar with publishing, so, as a point of contact I sought out Pickering & Inglis at 29 Ludgate Hill. I inquired about Spurgeon's Tabernacle and was told it was but a bombed-out shell. The managers, Mr and Mrs Gray, invited me to join them in their hall meeting (Brethren). I asked if there was not some evangelical center in London where I could hear the Word preached with power. They told me of Westminster Chapel and the effective work of the doctor. I straightaway made up my mind to hear this Dr Lloyd-Jones the following day. I had no idea I would be in for such a treat.

Problem after problem seemed to make it next to impossible to get to the Chapel. The final blow was when the cab driver delivered me to Westminster Abbey instead of Westminster Chapel. Running and walking down the Mall in a driving rainstorm, I finally arrived at the sanctuary and was seated in the center section, but a few rows from the very front. I had to look almost straight up to see the pulpit. After the singing had stopped the doctor began leading in the morning prayer. Never in my life had I heard a public prayer like that prayer. Then the message. What can I say? It was part of his series on the 73rd Psalm. Later I discovered his text that Sunday had been planned for the Sunday previous but that he was not able to finish it. He began dealing with verses 22 and 23, 'So foolish was I, and ignorant. I was as a beast before thee. Nevertheless I am continually with thee: thou hast holden me by my right hand.'

Every part of the message was directed to me. I had traveled across the United States from the west coast, boarding a ship to take me to England. I had been traveling for more than five weeks. I was in a backslidden state and my heart was full of fear. My spiritual condition made me fearful that God would finally disown me and I would find myself lost and without hope. It was as though the Lord had been in detailed conversation with the doctor concerning my condition. Everything seemed to fit. I was weakened, greatly humbled and yet thrilled to think that God knew where I was (even if I didn't), and that He was again at work in my soul.

As I reflect today on that November 29, 1953 experience at Westminster Chapel I have deep appreciation and gratitude to God for His leading me to hear that particular message. It was a life-changing happening. God's timing was perfect, as is everything He does. There is no way of my conveying what the ministry of Dr Lloyd-Jones has meant to me. It turned my life around. I'm sure this same acknowledgement could come from hundreds of others.

One of these 'hundreds' was Argos Zodhiates who, with his wife, was in Westminster Chapel on Sunday morning, October 21, 1957. Sad of heart, they were en route to Canada where they hoped to find a new home. Behind them lay a much-loved and fruitful work in the Greek Evangelical Church of Katerini which Argos had served since July 1946. The church at Katerini, on the Aegean Sea and not far from the ancient town of Thessaloniki, was one of the brightest lights for the gospel in Greece, and for that very reason it had incurred the anger of Bishop Barnabas, the local Greek Orthodox bishop. Persecution of various kinds had been increasingly directed against Argos and his preaching. When a dead bird was thrown down at his door with a threat of murder attached to it, the possibility that violence could proceed even to that length could not be dismissed. At length, in the midst of this sustained opposition, the Zodhiateses had come to the reluctant conclusion that it was time for them to leave, and passing through London on their way to North America they took the opportunity to visit Westminster Chapel. Their coming was, of course, unknown to ML-J who that morning 'happened' to be preaching on Ephesians 4:11, 'And he gave some apostles; and some prophets; and some evangelists; and some pastors and teachers'. In the course of his words on the pastoral office he was to say: 'The shepherd shepherds his flock . . . looks after their safety and guards them against enemies liable to attack them. It is a great office. A pastor is a man who is given charge of souls . . . he is the guardian, the custodian, the protector, the organizer, the director, the ruler of the flock . . .'[11]

---

[11] *Christian Unity: An Exposition of Ephesians 4:1-16* (Edinburgh: Banner of Truth, 1980), p. 193. He probably said more by way of application than is included in the

Argos Zodhiates and his wife felt that the word was direct from God to themselves, and turning to each other at the end of the service they said, 'That's our answer.' They went back to Greece, ready to battle it out, and Dr Lloyd-Jones heard nothing of the incident until he visited Katerini four years later.

Such experiences confirmed all that he believed about preaching. To use the words of Gardiner Spring, 'The results of a preached gospel are associated with the most interesting realities in the universe.'

* * *

In form the Sunday evening service at Westminster Chapel was virtually the same as the morning service already described. It was the nature of the sermon which constituted the main difference. In the morning the content of sermons ranged over many subjects arising out of the passage of Scripture currently being expounded as part of a consecutive series. In the evening the intention was narrower. Attention was focussed on such texts, or features of a text, as have pointed relevance to non-Christians. Not that such relevance was expected to be immediately apparent to his hearers; on the contrary he usually began (on Sunday nights) with the assumption that he was addressing those for whom Scripture might have no point or interest. It could well be some way into the sermon before the casual hearer began to come to the conviction that the text — perhaps from a book of Scripture that he could not even find — was speaking to him. Prior to that point, however, there was something in the preacher's introduction that had led the hearer into a train of thought and argument which was patently important enough to demand his attention. Perhaps the introductory words had to do with some familiar problem of the times and then, after the examination of popular but superficial proposals for the solution of that problem, it was related to the text and to the fundamental question of man's relationship to God.

But while ML-J's method of speaking to non-Christians was always logical and intended to engage their minds, it was in no sense based upon the idea that people can be reasoned into the kingdom of God. He believed absolutely that all saving hearing of Scripture

---

printed version of the sermon. The next sermon in this volume (pp. 196-208) gives one of ML-J's finest summaries on the work of the ministry.

came from God alone. That did not lead him, however, to suppose the exposition of any part of Scripture is as likely to be as effective as the preaching of any other part. Such a supposition he regarded as destructive of true evangelistic preaching. All Scripture is not equally profitable to the unconverted, rather there are certain primary truths which are essential to gospel preaching and which are most likely to be used in leading to conviction of sin and then to repentance and faith. The immediate purpose of evangelistic preaching is to drive men from all hope in themselves, and the scriptural means to that end is the proclamation of the truth about God and his holy law. Reflecting on Lloyd-Jones' Sunday-night preaching, and comparing it with the message of other well-known London pulpits, an observer once said, 'Soper preaches love, Weatherhead preaches Jesus, and Lloyd-Jones preaches God.' For ML-J his emphasis was not a matter of personal preference, it was *biblical*. He believed with B. B. Warfield that 'the staple of Paul's preaching was God and judgment'. That must be the starting point, for it is man's wrong attitude and his enmity to God which is the essence of his sin. Repentance is, primarily, a change of attitude to God. 'The worst sin of all is the false thinking about God of which the natural man is so terribly guilty.' 'The trouble with people who are not seeking for a Saviour, and for salvation, is that they do not understand the nature of sin. It is the peculiar function of the law to bring such an understanding to a man's mind and con-science. That is why great evangelical preachers three hundred years ago in the time of the Puritans, and two hundred years ago in the time of Whitefield and others, always engaged in what they called a preliminary "law work".'[12]

This proclamation of God he saw as much more than the teaching of orthodox statements. It required the sense and experience of God both in the preacher and, if hearers were to be saved, in the pew. The presence and power of God himself must be there. With reference to this, Jim Packer could speak many years later of what he remembered most about hearing nearly a year of ML-J's evangelistic preaching:

> I have never heard another preacher with so much of God about him . . . His approach is habitually Isaianic: having surveyed man's pretensions, his fancied greatness and adequacy, moral, religious,

---

[12] *Romans: An Exposition of Chapters 7:1 to 8:4, The Law: Its Function and Limits* (Edinburgh: Banner of Truth, 1973), p. 114.

cultural, intellectual, he punctures them, humbling man and exposing his weakness, futility and sin, in order then to exalt God as the only Saviour. The thrust of Lloyd-Jones' sermons is always to show man small and God great . . . Application has been going on throughout the sermon; in one sense, it has all been application. He will have searched us, analysed us to ourselves, diagnosed us into self-despair, shown up sin and weakness and failure in vivid forms. Now, in conclusion, he points us to the God of all grace. With intense compassion he urges us to cast ourselves on the mercy of God in Christ, and his last words are likely to be an assurance about the life and glory we shall find when we do. Thus the preacher slips out of the picture and leaves us with the God whom he would have us know.[13]

For Dr Lloyd-Jones to preach the real peril of man's guiltiness before God meant to preach the certainty of divine wrath, wrath which is already upon the unconverted and which is yet to come in the punishment of sin in hell. Far from believing that because modern man does not like this truth it should not be preached, he regarded warning as an essential part of biblical preaching. Hell is not a theory, and he saw the idea that for the ungodly there is no immortality (which was quietly gaining acceptance in some otherwise evangelical circles) as a dangerous error. 'Perish means perish; it does not mean go out of existence. It is the opposite to eternal life. It is the same as that place where their "worm dieth not and their fire is not quenched".'[14]

Another truth which he regarded as necessary to evangelistic preaching was that of human helplessness and inability in sin. To teach men that they possess the ability to turn from sin when they choose to do so is to hide the true extent of their need. Certainly the offer of salvation is to be urged upon all, and men must be shown the necessity of their believing and repenting if they are to be saved, but faith and repentance are given to those who come to an end of themselves. If men could choose to turn themselves from enmity to love, and from death to life, their conversion would not be the

---

[13] Quoted in *Twenty Centuries of Great Preaching*, vol. 11, Clyde E. Fant Jr. and W. M. Pinson Jr,.1971, pp. 269-71.
[14] *Romans: An Exposition of Chapters 2:1 to 3:20, The Righteous Judgment of God* (Edinburgh: Banner of Truth, 1989), p. 107.

immense and supernatural thing which Scripture represents it to be. Commanded to believe though he is, man's preference for self and sin is such that any saving change in his condition must come from the direct action of God. The true condition of every non-Christian is such that he cannot desire to love God, he cannot desire to obey him:

> he cannot choose to do so, he is totally incapable of any spiritual effort. I am not saying this; it is the Apostle Paul who says it. The popular teaching which says that we have to preach the gospel to the natural man as he is, and that he, as he is, decides to believe on the Lord Jesus Christ; and that then, because he has believed, he is given new life, is regenerated — this, I say, is a complete denial of what the Apostle teaches here.[15]

The time of regeneration is, therefore, not in man's control. What Scripture does make clear is that God first humbles through the truth those to whom he is pleased to impart life and a new nature. The proof that believing is genuine is that the *life* is changed. These simple facts he saw as having immense bearings on evangelism. For one thing, it means that an evangelist must exercise care lest by a mere appeal to self-interest he induces a 'decision' which, far from being saving, is perfectly consistent with a person remaining in an unregenerate condition. A presentation of the gospel chiefly in terms of its ability to satisfy man's need of happiness and other blessings, and which fails to show that man's wrong relationship to God 'is much worse than everything else' in his condition, may well receive a considerable though temporary success. A salvation conceived 'not as something primarily that brings us to God but as something that gives *us* something' requires no real conviction of sin in order to its acceptance. ML-J was not surprised that such evangelism could be carried on with glibness and lightness and that its result was to add the unspiritual and the careless to the churches. The true convert always wants deliverance from the power as well as the guilt of sin.[16]

---

[15] *Romans: An Exposition of Chapter 8:5-17, The Sons of God*, p. 14.

[16] 'In true conversion there is always some degree of realization of the horror of sin within and the desire to be delivered from it' (*Romans: An Exposition of Chapter 8:5-17, The Sons of God*, p. 215). Preaching which gives people the impression 'that all they have to do is to say that they believe in Christ' is 'a non-ethical message. True evangelism is always ethical' (*Romans: An Exposition of Chapter 6, The New Man* [Edinburgh: Banner of Truth, 1972], p. 195). See also his important sermon on

He viewed with sadness the type of evangelism which supposes that the ethical and moral change associated with sanctification is something which Christians can receive at some point later than their conversion and justification. Rather, the most decisive influence for holiness comes from the rebirth itself.[17] By obscuring the nature of regeneration, modern evangelism had separated two things which Scripture always puts together, namely forgiveness *and* a new life of fellowship with God. To suppose we have received one and to know nothing of the other is to be in a state of delusion. On the effects of this kind of teaching he spoke very strongly.[18]

An account of ML-J's preaching at Westminster was written by Dr Wilbur M. Smith in *Moody Monthly* (October, 1955) while spending six Sundays in London. In his subsequent article entitled 'Preliminary Thoughts on Contemporary Preaching in London' he wrote on W. E. Sangster, John Stott, and finally, at length, on Martyn Lloyd-Jones:

> Any minister of this church who expects week by week to hold the audience of Westminster Chapel and to draw to this side street men and women from all over London, must first of all be a preacher with unusual gifts. The present minister, Dr D. Martyn Lloyd-Jones, has had just such gifts abundantly conferred upon him by the Lord Himself.

'Sanctification and Evangelism' in *Sanctified through the Truth,* ed. C. Catherwood (Eastbourne: Kingsway, 1989), p. 323.

[17] 'There is nothing that is so unscriptural, so utterly wrong, as to place or create a division between justification and sanctification' (*Romans, An Exposition of Chapter 6, The New Man,* p. 217). For ML-J, it must be understood, regeneration is an instantaneous act of God that radically changes a man's nature: conversion (i.e., the exercise of faith and repentance) is the process following that hidden act. That the conversion is genuine is not to be judged by the time element (whether quick or slow), nor by the degree of assurance professed, but rather by whether or not the whole life has been made new. ML-J agreed with J. C. Ryle's assessment of the evangelism which became popular in the later nineteenth century. It was marked, says Ryle, by 'an extravagant and disproportionate magnifying of three points in religion — *viz.,* instantaneous conversion, the invitation of sinners to come to Christ, and the possession of inward joy and peace as the test of conversion' (*Holiness* [repr. London: Clarke, 1952], p. 74).

[18] See, *Studies in the Sermon on the Mount,* vol. 2 (London: IVF, 1960), pp. 247-8. 'There is no greater danger to our highest interests than this kind of "easy believism" which is not the work of the Spirit at all' (*Romans: An Exposition of Chapter 8:5-17, The Sons of God,* p. 212). Also 'Sandemanianism' in *Puritans,* pp. 170-90.

It is commonly said among evangelicals in London that he is the outstanding preacher in Great Britain today. I have heard it stated since coming to London, not by anyone connected with Westminster Chapel, that no less a person than Brunner himself, the Continental theologian, has stated that Dr Martyn Lloyd-Jones is the greatest preacher in Christendom today. This would be a great deal for Brunner to say about anyone, and especially about this person, because Dr Lloyd-Jones is a staunch defender of the plenary inspiration of the Holy Scriptures. After hearing him again, twice within three weeks, I am easily persuaded that both of these statements are probably true.

One Sunday morning I heard him preach his thirty-eighth consecutive sermon from the first chapter of Ephesians . . . Two weeks later, on a Sunday night, before a great audience, I heard him preach from a text that I had never noticed before: 'Heal me, O Lord, and I shall be healed; save me, and I shall be saved: for thou art my praise. Behold, they say unto me, Where is the word of the Lord? Let it come now' (*Jer.* 17:14, 15). Here, said this great defender of the faith, we have two contrasting attitudes toward the Word of God: in verse 14 the believer speaks; in verse 15 the scoffer and unbeliever speak.

He then went on to say how that these are the only two groups there are in the world in the sight of God. Men create various groups, according to our ancestors, the race to which we belong, intellectual training, wealth or poverty, etc., etc., but in the sight of God there are only two groups, those who believe His Word and those who disbelieve. No one can pronounce the word *Scriptures* with such force as this great expositor. You cannot hear him preach for three minutes without realizing that he believes God is speaking in His Word, that the Word is infallible, and that what we do with the Word of God will determine our eternal destiny.

Over and over again he illustrated the meaning of the scoffers' sarcastic challenge, 'Where is the word of the Lord? let it come.' 'Ah,' said Martyn Lloyd-Jones, 'it came.' What the prophet uttered came to pass, and it was not long before these people were in chains marching to Babylon. The Jews said the same thing when they heard Christ's prophetic words, 'Let it come.' Indeed, they went further and flippantly, with a shuddering boldness, cried out, 'Let his blood be upon us', and it came upon them! In forty years their city was in the dust, and those who were left from the terrible slaughter of Titus were being marched to Rome as slaves.

So, too, will come an end of this age. Man may speak scoffingly of the second advent of Christ and of the day of judgment, saying, 'Let it come', but, oh, it will come. Then he pleaded with the souls before him to believe *that very night* in the grace of God revealed in the cross of Christ.

I have not heard such preaching for years. One thing I determined in my own soul. I would never be satisfied again, as long as I live, with preaching anything but the very best that I have in deadly earnestness and, pray God, in the power of the Holy Spirit. This is preaching.

To a group of men who were paying compliments to her husband's powers, Bethan Lloyd-Jones once quietly remarked, 'No one will understand my husband until they realize that he is first of all a man of prayer and then, an evangelist.' It is certain that ML-J saw himself primarily as an evangelist. To a critic who once asked him, 'When did you last have a campaign at Westminster Chapel?' he could reply, 'I have one every Sunday'. It was his decided conviction 'that there should always be one evangelistic service in connection with each church every week'.[19]

Further, it should be clear that the difference between him and popular evangelicalism was not so much over methods and types of evangelism as over theology. 'It is our whole idea of evangelism that is wrong.'[20] He believed that the common view of gospel preaching could not be harmonized with the apostolic approach laid down in the Epistle to the Romans. Effective evangelism requires that biblical principles be held in their true relationships. When he came to be regarded as a 'teacher', not an 'evangelist', he saw the assessment not as a reflection on himself but on the current view of evangelism — 'a measure of the terrible spiritual aberration of these days', as he wrote to a friend.

He regarded the preaching of Christ to the unsaved as the most demanding of all work. For not only does it require a discriminating

[19] *Preaching and Preachers*, p. 63.
[20] *Sanctified through the Truth*, p. 30. 'The ultimate defect and error of the Arminian argument and all that has emanated from it is that it excludes the Holy Spirit from the real decision, and asserts that man is able to convert himself.' *Puritans*, p. 19.

understanding of the truth, it looks for an 'impossible' response as far as man is concerned. In the hope of attracting people, and to lessen the possibility of failure, the modern practice was not to start as Paul did with man in sin and under the wrath of God. 'Perhaps', it was said, 'you could do that sort of thing one hundred years ago, but you just cannot now.' In ML-J's view the supreme need was for men full of faith and the Holy Spirit who, sent by God, would be owned in the recovery of apostolic gospel preaching. With the word of the gospel there can be, there has to be, almighty power to awaken the dead. If he had not believed that, as he would often say, he would have given up in despair.

27. Interior of Westminster Chapel from pulpit.

TWENTY-THREE

Opposition

At the same time as Dr Lloyd-Jones was being given added influence in some circles he was losing it in others. After the initial welcome on the part of Nonconformist leaders on his coming to London, a growing coolness and finally open criticism developed. The change was early apparent in the columns of the *British Weekly*. After the end of John Hutton's editorship in 1946, news of the minister and ministry of Westminster Chapel gradually disappeared as the paper pursued a policy manifesting very different sympathies. The 1949 series of articles on 'Giants of the Pulpit', already mentioned, and the Correspondence columns, majored in praise of liberals with such statements as, 'In London, the most outstanding preacher is Leslie Weatherhead. He relates religion to life.'

The particular cause of the dislike is not hard to find: it was ML-J's insistence on a 'narrow' rather than 'broader' view of Christian belief. Although he was not responsible for the IVF's Basis of Faith, he became the party most blamed for that organization's refusal to co-operate with those who were not committed to the inerrancy of Scripture. An early instance of division over this issue came in the case of Dr Donald Coggan. Coggan, a friend of Douglas Johnson, was Principal of the London College of Divinity and a future Archbishop of Canterbury. In 1946, on the assumption that he could still sign the Basis of Faith, he was asked to become a vice-president of the IVF, a work with which he had long been associated. But this he now declined to do on account of its commitment to inerrancy. 'He pointed out', writes his biographer, 'that he had already, as part of his ordination vows, given his assent to Article 6 of the Thirty-nine Articles, would that not suffice? The IVF decided not; he and they parted company.'[1]

The same commitment to Scripture brought a more public loss to IVF's numbers in Edinburgh after ML-J was due to lead a Mission to the University with Alec Vidler in November 1948. Christian work among students in Britain at this date was divided between the Student Christian Movement (SCM) and the IVF. At this mission, it appears, there were to be speakers connected with both organizations. When Lloyd-Jones had to withdraw on account of a bad cold, another IVF speaker and author, Thomas F. Torrance, took his place. The organizing secretary for the mission was also an IVF man by the name of James Barr. Torrance, however, as was soon to become clear, was no longer in sympathy with the IVF position on Scripture. *The Scottish Journal of Theology*, which he launched that same year with J. K. S. Reid, was announced as a journal in which 'no theological position is represented exclusively'. Under Torrance's influence others in Scotland were to secede from the IVF, most notably in the Edinburgh Evangelical Christian Union.

Other evangelical agencies were also put under pressure on account of the same issue. In January 1948 the Evangelical Alliance, in its 101st year, held its annual 'week of prayer', with a main public meeting arranged for Monday, January 8, 1948 for which Westminster Chapel was hired. From the speakers announced it was clear that the society was no longer applying doctrinal tests in its choice of speakers. The man asked to chair this meetings was Dr W. R. Matthews, Dean of St Paul's, and 'the chief speaker' was Sir Stafford Cripps, a leading politician. These two men spoke in a general way of the need for Christian morality and prayer, but when ML-J rose to give a closing address it was evident that he was speaking from a different standpoint. It was a waste of energy, he declared, 'to try to induce man to apply the

[1] Margaret Pawley, *Donald Coggan, Servant of Christ* (1987), p. 87. Article 6 of the Thirty-nine Articles says nothing on the inerrancy of Scripture for the simple reason that there was no challenge to that belief in the sixteenth century. It is a slanted representation of what happened to say that Douglas Johnson 'had no hesitancy in disqualifying him'. Ian S. Rennie in *Evangelicalism: Comparative Studies of Popular Protestantism in North America, the British Isles and Beyond, 1700-1990*, M. A. Noll, David W. Bebbington, G. A. Rawlyk, eds., (Oxford: OUP, 1994), p. 341.

Christian ethics to his life'. The first need, he said, was for repentance in the church herself and a recovery of the power of the Holy Spirit. One evangelical hearer, Hector Brooke, who was present, wrote in his diary afterwards, 'He denounced those who weakened the authority of the Bible and urged us to pray that the Spirit might be manifested in a mighty revival. I trembled even to look at Cripps or Matthews.'

What a non-evangelical such as Matthews thought of Lloyd-Jones has been recorded by Professor F. F. Bruce who supplies this memory of what followed the Evangelical Alliance meeting:

> Some time later, in the dining hall of an Oxford college, I sat alongside Professor R. V. G. Tasker of King's College, London; on the other side sat Dr Matthews. The conversation turned to contemporary preachers. Professor Tasker sought and readily obtained my concurrence in his assessment of ML-J as 'extraordinarily good' (on his own confession his life had been revolutionized by an address which ML-J gave at a LIFCU mission in 1947). 'I should say extraordinarily bad', said Dr Matthews.[2]

In the published proceedings of that week of prayer nothing was said by various churchmen which remotely resembled ML-J's address. On the contrary, at a large luncheon gathering, sponsored by the Alliance, Leslie Weatherhead spoke of the uselessness of 'scrapping' over 'theological points'. 'What we ought to do above everything else is to unite in action.' H. Martyn Gooch, who had been the General Secretary of the Alliance for over forty years, concluded the luncheon speeches by referring to Cripps' 'very moving address' of the previous Monday, and he believed that 'the secret of all that has been said today is to be found in that word "Evangelical"'.

As Weatherhead's words above underline, the point which was to become the great issue in the years ahead was not so much *which* particular doctrines are necessary but whether *any* definite statements about the truth are to be regarded as essential. Christianity, it was said, depends upon experience, not 'propositions', and therefore any contention for theological principles is not only uncharitable, it constitutes a failure to understand the true nature of Christianity.

Using the word 'Fundamentalism' as a term to describe the viewpoint for which Dr Lloyd-Jones was the most conspicuous advocate,

[2] *Evangelical Quarterly,* 1991, p. 70.

'Ilico', a regular columnist in the *British Weekly,* wrote on 'Why Fundamentalism Will Not Do' (Dec. 29, 1949). With obvious reference to the work of IVF he said: 'Fundamentalism, which seemed to most to be a lost cause yesterday, gathers in many today, not least amongst an educated section of the community. Not "Liberalism" but obscurantism would seem the greater danger in these days.' Fundamentalists, he believed, were basically wrong in their view of doctrine or theology. 'Theology' is but the human attempt to state the 'unchanging gospel'. God has not revealed 'theological propositions'.

If there had been any doubt about the depth of this division it must have been made clear to those who met at what some regarded as a 'peace conference' between delegations of the SCM and the IVF meeting privately in London on March 1950. At the beginning of the century an evangelical SCM had been alone in its witness in universities, but as liberal influence gained strength, the IVF came into being and was distinguished by its adherence to the infallibility of Scripture and faith in Christ as the substitute for sinners. In the course of time the IVF would overtake the SCM in its role in the student world, and the 1950 meeting was designed by the SCM in the hope of bringing the two organizations nearer. The representatives were numerous from both sides, with Dr Nathaniel Micklem, Principal of Mansfield College, in the chair. Alan Booth, a Methodist and general secretary of SCM, led his delegation, with David Jenkins of Oxford (the future Bishop of Durham) and other staff and clergy in support. For the IVF there was Douglas Johnson and Oliver Barclay, with ML-J the most prominent individual among non-IVF staff.

The issue very quickly became whether Christian belief could be held to be final and unchangeable or whether it was inevitably bound to change (as the SCM side argued) on account of 'a growing understanding'.[3] Thus, although it was conceded that the original leaders of the SCM believed in the deity of Christ, it was not necessarily wrong for their successors to hold a different view. So, as Oliver Barclay pointed out, 'faith in Christ' did not mean the same for both of them, as was shown by SCM's readiness to include Unitarians. The

---

[3] For all the documentation of this meeting I am indebted to David Goodhew, 'Understanding Schism: The Peace Summit between the Student Christian Movement and the Inter-Varsity Fellowship' in *British Evangelical Identities Past and Present,* vol. 1, ed. Mark Smith (Milton Keynes: Paternoster, 2008), pp. 35-45.

discussion went on to reveal how different the priorities of each side were. For SCM the priority was to achieve 'unity' among Christians. 'We are bound as Christians', Booth argued, 'to seek to recognize each other in Christ.' Lloyd-Jones responded that to put that first, while declining a specific endorsement of leading articles of the faith, was to put a 'sentimental notion of unity' before the truth. A suggestion from Booth that they could at least meet together for joint Bible study, was supported by the supposedly neutral chairman, Dr Micklem, who commented that since the IVF used the Bible with non-Christians, they could do so with SCM. 'No,' replied ML-J, 'you preach to the unconverted. They are not in a position to discuss and I think we have made a great mistake often in discussing with such people instead of proclaiming to them.' Christian fellowship follows faith, it does not come before it.

Lloyd-Jones affirmed, 'You must state the truth in propositions; the human mind must have it in that form, not that we say it ends at that.' The other side disagreed and claimed that in their quest for infallibility the IVF were imitating Roman Catholicism. When Oliver Barclay stated, 'As a movement you do not stand for anything in particular', Jenkins replied that his argument was 'fantastic'. Johnson would later recall, 'David Jenkins — was a picture! He could scarcely contain himself at the enormities propounded by our folk. He was saying "No, No" and almost breaking his chair with exasperation.'

The meeting was, in Booth's view, 'a disaster'. Both sides differed over the reason why that was so. On the IVF side, it was because SCM were unprepared to treat Scripture as authoritative; on the SCM side it was, in Booth's words, because 'They believe more in theological definition than in Christian faith.' The discussion also brought out what would later become public controversy. A different understanding of what constitutes a Christian necessarily leads to a different understanding of what is a church. For the IVF the church might consist, at times, of only a 'remnant' of true believers, while for the SCM 'church' was to be considered as an inclusive, broad body; the IVF was 'schismatic and heretical'. Booth, Goodhew comments, 'now prepared for war'. The other side believed that a spiritual war already existed.

Lloyd-Jones made no public comment on the above meeting but without mentioning any names he had in mind the thinking of the other side when, again as president of the IVF, he addressed the annual student conference at Swanwick in 1952 on 'Maintaining the Evangelical Faith Today'.[4] This address remains crucial for an understanding of his thinking, and is a key to controversy which would mark the next fifteen years. Against the charge of 'intolerance', he insisted the believer 'must refuse to compromise upon any matter which is *clearly* revealed in Scripture to be the mind and will of God. He must not venture to modify such things at any point at all.' He rejected the claim that 'external unity' in a 'great, broad, and comprehensive ecclesiasticism' would make for strength. 'There are not wanting today men in teaching and preaching positions who are advising us to walk in "the broad way"; but our Lord and his apostles constantly affirmed that this is the opposite of God's will for us. We must not mind being thought "narrow". We must not be afraid of the charge that "You think that you *alone* are right."'

This address when published brought probably the first open attack on the preacher in the Christian press in a lengthy, unsigned editorial column in the *British Weekly* (March 19, 1953). The writer was Dr Micklem, the same man who had chaired the meeting of March 1, 1950, and with whom ML-J had lunch in Oxford in February 1941. Micklem characterized Lloyd-Jones' address as 'an apologia for the refusal of the Inter-Varsity Fellowship to co-operate with any Christians who do not agree with them in their opinions, and is an attack on the World Council of Churches and the British Council of Churches.' Its thesis was that

> the whole, full gospel is to be identified with Dr Martyn Lloyd-Jones' definition of it . . . Dr Lloyd-Jones writes in sincerity and charity, but it is time there was some plain speaking in this matter; for the Inter-Varsity Fellowship which, as utterly committed to the gospel, might well be the spear-head of the Christian challenge to the world, is, in some places and where in this matter it follows the lead of Dr Lloyd-Jones, divisive, schismatic, obscurantist and quite un-biblical.
>
> The kindest thing to say about Dr Lloyd-Jones' position is that it rests upon downright theological ignorance . . . no scholar could maintain that there is theological and doctrinal agreement between St Paul, St John and the writer 'to the Hebrews'. Nothing could be

---

[4] Reprinted in *Knowing the Times*, pp. 38-50.

more clear than that Dr Lloyd-Jones is a kind of Calvinist; and that the Apostle Paul was not. The gospel is not in the least indefinite, but being God's Word to man, it can never be fully and adequately and finally caged and set forth in any human formula.

The sober truth is that Dr Lloyd-Jones offers a more or less arbitrary selection from the tenets of scholastic Calvinism, and tells us that if we presume to criticize these doctrines we deny the gospel. 'We must be like Martin Luther', he tells us, 'when he stood alone against the authority of the Roman Church, which had arrogated to itself such dictatorial powers for so many long centuries.' Quite, and unhappily we must follow Martin Luther and resist the authority of the IVF which, in the person of Dr Lloyd-Jones, arrogates to itself the same dictatorial powers.

ML-J in replying in the Correspondence columns of the *British Weekly* made only two points:

I have always asserted and argued as strongly as I could that evangelicals should not separate on the question of Calvinism and Arminianism. In the IVF, both here in Great Britain and on the international level, Arminians and Calvinists work most happily and harmoniously together, and it is my privilege to co-operate with all such . . . I pleaded for the maintaining of that Biblical Evangelical Faith to which Arminians, Lutherans and Calvinists subscribe. That is my position and for that I make no apology.

Neither do I make any apology for the 'ignorance' which hitherto has led me to believe, unlike you, Sir, that there is 'theological and doctrinal agreement between St Paul, St John and the writer to the Hebrews'.

Either no well-known evangelicals wrote to the Correspondence columns of the *British Weekly* in the weeks following Micklem's attack, or any such letters were unpublished.

By this date it was becoming clear that the opposition of what Lloyd-Jones stood for was settled on the lines of attack. His 'dogmatism' was due to 'downright theological ignorance'. Likewise Alan Booth characterized the IVF spokesmen at the discussion with SCM as men who had 'no theological training at all'.[5] This charge would come to be taken up by others. Martyn Lloyd-Jones was an amateur.

[5] *British Evangelical Identities Past and Present*, ed. Mark Smith, vol. 1 (Milton Keynes: Paternoster, 2008), p. 41.

He 'had undertaken no formal study of theology, but neither had he any formal qualifications or academic standing as a biblical scholar'.[6] This line of criticism brings us to a real fault line. It is true that Lloyd-Jones, together with Douglas Johnson and Oliver Barclay, held doctorates in science, not theology, but the assumption of their opponents was that no one could understand the present state of 'theological scholarship' unless they were trained according to its mentors. 'Scholarship' had long decided that being controlled by the authority of Scripture in order to right understanding was outmoded obscurantism. In the words of one of their number, Dr T. R. Glover, 'verbal inspiration is a monstrous belief', and he was thankful, as he wrote in *The Times* (March 11, 1932), 'Today if you want a real old obscurantist college, you have to found one.'[7] Lloyd-Jones' procedure was challenging the whole modern edifice of theological education. 'Theology' for his critics meant the contemporary academic establishment and its professionals. To their mind how could the disagreement they met be explained other than in terms of ignorance? Dr Lloyd-Jones' explanation of the disagreement was intolerable; it was that the academic theologians had commonly become false prophets.

I have noted earlier how the possible appointment of ML-J to teach at the Bala College in 1938 was blocked. In view of the hold which belief in the Bible still had on numbers in the Calvinistic Methodist Church, there was no acknowledgement by church leaders of a chief reason for their opposition. But it was voiced in the Welsh press. Lloyd-Jones was not acceptable because, like Amos, he did not come from the normal 'school of the prophets':

> After the manner of the Hebrew prophet he has sprung from the laity and consequently he lacks those traditional accoutrements as regards training, deportment, and jargon, which have come to be regarded as the hall-mark of preachers as a class. That is why so many of them are ready to regard him with disfavour . . .
>
> The fact that the most popular preacher in Wales is one who has never undergone a theological training, after their example, manifestly serves to demonstrate to the point of proof that such

---

[6] T. A. Noble, *Tyndale House and Fellowship: The First Sixty Years* (Leicester: IVP, 2006), p. 70. These were surprising words in an IVP publication.

[7] See my title, *Archibald G. Brown, Spurgeon's Successor* (Edinburgh: Banner of Truth, 2011), pp. 279-80.

training is not really necessary for a successful ministry. It is that consideration which has upset their professional equilibrium and made them jealous of his phenomenal success. They would rather see him leave the connexion than remain in it as a perpetual reproach to the men who have emerged from the denominational colleges with the full flavour of academic distinction, but who, notwithstanding, are utterly unable to attract the masses to their half-empty churches.[8]

An appointment of Lloyd-Jones would have given credence to a dangerous anachronism in an age when, as the scholars believed, the credibility of Christianity depended on a far more 'flexible' approach to Scripture. To insist on *all* biblical testimony, to accept the Old Testament as though it were as dependable as the New, or Paul's words as though they were equal with Christ's, would be to turn the clock back with a vengeance. It would be to condemn no small part of the very work which theological colleges existed to promote.

Dr Lloyd-Jones' subject at the annual meeting of the IVF in London on October 1, 1954, bore on this issue. There was no common ground, he argued, with those who claimed that it is 'experience' of Christ which unites and not any common body of truth. For the issue behind that claim was really this: 'In spiritual affairs, does theology really matter at all? Does it, in the last analysis, matter what a man ultimately believes?' An avoidance of that question, he believed, lay at the heart of the ecumenical movement which was now gaining the support of the denominations. But that movement was not facing the real problem. Certainly church attendance was about a third of what it had been in 1901, but why was this?

We have been repeatedly told that the cause of the state of the church today was the result of two world wars and their consequent aftermath of political, economic and social changes. Obviously, they say, increasing social pressures of various kinds, greater movements of the population and a hundred and one other factors have all combined to take people away from places of worship. Such an explanation is constantly given and this superficial diagnosis all too easily accepted. But is it *true*?

There is only one adequate explanation for the state of the

Christian church today, it is the *apostasy of the church herself*. The crucial damage was done by that fatal destructive Higher Criticism movement which came into being during the nineteenth century. The one essential question in the mind of anyone who investigates such a matter must be, 'What robbed the church of its authority?' The certainty of its message was undermined. This is why the church lost its hold upon the masses. That is the real explanation of the present position.

In Jude 3, we read, 'Beloved, when I gave all diligence to write unto you of the common salvation, it was needful for me to write unto you, and exhort you that ye should earnestly contend for the faith which was once delivered unto the saints.' Here we are given a stirring call to the defence of the Faith. Such a call is not popular today. It is not popular today even in some evangelical circles. People will tell you that it is all 'too negative'. They continually urge that we must keep on giving positive truth. They will tell us that we must not argue and we must never condemn. But we must ask, 'How can you fight if you are ever afraid of wounding an enemy?' 'How can you rouse sleeping fellow-warriors with smooth words?' God forbid that we find ourselves at the bar of judgment and face the charge that we contracted out from love of ease, or for fear of man, or that we failed to do our duty in the great fight of the Faith. We *must — we must* fight for the faith in these momentous times.[9]

It is hardly surprising that opposition to ML-J increased. Dr Packer has written:

His peers in official Christianity treated him as scarcely more than an extremely able freak. Being themselves consciously and complacently 'progressive' they saw him as a throwback to a type of ministry that as a general pattern had long since ceased to be viable . . . deep level isolation from most of his ecclesiastical peers was a permanent part of the Doctor's experience.[10]

While Dr Lloyd-Jones was conscious of this, he by no means enjoyed standing apart, or speaking to issues on which others were silent. He felt keenly the lack of like-minded men. When Philip

[9] 'A Policy Appropriate to Biblical Faith', *Knowing the Times*, pp. 55-59.
[10] C. Catherwood, ed., *Martyn Lloyd-Jones, Chosen by God*, (Crowborough: Highland Books, 1986), pp. 42-3.

Hughes, after being in touch with Continental Calvinists, wrote to ML-J about the hope of starting an English committee to co-operate with them, ML-J was not optimistic, in part, as he explained in a reply to Hughes, dependable Englishmen able to make up such a committee simply did not exist: 'As far as names of other Reformed persons, there are really none that I know of of any standing at all, except Kevan.'

Yet there were times when prominent individuals came to his side from unexpected quarters. One such was the Rev. R. V. G. Tasker, Professor of New Testament Exegesis at King's College, London. In an address for the IVF in May 1951 on 'The Biblical Doctrine of the Wrath of God', Tasker confessed that his life had been 'revolutionised' by hearing Dr Lloyd-Jones in 1947. Tasker happened to comment on ML-J to the Rev. Edwin King afterwards, 'I think he is a very lonely man in need of fellowship.' A few months later King spoke with Tasker on the steps of Westminster Chapel (where the professor now attended in the evenings). 'This is preaching in the grand style,' exclaimed Tasker, 'by the time we Anglicans have concluded our little homilies the Doctor is just emerging from his introduction.' As they talked further, King referred to Lloyd-Jones' concern over the loneliness which, he believed, the professor was experiencing. The assessment was not far from the mark; for, after taking a stand on the Word of God, as Tasker once told Douglas Johnson, he felt as though he had been 'sent to Coventry' by his colleagues. But his response to Edwin King was to say, 'You know I think he is speaking out of his own heart's experience. He is the lonely man.' The truth is that both men knew what faithfulness to Scripture involved.[11]

* * *

At the time of this liberal opposition to evangelicalism few saw that the whole structure of English evangelicalism was soon to be in danger from another direction. As already noted, since the decline of historic Christianity in the nineteenth century, while generally

[11] *The Gospel in the Epistle to the Hebrews,* an address given by Tasker for the IVF in Cambridge in August 1949, was published by them in 1950. His most influential literary work was to be in editing and contributing to the Tyndale series of New Testament Commentaries.

continuing in their respective denominations, evangelicals had found their chief support and encouragement in activities which lay outside the control of the denominational bodies. Accordingly, their main influence was exercised not in the denominations as such — where they were commonly ignored or criticized — but rather in such evangelical institutions as Keswick, the non-denominational missionary societies and the Inter-Varsity Fellowship. Here, if not elsewhere, evangelicals could insist and act upon an acceptance of the Bible as the inerrant Word of God.

'Fundamentalism' (i.e. Evangelicalism), James Barr was to argue, 'produced its own special forms of organization, and these are of the greatest importance in any attempt to understand fundamentalism as a phenomenon . . . though undenominational in this sense, they are commonly very exclusive and non-co-operative towards non-conservative evangelical organizations which work in parallel with them. The classic case is . . . the Inter-Varsity Fellowship.' [12]

In other words, evangelicals put the Bible and fellow evangelicals first, even though it frequently brought the accusation that they lacked loyalty to their denominations. Painful though that charge was, evangelicals at least had the consolation of believing that they were putting *Christian* unity before denominational unity. But it was precisely that belief which the ecumenical movement challenged, for it also claimed to represent a greater Christian unity which transcended all denominational differences. If Evangelicalism was going to meet the accusation that it represented an exclusive sectarianism, there was need for a justification of its position.

Evangelicalism was at a crossroads and was about to be put under pressure for which it was not prepared. The Evangelical Alliance, with its stand for evangelical unity, was one of the first agencies to face this difficulty. Following the mixed nature of its speakers in 1948, ML-J had a private meeting with Martyn Gooch, the General Secretary of the Alliance. Perhaps Gooch had listened to what he was told on the danger of ecumenism when he wrote to ML-J on March 25, 1948, 'How greatly I enjoyed that talk with you, and how important I feel the present to be in relation to the future!'[13] A further private meeting

---

[12] *Fundamentalism* (London: SCM, 1977), pp. 21-22.

[13] Gordon Landreth, a later General Secretary of the Evangelical Alliance, says of ML-J: 'It is not generally known that in the immediate post-war years it was his

was arranged with a number of key men, the Rev. Hugh R. Gough of Islington (soon to be Bishop of Barking) representing the officers of the Alliance, and Lloyd-Jones being asked to invite others whose names he had evidently mentioned.

They met in April, 1948 when nothing seems to have been settled. After the World Council of Churches was founded later that same year, the Evangelical Alliance was asked to state publicly its policy on ecumenism. It replied that its attitude to the World Council of Churches was one of 'benevolent neutrality'. When Poole-Connor wrote a letter to the *Christian* expressing his regret over this statement, the publication of his letter was declined. 'I then', writes Poole-Connor, 'inquired of the Editor of the *English Churchman* whether he would print it, and he cordially agreed to do so. But once more my efforts were frustrated, for the Bishop of Barking (Hon. Clerical Secretary of the Alliance) intervened, with neither apology nor explanation, to prevent its publication.'[14] Later Poole-Connor came to believe that the Alliance 'had made up its mind to follow a policy of "benevolence" toward the World Council which carries it far beyond "neutrality"'. When an article appeared in the Alliance's magazine *Evangelical Christendom* (May 1952) which, in Poole-Connor's words, 'conveyed the impression that the World Council was strongly swinging over to Evangelicalism', he resigned his Alliance membership.

Soon there came another development which was to have major significance. On 16 June 1953 Roy Cattell, the new General Secretary of the Alliance, sent ML-J a circular-type letter, expressing 'little doubt that the existence of the World Evangelical Alliance is known to you', together with a booklet on 'Put in Trust with the Gospel' by Dr Billy Graham. The Alliance, supported by Bishop Gough, was now to take an evangelistic role, and when there was no support from denominational leaders for the little-known American evangelist to preach in London, the Evangelical Alliance had stepped in.

---

initiative which led to the strengthening of biblical convictions within the Evangelical Alliance leadership at the time, indirectly preparing the way for the subsequent invitation to Dr Billy Graham to conduct the Harringay Crusade of 1954, though Dr Lloyd-Jones himself did not publicly support that event.' *Idea, the Quarterly Bulletin of the Evangelical Alliance,* Summer 1981.

[14] *E. J. Poole-Connor,* D. G. Fountain, 1966, p. 182.

Under Gough, an Executive Committee was formed to back 'the Billy Graham Greater London Crusade'.

After widespread publicity the Crusade began at Harringay arena in North London on March 1, 1954. It continued for eleven weeks during which time Shaun Herron, editor of the *British Weekly*, warned Graham that he would have to choose whether he wanted the support of evangelicalism or of the denominations. He could not have both. Accordingly the *British Weekly* opposed Graham's coming.

But the success at Harringay brought a remarkable change in the attitude of non-evangelicals. As the Crusade progressed to the point when, during eleven weeks, 37,600 people responded to the evangelist's invitation to go forward to 'receive Christ', church leaders, hitherto never known to stand for biblical convictions, suddenly offered their support and approval. Men not previously identified with evangelicalism (including Leslie Weatherhead) were now to be found as distinguished visitors welcomed to the platform of the Harringay arena. Herron also changed his mind and promised the goodwill of ministers all over the country, with the hope that the Crusade might 'become something of great value to *all* the churches', provided Graham would distance himself from the 'self-righteous censoriousness' of his 'followers' who were 'denouncers of their fellow Christians. You still have time to make it clear to the zealots that the consignment of all other Christians to hell is not a part of what you preach or what you wish . . . You should say it loud and clear, at Harringay, every night, and wherever else you may.'

Herron's words were a typical caricature of what had been evangelical policy. But, with the comprehensive policy of co-operation which the Graham organization was now adopting (and with such apparent success), the old policy was now to be questioned from within as well as by non-evangelical critics. Instead of the cold-shoulder there came the tempting invitation from former opponents to form more 'charitable' judgments, to accept the broader co-operation, and the suggestion that it had been a bad dogmatic spirit which explained why they had not been more successful. As Herron promised, for greater success all that was needed was for evangelicals to have a 'better' relationship with others. As the Crusade came to its conclusion, with the platform now open to divers church leaders, Jerry Beavan, its Executive Secretary, affirmed his hope that no 'divisiveness' would 'be stimulated by the campaign'. As though to confirm the same point, when the great final meeting was held at Wembley Stadium on May 22, Geoffrey Fisher, the Archbishop of Canterbury, was there to give the benediction. Henceforth, in Britain (and elsewhere), the Graham crusades would be open to the co-operative support of all churches and their leaders irrespective of theology.[15]

Whether or not they would believe the Herron argument was the question for British evangelicals. Evangelicals had either to justify their former intransigence, with the alleged 'partisanship' of their separate identity — so contrary to the new ecumenical spirit — or they had to abandon it.

For different reasons, the Graham Crusade also put Lloyd-Jones in some difficulty. On the one hand he regarded the Herron argument as based on a total misreading of the situation, on the other he had meant what he had written in the *British Weekly* that evangelicals 'should not separate on the question of Calvinism and Arminianism'. Graham held Arminian belief,[16] but his message of sin and of rec-onciliation with God through Christ's shed blood was one which ML-J believed and which liberals did not. He publicly prayed for the Crusade, attended one meeting *incognito,* and personally befriended Graham whom he regarded as 'an utterly honest, sincere and genuine man'. At the same time, while he did not doubt that true conversions took place at Harringay, he believed that the method of calling for public decisions was calculated to mislead many, and that, along with the opening of the door for the co-operation of non-evangelicals, was his reason for declining the evangelist's invitations to give his personal support to the Graham organization.[17]

[15] Graham's 'fundamentalist' beliefs did not worry Weatherhead or the Anglican leaders who now gave their support. 'Graham is helping to fill our churches. We can teach people theology when we have someone to teach.' K. Weatherhead, *Leslie Weatherhead* (London: Hodder and Stoughton, 1975), p. 199. A. M. Ramsey, who became Archbishop of Canterbury in 1961, similarly urged his clergy to receive those referred to them by the Graham crusades, 'whatever we think of the theology' *(Canterbury Diocesan Notes,* April, 1966), p. 2.

[16] 'God has given to every man the ability to believe', *Peace with God,* 1954, p. 134.

[17] 'If ten percent of the converts in a crusade are faithful after a year, evangelists and pastors pronounce it a great success.' David F. Wells, *Turning to* God (Grand Rapids: Baker, 2012). Lloyd-Jones believed those truly converted were so changed by the grace of God, not by the public decision. The public 'decision' by the many who do not stand is calculated to mislead both them and those who believed the publicity on the

Other evangelicals responded to the Graham Crusade and Herron's appeal differently and a new alignment was introduced into the British evangelical scene. From now on there would not be two opposing views — comprehensive 'unity' or evangelical separation from non-evangelical work — but a third, namely, evangelicals who would not require certain doctrinal standards as a basis for co-operative effort but would practise, in the new phrase, 'co-operation without compromise'. This would be, in the words of the founders of *Christianity Today*, 'an entirely new approach'.[18]

The organizers of the British Council of Churches were particularly interested in this development and were not slow to take the opportunity created by a dilemma among evangelicals. On October 6, 1954 the Rev. Kenneth Slack, as its General Secretary, sent a letter to Dr Lloyd-Jones and a few other key evangelical leaders, asking for discussions. Slack reported that the Council had received a report from their Committee on Evangelism proposing a consultation 'between those with differing biblical presuppositions to discover what co-operation in evangelism may be achieved despite such differences'. In all twenty-one private meetings for this discussion took place over the next five years, Dr Lloyd Jones being in constant attendance. The discussion paralleled that of the talks with the SCM leaders in 1950, only on a larger scale and without the unanimity on the evangelical side which there had been at the earlier day. On the definition of a Christian, Hugh Gough, Bishop of Barking, thought that it was essentially a matter of 'the spirit' and that people could be one 'in Christ' though differing profoundly in theological beliefs.

At one meeting, when Dr Lloyd-Jones affirmed that his whole theology rested upon the historicity of Adam as a person, Principal Huxtable 'wondered how Dr Lloyd-Jones reconciled his position with what the scientists say'. Possibly the only scientifically-trained person in the room, ML-J replied that 'scientists are very fallible gentlemen'.[19]

---

scale of the success. See his chapter, 'Calling for Decisions', in *Preaching and Preachers*.

[18] For the first two years of its existence. *Christianity Today* 'would emphasize points of commonality with ecumenical Christians, thus establishing the widest possible hearing for the magazine'. See *The Fight of Faith*, p. 304, and my book, *Evangelicalism Divided: A Record of Crucial Change in the Years 1950 to 2000* (Edinburgh: Banner of Truth, 2000) where I deal with this much more fully.

[19] The theory of evolution was 'the biggest hoax in the world in the past 100 years'.

After twenty such meetings from 1954 to a twenty-first (on April 17, 1961) it was decided to recommend to the Committee on Evangelism that it wished to disband. In ML-J's opinion the group had been called together by the other side with the idea in mind that they were only divided by the question of the authority of Scripture. But as successive doctrines came under review, disagreement occurred all along the line. When, towards the end, Kenneth Slack spoke of the Old Testament claim that Uzzah was struck dead as 'not only shocking, but immoral', and ML-J answered him, the conclusion was reached that they differed even on the nature of God. 'We had demonstrated', ML-J believed, 'that no co-operation was possible'.

As these meetings were never publicised, the way in which ML-J had patiently and courteously debated the biblical position with those of differing views over five years, was never known. Some in the mid-sixties would come to regard him as an unrelenting opponent of Christian unity who had not sought to avoid misunderstandings or to find out whether the differences were real and fundamental.

* * *

No one in England in 1954–55 anticipated precisely what the new coalition which emerged from the Graham Crusades would do to evangelicalism. The Evangelical Alliance, again under new personnel, soon faced the challenge. When the Rev. Gilbert W. Kirby, a Nonconformist minister and member of the Westminster Fellowship, became its General Secretary in 1956, he sought to renew the old role of the Alliance in the promotion of evangelical unity. On this subject and others he was in frequent consultation with Dr Lloyd-Jones and, for a time, Lloyd-Jones was to return to being a principal speaker for the Evangelical Alliance. Already, however, there were signs of tensions which lay ahead. After Dr Lloyd-Jones had been the main speaker at a day conference of the Alliance held at Westminster Chapel on June 18, 1957 Poole-Connor wrote to him: 'I do so heartily thank God, and thank you, for your address at the Alliance meeting on Tuesday last! You always manage to say the thing that needs to be said, but which nobody else will say. I attended the morning meeting; and while Kirby was excellent, and Sir Arthur [Smith] good, Bishop Gough

---

Further on Genesis chapters 1 to 3 as history, see *Knowing the Times,* pp. 291, 343 ff.

presented the vaguest platitudes; except that he hinted at kinder feelings toward Rome, and left the door wide open for co-operation with the World Council — all in the most dulcet of tones.'[20]

For the time being at least the old attitude towards non-evangelical Christianity was prominently represented in the Evangelical Alliance and the Alliance was agreed about the danger of the new openness towards the Church of Rome in the Church of England. Changes in the Canon Law of the Church of England, in order to allow the use of vestments identified with the idea of a sacrificial priesthood, were currently being put forward, and Kirby, on behalf of the Alliance, drafted a letter to the Archbishop of Canterbury expressing 'the apprehension that is felt by evangelicals generally'. 'We deplore', he wrote, 'any revision of the Canons which would make co-operation between the established Church and the Free Churches more difficult, or which would in any sense compromise the reformed character of the Church of England . . . We are concerned that the position of the Bible as the supreme and final authority in all matters of faith and conduct should be zealously safeguarded.' If this proposed Alliance letter was sent it was probably the last time that evangelicals unitedly attempted to affirm what had been the traditional evangelical view of the Protestantism of the national Church. Archbishop Fisher, to whom the protest was addressed, as well as giving his blessing to the Graham Crusades, was soon to be the first man holding his office to visit the Pope since the Reformation.

Precisely the same tension was now emerging in connection with the whole work of overseas missions. For many years strategists in the missionary world had seen the need for far greater unity. Too often traditional denominational differences between Protestants had been maintained on the mission field to the injury of young churches. Evangelicals did not doubt that a greater measure of biblical unity would dearly be to the advancement of the gospel. But by the 1950s there were missionary statesmen already convinced that the movement represented by the WCC provided the best hope for

[20] Gough became Archbishop of Sydney in 1959, a position which he did not occupy very happily. He was 'more comprehensive' and 'had a stronger sense of the legitimate place of other schools of thought in the Anglican Church than many conservative Evangelicals in Sydney desired.' S. Judd and K. Cable, *Sydney Anglicans* (Sydney: Anglican Information Office, 2000), p. 265. Gough resigned in 1966 aged 60.

greater unity. They accepted that the ecumenical movement was, in the words of the WCC statement at Evanston (1954), a response 'to the call and action of their Divine Lord'. When a London Mission Convention of sixty British missionary societies was held in March 1957, this viewpoint was strongly presented by Bishop Stephen Neill. Surveying the forces arrayed against the Christian message, he argued that it would be folly not to commit the whole missionary effort to the ecumenical principle.

The Evangelical Alliance responded to this with the formation of the Evangelical Missionary Alliance. Gilbert Kirby reported to Dr Lloyd-Jones (Feb. 12, 1959): 'There are just on forty Societies in membership, plus a further eight Training Colleges. I thought you might be interested to see the draft constitution. You will notice that we have adopted the IVF basis.'

But despite this move to create an alternative to ecumenism in missionary endeavour it is significant that not all its participants assessed the situation in the same way. A number of evangelicals apparently saw no conflict between adherence to the IVF Basis of Faith *and* participation in the World Council. In his book, *What of New Delhi?* Rev. A. T. Houghton, a leader in the most orthodox of the Anglican Missionary Societies (the Bible Churchmen's Missionary Society), argued that the only alternatives were participation in the WCC or 'splendid isolation'. In favour of evangelical participation, he believed that the day had passed when evangelicals 'who spoke the truth as they saw it were neither welcomed nor tolerated'.

Further, Houghton urged the illogicality of staying outside new developments, remarking that evangelicals in the Church of England were already committed by their denomination 'to indirect membership and involvement in the World Council of Churches'. To avoid that membership they would need to leave the Church of England altogether. They also faced the inconsistency, he believed, of not objecting to participation in Anglican diocesan affairs, yet drawing the line at the WCC: 'the former participation may be more frustrating and even "compromising" than the latter, for it is possible for the Church of England to take official action of which we thoroughly disapprove, but which we have to accept whether we like it or not'.[21]

[21] A. T. Houghton, *What of New Delhi?* (Bible Churchmen's Missionary Society, 1962), p. 22.

These words, as we shall see, are a key to understanding what was to be the new evangelical policy of the 1960s. A. T. Houghton was presenting views which would soon be popularised.

While the pressure for wider co-operation with non-evangelicals was perhaps most acutely felt by Anglican evangelicals, evangelicals in the Free Church denominations were not immune. An illustration of this occurred in the weakening of the once close connection between ML-J and the leadership of London Bible College. Since its small beginnings the College had prospered. By 1953 its old building on Marylebone Road was 'bursting at the seams' with 100 full-time students and another 400 attending evening classes. In a sense it was the increased numbers which gave rise to a difference in view between ML-J and Principal Kevan. Since the College was non-denominational its men had no ready access into the ministry of any denomination, yet success in placing students in churches within the mainline denominations was crucial to its reputation. Ernest Kevan, though of Strict Baptist background, saw a future for his students in the Baptist Union churches. Initially the Baptist Union would not accept London Bible College men for its ministry and it had become an object of Kevan's policy to change that decision. Putting as many as possible of his students through the Bachelor of Divinity course of London University was a part of that policy. He wanted to win recognition for the College as an educational establishment. The outcome was that the Baptist Union opened its doors and by the 1960s the leadership of the London Bible College was on good terms with members of the Baptist Union Council. Even so, the Union retained one or two special stipulations for candidates for its ministry from the LBC.

Concerned at the common view that 'the typical conservative evangelical is seldom a good denominational man', Kevan expected his men who entered the Baptist Union to live down that reproach and promised: 'When our men settle in Baptist pastorates they never cause trouble.'

Lloyd-Jones did not share Mr Kevan's confidence in this policy development. In the first place, he believed it involved the encouragement of a non-evangelical loyalty at a time when the distinctiveness of evangelical convictions was under threat. In the Free Churches, as well as in the Church of England, it was becoming virtually impossible to be pro-denominational without also being pro-ecumenical. In the second place, he did not believe that the London University Bachelor of Divinity course was the best means of preparing men for the work of the ministry. He recognized that to bypass the credentials conferred by theological degrees could exclude students from some places of influence, but he feared that a greater influence for usefulness was being jeopardized by subjecting future preachers to the unbelieving and liberal studies approved by the universities.

This background is necessary to understand the implications of an address which ML-J gave on the occasion of the opening of the new premises of the London Bible College at 19 Marylebone Road on Saturday, May 10, 1958. A fine day in early summer, it was a grand occasion in the evangelical calendar of that year. Earlier in the week Professor E. J. Young of Westminster Theological Seminary had given four 'Inaugural Lectures'. On the day itself the crowds of visitors were welcomed with the gift of a splendid brochure on the College, but for many there was no hope of getting a seat in the Chapel which was early crowded with official guests for the service at which Lloyd-Jones was to preach. Every corner of the whole building seemed to be crammed with people and, happily, the proceedings from the Chapel were relayed by loudspeakers. It was one of the most powerful sermons which ML-J ever gave. His text was 2 Timothy 2:15, 16, 'Study to shew thyself approved unto God, a workman that needeth not to be ashamed, rightly dividing the word of truth. But shun profane and vain babblings . . .'

In the course of this address he spoke of the contemporary lack of concern over error in the religious world, yet Paul says it 'will eat as doth a canker' (*2 Tim.* 2:17): 'It kills, robs of life and leaves a festering mass at the end. The church today is a travesty of the word "church" all because of this cancer.' The call to evangelicals, he went on, is to concentrate on 'the word of truth'. 'Our message is not uncertain. Men are not all going the same way, worshipping the same God. We are to teach *revealed* truth and not shift our position according to the state of the world . . . It is because it believes that, that this institution is called the London *Bible* College. If our Lord's return does not take place for a hundred years I hope it will still be teaching the same thing.'

ML-J's application of his message that day consisted in pressing the question, 'How may the College know if it is attaining this object and 'rightly dividing the word of truth'? The tests, he said, are these:

> Are the men more certain of the truth at the end of their studies than at the beginning? Are they more steadfast? Do they know God better and desire to serve God better than when they came in? Ah, how many lose this! Have they a greater zeal for God? a greater love for the lost and perishing? What is the purpose of doctrine and knowledge if it is not to know God? . . . You may have more B.D.'s than any College in the country but *only* if the result is that your people know God better!
>
> We are a remnant today, but others have been through the same situation — 'If we suffer, we shall also reign with him.' Paul encouraged Timothy with this, 'The foundation of God standeth sure, having this seal, The Lord knoweth them that are his.' Remember that he is taking special interest in you. He will be with you in some lonely village, and when the end seems to have come, remember that you are preaching a Saviour who rose again; 'Remember that Jesus Christ was raised from the dead.'

It was a thrilling peroration. E. J. Young told a group of students afterwards that he had heard nothing equal to it since the death of Gresham Machen. But Professor Young, and no doubt others present, had not seen the implications for the College which might lie behind the preacher's theme. The Faculty certainly saw them and received the sermon coolly. When the possibility of its publication was discussed at the next Faculty meeting, it was firmly turned down. After 1958 ML-J was asked to take little part in London Bible College affairs.[22]

Behind the evangelical differences there existed a major underlying difference over the present condition of evangelical Christianity. Dr Lloyd-Jones believed that as well as a serious decline in the churches, evangelicalism was itself weakening rather than gaining in spiritual power. His words, 'We are a remnant today', were out of line with

---

[22] For a fuller, and sympathetic account of Dr Kevan's thinking, see, Paul E. Brown, *Ernest Kevan: Leader in Twentieth-Century British Evangelicalism* (Edinburgh: Banner of Truth, 2012). The issue of theological degrees from secular universities arose also at the 1958 Puritan Conference when, in the course of discussion on the existing state of theological education, Jim Packer expressed the conviction that even the evangelical colleges 'turned out anything but preachers of the Word'. It was a general statement, but Kevan rose to deprecate it and to speak of the usefulness of the framework of the B.D. course.

what was becoming the popular evangelical mood. Even in 1951, when Poole-Connor's *Evangelicalism in England* was published, a reviewer in the *Christian* took exception to the statement, 'In most Protestant denominations some evangelicals are found but they are in a minority.' On the contrary, the reviewer believed, 'At no time have evangelicals been so numerous in the world as they are today.' After the Graham Crusades this hope was greatly increased. People spoke of 'harvest time in England'. Graham himself offered the belief, 'that Britain is on the verge of the greatest spiritual awakening in her history.' Gough, when Bishop of Barking, spoke of 'the glorious possibilities these coming years hold for us'.

This was not to say that evangelicals in the main denominations denied the need for change in the churches, but there was reluctance to admit the need for change at a fundamental level. There was the recognition of the need for evangelicals to attain a higher standard of scholarship. There was also the development of a feeling soon to sweep all before it, that a main hindrance to the church effectively reaching the world was her out-of-date appearance in the contemporary culture. Her Bible version and her forms of worship had remained little changed for centuries. The climate of thought — not uninfluenced by the secular world — was swinging against all things 'traditional' and 'old-fashioned'.

For Dr Lloyd-Jones what he had feared when he had spoken on 'Maintaining the Evangelical Faith' in 1952 was coming to pass: 'To concentrate upon external expansion to the neglect of the biblical requirements of doctrinal and ethical purity is to risk internal disloyalty, disunity, and confusion.' In the next decade, as we shall see, he was to be accused of dividing evangelicals. Such opinion overlooks the fact that division developed in the 1950s and he was not its source.

28. The family with Bethan's mother, Mrs Phillips.

TWENTY-FOUR

—————————

An Awakening of Books

I have commented on the change of thought in the recovery of Calvinistic convictions in a number of young people in the early 1950s. It had come in connexion with two means, the spoken word of one man, and the rediscovery of Puritan books. But that second means was not common at the beginning of that decade, for Reformation and Puritan literature was rare in England and scarcely to be found except, at times, in second-hand bookshops. Years earlier these shops had found such stock unsaleable. With no demand for old and unknown authors there was no reason to retain them in stock. Yet before Spurgeon, the so-called last of the Puritans, had died in 1892, he had asserted, 'Books written for the Master and his truth, though buried in obscurity are sure of a resurrection.' The decade from 1950 to 1960 was to see just such a resurrection. The contrast within ten years was to be striking. In 1950 there were no British publishers committed to Puritan or Calvinistic theology. When James Clarke reprinted Calvin's *Institutes* in 1949, and when Marshall Morgan and Scott re-issued Warfield's *Inspiration and Authority of the Bible* in 1951, they were resting on ML-J's belief rather than their own. In the words of the latter, the hope was to 'try to create a new interest'. Clarke went on in 1952, again at Lloyd-Jones' suggestion, to reprint *Holiness* by J. C. Ryle, but Marshall Morgan and Scott declined to proceed to Warfield's *Biblical and Theological Studies*. While Christian publishers admired Lloyd-Jones's ministry, and observed its evident influence, they did not share his vision for the theological change which was needed in the church at large. Even the IVF in measure shared in this limitation. While they did much for a recovery of evangelical reading, 'they were', in Dr Lloyd-Jones' words, 'very careful to say that this was not a theological matter primarily, but of biblical studies, so they concentrated on commentaries and books of a general apologetic nature'.[1]

Further, living British Christian authors who were representative of the older theology were virtually unknown in 1950. The writings of Arthur W. Pink were of no interest to any British publishing house and when he died unnoticed in Scotland in 1952 there was no expectation that they would ever be reprinted with a global readership. Yet by 1959 Dr Lloyd-Jones could speak of the 'tremendously encouraging fact' that 'there is obviously a new interest in Reformed literature and this seems to me to be true right through the world'.[2]

While preaching and books were at the forefront in this change, to trace the source only to them would be to miss its real nature. God was answering the prayer that he had himself prompted.

It may sound surprising in view of what would later happen, that in the recovery of a more scriptural and doctrinal Christianity Dr Lloyd-Jones played a comparatively small part as an *author*. There was very little by him in print in 1950 apart from a monthly sermon in the *Westminster Record*. The explanation lies chiefly in his conviction that ministers are called to be preachers, not writers. The readiness of contemporary Christianity to allow the preaching to be overshadowed by other means of communication he saw as a loss of faith rather than a wise adjustment to modern conditions. The testimony of John Knox was no longer commonly believed: 'What efficacy hath the living voice above the bare letter read, the hungry and thirsty do feel to their comfort'.[3]

It may, however, be asked why ML-J's sermons, once preached and recorded, could not then be printed — as in the *Westminster Record* month by month?[4] The answer lies in the whole practical problem which arises when the spoken word is transferred into literary form.

---

[1] *The Annual Meeting of the Evangelical Library,* 1966, p. 27.

[2] *The Annual Meeting of the Evangelical Library,* 1960, p. 13.

[3] *Works of John Knox,* (Edinburgh: Johnstone and Hunter, 1856), vol. 5, p. 519.

[4] His sermons at Westminster Chapel were first taken down in shorthand by Mrs Edith Burney. Only towards the mid-1950s were they regularly recorded.

Some of the features of the most effective speech become blemishes when put into print and therefore even in literature where the sermonic form is retained — as, for instance, in the case of Spurgeon's published sermons — a great deal of revision is necessary. Despite Mrs Lloyd-Jones' aid and later that of their daughter, Elizabeth, Dr Lloyd-Jones was often hard pressed to find the time to do the minimum work required on the monthly published sermon. On his voyages to the States in 1956 and to South Africa in 1958 it was this kind of work which he had to take with him.

Although several publishers asked ML-J for books they all entertained the view that material patently sermonic in form — as in the *Westminster Record* — would be unsaleable and that considerable changes would have to be made in order for it to reach a wider readership. This view was demonstrated by more than one publisher. In 1946 Pickering and Inglis were eager to print nine sermons which he had preached from Ephesians on 'God's Plan for World Unity' and then published in the *Westminster Record*. After Arthur Marsh, on ML-J's behalf, had entered into negotiations with these London publishers they had returned the sermons (as printed in the *Westminster Record)* so that the author could 'look them over'. But ML-J determined that more than a 'look over' was needed and he had no time to attend to it. They found a final resting place in a bottom drawer in his study.

Lutterworth Press fared worse than Pickering and Inglis. Through Arthur Marsh they negotiated a contract with Dr Lloyd-Jones for his sermons on 'The Soul's Conflict' from the *Record* and to avoid, as they hoped, the problems of which they had probably heard rumours, they proceeded to have the type set without giving ML-J the opportunity to 'look over' what they had taken upon themselves to do by way of editorial revision. 'I think', wrote their editorial secretary, 'that when you see the book in proof and look at the way in which our very skilled editor has brought the material into the right compass you will be very pleased indeed.' Far from being 'pleased' when he saw the proofs, Dr Lloyd-Jones terminated the whole proposal!

The main problem in this oft-repeated difficulty was not any wish on the preacher's part to retain his exact words. He understood the need for some revision very well. Disagreement centred on the extent to which the authoritative preaching style, at times discursive and repetitious, ought to be retained. Dr Lloyd-Jones was himself unsure how effectively he could be put into print, and he preferred to forego publication altogether rather than accept the extent of the curtailment which publishers commonly considered necessary. His five addresses given at Wheaton on 'Truth Unchanged, Unchanging' in 1947 were less sermonic in form and that may be part of the reason why they were his first post-war book to be printed. Yet even this small book did not appear until four years later.[5] In 1951 Fred Mitchell also attempted to encourage the publication of a major volume of sermons by ML-J. By December of that year the first nine sermons of his long series on 'The Sermon on the Mount' had been printed in the *Westminster Record*. Mitchell, having ascertained that Leslie Lyall — a CIM missionary well accustomed to editorial work — was willing to help, wrote to ML-J proposing that Lyall start work on these sermons. The preacher was willing to give it a try but once again the revision foundered on the fundamental issue of how far the chapters would keep their original character.

As a result of this persistent difficulty, coupled with ML-J's own lack of time, it was not until 1959 that volume one of *Studies in the Sermon on the Mount* was published. The text stayed close to what was first printed in the *Record* and the Preface included the words of apologia, 'A sermon is not an essay and is not meant, primarily, for publication, but to be heard and to have an immediate impact upon the listeners.'

ML-J's slowness over his own books cannot be related to any doubt over the influence of literature. These pages have already made that clear. He was looking for writers. In that regard he encouraged speakers at the Puritan Conference and elsewhere, and for the aid of such men he knew no more vital asset than the Evangelical Library. We noted its opening in London in 1945. In 1948 it was moved to 78 Chiltern Street, which is close to Baker Street, in the heart of the West End, and only a few hundred yards from the London Bible College in Marylebone Road. The Library premises were in many ways an extraordinary place, situated on the third floor of an old building and to be approached only by flights of stone steps akin to the entrance of some Victorian workhouse. A notice on a landing two-thirds of the way to the top advised the climber to 'Pause and Pray'. The top

[5] London: James Clarke, 1951.

landing once reached, a heavy door opened into a large upper room, some seventy feet long by twenty broad, with a pitched roof rising immediately from the high walls to an apex twenty-two feet above the floor, and windows letting in some light on the southern slope of the roof. It would have been comparatively airy had it not been for some 25,000 volumes, crammed into the shelved partitions which divided the floor space, and climbing like creepers up every conceivable inch of wall with the exception of the spaces occupied by portraits of the old divines. Immediately inside the entrance door, on the right, was an office where at almost any time Geoffrey Williams and Marjorie Denby, his secretary, could be found with barely enough room to sit amidst books and papers and, if it happened to be lunch time, the delicious smell of toasted brown bread. Williams was 70 in 1955. Miss Denby, six years younger, was a member at Westminster Chapel and was often to be seen carrying books that ML-J needed to his vestry on a Friday night.

29. The Evangelical Library, Chiltern Street, and Geoffrey Williams.

However improbable it might sound, it was to this archaic place that young people were now coming in increasing numbers. Although not the finest Puritan library in England, it was probably the only one where the works of many seventeenth-century authors could be seen and even, given a careful use of ladders, handled and read. Ten years later Dr Lloyd-Jones was to look back on the mid-1950s as a time when the Evangelical Library made 'a massive contribution' to the beginning of something new, and he regarded its work as 'a living illustration of the fact that out of the smallest — almost despicably small — beginnings, God can bring a great power into being'.[6]

It would appear to be from the year 1955 that we have ML-J's first recorded conviction that a major spiritual change had begun. By that date it had become a tradition that, as President of the Evangelical Library, he should speak to the group of friends who gathered there once a year for an Annual Meeting. In numbers they were few, but ML-J regarded them as an inner circle (both of the Library and of his ministry) and he would often express his personal thoughts to them in a manner which he would seldom do anywhere else in public. His words at the 1955 Annual Meeting included the following:

> There is another remarkable thing to which I must refer; I feel that we are witnessing a true revival of interest in the Puritans, and a number of young men are studying their literature constantly. There is held annually a Puritan Conference which is attended by some sixty people, and this library has played a very central part in it. All the men involved come here, or to the branches, in the course of their quest. As I see things, it is of supreme importance for the future of the Christian faith in this country that we should experience a revival of interest in the literature of the great Puritans of the seventeenth century, and to this end the library is absolutely central and invaluable.

Twelve months later he reported to the same gathering that what they were beginning to see in Britain was also to be found across the Atlantic:

> I spent some time in the United States and Canada recently and I can tell you something about the religious situation there. I found one thing there which is the most encouraging trend I have encountered for many a day. Among the leaders in evangelical work, and especially among the students, I found something which really did amaze me. After a meeting a number of young men came forward

---

[6] *The Annual Meeting of the Evangelical Library*, 1966, pp. 27-30.

to speak with me, and every single one talked to me about Puritan literature and asked whether there was a possibility of getting Puritan books from this country. It is true of increasing numbers of them; they, like us, are turning to the Puritans, and for the same reason. We are all tired of the typical periodicals and books and are not being helped by the literature of today. They felt that they wanted something solid for their souls.

I am sure this library is playing a part in bringing this conviction into being, and I rejoice in it. For, it seems to me, we shall never see a spiritual revival except along these lines — as people come back to these works and are searched by them.

It was at this point that another agency came into prominence which was destined to carry forward on a larger scale what had already begun. Mr D. J. W. ('Jack') Cullum was a well-known acoustic consultant in London and the head of two London companies which he largely owned. Financial success and international business had followed his invention during the Second World War of mufflers to reduce the noise of jet aircraft when they were being tested on the ground. Yet this prosperity had brought no inner peace to the nominal Methodist who had long since ceased attending church. Only when two evangelical Christians, Mr and Mrs Stanley Clarke, spoke of Christ to him during a trans-Atlantic crossing on the 'Queen Elizabeth' in March 1953 did the message touch his heart. On returning home from New York, Jack Cullum resumed church attendance in his former denomination, but, after trying one or two Methodist churches in North London he remained confused and under conviction of sin until December 1955 when he accepted an invitation from the Clarkes to visit them in their home at Jerusalem. It was there that he received assurance of salvation.

In 1956, when I became Assistant to Dr Lloyd-Jones at Westminster Chapel, and one of my duties was to take a Wednesday night meeting with addresses on church history, I first met Jack Cullum, who was now attending Westminster Chapel. Six feet four inches in height with jet-black hair, it was impossible not to notice him and his rapt attention when these Wednesday night meetings began in October, 1956. It was a few months later that we first talked personally when my wife and I accepted an invitation to visit his home in Highgate on January 26, 1957. As we walked that day close to Hampstead Heath he put a question to me the repercussions of which were, in due time, to touch the ends of the earth. He was thankful for a growing understanding of how salvation is all of God, and also finding the witness of church history to be full of excitement. His question was, 'Why is it that all the history and teaching of the English Reformers and Puritans is so little known today?' When I replied in terms of the long period during which their works had been unavailable, I had no idea that I was speaking to someone whom God was calling to support their republication. Since his conversion Jack Cullum's prayer had been that he might be enabled to do something useful for the remainder of his life. At first he had thought of giving of his considerable means to advance evangelical agencies in general, and he had founded a charitable trust with that in view, but the testimony of leaders from the sixteenth and seventeenth centuries had stirred him deeply and, on hearing of the vision of a new publishing venture for the advancement of historic and Calvinistic Christianity, he was almost instantly committed to it. By mid-March 1957 plans were developed between us, and ML-J gave his approval to a publishing work which, as its existence was unrelated to any question of financial profit, should also be a charitable trust. The intention was to continue on a larger scale the message of the magazine I had edited since 1955, hence the name we adopted in 1957 was 'The Banner of Truth Trust'.

By November 1957 two books were printed and at the binders, with a further nine in the course of production. When the first two books became available early in 1958 their sale was remarkably rapid, and especially at Westminster Chapel, where ML-J said on the first Friday evening after they became available:

> I want to call your attention to two books available in the Book Room. *A Commentary on the Song of Solomon* was published at my personal suggestion. It is one of the choicest books I have ever read in my life . . .[7] I cannot speak too highly of this book and exhort you all to read it. It is republished by a new Trust and the price of ten shillings and six pence is quite amazing. Old classics are to be reprinted at a cheap rate. The second book is Thomas Watson's

[7] George Burrowes, *The Song of Solomon,* first published in 1853. The 1958 reprint did not include the author's lengthy Introduction. This was put right in the 1973 edition and remains in print.

Body of Divinity, sermons on the Westminster Catechism. As you read this book you will be brought face to face with the essentials of the Christian Faith. I am not a member of this Trust; I am speaking warmly of these books because of my esteem for them. I am extremely happy that this is being done so that modern Christians can read some of the great Christian classics.

Dr Lloyd-Jones did not want the publishers identified with Westminster Chapel, hence the words, 'I am not a member of this Trust'. He did not say that his Assistant and one of his members were the founding trustees, or that he had suggested to the deacons that the Chapel premises could be used for the storage and dispatch of books till a permanent base was found.[8]

These first books were quickly followed by *The Select Sermons of George Whitefield* and *The Select Works of Jonathan Edwards,* vol. 1. The latter work Dr Lloyd-Jones recommended to the congregation on Friday evening, March 7, 1958, and pointed out that the month marked the bicentenary of Edwards' death. It was this same month that he wrote a Foreword to Robert Haldane's *Exposition of the Epistle to the Romans* which the Banner of Truth Trust had in hand for publication. In this Foreword he quoted the words of Dr Reuben Saillens concerning the revival which had followed Haldane's work on the continent of Europe. The quotation also expressed very clearly the objectives both of ML-J's own ministry and that of the Trust:

> The three main characteristics of Haldane's Revival, as it has sometimes been called, were these: (1) it gave a prominent emphasis to the necessity of a personal knowledge and experience of grace; (2) it maintained the absolute authority and divine inspiration of the Bible; (3) it was a return to Calvinistic doctrine against Pelagianism and Arminianism. Haldane was an orthodox [preacher] of the first water, but his orthodoxy was blended with love and life.

Two years later, at the Annual Meeting of the Library on November 29, 1960 Dr Lloyd-Jones could say:

---

[8] In February 1958 the Trust rented its first headquarters on the ground floor of the same building as the Evangelical Library, 78 Chiltern Street. Members at Westminster Chapel commonly assumed ML-J's link with the Trust, even to the point of his being given a complaint that the print was too small in one early volume!

We rejoice in the fact that now we can get so many really good books, brand new and beautifully produced, with glossy, shiny covers. You see, the daughters are much more up-to-date and attractive in appearance than the older ones. But do not forget the mother! The best books were available here, and almost exclusively here until two or three years ago.

Crusade magazine, reviewing developments in evangelical life in the previous twenty-one years, referred in 1971 to 'the revival of Reformed theology sparked off largely by the setting up of the Banner of Truth Trust which flooded the market with inexpensive reprints of Puritan classics'. As the preceding pages have shown, this is not an accurate statement of what occurred. The Trust's work met with success in 1958 because a hunger already existed. No one can flood a market with unwanted books. The change was already there, stimulated by the few reprints previously available and by the older books to be found at the Evangelical Library and elsewhere.

But pre-eminently it was the preaching and teaching of ML-J which had prepared the way for a new climate of opinion. The seemingly sudden demand for a different type of book was directly connected with the pulpit of Westminster Chapel and confirmed what he had once said: 'It is very interesting to note how the type of theology you hold will decide whether you are a reader or whether you are not.' The theology he preached made people *readers*. The preaching had to come first, and had it not done so the response to the older literature might well have remained as feeble as it had been ten years earlier. The spoken word had opened the way.

ML-J's hopes were by no means confined to the writers of former generations. While he encouraged the importing of such living authors as A. W. Tozer from the United States, he looked, as I have said, for young men in England with a gift to write. Jim Packer was one of the first whom he recognized in that connection. Packer was asked to give the Evangelical Library Lecture in 1952 on 'The Practical Writings of the English Puritans', and the typescript subsequently circulated by the Library was the first taste of much that was to come from the same author.[9] It was an initial fulfilment of ML-J's hopes for a new school of authors. If the Packer lecture of 1952 was noticed by

[9] With some revision it will be found in *A Quest for Godliness: The Puritan Vision of the Christian Life* (Grand Rapids: Crossway, 1990).

comparatively few, it was otherwise when his critique of the Keswick theology of sanctification was published in the *Evangelical Quarterly* in July 1955. 'I expect some criticism from Keswick supporters', F. F. Bruce, the editor, wrote to ML-J. This was followed by Packer's joint work with Raymond Johnston in a new translation of Luther on *The Bondage of the Will* (London: James Clarke, 1957). An Introduction' of nearly fifty pages concluded: 'Much modern Protestantism would be neither owned nor even recognized by the pioneer Reformers.' Packer went still further in his 'Introductory Essay' to John Owen's *The Death of Death in the Death of Christ* (London: Banner of Truth, 1959).

There was by this time a considerable disturbance over what was, for most, the unheard of teaching that Christ died to save the elect. Evangelist Tom Rees believed that evangelicalism was being divided and warned that, 'Extreme Calvinism has spread to many parts of the country, particularly amongst the younger evangelical ministers and undergraduates'. It was feared that this would put an end to evangelism, a fear well and wisely countered in Packer's *Evangelism and the Sovereignty of God* (1961).[10] But controversy did not abate quickly. At one point, a senior IVF committee, anxious to see it end, entertained a proposal that anyone belonging to 'a party' [i.e. a 'Calvinist'] should be excluded from speaking to the Christian Unions; ML-J immediately indicated that such a ruling would put them all out, for they all belonged to parties in matters of belief.

Dr Lloyd-Jones was himself blamed for the turmoil which young men associated with him were causing in some places. In reality he was giving more time than ever to guiding, advising and, often, restraining them. But he exercised no dictatorial control, and the new circumstances certainly placed him in a difficult situation. He wanted evangelical unity. He eschewed any kind of Calvinistic sectarianism which would break fellowship with fellow Christians of Arminian persuasion and, in this regard, he often pointed to the example of Whitefield's brotherly relationship with John Wesley. Yet at the same

---

[10] This important book was an expansion of an address given to students in London on October 24, 1959, prior to a mission held by the London Inter-Faculty Christian Union. It faced the necessity and urgency of evangelism, argued that belief that God is sovereign does not affect the genuineness of gospel invitations, and made discriminating distinctions, i.e., 'Evangelism is man's work, but the giving of faith is God's.'

time he had worked and prayed for evangelicalism to be moved to a stronger doctrinal position and he believed passionately that the greatest need of the church, namely a true revival, was closely related to a recovery of those biblical truths associated with the Calvinistic tradition. It was thus his belief that, despite some excesses among the younger men, the return to the older tradition was of God.

He urged that truth should be kept in its biblical balance and be presented in a devotional not a polemical spirit. The further recognition of that need led to another literature work starting from a member of Westminster Chapel in 1958. This was Elizabeth Braund who in 1956 and 1957 had given addresses at the Puritan Conferences. Miss Braund had been converted earlier in the 1950s, in connection with the ministry at Westminster Chapel, at a time when she was preparing the script for a BBC programme on the history of the transmission of the Bible. In September 1959, encouraged by ML-J and in conjunction with 'consulting editors' Jim Packer and Elwyn Davies, she launched the *Evangelical Magazine,* a bi-monthly with a strong devotional and pastoral emphasis. It was largely from a series of articles by Packer in this magazine that his book, *Knowing God,* would come and be one of the most widely read Christian books of the twentieth century. After the publication of those articles in book form in 1973 the sales went to more than three million copies.

* * *

It was characteristic of ML-J that he was not bound by any programme in his preaching, but I do not know that he ever interrupted a series in the way he did for Sunday mornings in 1959. At the beginning of that year he was due to continue in the midst of his exposition of Ephesians chapter 5. But he set Ephesians aside until November of that year, and instead took up a series on the subject of Revival. For an understanding of his thinking this series remains one of his most important.

As ever, in preaching on revival ML-J was affected by the situation as he saw it. Several different factors combined to prompt him to take up this subject. First, although it happened to be one hundred years since the last widespread awakening of 1859 in Britain, he was not greatly interested in a commemoration. There were some who were, and to the point of having all night prayer meetings for revival.

They were surprised when ML-J did not join in. He did not believe in laying aside the normal work of the church to await the extraordinary.[11] Prayer for the Holy Spirit was part of the regular life of the church at Westminster Chapel, and he considered the special activity proposed in all-night meetings had about it the error that we can *do something* to induce revival. These were well-meaning people who needed clearer teaching.

But a second group he had in view was much larger in number, and more representative of the general evangelical scene. They did not see any urgent need for revival: 'They do not think about revival, and they do not feel it necessary, and they do not pray for it. "All we have to do," say they, "is to keep on as we are. God is blessing us. Everything is all right."'[12] They needed to learn from the mighty works of God recorded in Scripture and in history, that revival was not a present experience. A main burden of the revival series was to address this kind of complacency: 'I am not despising the day of small things — I just want us to realize that we *are* in the day of small things.'[13]

Nearer home, he also meant to speak to the young men who were in danger of misreading the doctrinal resurgence in which they were sharing. They were seeing numbers swelling — the Westminster Fellowship had needed to move from the church parlour to the large Institute Hall; the 60 at the Puritan Conference in 1955 had grown to about 200; and the same feature was clearer still in the Sunday services at Westminster. David Potter, who came to London to study theology in the late 1950s, has written: 'At first I resisted the pressure to join the crowds to Westminster Chapel each Sunday. Eventually I succumbed, but made my way alone to "the Chapel". Many things surprised me. The size of the congregation was quite new to me, and the hymn-singing was moving in a way I had rarely experienced. And there seemed to be hundreds of other students.'

[11] Speaking in December 1959, he criticised people 'who always talk about revival and only about revival. They are only interested in the exceptional and unusual, and they tend to "despise the day of small things", the regular work of the church and the regular work of the Spirit in the church.'

[12] D. Martyn Lloyd-Jones, *Revival, Can We Make It Happen?* (Basingstoke, Hants: Marshall Pickering, 1986), p. 176. The U.S. edition (Wheaton, IL: Crossway, 1987) has the same pagination, but rightly drops the words of the sub-title which were no part of the author's original.

[13] *Ibid.,* p. 179.

This was a situation which could too easily prompt an unwarranted satisfaction among the young. Reasons why those belonging to the Reformed tradition could be tempted to miss the need for revival he summarised at the 1959 Puritan Conference as: (1) Resting in orthodoxy and 'growing negligent about your own spiritual life and the life of the church'; (2) An over-concern with apologetics in answering Modernism; (3) The dislike of 'emotion' and 'an excessive reaction against Pentecostalism'; (4) A wrong deduction drawn from the Puritans, as though this was a subject which did not interest them.

He also said at that same conference that it had been the decline in Reformed theology in the previous hundred years which had contributed most to the lack of interest in revival. He did not use that label in preaching the revival sermons but he was referring to it when he said:

> Look at many books which have been written in this present century on the doctrine of the Holy Spirit and try and find for me a paragraph, or a section, or a chapter, on revival . . . Now if you go back and read books which were written on the person and the work of the Holy Spirit, say, round about 1860, by Smeaton, for example, and others, there you will find sections on religious awakenings, religious revivals. They deal with it specifically. In the past they always did, but during the last seventy to eighty years, this whole notion of a visitation, a baptism of God's Spirit upon the church, has gone.[14]

He was asserting that the older evangelical and Calvinistic writers had an understanding of revival different from contemporary ones. The common evangelical idea was that there was one baptism of the Spirit at Pentecost, into which all Christians come at their conversion, and so their one duty was to believe what they already have. But the old writers believed that there is an on-going baptizing work

[14] *Ibid.,* pp. 53-4. George Smeaton, *The Doctrine of the Holy Spirit* (1882; repr. London: Banner of Truth, 1958) was one of the Banner of Truth's first reprints and remains in print. It should not be thought that the thinking he represents belonged only to those of a distinctly Reformed persuasion. Bishop H. C. G. Moule, for instance, says on Ephesians 1:17: 'We are not to think of the "giving" of the Spirit as an isolated deposit of what, once given, is now locally in possession. The first "gift" is, as it were, the first point in a series of actions.'

of Christ — further enduements and times of refreshing when the Spirt is given in larger measure to individuals or to churches. 'Baptisms', 'outpourings', 'revivals', were synonymous terms — Jonathan Edwards repeats the same idea in speaking of 'remarkable effusions [of the Spirit] at special seasons of mercy'. This, as ML-J pointed out, was the common understanding of the older writers. Thus John Knox explained what he saw at the Reformation in the words, 'God gave his Holy Spirit to simple men in great abundance.' This is the sovereign action of God. Christians are ever to pray for more of the Spirit's grace and influence, but the measure and times in which the prayer is answered belong to God.

Given the existence of such a diversity of thought it might be wondered how the Revival sermons could speak to all. Lloyd-Jones' answer was that underneath there was just one great need, a clearer vision and consciousness of God. Not so much changed opinions, as a higher realization of the glory of God. This is what the Spirit teaches, and at times when he teaches this with special power the fear of God takes hold of people and churches: 'They begin to see what an appalling thing sin is in the sight of God. Never has there been a revival but that some of the people, especially at the beginning, have had such visions of the holiness of God, and the sinfulness of sin, that they have scarcely known what to do with themselves.'[15]

So if there was a chief hindrance to greater blessing it was that 'the Christian church is still so healthy, so confident in herself, so sure she only needs to organize yet another effort, some further activity'. That being so, there could be no assurance that revival was near: 'It may be that things infinitely worse than what we have already known will yet have to happen to us.'

* * *

In Geoffrey Williams' little office, the inner sanctum of the Evangelical Library, there was a disused fireplace and in the corner to the left of the fireplace a glass bookcase containing his favourite books. In a sense the whole purpose of the Library was contained in that small space. Here were his select books on revivals and biographies of men who had been leaders in such times. Some of the books Marjorie

[15] *Ibid.,* p. 157.

Denby would carry to ML-J probably came from there and certainly some of the titles the Banner of Truth Trust were reprinting did. Dr Lloyd-Jones' sermons on Revival were not to be in print until 1986, but numbers of books on the subject which he prized had been spread round the world by that date. He knew that books of themselves do not bring revival but, whenever a revival comes, the consolidation of the work in the churches stands related to right reading beforehand. It meant much to him that, at the Library annual meeting of 1960, Geoffrey Williams could report 6,700 books borrowed that year from Chiltern Street and 84,077 books sent to overseas branches. The prayer with which ML-J concluded that meeting is a fitting conclusion to this chapter:

> And now, O Lord our God, we ascribe unto thee all praise, all honour and all glory, and it is thine alone, and we do not desire to give any portion of it to anybody else. Lord, it is thine; we but humbly thank thee that thou hast ever given any of us a part and a place in thy great purposes of grace.

TWENTY-FIVE

Unity: Ecumenical or Evangelical?

For Dr Lloyd-Jones the 1960s were undoubtedly to be the hardest decade in his life. In general he was convinced there was a worsening of spiritual conditions in Britain and, instead of sharing in the self-confidence of an evangelicalism which spoke as though revival was at hand, he feared 'we still have a long way to go'.[1] There were now problems to be addressed on several fronts at once. Some had to do with excess among those with whom he had much in common. Among the younger men who had shared in the doctrinal recovery of the 1950s there was now a dangerous tendency to think too exclusively of orthodoxy. In reading Lloyd-Jones, to understand his variation in emphasis, it is well to keep in mind to whom he was speaking and at what date. 'I spend half my time telling Christians to study doctrine and the other half telling them that doctrine is not enough.'

But the main difficulty lay elsewhere. The ecumenical movement was not only questioning the priority of truth, it was challenging the argument of evangelicals that, because the New Testament requires only the spiritual oneness of believers, they could remain scattered in various denominations. A flood of ecumenical articles, books, 'conversations', commissions and conferences argued that a purpose to transform the existing denominations into one church was a good and proper thing. In 1964 a Conference of the British Council of Churches at Nottingham committed itself to 'one Church not later than Easter

---

[1] *Revival*, p. 182.

Day, 1980'. All that remained, it seemed, was discussion over the means by which this was to be brought about. For evangelicals, however, the fundamental questions were only beginning to be faced.

How the need for true unity was to be met was much more important to Dr Lloyd-Jones than mere opposition to the ecumenical movement, yet, holding the position which he did, it was inevitable that he would have to take a leading role in opposition to the latter. He differed with ecumenism on its fundamental principle, namely, that all dialogue should proceed on the understanding that it was between fellow *Christians.* He objected to this because it gave a breadth to the meaning of 'Christian' which was unknown in the New Testament. The fact was that the movement for the reunion of the denominations had grown up in conditions where the liberal view of Scripture was so pervasive that the idea that anyone needed to *believe* certain definite truths in order to be a child of God was no longer taken seriously. In theory some kind of recognition of Christ as 'the Son of God' might be required as a statement of belief, but there was a general willingness among church leaders to dispense with any doctrinal test of Christian profession. In practice this meant that when Aneurin Bevan MP died in 1960, despite his atheism and public indifference to Christianity, a memorial service was held in Westminster Abbey. The following year Michael Ramsey, Fisher's successor as Archbishop of Canterbury, was reported to have pronounced: 'Heaven is not a place for Christians only . . . I expect to meet some present-day atheists there.'[2]

Such a view was not the temporary aberration of one leading Anglican. The same basic attitude was in all the mainline churches, as may be seen by the way in which Albert Schweitzer, Nobel Prize winner and medical doctor at Lambarene in Gabon, was commonly regarded as a very eminent Christian. Yet Schweitzer was a self-confessed agnostic without a shred of Christian belief. A prominent article in the *British Weekly* (July 28, 1960) by Professor John G. McKenzie discussed, 'Is Schweitzer a Christian?' and concluded that there ought to be no hesitation in saying that he was. 'Life is bigger than intellect', McKenzie wrote. Schweitzer had 'the spirit of Christ' and anyone who has that is a Christian regardless of what is believed or disbelieved.

[2] *Daily Mail,* Oct. 2, 1961.

Instead of regarding this interpretation of unbelief as a happy advance in the spirit of charity, ML-J saw it as an error denying the exclusiveness of the Christian message and threatening the very life of the churches. He took up this subject at length in two addresses which he gave to the Westminster Fellowship at the annual outing to Welwyn in the summer of 1962. In expositions of John 17 and Ephesians 4 he showed that the biblical definition of what it means to be a Christian must precede an understanding of the unity in which Christians share. In the definition of 'Christian' he stipulated the necessity of both belief and experience. Christians are people who have experienced conviction of sin, who know repentance and who possess new life as the result of a rebirth. But the experience and the doctrine they believe belong together. If a person does not love fundamental truths, and desire to know them more, he has no claim to be regarded as a Christian. These addresses were published by the IVF in December 1962 under the title *The Basis of Christian Unity.*[3]

Christian unity is the result of a common faith in the gospel of Christ and while he did not regard *all* beliefs associated with evangelicals in the 1960s as tests of a person's Christianity, he considered the word 'evangelical', rightly understood, to be synonymous with 'Christian'. Evangelicals, in the historic sense of the word, are 'gospellers'. Certainly he believed that a man might be a Christian who did not employ the name 'evangelical', and he knew that it does not belong to us to be the final judges of a person's Christian profession. But the fundamentals of evangelicalism are the fundamentals of the gospel, and to concede the title 'Christian' to those who deny those fundamentals is to undermine Christianity itself: 'Those who question and query, let alone deny the great cardinal truths that have been accepted through the centuries, do not belong to the church, and to regard them as brethren is to betray the truth.'

It was pre-eminently because of this point that ML-J drew such criticism from ecumenists. He was denying the validity of their main presupposition. We noted the antagonism of the *British Weekly* to his 'Maintaining the Evangelical Faith Today' in 1952. In the 1960s the opposition was to increase. When some evangelicals shared in the ecumenical discussions of the First British Faith and Order Conference at Nottingham in September 1964, they spoke of

[3] Reprinted in *Knowing the Times,* pp. 118-63.

being 'keenly conscious of the prejudice and even hostility' towards the IVF's position (of which ML-J remained the chief spokesman). At that Nottingham Conference it was ML-J's convictions which Principal John Huxtable attacked: 'Not the least of my difficulty with the Conservative Evangelicals', he said, 'is their characteristic insistence that, unless the Faith is expressed in their particular way, it is not truly expressed at all . . . that, unless we believe in a sub-stitutionary theory of atonement, it is doubtful if we believe in salvation at all.'

Huxtable was more guarded than another ecumenist, Douglas Jones, Lightfoot Professor of Divinity at Durham University. In his book, *Instrument of Peace*, Professor Jones deplored that ML-J's 'influential book, *The Basis of Christian Unity*,' taught that 'the true believers are those who believe in the historic fall, the wrath of God against sin, the substitutionary atonement, the physical resurrection of Jesus Christ, and . . . a fundamentalist approach to the Scriptures'. Instead he applauded the words of the Archbishop of Canterbury that, 'Christians do not "believe in the Creeds" but, with the Creeds to help them, they believe in God.' 'Dr Martyn Lloyd-Jones', he complained, 'is trying to persuade us that there are precise doctrinal distinguishing marks of Christians, that we can distinguish him who believes from him who does not believe . . . In this respect he has learnt nothing from the greatest evangelical theologian of modern times . . . [i.e., Karl Barth]. There is no greater scandal in this com-plex situation than the refusal of Christians to accept their fellow Christians.'[4]

It is plain that the Durham Professor of Divinity differed in his whole conception of salvation. Denying ML-J's conviction of the church as separate from the world, he argued, 'The church is the emergence within the body of mankind of the unity to which not only Christians but all men are called — more than that, in which they already exist in Jesus Christ. Christ is the head of every man . . . the church is . . . never possible to define.'

Still stronger words were to follow. Dr Lloyd-Jones' position, it was to be said, was akin to that of the self-righteous Pharisees. Such antipathy was to persist. A decade late James Barr was to direct his readers to ML-J's *Basis of Christian Unity* 'for an example of a harsh

[4] Quotations from *Instrument of Peace* (1965), pp. 69-74.

and rigid opposition to any participation by conservative evangelicals with non-conservatives'.[5]

Censure of this kind did not worry ML-J but what did concern him deeply was the cleavage appearing within evangelicalism on how the ecumenical movement should be treated. I have already touched on the background to a major shift in evangelical opinion which was now taking place. Clearly change of some kind in English evangelicalism was inevitable, for ecumenism had raised new issues and was aiming to alter the denominational boundaries in a manner hitherto unknown. Congregationalists were in active discussion with English Presbyterians with respect to union; the Church of Scotland (Presbyterian) was in consultation with the Church of England, and the Methodists were likewise engaged in plans for reunion with the Anglicans. If church structures were radically changed there was no way in which evangelicals could remain exactly as they were. Uneasy though they had often been in staying in their respective denominations, at least they had known for what those denominations originally stood. For long years the boundary lines had been static. Now, amidst the general call for new alignments and for visible 'Christian unity', the old evangelical *status quo* was scarcely tenable. One way or another there was bound to be movement.

Dr Lloyd-Jones believed that this situation presented evangelicals with a great opportunity. Instead of simply adopting delaying tactics within their denominations, evangelicals should themselves take up the New Testament emphases on unity. He argued that opposition to error, and warnings over the growing doctrinal indifferentism, were not enough in this new situation: if men were orthodox and yet content to remain divided from one another at the church level, were they, he asked, taking the New Testament with sufficient seriousness? Evangelicals said that they were 'one in Christ' at such gatherings as the Keswick Convention, and 'one' in the many evangelical organisations (whose work had been too important to allow the membership of non-evangelicals), yet in the corporate responsibility for unity required of *churches* in the New Testament they were not one at all. Now, with the denominations themselves in a ferment, he believed that evangelicals should translate their oft-affirmed oneness into practice:

[5] *Fundamentalism*, p. 362.

We have avoided the church problem by contenting ourselves with movements. Our testimony has been inevitably inconsistent because it is scripturally defective. We have criticised those in error yet continued to belong to the same church and have acknowledged them as members and dignitaries. This more or less nullifies our criticism.

Non-evangelicals are generally consistent. They say the same things at all levels. We do not. For example, evangelicals advocate separation at the student level (recommending attachment to IVF, not SCM) and then at the church level evangelicals do the exact opposite and advocate participation in the WCC. If separation is right on one level should it not be right on the other? This makes the evangelical position almost untenable.

The above was part of an unpublished address to the Westminster Fellowship on June 19, 1963. It revealed what he already knew: evangelicals were divided on the whole subject of unity.

One cause of this difference has already emerged in the preceding pages. Within English evangelicalism there was now a major difference in mood with respect to the contemporary scene. Dr Lloyd-Jones had travelled the country ceaselessly for over thirty years and he knew the general conditions as did few others. In addition, instead of spending long summer breaks abroad (as many wished him to do), he was generally in many different parts of Britain and seeing churches from the pew rather than from the pulpit. As an ordinary member of the congregation attending for worship on a Sunday, the impression he received was often very different from that of a mid-week service where many came from other places when he was preaching. His summer holidays in 1960 and 1962 sharpened his conviction that the whole country was involved in a spiritual decline of vast proportions. Whether in East Anglia or Oxfordshire, Cornwall or Somerset, the north of Scotland or Wales, everywhere conditions were much the same. 'The tragedy', as he told members at Westminster, 'lies not merely in the smallness of the congregations, but in their utter deadness and their apparent dislike of the truth when presented to them.' Meeting with forty or more ministers in the Highlands of Scotland, he noted their view that 'even in the last five years there had been a deterioration in the situation'.

Almost everything he saw outside London confirmed his impression that the situation was profoundly serious. To his friends at the

Annual Meeting of the Evangelical Library in 1961 he said: 'I think it is more than likely that the times will get worse and that there will be a great searching even amongst us who are called evangelical. We will be driven back to certain foundations; we may become a very small company.'

The basis for these opinions, and the fact that these were held by a man who ministered in one of the largest regular congregations in London, were things passed over by most evangelicals who believed that evangelical influence was growing. Far from accepting ML-J's diagnosis, they thought that evangelicalism with a modern image, and an up-to-date presentation of the Christian Faith, could even yet win the centre ground in the mainline denominations. What was needed, then, from evangelicals was more involvement in their denominations, not any kind of 'withdrawal'.

Conservative evangelicals in the Church of England were the most prominent in advancing this opinion and, because of their numbers, their colleges and their traditional place of leadership in English evangelicalism, their decision with respect to ecumenism was bound to be widely influential. From 'the benevolent neutrality' favoured in the early 1950s, numbers of Anglican evangelicals now began to move to accept the active involvement in ecumenism advocated by A. T. Houghton. If the evangelical voice was to be heard in the corridors of power where it could count, there was, they argued, no other alternative. The headline report of an address by A. T. Houghton was, 'Choice before evangelicals, Isolation or Involvement'. Ecumenism was the discussion of the age and if evangelicals did not speak from *within* that discussion their opinion would count for nothing. 'The fault of evangelicals who eschew dialogue', wrote John Stott in the *Church of England Newspaper* (Nov. 1, 1968), is to assert their evangelicalism in an 'inflexible way which is quite irrelevant to the modern confusions and perplexities of the Church.'

Those who took this view were confirmed in their belief in its rightness by the welcome now being accorded to them in various congresses and commissions for ecumenical discussion. J. D. Douglas (a Church of Scotland evangelical) applauded the 'notable gesture' of the organisers of the 1964 Nottingham Conference who 'encouraged the attendance of a number known to be conservative evangelicals'. He believed that the Nottingham invitation 'reflects a graciousness of spirit that augurs well for the future', and noted that 'one of the evangelicals, the Rev. A. T. Houghton, was asked to give one of the major addresses'. Anglican evangelicals similarly received invitations to join the various forums for ecumenical discussion within their church. Soon it was to seem a far cry from the comparatively recent days when evangelical Anglicans, in Stott's words, were 'a rejected minority, a despised minority movement'. In 1964 the Rev. John Weller, Secretary of the Faith and Order Department of the British Council of Churches, could report that: 'The dialogue between "conservative evangelicals and others" is going on at the moment here in Britain more widely, more vigorously and more fruitfully than perhaps at any time in these last few years.'

Instead of believing that those who took this optimistic view were gaining a real influence for biblical Christianity, ML-J considered that they were unwittingly contributing to the existing decline and confusion. The main problem in the nation was the unbelief established in the mainline churches. Archbishop Ramsey's words on meeting atheists in heaven were far from uncommon. By the mid-sixties the Labour leader in the House of Lords could not be contradicted when he said that there was not one bishop holding to a Protestant position; mass vestments, prayers for the dead and stone altars had the approval of all. In the Methodist Church, involved in reunion negotiations with the Church of England, one of its best-known leaders, Dr Donald Soper, proposed a ban on Bible-reading for the year 1965 because, 'The present situation with regard to the Scriptures is intolerable. They represent an incubus that cannot be removed until an almost completely new start is made.' In an article entitled, 'The Methodism Gone Forever', published in *The Methodist Recorder*, John J. Vincent argued that all the doctrines of justification, of saving faith, assurance and holiness, 'belong to an intellectual and theological world which is no longer ours. They describe experiences which are no longer normative for Methodist people.' When an evangelical at the Methodist Conference in Plymouth in 1965 moved an amendment to recall the Church to its *own articles of faith* it was defeated by a vote of 601 to 14.

But the price for ecumenical dialogue was that the very men who tolerated, or even approved, this state of affairs had to be regarded by evangelicals as fellow Christians. As one of the evangelicals after the

Nottingham Conference of 1964 was to declare: 'The real question at issue in the whole discussion of the ecumenical movement is one of trust. Are we or are we not willing to trust the Christian sincerity of those who name the name of Christ, who call Jesus Lord, but differ from us in doctrine?' This was indeed the question, and many evangelicals — led by Anglicans — decided there had been a serious mistake in the way in which they had previously answered it. The issue was thus becoming clear: either the former evangelical attitude was wrong, narrow and bigoted, or the new policy was a move away from Scripture. If it was the latter, what could account for such a change of direction?

One reason was that doctrinal commitment had become weakened in evangelical circles as the policy of leaders came to be shaped by considerations of achieving success and wider influence. The position of Dr Billy Graham, who was now emphasising, 'The one badge of Christian discipleship is not orthodoxy but love', made a critical difference at precisely this point. Under the cover of such words religious leaders, whose teaching had been disastrous in its spiritual effect, were being identified with a message which their ministries opposed. On this point ML-J talked with Graham face to face. They met in the vestry of Westminster Chapel early in July 1963, and at the request of the American evangelist who wanted ML-J to be chairman at a 'World Congress on Evangelism' then being planned to take place in Europe. The latter replied: 'I said I'd make a bargain: if he would stop the general sponsorship of his campaigns — stop having liberals and Roman Catholics on the platform — and drop the invitation system, I would wholeheartedly support him and chair the Congress. We talked for about three hours, but he didn't accept these conditions.'[6]

On the contrary, Graham went on to confirm the policy of gaining wider influence. In a televised interview with Cardinal Cushing of Boston, he spoke of the 'new day of understanding and dialogue'. 'You've made a great contribution to this ecumenical spirit', Cushing replied. When Graham returned to London in 1964, for preliminary talks on a further Crusade, his biographer tells us that his first engagement was with Archbishop Ramsey and that soon after he was

---

[6] Dr Graham had been suffering from throat trouble when he saw Lloyd-Jones on this occasion and the latter took him to see a medical friend.

to see the Bishops of London and Southwark. The latter (Mervyn Stockwood), a supporter of reunion with Rome, was asked to serve on the Council of Reference which was to support Graham's 1966 Earls Court Crusade.

The acceptance of this ecumenical patronage on the part of Graham could only have one effect upon those who had confidence in his judgment. If the evangelist was so impressed by the 'brotherliness' of non-evangelicals, then there was surely reason to say, 'Well, I wonder whether these doctrines we've been emphasizing are so important after all.'

To say this is not to make Dr Graham out to be the main cause of the doctrinal weakening in Britain. If weakness had not already been present, evangelicals would never have been carried away, as they were, by the new policy of co-operation. What would once have been called compromise was now being openly justified. An example from the realm of Christian literature will illustrate this. Dr William Barclay of Glasgow was one of the best-known religious figures of the 1960s. As an author and broadcaster he had mastered the art of communicating ideas in a popular manner to the average person. But although Barclay spoke much about the Bible he had no belief in its authority as the Word of God and his views on the person and the birth of Christ were not those of historic Christianity. Barclay's biographer quotes ML-J as saying that Barclay was 'the most dangerous man in Christendom'.[7] It is probably an accurate quotation. ML-J believed that people were confused by the attractiveness of Barclay's presentation, and because of some of the good things which he did say. But what concerned him more, in terms of encouraging confusion, was that Professor F. F. Bruce was now working in harness with Barclay in the production of a series of 'Bible Guides' of which Lutterworth Press were the publishers. Bruce, Rylands Professor of Biblical Criticism and Exegesis at the University of Manchester, remained a signatory to the IVF Basis of Faith and yet saw no inconsistency in being publicly identified with one whose beliefs were far removed from that basis. This was the kind of action which led ML-J to press the question, 'What is the value of evangelicals affirming a statement of faith if they see no harm in making common cause with those who teach the opposite?'[8]

[7] Clive L. Rawlins, *William Barclay, The Authorised Biography*, (1984), p. 651.
[8] Bruce's autobiography does not address this question either. He speaks of the

Another factor which ML-J saw as contributing largely to this change in direction among evangelicals is closely related to the above. Alongside a willingness not to insist on Scripture, there came an excessive fear of being thought negative, controversial and belligerent. Criticism of almost any kind had become unpopular, and a 'loving attitude' which accepted everyone for what they appeared to be was in vogue. If discernment between truth and error, and the need to 'beware of men', were still counted as Christian virtues they were now low down the list of priorities. The duty of 'contending earnestly for the faith' was put still lower. To emphasise these things was to risk losing the increased acceptance for which evangelicals hoped. Those who defended this greater toleration generally did so in terms of the hard, unattractive contentiousness which, they claimed, had formerly too commonly prevailed. It is true that there have always been cases of orthodoxy divorced from compassion, but it was now implied that anyone who took 'the fight of faith' seriously was such a person. If there was one thing left which was still considered worthy of outright condemnation it was 'lack of love'. Such was the atmosphere into which evangelicals were being drawn in the 1960s, and it goes far to explaining why Dr Lloyd-Jones was so often unsupported in what he said.

It is to the credit of F. F. Bruce, differing though he did with ML-J in this area, that he defended him from the charge of proud dogmatism which was increasingly brought against him: 'He was a thoroughly humble man. Those who charged him with arrogance were wildly mistaken. His confidence was based on the message he was commissioned to proclaim . . . He was a man of prayer, a powerful evangelist, an expository preacher of rare quality, in the fullest sense a servant of the Word of God.'[9]

It is not insignificant in this connection that Dr Lloyd-Jones' Sunday morning sermons in the early 1960s gave much time to an exposition of 'the wiles of the devil'. The Bible, as he reminded his people, warns us that things are often not what they *seem* to be and

---

IVF needing to be 'specially sensitive to the climate of opinion in the evangelical world' because of 'its constitution and clientele' but expresses thankfulness for the 'academic freedom' of Universities 'where it is quite irrelevant whether a man is conservative or liberal in theology'. *In Retrospect, Remembrance of Things Past,* (1980), pp. 187, 143.

[9] *Evangelical Quarterly,* 1991, p. 71.

that vigilance and a suspicion of human nature, because of the fall, are constant duties for the Christian. Included in these sermons were several on the Devil's use of error and deception and when one of these, on Roman Catholicism, was printed in the *Westminster Record*, it caused much comment. The minister of Highbury Quadrant Congregational Church feared it hindered the reconciliation of churches. More strange was the attitude of those who regarded the warning in the sermon as unnecessary. At the Islington Clerical Conference of 1960 the Rev. M. A. P. Wood saw no danger from Roman Catholicism and, as late as 1962, the Rev. A. T. Houghton was denying that the direction of ecumenism was towards reunion with Rome. But the ecumenical argument to justify a positive response to the overtures which came with Vatican II — the existence of a 'shared spiritual experience' — was one soon to be used by evangelicals.

It should be said that ML-J read Roman Catholic authors both in books and journals. He was familiar with such authors as Hans Küng and even read the monthly *New Blackfriars* edited by English Dominicans, of which most evangelicals had never heard. Mr H. W. J. Edwards, a frequent contributor to Roman Catholic journals, records how he went to hear ML-J preach on one occasion and afterwards 'dared' to enter the vestry: 'to my very great surprise Dr Lloyd-Jones beamed upon me and said (in Welsh), "H. W. J. Edwards? Why, I am so glad to meet you."' ML-J was never an advocate of any personal hostility to Catholics and the possibility of being a Christian and a Roman Catholic he would never deny, 'such people are Christians in spite of the system to which they belong and not because of it'. But he regarded the Roman Catholic system as the ultimate form of anti-biblical comprehensiveness. The only change in Rome was of a kind that had been seen many times before, in her ability to accommodate to different circumstances. Evidence that would justify a new hopefulness, that is, a change in her fundamental doctrine of salvation through church and sacraments, did not exist.

By 1964, for the reasons we have considered, Dr Lloyd-Jones knew that there could be no expectation of any general evangelical unity. The truth was that evangelicalism itself was already dividing. But he still entertained hopes that a new grouping might emerge which would rise to the challenge of the hour.

TWENTY-SIX

Crisis Years

We have seen how the subject of unity was taking increasing amounts of Lloyd-Jones's time. A change in the meetings of the Westminster Fellowship illustrates this fact. Until January 1960 the Fellowship usually met monthly on a Tuesday afternoon. With the larger numbers now attending, it became difficult for Westminster Chapel ladies to serve tea on Tuesdays when a women's gathering was meeting elsewhere on the premises at the same time. The ministers' meeting was accordingly moved to a Monday afternoon. Then, at the meeting of June 1963, it was proposed and agreed that, in view of the need for more time to discuss the pressing issues of ecumenical or evangelical unity, the Fellowship should add a morning session to its regular meeting. This meant for ML-J that once a month he went straight from his heavy weekend of ministry at the Chapel to virtually a full day of meetings as well as to interviews, for there were always ministers from a distance at the fraternal who sought his advice over particular problems while they were in town.

With the introduction of this morning meeting of the Fellowship, there was also a new arrangement in the meetings themselves. In order to follow up his June address of 1963[1] it was arranged that a number of speakers from within the membership of the fraternal would give addresses at the morning session as a basis for discussion. These men represented the denominational differences to be found

---

[1] See pp. 367-8.

in the Fellowship, the intention being to re-examine these differences from Scripture in the hope of there being sufficient common ground to lead to a much wider and closer association. ML-J selected those who spoke but, in part through pressure of time, there was insufficient planning. The addresses once given were never made available. The same points tended to re-emerge and to be left unresolved. No drafting work was ever done by committees. In part the slowness of the procedure was deliberate, for ML-J wanted to give men time to think and confer. By the autumn of 1964 he had made up his mind to make the mid-summer meeting at Welwyn in 1965 the occasion when he would give a final challenge to men to put evangelical unity *before* traditional denominational affiliations. In some cases, at least, he knew that such a decision would necessitate men leaving their present denominations and what this would cost some men weighed heavily upon him. He thought much about the question of timing and was critical of the Elizabethan Robert Browne's attitude of 'Reformation without tarrying for any'. 'There is a timing in these matters; history proves that very eloquently . . . We must always consider the preparation and readiness of the people. Do not rush them . . . Educate them, train them, show them the dangers. I am sure that we need to exercise great patience.'[2] Such was the advice he would give to enquiring pastors. If there was to be a withdrawal from denominations it should be of congregations, not simply of ministers.

There was, however, a factor besides patience which now held ML-J back from what might have become a more definite challenge in the summer of 1965. Counter-proposals (which is basically what they were) emerged from men within his circle and with whom he had long had close relations. The Evangelical Alliance, of which Gilbert Kirby remained the General Secretary, had begun to take its own steps to meet the problem of the endangered unity of evangelicals. It announced a 'National Assembly of Evangelicals' to be held in London at the end of September 1965 — a move which was linked with a significant change in the organisation of the Alliance. Hitherto it had stood for 'spiritual unity', with membership restricted to individual Christians. Now, to help meet the charge that such unity was a great deal less than what is required by the New Testament, local

---

[2] *WR*, July 1963, pp. 109, 110.

churches or assemblies could become associate members of the Alliance and the National Assembly conference sessions (as distinct from public evening meetings) would be 'reserved for those who come as representatives or delegates of local churches or of Christian societies'.

Instead of regarding this as a move in the right direction, ML-J believed that it would bypass the issue of whether a true unity of evangelicals could be maintained if it included those who *simultaneously* believed in the possibility of ecumenical unity. His belief was confirmed by his observation that the programme for the Alliance's 'National Assembly' contained no mention of anyone speaking on this issue. He saw the change as a compromise which was bound to fail.

The Spring of this same year 1965 saw the publication of a book *All in Each Place* which came as a blow to ML-J. As we have seen, in the debate over participation in ecumenical proposals much depended largely on the position taken by evangelical Anglicans and, notwithstanding the policy of what seemed to be a new majority, ML-J had until now been hopeful that Jim Packer would lead a minority of the more Calvinistic of the younger Anglican evangelicals. But between 1963 and 1965 (when he became a member of the Anglican-Methodist Unity Commission) something happened to Packer's assessment of the situation, as was apparent in *All in Each Place, Towards Reunion in England, Ten Anglican Essays, with Some Free Church Comments*.[3] Dr Packer edited this work and contributed the major opening chapter on 'Wanted: A Pattern for Union'. Along with much that was good, the book showed unmistakable signs of a major shift towards the very position which Packer had earlier criticised as inconsistent with evangelicalism. He now wrote of 'the debate on union between evangelicals and others', the 'others' being described as our 'catholic' brethren (meaning Anglo-Catholics) and 'non-episcopal brethren'. The non-episcopal included such Free Churchmen as John Huxtable (who contributed to the volume), although he had chided evangelicals at Nottingham for holding 'a substitutionary theory of the atonement'. To Anglo-Catholics the book promised that the authors intended to create no 'conscientious difficulties' for them; all plans for reunion must 'safeguard' the consciences of Anglo-Catholics, even to the point of allowing 'the

[3] Abingdon: Marcham Books, April 1965.

right of Anglo-Catholics to abstain from eucharistic fellowship of which as individuals they cannot approve'. The 'deeply unorthodox' should be excluded from official positions in a united church but who such people might be was left in obscurity. The overall impression given by *All in Each Place* was that the majority quest for unity with non-evangelicals was right after all.

At the Westminster Fellowship outing to Welwyn on June 16, 1965 ML-J gave the reasons why he had no expectation of an emerging evangelical unity and his address concluded with words of an unusual personal nature. He explained that he was being forced to say some things and denied 'rumours' that he was about to launch a new church. He went on:

> I have no *personal* interest in all we are discussing. I have not proposed a new church. I am not an organiser — it is probably one of my greatest defects. I am almost driven to think I ought to write an autobiography in the interests of truth! I could have been President of the Free Churches Council or the Congregational Union years ago. I could have had it all.[4] Every man will have to answer to God for himself.

> I still feel that evangelicals are missing an opportunity which will probably never recur. A world church is coming and evangelicals will be faced with a *fiat accompli*. The situation is not hopeless but it is very grievous. I never expected anything else, but I am sad. What do we do? All I have to do is to go on preaching the gospel. 'Fight the good fight of faith' — it is the whole fight of forty or fifty years ago but we have to fight it this time in evangelical circles. What amazes me is that any evangelical should think there is anything new in this situation! We have to exhort the people to pray for revival . . . I am going to spend my time urging people to pray for the outpouring of the Spirit. Many of these difficulties would then be swept out of existence. We need to encourage the formation of local independent evangelical churches . . . Greater London is not representative of the country.

> I know I shall be misquoted. That does not worry me. We shall all stand before the judgment seat of Christ, and knowing something of the terror of the Lord I have tried to persuade you concerning some of these things.

---

[4] Others beside J. D. Jones had wanted him in these roles.

This Welwyn outing (the last of many happy summer days at the beautiful 'Guessens' location) concluded in a very sombre spirit. ML-J was of the opinion that the Fellowship in its present form had fulfilled its usefulness. No further meeting was to be held until Monday, November 29.

Dr Lloyd-Jones did not go to the Evangelical Alliance's National Assembly of Evangelicals in September 1965 but a report of that Assembly, followed by discussion, occupied the Westminster Fellowship at its one further meeting in 1965 on November 29. ML-J already knew the main facts. Although not convened to discuss church issues, the National Assembly had accepted a resolution from the Rev. Don Davies (a member of the Westminster Fellowship) for the setting up of a Commission 'to study radically the various attitudes of Evangelicals to the Ecumenical Movement, denominationalism and a possible future United Church' (i.e., a United Evangelical Church). Gilbert Kirby had informed ML-J of this decision in a letter of October 14, 1965 and asked for his participation in the discussions which the Commission intended to set in motion.

Dr Lloyd-Jones and other members of the Westminster Fellowship, including the present writer, accepted invitations to speak to the nine-member Commission and it was therefore agreed that the Fellowship would postpone any move of its own until the Commission's findings were published. The date already fixed for publication was October 1966 which would coincide with a Second National Assembly of Evangelicals again organised by the Evangelical Alliance. In the meantime the fraternal would continue its own discussion of the issues and, accordingly, the usual monthly schedule of meetings was arranged for 1966.

The theme which had been receiving such attention during the previous twelve months was also the subject for the addresses at the Puritan Conference for 1965, 'Approaches to Reformation of the Church'. With one exception, the papers given dealt with the history of the sixteenth century and were predictable in content. The exception was ML-J's concluding address, 'Ecclesiola in Ecclesia', which broke new ground. He traced a number of examples from the Reformation onwards of evangelicals who had sought to organise a nucleus of churches within a larger territorial church ('little churches within a church'). In his view these attempts at reformation from within had all failed to come to grips with the New Testament teaching on the nature of the church. They had put expediency before principle and he was convinced that current events were again illustrating the decline which occurs when a concern for influence is put first: 'We are forgetting the doctrine of the remnant. We are trusting to expediency and expedients and not saying that, if we are faithful, the Holy Spirit has promised to honour us and our testimony however small our numbers and however despised by 'the wise and prudent'.[5]

For Dr Lloyd-Jones, at the end of 1965, the lines of a coming division were clearly drawn. He wrote to Philip Hughes in the United States, 'I am sure that we are heading up during this next year to a real crisis.'[6]

There is one point which needs to be stressed if the reader is to grasp ML-J's thought in what is to follow. It must be understood that neither now nor at any time was he advocating the formation of a new evangelical denomination as the right response to ecumenism. To the question, 'Are you proposing to set up a new denomination?', he could reply, 'That is the very thing I am not saying'.[7] If he had given his weight to supporting one denomination — either one already existent or one to be newly formed — and pressed his own view of church order, namely Congregationalism or Independency, there can be no doubt that he would have received considerable support. But he was against such a procedure for a fundamental reason. The crisis in the church was not over different forms of church government, a subject about which, in his view, the Scriptures allow no final certainty. It was over the gospel itself and the question, 'What is a Christian?' The need of the hour, therefore, was not for the emergence of a new denomination which would either enforce one view on church government or convince all participants to accept some kind of compromise over traditional denominational distinctives — excluding all others. Such a course of action would never achieve greater evangelical and Christian unity. It would only perpetuate the mistakes of the past. Greater unity would not come by attempts to remove all secondary differences. 'I do not care whether a man is

[5] *Puritans*, p. 147.

[6] Letter of Dec. 21, 1965, *D. Martyn Lloyd-Jones: Letters 1919–1981* (Edinburgh: Banner of Truth, 1994), p. 167.

[7] *Revival*, p. 167.

a Presbyterian or a Baptist or an Independent or Episcopalian or a Methodist, as long as he is agreed about the essentials of "the faith".' The way to unity was not through the removal of all secondary differences. It was for churches to submit themselves to Scripture on all the fundamentals and, provided that submission existed, ML-J could say, 'I have no interest in denominations.' 'Belong to a denomination, but do not stand fast in denominationalism.'

* * *

On Thursday, January 20, 1966, the first Westminster Chapel members' meeting was held of the new year. It included a baptism, a financial statement, report on news of members and, finally, an address by ML-J on the question of the Chapel's relationship to the proposed new 'Congregational Church' — the constitution of which he had already studied and considered with the deacons. According to this constitution, one of the Church's aims would be 'to further the unity of the Church and to foster ecumenical relationships with other Christian Churches and communities through such agencies as the Free Church Federal Council, the British Council of Churches and the World Council of Churches'.

When the motion was proposed and seconded that Westminster Chapel should not enter into covenant with other churches to form the proposed Congregational Church in England and Wales, it was overwhelmingly carried, not a hand being raised against it.

In the same Institute Hall in which this meeting was, as usual, held, the Westminster Fellowship also met on March 21, 1966 for what was to be the last in the whole series of addresses on questions of church polity and evangelical unity. For this Dr Packer had been invited by ML-J to speak. He came with a well-prepared address. He knew that *All in Each Place* had not been well received by the majority of those listening to him and took evident care not to say anything which would add further tension to a relationship already strained.

The case which Dr Packer put for involvement in the Anglican ecumenical agenda and for not making common cause with ML-J's plea for a new visible unity between evangelical churches was two-fold. First, he argued that evangelical Christians were already united in the great matters of the gospel and that a formal, organisational or denominational unity was not essential. Second, as evangelicals differed over secondary matters, such as church order, he believed that they were justified in remaining in denominations which accorded with their views on those secondary matters provided they retained their freedom to preach the gospel. 'Am I', he asked, 'separated from my friends in a way which is needless and which could be remedied? I am not sure that I am. Though we agree on essentials, there are other points on which we are divided . . . I do not see how the facts of the case can be met except by evangelicals maintaining fellowship while at the same time [continuing in] different denominational alignments.'

Packer's address on March 21, 1966, had no alternative to offer with respect to evangelical unity. His hopes lay in what might be obtained from working within the ecumenical programme, and he asked those of a contrary view to set forth the more biblical form of visible unity which they envisaged.

On March 22, 1966, the day following the Westminster Fraternal, ML-J was engaged to preach at a combined meeting of churches in the market town of Melton Mowbray in the English Midlands. It was one of the occasions when I drove him, partly to give us time to talk and partly so that he could be back in his own home by the early hours of the following morning. Our conversation included the fraternal of the previous day and the form which any new grouping of evangelical churches might take. But the message he preached that night overshadowed all else. His text was Acts 24:24-26, especially verse 25, 'And as he reasoned of righteousness, temperance and judgment to come, Felix trembled . . .' The congregation which had come to the parish church in Melton Mowbray that evening were as affected as everyone else at that date by the excitement over the General Election to Parliament which was to be held the following week. But as Paul's message to Felix was preached all else suddenly seemed trivial. The silent and packed congregation, whose feet rested on ancient flagstones covering the dead of other centuries, were not being addressed as voters but as immortals whose chief interests belonged to another world. The preacher remained an evangelist before everything else.

* * *

Dr Lloyd-Jones was asked to be the speaker at the opening meeting of the Second National Assembly of Evangelicals at Westminster Central Hall on October 18, 1966. A second day for addresses and discussions was to follow, with a communion service at the conclusion. The main subject before the Assembly was the question of Christian unity and, particularly, the finding of the Commission set up after the First Assembly. In a twelve-page Report, published in time for the Second Assembly, the Commission announced its finding:

> There is no *widespread* demand at the present time for the setting up of a united evangelical Church on denominational lines . . . This does not mean that there could not be an effective fellowship or federation of evangelical churches at both the local and national level.

Part of the confusion which was to follow ML-J's address was the assumption on the part of numbers present that he was speaking either for or against this finding when he was doing neither. It has to be remembered that thus far his thinking had been very largely expressed in private meetings such as the Westminster Fellowship and nothing of it was in print. The purpose of the Evangelical Alliance in asking him to speak was that he should be 'asked to say in public what he had said in private', and, knowing that he would not speak for all evangelicals, they also invited John Stott, who was to chair the meeting, to give ten minutes on the Anglican evangelical view of unity. The Lloyd-Jones address, which followed Stott's shorter words, summarized his belief as already given in these pages: evangelicals could no longer simply follow their existing practice on unity because the ecumenical movement had put them in a new position: 'We are confronted by a situation today such as has not been the case since the Protestant Reformation.' Yet, instead of facing the doctrine of the church, 'The impression is given that evangelicals are more concerned to maintain the integrity of their different denominations than anybody else in those denominations.' If evangelicals were prepared to continue as 'evangelical wings' in their denominations, the question they needed to face was whether they would also be an 'evangelical wing' in a national, ecumenical and, eventually, Roman Catholic Church.

The main issue, as he saw it, was whether evangelicals should try to modify and improve the existing situation in the denominations, or meet the ecumenical challenge head-on by going back to Scripture and asking, 'What is the Christian church?' 'Here is the great divide. The ecumenical people put fellowship before doctrine. We, as evangelicals, put doctrine before fellowship.' The church is the body of those who have believed and experienced the fundamental truths (*Acts* 2:42); they are people who give daily evidence by their lives that they are Christians,

> That is the evangelical view of the Christian church . . . the church consists of living people. If you don't believe a certain irreducible minimum, you cannot be a Christian, and you are not in the church. Have we reached a time when one must not say a thing like that? Have evangelicals so changed that we no longer make an assertion like that?

The reader is advised to study the whole of this address of which I can only give a part.[8] (Further his address should be understood in the context of all *three* addresses which he gave at the large Evangelical Alliance meetings, the other two being in 1947 and 1957.)[9] Did Lloyd-Jones do what he was asked to do on the night of October 18, 1966, or did he do something more? The chairman believed he had done more; he had presented conclusions, and an appeal, which, he thought, should have come *after* the discussions planned for the following day. Instead, therefore, of rising to close the meeting, John Stott gave further impromptu counsel:

> There, brethren, is dialogue . . . We are here to debate. I would think appeal should have come at the end [of the Assembly]. I believe history is against what Dr Lloyd-Jones has said . . . Scripture is against him, the remnant was within the church not outside it. I hope no one will act precipitately . . . We are all concerned with the same ultimate issues and with the glory of God.

[8] 'Evangelical Unity: An Appeal' in *Knowing the Times*, pp. 246-57.

[9] The 1957 addresses, in which an Anglican, Frank Colquhoun, spoke on the truths which are the basis of evangelical co-operation and unity (available from MLJ Recordings Trust, MLJ 5714). The significance of the 1957 address had been generally overlooked; Roger Steer, writing on 'Martyn Lloyd-Jones and Anglican Evangelicals', is so ignorant of it, and of 1947, that he says, 'The 1966 Assembly was the first major gathering of British Evangelicals since 1846 to be organised by the Alliance.' There was, of course, also the Assembly of 1965. Steer, *Guarding the Holy Fire: the Evangelicalism of John R. W. Stott, J. I. Packer, and Alister McGrath* (Grand Rapids: Baker, 1999), p. 224.

30. In conversation with John Stott (by courtesy of Maurice Ambler).

Though calmly spoken, and without disrespect for the speaker, John Stott's intervention to repudiate the case which had just been presented could not be other than dramatic. It polarised the packed meeting, few of whom could be present for the daytime discussions of the next day. Many, only beginning to consider the issues under debate, were to take the easier choice of following one evangelical leader or the other. Feelings were profoundly stirred. Perhaps, as John Stott evidently thought when it was too late, it had been a mistake to pre-empt debate by having Dr Lloyd-Jones speak at the Assembly's first meeting. As ML-J and Stott left the tense gathering, the latter murmured apologetically that he was afraid that some of the Anglican clergy might have left their churches the next morning had he said nothing at the end. Probably both Stott and the Evangelical Alliance leaders had underestimated the difference between hearing the Doctor's views in private and the same views *preached* at the Central Hall.

The second day of the Assembly was designed to give further time to the subject of unity, but there was no real continuance of the issues opened the night before. The major address relevant to the matter was by a young Anglican, the Rev Julian Charley, who was obviously given time to balance the time given to ML-J. His case that they should all be seeking 'a united, territorial church rather than advocating secession' was far removed from reality and debate fell flat.

ML-J was there for some of the day but he took no part. The organisers were mightily relieved that the remainder of the Assembly passed without further controversy. The fact was that numbers believed the line had already been drawn and many nonconformist evangelical churches proceeded to withdraw from the Evangelical Alliance.

Inevitably the religious press concentrated all their interest on the public division revealed on the night of October 18, and presented the crux of the difference as secession or non-secession from the mainline denominations. Under a bold heading, 'Evangelicals — Leave your Denominations', the *Christian,* October 21, announced that Dr Lloyd-Jones had given 'an impassioned plea . . . to form a united church'. Most reports presented the speech in the same light. It was thirty-five years later before anyone on the Stott side of the division went into print with a different judgment. Timothy Dudley-Smith in his magisterial biography of John Stott, wrote of Lloyd-Jones' 1966 address, that it was not entirely clear what step he was urging ministers and clergy to take, 'but it is plain that to say — as the *Christian* and *Christianity Today* reported — that he was urging them "to leave the major denominations and to form a united church" was quite mistaken. Rather he seems to have pleaded that "what we need above everything else at the present time, is a number of such churches, all in fellowship together."'[10]

The first meeting of the Westminster Fellowship after the Evangelical Alliance Assembly met on November 28, 1966, and it was evident from the abnormally large attendance that an important occasion was anticipated. After some free-flowing comment Dr Lloyd-Jones rose to give his own conclusion. The time had come for action and the first practical step, he believed, was to bring the present Fellowship to an end: 'At Welwyn eighteen months ago I said I saw no hope of evangelical unity and said that this Fellowship had come to an end. I postponed that decision . . . When we met in November

---

[10] Timothy Dudley-Smith, *John Stott, A Global Ministry* (Leicester: IVP, 2001), p. 67. Notwithstanding this difference, the biographer shows the 'warm personal respect and friendship' maintained between the two men. On one occasion, as the congregation was departing from All Soul's, Stott greeted a student with the words, 'Hello, I thought you went to Westminster Chapel.' To the reply, 'No, I am not a follower of the great Doctor,' Stott said, 'Aren't you? I am.' At the age of 70 he put ML-J in his list of seven people 'who have influenced me'. *John Stott: The Making of a Leader* (Leicester: IVP. 1999), pp. 233-4, 260.

1965, in view of the proposal of a Commission arising out of the first Evangelical Alliance Assembly, I said I was prepared to wait for another year to see if the Commission could do what we failed to do. We have waited. The issue has been settled: there is a fundamental cleavage among us.'

If the Fellowship continued without change, he believed there would be the danger of the gathering degenerating into strife and wrangling: 'There has been strife already in these discussions; some of us have been given grace and restrained ourselves with difficulty.' The gathering, he further explained, had never possessed any constitution and it was an embarrassment that it should centre round him:

> I am not surprised at what has happened. I am saddened but not surprised. I am very ready to do anything to help men who are out of the denominations or who are thinking of moving out, but I cannot see the point of meeting with men who are adamant on staying in. We must never lose charity. We must recognise the honesty of those with whom we differ and recognise that others do not see it as we do. People say, 'He is quite right but . . .' I am prepared to accept that. Our personal relationships will remain what they were before. We can help one another, but we cannot go on in regular association.

With respect to any future fraternal, as he told the morning meeting, he had no plans. If men wished to discuss further they could have the use of the room or another room after lunch but he would not be present. If any further meeting was able to draw up a basis with which he felt free to be associated he would give support. But, he concluded, 'the present Westminster Fraternal must be considered as disbanded'.

A further meeting was held after lunch that day in ML-J's absence and, after lengthy discussion, a resolution was carried 'to endorse the appeal made by Dr Lloyd-Jones at Westminster Central Hall'. The vote was 96 for, 13 against, and 31 abstentions. The figures reflected the uncertainty of some over what the appeal entailed. A few of those who abstained would stay closer to ML-J in days ahead than some who voted in favour. The outcome was a re-constituted Fraternal meeting in the New Year on a more definite basis of membership.

31. *Conference group at Tyndale House, Cambridge, 1956. Front centre, John Wenham [left] and Philip Hughes. ML-J behind Wenham. Derek Swann behind Hughes, with Ernest Kevan behind to left, and Alan Stibbs to right. Extreme left, 2nd row, J. I. Packer.*

32. *Kelvin Hall, Glasgow, April 22, 1963. Throughout his ministry ML-J continued to preach to gatherings small and large across Britain.*

TWENTY-SEVEN

Controversy

The charge against Lloyd-Jones after the Evangelical Alliance Assembly of 1966 was that he was 'wrecking evangelical unity'.[1] For years to come this was to be a widely-held opinion, even supported by some who would have been expected to think differently. In response we have to return to the confusion to which we have already referred. How did it come to exist and, I believe, to mislead many?

First, there was the spread, deliberately or accidentally, of inaccurate information. This was the case with regard to press reporting as already indicated. But why was not more done on the ML-J side to set the record straight? Instead he declined to put his address into print. I think that may have been because he had no time to give to it. Further, if the larger picture was not also stated, so that his address was put in the wider context, it might not be rightly understood as the post-Assembly controversy has shown. Of one thing I am certain: the reason for his not putting his address into print is not the one aired by John Brencher and supported by R. T. Kendall. Brencher writes on the events of 1966:

> Whether he would have formed a new denomination given the chance is a moot point. Publicly he denied any such intention, though some who were close to him are not so sure. R. T. Kendall,

[1] Alister McGrath, *To Know and Serve God, A Life of James I. Packer* (London: Hodder and Stoughton, 1997), p. 126.

for example, feels that, when nothing happened, 'he was very disappointed. He could have done it. I think the only reason he did
not have the courage to do it was he thought it might fail.'[2]

No one with an understanding of ML-J could have written such
words.

Second, the fact that Lloyd-Jones said very little about the form
of the unity to which he called evangelicals left it open for those,
unacquainted with his thinking, to suppose that he really did have
some 'united church' in view. It was some time later that John Stott's
biographer, Timothy Dudley-Smith, stated his thought correctly, as
mentioned already.[3] The truth is that ML-J was not more definite,
and formulated no plans, because he believed that such responsibility now belonged to others. At the meeting of the Westminster
Fellowship on November 28, 1966, following the critical Central Hall
meeting, when Leith Samuel had offered his sympathy to ML-J, the
latter replied, 'I don't need any sympathy. I am not an ecclesiastic and
never had any ecclesiastical ambition. I am not going to organise,
lead, or suggest anything. I feel I have done what I've been called to
do. The question is what are you going to do?'

At the same time Lloyd-Jones was not without thoughts of possible future developments. From 1964, and probably earlier, he had
spoken in private of the possibility for a unity of evangelical churches
and denominations which might include such bodies as the FIEC in
England, the Free Church of Scotland, the Irish Evangelical Church,
and the Evangelical Movement of Wales. This he discussed with one
or two leaders, including one of the best-known pastors of the FIEC,
the Rev T. H. Bendor-Samuel, a member of the Westminster Fellowship. Bendor-Samuel was also a leader of the British Evangelical
Council (BEC), an organization launched in 1953 in order to represent churches and bodies that were unwilling to be connected with
the World Council of Churches. E. J. Poole-Connor, another of the
founders of the BEC, had resigned from the Evangelical Alliance in
1952, as noted earlier.[4] Hitherto Lloyd-Jones had never participated
in the BEC, chiefly on account of a concern lest its primary purpose

[2] John Brencher, *Martyn Lloyd-Jones and Twentieth-Century Evangelicalism* (Carlisle, Cumbria: Paternoster, 2002) p. 132. Hereafter cited as Brencher, *Lloyd-Jones,*
[3] See above, p. 386.
[4] See above p. 335.

should prove too negative. The BEC had small support in England but, including as it did the Free Church of Scotland and the Irish Evangelical Church (those denominations being represented on its Council by two of ML-J's friends, the Rev. G. N. M. Collins and the Rev. W. J. Grier), there was the potential for it having a wider appeal; perhaps the BEC, and its member churches, could provide the structure for a move towards a greater unity of evangelical churches. At least one or two BEC leaders seemed to have believed that it could.

This idea, which surfaced among men connected with the Westminster Fellowship in 1967, seemed to provide an answer to the point Packer had put to that fraternal in March 1966 when he asked those of a contrary view to explain the more biblical form of visible unity which they envisaged. At a public meeting in Westminster Chapel on November 1, 1967, under the auspices of the BEC, the beginnings of this new public alignment had a much-publicised send off when ML-J spoke to a large number on 'Luther and his Message for Today'.[5]

But the BEC solution, as yet only in its early stages, had a serious flaw. Part of ML-J's case for evangelicals standing together was that they were guilty of schism if they did not do so. He insisted that the spiritual unity of evangelicals was not enough. The 'guilt of schism' had to be removed by evangelicals belonging to a visible unity. This 'schism' argument was part of his case and had been repeated in the 1966 address. But as the BEC began to emerge as the representative of true unity two objections followed: (1.) Despite the large numbers at the Westminster Chapel meeting, evangelical churches belonging to the BEC represented only a small part of the evangelical ministers and congregations in the UK; were the larger number to be considered 'schismatic' because they did not belong to it? The ML-J argument would appear to point to that conclusion. (2.) The assumption that there could not be true evangelical unity unless it had a more visible church form of expression, appeared to be against what ML-J himself had previously urged in opposing the ecumenical insistence on visible unity, namely, that unity is essentially spiritual, not organisational and formal. The long-held evangelical and Protestant belief was that the church, the body of Christ, exists *wherever* there are

---

[5] H. R. Jones ed., *D. Martyn Lloyd-Jones: Unity in Truth: Addresses given under the auspices of the British Evangelical Council* (Darlington: Evangelical Press, 1991).

true Christians, and that their unity lies in their relationship to him, not upon their place in an external oneness (as Roman Catholicism teaches). If the existence of unity with evangelicals remaining in the mainline churches was being denied, it looked as if the former belief was being abandoned. In which case, it was not the evangelicals who did not respond to his appeal who were disrupting evangelical unity but Lloyd-Jones himself. Thus Dr Packer would later write of ML-J: 'He, rather than I, was the denominationalist for insisting that evangelicals must all belong to this grouping and no other. By contrast, I do not believe that the claims of evangelical unity require ecclesiastical separation.'[6] This argument was to be repeated by many others. In John Brencher's words, 'While he [ML-J] favoured unity among believers his separatist ecclesiology only exacerbated the situation and left evangelicals more divided than before.'[7]

The claim is that Lloyd-Jones was not only responsible for confusion, his appeal was against the best interests of evangelicalism. In the opinion of some, it was a mistake which lost him his place as an evangelical leader.

This case against ML-J looks impressive *only* so long as 'secession to avoid schism' is treated as the heart of his message. It was not, as a reader of his 1966 address ought to see. Whether right or wrong in what he said about schism (and I think he was mistaken in the way he applied the subject), the burden of his message lay elsewhere. It was that the gospel was being endangered by the failure of evangelicals in the mainline denominations to face the question 'What is a Christian?' as the primary issue. Instead they were entering into co-operation with teachers who denied biblical truths.

The ML-J issue should not be confused with a different question, namely, 'What should evangelicals do in a denomination where error cannot be disciplined?' That question had long been a matter of disagreement between evangelicals and yet hitherto it had not prevented recognition of their wider unity. But that wider unity included the shared conviction that *opposition*, not collaboration, had to be the response to false teachers. Now, however, a different principle was operating, popularized by the ecumenical movement, namely, that

---

[6] *Chosen Vessels, Portraits of Ten Outstanding Christian Men*, ed. C. Turner (Ann Arbor: MI: Vine, 1985), p. 112.

[7] Brencher, *Lloyd-Jones*, p. xiii.

all who 'profess to be Christians' should be regarded as being so, irrespective of what they believe or deny. This principle, as noted earlier, was long held by liberals and it underlay the ecumenical slogan that 'fellowship, not belief, unites', but it was *new* among evangelicals. Evangelicals in the Church of England had long stood against any idea that non-evangelicals and Anglo-Catholics were equally entitled to their place in the Church.[8] The Thirty-nine Articles are indisputably against Roman (and therefore Anglo-Catholic) beliefs. Yet in the 1960s Anglo-Catholic and liberal beliefs were both widely established in the Church of England, with the latter in the majority. In the words of Packer, 'the gospel of the Anglican mainstream says: though everyone is fundamentally good, what we all need and what Christ gives us is help'.[9]

What was happening in the new policy was that the terms of evangelical unity and co-operation were being changed. The basis of that co-operation had been rightly repeated by the Anglican, Rev. Frank Colquhoun at the 1957 Evangelical Alliance meeting, with whose statement ML-J was in full agreement. Evangelicals such as Colquhoun repudiated any charge of their being inconsistent by being in the Church of England. They insisted that their position — unlike that of others in the Church of England — was that of the Thirty-nine Articles. Article 19 defined a church as 'a congregation of faithful men' (i.e., men of faith, or believers), implying, as Philip Hughes has written, that 'we have a right to expect, and to require, that a man's profession of faith should be credible'. Yet the situation in 1966, Hughes went on to say was one of 'prevailing indiscipline'.[10]

[8] See J. C. Ryle, *Knots Untied* (repr. Moscow, Idaho: Nolan, 2000). How the older generation of evangelicals regarded Anglo-Catholic and Roman belief is well illustrated in J. S. Reynolds, *Canon Christopher of St Aldate's, Oxford* (Abingdon: Abingdon Press, 1967). In 1927 when a Prayer Book Measure was designed to give greater liberty to Anglo-Catholic teaching, 1,000 evangelicals 'joined in a solemn pledge to leave the Church of England if the Prayer Book Measure was passed'. Marcus Loane, Archbishop of Sydney, went on to describe this as 'the high water mark of Evangelical strength' between the two World Wars. (Marcus L. Loane, *These Happy Warriors: Friends and Contemporaries* [Blackwood, South Australia: New Creation, 1988]).

[9] 'The Gospel and the Lord's Supper,' *Collected Shorter Writings of J. I. Packer* (Carlisle; Paternoster, 1998), vol. 2, p. 46.

[10] J. I. Packer ed., *Guidlines: Evangelical Anglicans Face the Future,* (London: Falcon, 1967), p. 162.

It was in this situation that different terms for co-operation were now accepted by Anglican evangelicals at the Keele Congress — not the Articles, with their clear statements on 'church', 'justification' (Article 11) etc., but rather that the Christian standing of none in the Church should be questioned. All clergy had professed 'faith' and that was enough for co-operation. It was the ecumenical principle that 'fellowship' may exist without unity in belief. Evangelicals were thus to accept that denominational unity be taken as synonymous with 'Christian unity'. Inevitably, therefore, ML-J's question, 'What is a Christian?' was disruptive of this agenda. It could not be answered without upsetting the primary condition for ecumenical unity. This is not to say that evangelicals ceased to give the answer from pulpits; the silence was in the forum of Church politics where the new relationship with non-evangelicals was to operate.

In understanding what was happening dates are important. It may be asked how Lloyd-Jones by his Appeal in 1966 could be seen as disruptive of the Keele agenda of 1967. The answer is that the Keele agenda was in the process of being formed from 1964 and was well advanced by 1966. ML-J had discussed the issue with Stott in 1965. Recent research shows that it was not so much 'evangelicalism' which the Keele leaders feared ML-J might 'wreck' by his words in 1966 but the new policy which they were soon to publicise.[11]

It would be truer, however, to say that the new policy was assumed rather than accepted at Keele. The remarkable thing was that such a change in Anglican evangelical thought could be brought in without any reasoned explanation to the evangelical rank and file. As David N. Samuel, at that time Rector of East Ravendale, Grimsby, would later write: 'How such a profound change in how Evangelicals understood themselves and their role in the Church of England was so quickly and easily accomplished will remain perhaps one of the great mysteries of church history, but it is unquestionably a fact.'[12]

---

[11] See Alister Chapman, *Godly Ambition: John Stott and the Evangelical Movement* (Oxford: University Press, 2012), chapter 4. The Keele statement said, 'We do not believe secession to be a live issue', *Keele '67, The National Evangelical Anglican Congress Statement* (London: Falcon Books, 1967), p. 38. But it was a live issue as Andrew Atherstone has recently shown, writing on 'Lloyd-Jones and the Anglican Secession Crisis', in *Engaging with Martyn Lloyd-Jones*. One thing Keele was intended to do was to head off secessions.

[12] *Evangelical Magazine*, Nov. 1972, p. 16. Dr Samuel would subsequently secede.

The truth is that the reason for the change was not a biblical or theological one, it was political, or, as Packer and Stott, would both subsequently say, 'tactical'. Their concern was that, as evangelicals, 'we might appear to others as representing an extreme wing of the Church of England'. Given that image, they could do nothing to influence the mainstream of events in their denomination; some kind of move into 'the centre' was necessary if they were to exercise the influence for the gospel which they desired. Keele was intended to impress upon fellow Anglicans that just such a move had been made. In the words of Stott, there was repentance for 'narrow partisanship': in that regard the Congress was a 'watershed'.[13] Similarly Packer described Keele as, 'a milestone in twentieth-century evangelical history, for it broke with a long prevalent pietist and sectarian mood'. The intention of Keele was to see evangelical 'ecclesiastical isolationism . . . swept away'.[14] 'We desire to enter this ecumenical dialogue fully', the Keele statement read. As though to prove the change, Archbishop Michael Ramsey, the liberal Anglo-Catholic who expected to see atheists in heaven, was the guest invited to address them.[15] Henceforth there were to be no bars to co-operation, and the Congress agreed that all who 'confess the Lord Jesus Christ according to the Scriptures' (World Council of Churches Basis) 'have a right to be treated as Christians'.[16] This statement could only have sounded sufficient to those who did not know how it was interpreted within the World Council of Churches where Unitarians and liberals were all in membership. The WCC Basis did not say that the word, 'Lord' was to be interpreted by 'the Scriptures *alone*'. Yet in a day when all kinds of error were tolerated in the Church, the WCC Basis was treated as enough for a new unity. John King, an editor of the *Church of England Newspaper* (a mouthpiece for the changed policy), was pleased that at the Keele Congress, 'monolithic evangelical unity' had given way to a new 'church consciousness'. Oliver Barclay saw it

[13] Noble, *Tyndale House*, p. 143.

[14] 'Taking Stock in Theology', in *Evangelicals Today: Thirteen Stock-Taking Essays*, ed. John C. King (Guildford: Lutterworth, 1973), pp. 15-16. 'Pietist' and 'sectarian' refer to the former Anglican evangelicals but look like pejorative terms.

[15] For Ramsey's view of both the Reformation and Scripture see his *The Gospel and the Catholic Church* (London: Longmans, 1961). It would appear that Ramsey was not impressed by Stott's supposed change. See Chapman, *Godly Ambition*, p. 111.

[16] *Keele '67*, p. 37.

differently when he commented, 'Evangelicals had their own ecumenism, bounded by the authority of Scripture.'

The controversy as it involved ML-J took a new turn in 1970 when Dr Packer, with another evangelical and two Anglo-Catholics, published *Growing into Union: Proposals for Forming a United Church in England* (London: SPCK). This 221-page book endorsed Roman Catholic positions such as, 'both Scripture and Tradition must be seen as derived from Christ'; and, on saving grace conveyed through sacraments, 'The gospel makes us one in the Second Adam by baptism.'

Packer has explained that the reasoning behind this move was also 'tactical'. It came about at the juncture when a proposed merger between the Church of England and the Methodist Church looked likely to happen. Not for identical reasons, both Anglo-Catholics and evangelicals were against a union which would bring more liberals into the Church, and *Growing into Union* represented a theological accommodation to justify their combining to defeat it. For the evangelicals it meant a truce over 'lesser errors' in order to prevent the spread of greater. But there was good reason to question whether Anglo-Catholic deviations from evangelical orthodoxy could be so described and the consequences involved in this alignment were not minor. Until now assent to the Thirty-nine Articles, and their definite Protestantism, had been required of all clergy. This assent had long been a dead letter but as long as the Articles stood, in theory at least, the constitution of the Church of England remained Protestant. But a truce over Anglo-Catholic beliefs could not co-exist with a firm defence of the Articles and this has to be one reason why, when 1975 legislation officially ended the authoritative status of the Articles, the Keele leaders proposed no resistance. The end of the Protestantism of the Church of England came very quietly. Both at Keele, and at the Second Congress at Nottingham (1977), the Conference statements made no reference to what had for so long been the doctrinal standard of the Church. The Anglican theologian, W. H. Griffith Thomas, pointed out that more than eight of the Thirty-nine Articles are specifically against 'the errors of the Church of Rome', a Church he described as 'marked by grievous and fundamental errors'.[17] Evangelicals had never believed that a connexion with that Church was

[17] W. H. Griffith Thomas, *Principles of Theology: An Introduction to the Thirty-Nine Articles* (London: Longmans, 1930), p. 273.

enough to be regarded as a Christian (the Homily for Whitsunday even went as far as asserting that Rome was not to be regarded as a Church). But in contrast, at Nottingham, where Stott again chaired, he affirmed: 'Seeing ourselves and Roman Catholics as fellow Christians, we repent of attitudes which seemed to deny it . . . We shall all work together towards full communion between our two churches.'

By 1977 Packer believed that something was going wrong in their midst and he wondered if Nottingham was not a 'mistake'.[18] Evangelical Anglicans were losing their 'common purpose' and 'while the total number of evangelicals in the Church increases, the number of campaigning evangelicals declines'.[19] It was not, however, over Anglo-Catholic or Roman error that he expressed concern, but over a weakening resistance to liberal unbelief. He had not himself been immune from pressure from that quarter. Serving on the Church of England's Doctrinal Commission he was a signatory to *Christian Believing* in 1976, in which all were identified 'followers of a common Lord' in spite of an absence of unanimity on the deity of Christ.[20] After Nottingham the policy of inclusiveness would go on apace among Anglican evangelicals. In *Essentials*, John Stott, accepted that while such truths as the virgin birth of Christ and his bodily resurrection are 'essential', this did not mean 'essential' to the right to be regarded as a Christian.[21] Accordingly, he said, the 'kindly David Jenkins' was to be seen as a Christian, even though the bishop denied the fall of man, the virgin birth and the resurrection of Christ.

Dr George Carey, once committed to the IVF basis of faith, and prominent at Nottingham, was like others who became bishops and who were different men before their elevation to higher office. He was to publish in favour of reunion with Rome in his book, *A Tale of Two Churches: Can Protestants & Catholics Get Together* (Downers Grove, Ill: IVP, 1985),[22] and to express his view of the Church of England

---

[18] *Collected Writings,* vol. 1, p. 74.

[19] *The Evangelical Anglican Identity Problem* (Oxford: Latimer House, 1978), pp. 30-1. 'For political reasons I was not free to say what I thought', he has said of Nottingham, 1978.

[20] *Lloyd-Jones, Fight of Faith,* p. 658. I refer readers to that volume and to my *Evangelicalism Divided*, for fuller information and references.

[21] *Essentials,* David L. Edwards and John Stott (London: Hodder & Stoughton, 1988), p. 228.

[22] Foreword by J. I. Packer. Carey's hopefulness, and Packer's mild disclaimer, are

in the words: 'I am convinced it is a broad church combining the catholic, evangelical, charismatic and liberal in joyful harmony.'[23]

This may seem a long digression from the life of Dr Lloyd-Jones but it is all very closely tied to the 1960s, controversy over which he has been widely blamed for being 'anti-Anglican' and sectarian. Yet in reality he was the one standing closer to the historic Articles of the Church of England. One 'proof' of his bad spirit has been adduced from his termination of the Puritan Conference in 1970, which one critic has described as a '*putsch* which ousted Packer and others who did not share the required beliefs about separation and a pure church'.[24]

This is a complete misrepresentation. The break with Packer — one of the saddest experiences of ML-J's life — did not come after Keele in 1967. It was occasioned by Packer's book, *Growing into Union,* which patently endorsed Anglo-Catholic teaching contrary to the Thirty-nine Articles. To claim that Stott and Packer were defending the gospel issue over against Lloyd-Jones' ecclesiology is to stand the truth on its head. This is not to say that the leaders of the new policy did not mean to uphold the gospel. They did. They hoped, by leading evangelicals to a more central position in the Church of England, to increase influence for the gospel. Dr Lloyd-Jones argued that it could not succeed: being evangelical and ecumenical at the same time could only weaken the evangelical position because there was a basic incompatibility. If there could be unity with non-evangelicals, *without* evangelical belief, how could that belief continue to be held

---

in marked contrast to J. C. Ryle: 'A Church which regards Romanism and Protestantism with equal favour or equal indifference, is mere Babel, a "city of confusion," and not the city of God.' 'The Church of England had better be disestablished, disendowed, and broken in pieces, than reunited with the Church of Rome.' *Charges and Addresses* (repr. Edinburgh: Banner of Truth, 1978), pp. 333, 170. Packer has also said elsewhere that the Church of Rome is 'irreformable'.

[23] *Bath and Wells Diocesan News,* March 1988, p. 5. Carey became Archbishop of Canterbury in 1991.

[24] Gaius Davies, *Genius, Grief and Grace* (Fearn, Ross-shire: Christian Focus, 2001), p. 368. Davies says that word of the termination of the Puritan Conference came to Packer in a letter from ML-J 'rather like being sent a Papal Bull'. How far the letter, beginning, 'My Dear Friend,' and ending with, 'I sincerely hope we shall be able to maintain some personal contact . . . with warmest regards', deserves such a description, readers can judge for themselves. It is printed in my *Lloyd-Jones: Messenger of Grace,* pp. 205-7.

as vital? The pressure for an acceptance of a multiformity of beliefs within the Church of England was so strong that it needed very definite statements to the contrary to withstand it. But by the very terms of the alignment any such definiteness was precluded. Collaboration necessarily inhibited open opposition; the very 'ground rules' for ecumenical partnership were against it. Bishop Mervyn Stockwood was only one of the many who said that the 'new-school evangelicals' could only make their 'distinctive contribution' if they were 'open-minded and flexible'.[25] So universally accepted were these grounds of co-operation that James Barr thought one sentence quoted from Lloyd-Jones was enough to prove the man 'harsh and rigid'; the Lloyd-Jones' sentence was, 'If people query or question the great cardinal truths, "to regard them as brethren is to betray the truth."'[26]

To ML-J's grief evangelical friends in the Church of England could not see that doctrinal drift must inevitably follow the new thinking. He warned what would be the outcome even in 1965:

> We have evidence before our eyes that our staying amongst such people [i.e., opponents of evangelical truth] does not seem to be converting them to our view but rather to a lowering of the spiritual temperature of those who are staying amongst them and an increasing tendency to doctrinal accommodation and compromise.

Francis Schaeffer would make the same point: 'If one gives in to ecclesiastical latitudinarianism which becomes a co-operative comprehensiveness, there is a tendency to drift into doctrinal comprehensiveness and especially to let down a clear view of Scripture.'[27]

I do not think my friend Jim Packer meets this case head on.[28]

[25] Stockwood, *Chanctonbury Ring*, p. 154, quoted by Manwaring, *Controversy to Co-Existence* (Cambridge: Cambridge University Press, 1985), p. 145. Stockwood actually scorned evangelical belief. So meekly was Stockwood's qualification accepted, that the evangelicals in their book, *Evangelical Anglicans: Their Role and Influence in the Church Today* (London: SPCK, 1993), gave the last chapter to Bishop Richard Holloway who rubbed in the same lesson: an Anglican must 'affirm expressions of the common faith that may not be entirely sympathetic to his or her own tastes . . . Churches balance contrarieties and disagreements' (pp. 178-9).

[26] Barr, *Fundamentalism*, p. 362.

[27] Schaeffer, *The Church before the Watching World* (Leicester: IVP, 1972), p. 97.

[28] I say 'friend' deliberately, for those who have disagreed with him in this controversy have been otherwise described by some commentators. He and I have valued meeting together after the disruption of 1970 and have kept in touch through the

Instead he speaks of ML-J's appeal of 1966 as consisting of two arguments, which he called 'bad arguments': 'Bad argument number one was that if we stay in the Church of England we're guilty by association of all the theological errors that any Anglican may be promoting anywhere at all.'[29] Dr Lloyd-Jones, he wrote again, believed in 'second-degree' separation, and thought that 'opposing and repudiating' error within a mixed denomination, 'does not clear one of guilt unless one actually withdraws.'[30] I do not know documentation to show that such was Lloyd-Jones' belief. If men were resolute for obedience to Scripture within mixed denominations, and opposed the opposite, they had his sympathy. To the end of his life, as I have shown elsewhere, he kept in fellowship and sometimes publicly helped Anglican evangelicals. His case was when evangelicals *condoned* a policy of standing together with men who taught serious error (Archbishop Ramsey, for instance) there was guilt. He did not hold that Anglicans such as Frank Colquhoun, with whom he happily co-operated, were guilty *per se* for being in a 'mixed denomination'. It was only after Keele that his language stiffened, and it was then that, as far as I know, he first used the term "guilt by association" in connection with those who were ready to be 'yoked together with others who deny the very elements of the Christian faith'.[31] Packer argued, 'As long as we are free to raise our voices against errors and seek to correct them from within we are not guilty of them.' If this had been done, to any degree as Paul who 'withstood Peter to the face', the Keele policy would have instantly collapsed. What Packer did by opposing wrong teachers *openly* before Keele I do not see him doing in England over the following ten years.

The words of Professor Douglas Jones are a case in point. As noted above, in 1965 he condemned Lloyd-Jones for saying that Christian unity exists only where the central doctrines of Paul's gospel are

---

years. The admiration numbers of us had for him in the 1950s has not been lost.

[29] Roger Steer, *Guarding the Holy Fire* (Grand Rapids, MI: Baker, 1999), p. 225. The second ML-J argument Packer states as: 'Don't you see that the times call us to leave all the doctrinally mixed congregations and form a pure new one.' To which he saw a different call, to 'work for Reformation, renewal and fresh life in the church that has this rich heritage'.

[30] Packer, *The Evangelical Anglican Identity Problem* (Oxford: Latimer House, 1978), pp. 31-2.

[31] *Unity in Truth*, p. 41.

believed. You could have 'faith in Christ' without believing doctrines concerning Christ. Packer replied to him that Lloyd-Jones knew as well as he did that it was possible to have belief in doctrines without faith in Christ but that was not the point: 'That you can have belief in doctrines without faith in Christ was not in dispute. Dr Lloyd-Jones' thrust was rather that you cannot have faith in Christ without faith in the doctrines of the gospel . . . in principle Dr Lloyd-Jones' position is unchallengeable.' These words were published in 1966.[32]

But to these words Packer introduced a qualification over how 'heretics' are to be assessed, and the words play a part in the subsequent divergence between him and ML-J:

> It is beyond our power to determine how much false doctrine, or how little true doctrine, concerning Jesus is compatible with 'justifying faith' in any particular case. No doubt we must be cautious in judging the spiritual state of heretics.

The statement is true, but it is never used in the New Testament to excuse outright confrontation with false teachers and their discipline. It was ecumenical leaders, as noted earlier, who popularised the argument that the Christian standing of anyone is not be judged by their *words,* for they might be wrong in their heads but right in their hearts.[33] Evangelicals, including Packer, were, I think, to misuse this language. Scripture knows no such separation of head and heart when it comes to the acceptance or denial of fundamental truths. As J. C. Ryle wrote, 'When a man's tongue is generally wrong, it is absurd, no less than unscriptural, to say his heart is right.' The test which Scripture gives us is: 'He that is of God heareth God's words: ye therefore hear them not, because ye are not of God'; 'He that knoweth God heareth us; he that is not of God heareth us not. Hereby we know the spirit of truth and the spirit of error (*John* 8:47; *1 John* 4:6).

How much a person needs to understand to be considered a Christian, important as it is, was not, however, the main issue here.

---

[32] See *Collected Shorter Writings,* vol. 2, p. 36.

[33] Stott uses the argument in *Essentials*: 'Our heart may be better than our head, and salvation is by faith not by orthodox formulation' (p. 228). 'Radicals who query the truth and worth of much of Scripture are yet devout Bible readers and vigorous preachers of the gospel.' Packer, *'Fundamentalism' and the Word of God* (1958; repr. Grand Rapids, MI: Eerdmans, 1982), p. 124.

Lloyd-Jones was not speaking against the acknowledgement of weak Christians but of men who were *teachers* and *leaders* in the churches. He saw the New Testament instructions regarding such people as unmistakable (*Gal.* 1:8; *Titus* 1:11; *2 John* 10; *Rev.* 2:20).

* * *

Although this controversy for Dr Lloyd-Jones was a momentous issue, and remained so, I will not return to it in subsequent chapters. It did not deflect him from the continuance of his main work of positive preaching. The sadness which the differences brought he felt keenly; the more so because it involved a parting of friends in public work. In the case of Jim Packer, his younger colleague of many years, he felt this most keenly. At no point was his opposition to ecumenism and the Keele policy a personal matter. Nor was he in that opposition prompted by others. He led, he did not follow lesser men. His position was the outworking of the convictions of forty years. That he acted as he did because he liked to lead, as has been suggested, is to misunderstand him utterly. Before leaving the matter, however, I will attempt some concluding observations:

1. All those engaged in the controversy were fallible men. I have not claimed that Dr Lloyd-Jones' judgment was faultless and, at one point at least, time has proved him wrong. He feared the coming of a comprehensive church, favourable to all except definite evangelicals, and inclusive, perhaps, of the Church of Rome herself. In his thinking it was therefore urgent that evangelicals should be prepared and united to face this likelihood. As we know, the ecumenical 'success', so confidently predicted by its own advocates, never came about. So, some had said, ML-J's fear was prompted by an illusion.

But the fact that the commonly accepted time scale, in which he shared, was wrong does not mean that such danger cannot exist. Further, the reason the ecumenical programme failed underscores ML-J's conviction that it was not of God. Its motivation sprang too largely from the worldly notion that bringing the denominations into one 'super' church would regain the influence which Christianity was losing in the world. It was centralization for the power of numbers. Before the twentieth century ended that thinking was undermined by realities, for, where the union of denominations did succeed, their decline was in no way arrested.

2. Was the attempt to place evangelicalism in the centre of the Church of England as planned at Keele a success? Here, I think, there is a measure of agreement between both sides of the controversy. They disagree on *why* it did not succeed, but they seem to accept the fact. Packer would write in 1984:

> I hope I am wrong to suspect that with this enhanced participation has come a lessening of theological seriousness; for if I am right, then however evangelical numbers grow (and numerical growth since 1950 had been spectacular) evangelical thought will hardly be able to maintain its own integrity.

By 1978, he believed, as already noted, that evangelicals were losing their 'common purpose'.[34] That same year he said: 'Realism compels us to recognize that judgment, theological, moral and spiritual, has overtaken English Protestantism.'[35]

Before 1984 the evangelical grouping which had made the two Evangelical Anglican Congresses had fractured. Packer, 'the brains behind much Anglican evangelical policy, had gone overseas in 1979.'[36] In a brief autobiographical comment, he wrote that after fifteen years' work in England: 'I found myself marginalized, isolated, and required to work to unfulfilling, and, I thought, flawed agendas.'[37] John Stott, his 'coalition undone',[38] was to turn to gospel fields more promising than the reformation of his denomination. Alister Chapman, after detailing more of this story, goes on to say that Stott and others 'did much to relegitimate evangelicalism in the established church.' 'More evangelicals became bishops, and even archbishops.' That is true, but

[34] *The Evangelical Anglican Identity Problem*, p. 31. 'Is Anglican comprehensiveness a matter of not insisting on more than the gospel as a basis of fellowship, or of not insisting on the gospel at all? No outsider could be blamed for concluding that it is the second, for that is what you see when you look at the Church today' (p. 35). 'If the Christianity of the Church of England is in process of becoming something different from the dogmatic evangelical faith of the Articles, is not deep involvement in the set-up a bit perverse?' (p. 36).

[35] *Collected Writings,* vol. 1, 81.

[36] Alister Chapman, *Godly Ambition*, p. 104.

[37] Packer, *Truth & Power* (Guildford: Eagle, 1996), p. 204

[38] *Godly Ambition*, p. 109. 'On the face of it, Stott's attempt to unite Anglican evangelicals around a theologically conservative program to change the church was a failure' (p. 107).

with rare exception, the men so advanced all ceased to be identifiable as evangelicals in any historic sense of that term. The harvest of the Keele policy was not that for which its originators had hoped. Oliver Barclay, friend of John Stott, has this insightful comment:

> There was often an assumption that sheer force of numbers would somehow shift the churches in an evangelical direction, when there was no strategy to ensure that they themselves remained solidly evangelical in the face of growing pressure from those with whom they sought to work.[39]

To say this is not to discount the number of Anglican churches where evangelical preaching continued through this period, and was owned with conversions, notably, at times, in congregations led by men such as Dick Lucas of St Helen's, Bishopsgate, who had not been identified with the Keele policy. But no one claimed that these congregations were representative of the denomination's life, nor did they need to be in order to possess the spiritual influence which they had.

Packer has briefly given his own reasons why the Keele vision was unfulfilled. Interviewed on the subject in the year 2000, he believed the vision had not been maintained because the leaders, gaining wider involvement in the running of the Church, had been over-taken by the pressure of administrative responsibilities, and 'the charismatic tidal wave' had swept away more doctrinal awareness. He does not comment, as far as we are aware, on the crux question. He has written 'what makes an evangelical will be that which in the eyes of the New Testament writers makes a Christian'.[40] If that is so, how could the Keele policy of engaging with non-evangelicals for unity be right to pursue?[41] Eleven years after Lloyd-Jones had pressed the question, 'What is a Christian?', at a press conference at Nottingham, when John King asked Stott 'to tell him what exactly it meant to be an evangelical', the *Church of England Newspaper* reported, 'Stott had looked somewhat dazed in response.'[42]

---

[39] *Evangelicalism in Britain*, p. 101.

[40] *Collected Writings*, vol. 1, p. 75.

[41] Explaining the Keele programme, Chapman writes: 'Over time, Stott had become much more open to other points of view. He was now convinced that engaging with non-evangelicals was the right thing to do.' *Godly Ambition*, p. 99.

[42] *Ibid.*, p. 102.

3. We have noted how the policy of Keele necessitated 'tactics' and expediency in the attempted improvement of the evangelical image. Both Stott and Packer were thrown into church politics. It was a course of action which, however well intentioned, possessed greater dangers than either men seemed to realize at the first. It entailed, as I have already said, toleration of supposed lesser errors in the hope of overthrowing the greater. The older evangelicalism would have given a scriptural critique of that 'tactical' approach. Scripture warns to beware of seemingly small beginnings of error: 'A little leaven leavens the whole lump' (*Gal.* 5:9). 'Small' concessions, arrived at by expediency, commonly lead to consequences which were not intended.[43] 'As with Jim Packer,' Chapman writes, 'Stott gave himself to Anglican politics but in the end tired of them.'[44]

4. Almost forty years after Jim Packer wrote '*Fundamentalism' and the Word of God*, he gave this valuable opinion in retrospect:

> In the ongoing North American debate between evangelical and liberal Protestants . . . biblical inerrancy was from the first made the touchstone more directly and explicitly than was ever the case in the parallel debates in Britain. This, I now think (I did not always think so), argues for clear-sightedness in the New World, for without inerrancy the structure of biblical authority as evangelicals conceive it collapses.[45]

This is surely relevant to the controversy we have sketched. The Keele policy and its statement of faith had no mention of inerrancy. That was not accidental. Had it done so there could have been no question of gathering the numbers, or an archbishop, to support the Congress. Inerrancy, thought the religious world, was a belief owned by none but obcurantists and fundamentalists. A new image would have been impossible on that foundation. But if the presence of that doctrine would have made for much smaller numbers it would have

---

[43] 'We do not tolerate quietly a little dishonesty, or a little cheating, or a little lying: just so, let us never allow a little false doctrine to ruin us, by thinking it is but a "little one" and can do us no harm. The Galatians seemed to be doing nothing very dangerous when they "observed days and months, and times and years"; yet St Paul says, "I am afraid of you" (*Gal.* 4:10-11).' J. C. Ryle, *Knots Untied* (repr. Moscow, Idaho: Nolan, 2000), p. 354.

[44] *Godly Ambition*, p. 111.

[45] *Truth & Power* (Guildford: Eagle, 1996), p. 91.

cleared the ground for a definite message, uncluttered by debates on such things as women clergy,[46] and on how far 'hermeneutics' might explain how liberals could yet be Bible believers.[47] On inerrancy, at least, Keele gave an uncertain sound which cannot be unrelated to the eventual demise of the movement. It is not clear that the Congresses were clear of the blame of 'calculated laxity in handling the authority of Scripture' which, Packer says, belonged to the Anglican-Methodist conversations of 1963.[48]

Why Dr Packer was willing to confront liberal unbelief with inerrancy, and not also to face Catholic and Anglo-Catholic error with the doctrine of Scripture *alone,* I do not know. One judges that he supposed their common commitment to the supernatural was too necessary to endanger the alliance. But allowing 'tradition' to stand beside Scripture, and equally part of God's revelation (as publicly acknowledged in *Growing into Union*), was by no means the toleration of a little error: it was the very teaching which brought on the corruption which necessitated the Reformation.

* * *

In brief, it may be added that larger numbers of evangelical Anglicans did not support the Keele policy than was previously thought. Andrew Atherstone, himself an Anglican, has shown that 'Lloyd-Jones's heartfelt appeals for evangelical unity in the face of ecumenical confusion had a stronger groundswell of support within the Church of England than has previously been recognised.'[49] A larger number of clergy seceded than was recorded at the time and

[46] There was no voice from Keele or Nothingham against women clergy, and Stott was finally to concede a legitimacy to women bishops. *Godly Ambition*, p. 124.

[47] Hermeneutics is concerned with how the Bible is interpreted. Chapman records Stott's change of view on this subject; he came to believe that people's cultural places and perspectives come largely into their response to Scripture. *Ibid.,* pp. 104-5. While Packer regarded the new interest and promotion of hermeneutics as tending to the support of liberal theology, Stott saw it as a route to unity. If Roger Steer is reliable, Stott would have been hesitant in defending inerrancy. *Holy Fire*, p. 332.

[48] *Collected Shorter Writings*, vol. 2, p. 42.

[49] 'Lloyd-Jones and the Anglican Secession Crisis', in *Engaging with Martyn Lloyd-Jones*, p. 292.

others who remained sought to protest the change of direction. Alan Stibbs and Oliver Barclay spoke to the Church of England Evangelical Council (the policy-making group chaired by John Stott) in 1970 and 1971, but their words, as Atherstone reports, 'did not win a sympathetic hearing and Packer said their attitude reflected a "siege mentality"'.[50] Dr Barclay has written: 'When Alan Stibbs and I were invited to attend a meeting in 1971, he left almost in tears at what he felt was its departure from his hopes for it.'[51] Another who remained in the Church of England was Dr Gerald Bray whose teaching at Oak Hill College was terminated by ecclesiastical pressure in 1992. Thereafter he took the trail which other theologians in the denomination had taken before him to North America. Bray's review of Alister McGrath's biography of Packer is an insightful piece of writing. He believed McGrath failed to convey what the 'misunderstood and despised remnant' of evangelical Anglicans were — with their sense that 'they alone were charged with bringing the gospel to a benighted nation'. Before the new image brought in by Keele: 'It was a narrow world, but had its attractions as a company of true believers who were prepared to accept ridicule for the sake of the truth as they saw it. Dr McGrath may know this in his head, but he does not feel it in his bones, and so it does not come across to his readers in a coherent or convincing way.' Bray goes on to say:

> What Dr Lloyd-Jones saw clearly — more clearly, one feels, than either Dr Packer or John Stott did — was that Anglican Evangelicals were in danger of losing their cutting edge if they got too involved in the structures of the Church of England. This was a time when a younger generation of Anglican Evangelicals was beginning to feel that such involvement was both right and necessary, and in this they were supported by Packer and Stott. Trying to decide who was right in this debate is not easy, because much depends on one's point of view. The Packer-Stott line would have had a good deal to commend it had Anglican Evangelicalism been united around a coherent Reformed theology, but it was not. Those who wanted to 'go into' the Church of England, as they put it, were often quite happy to ditch whatever theology they possessed, especially if it could get them a bishopric. Whether Dr Lloyd-Jones

[50] *Ibid.*, p. 290.
[51] Oliver Barclay, *Evangelicalism in Britain 1935-1995* (Leicester: IVP, 1997), p. 85.

407

realized this or not, subsequent events have shown this — his was the prophetic voice.[52]

The gospel, not churchmanship, was the main issue in the division for which Lloyd-Jones was blamed in 1966. His hope did not lie in new church alignments but in the bold, unfettered preaching of Christ, in the power of the Holy Spirit. Concessions to ecumenical thinking led, he believed, in the opposite direction. But controversies are ever accompanied by confusion and that is the only way I can explain the mistaken words: 'Jim Packer's writings have shown, the Doctor's views on ecclesiology led to a parting of the ways.'[53] Again: 'While many evangelicals deeply sympathised with the Doctor's position, they felt that to make ecclesiastical issues the priority — however understandable the motive might be — was a mistake. What mattered was the continuing defence of the gospel.'[54]

---

[52] *Churchman*, vol. III, No. 4 (1997), pp. 359-60. ML-J's warnings as they related to the Church of England have often been avoided by the charge that he was inherently and temperamentally, anti-Anglican. 'For the record,' Bray writes, 'I can testify that Dr Lloyd-Jones was not anti-Anglican as such, because when he found out that I was going to seek ordination in the Church of England he came to see me and encouraged me in my vocation. The one thing he warned me about was the danger of becoming an ecclesiastical politician.'

[53] C. Catherwood, *Martyn Lloyd-Jones: A Family Portrait* (Eastbourne: Kingsway, 1995), p. 172.

[54] C. Catherwood, *Five Evangelical Leaders* (London: Hodder & Stoughton, 1984), p. 91.

TWENTY-EIGHT

The End of an Era

I t might be supposed that the controversy of 1966–67 was so major that it entered into Dr Lloyd-Jones' entire ministry. This is far from being the case. His normal work proceeded as usual and in a number of meetings where he might have taken up the issues he dealt entirely with other subjects. To the 'inner circle' at the Annual Meeting of the Evangelical Library on December 6, 1966, he spoke of the great improvement which he had seen in England with reference to serious reading over the previous thirty years. He attributed the change to the work of the IVF, the Evangelical Library, the Puritan Conference, and to the Banner of Truth Trust. At the same meeting the following year he was to speak of the United States. For his address at the Puritan Conference in 1966 — the year being the 350th anniversary of the founding of the first Congregational Church in England — he spoke on 'Henry Jacob and the First Congregational Church'.

As already said, there was no let up in his preaching engagements. I recall the conversation we had as I drove him from London to a service near Tintern, Monmouthshire, in July 1967. I expected him to be somewhat tired, for it was Tuesday, and the previous day — immediately after his Sunday work — he had given the major address at the Westminster Fraternal meeting. But far from being tired he was in fine spirits and reminded me that while physical effort exhausted him, he had great stores of nervous energy. Mrs Lloyd-Jones was more tired on Sunday nights than he was! From his childhood and the death of his brother Harold in 1918, conversation went on to his first visit to Canada in 1932. Then the subject of books came up. Though he read all through the year he looked forward to his summer break to get through some larger works. The books he was looking forward to reading that summer were A. F. Scott Pearson's *Thomas Cartwright and Elizabethan Puritanism* and a major biography of Napoleon by a Dutch author. Observing my surprise at the latter choice, he confessed to his enjoyment of books on battles and that there was still enough of the boy in him to have heroes and to regret their falls. He illustrated this same point from his recent experience in watching a cricket match. A few weeks earlier, on his annual day outing to Lord's, he had looked forward to seeing the Indian celebrity, the Nawab of Pataudi, who had batted brilliantly at Leeds. But to his regret the famous batsman was out quickly before they could see him in action. His disappointment, however, was more intense, he recalled, over a similar incident in 1948. In that year he had the opportunity to see Don Bradman bat for Australia against Middlesex in one of his last matches in England. Bradman had scored over 2,000 runs that summer but on this occasion Compton caught him at backward short leg for a mere 6 runs: in ML-J's view the crowd were 'fools' for erupting in applause instead of realizing what they had missed seeing from the world's greatest batsman!

As usual, he made many visits to Wales in 1967. One of these engagements he was to describe as the most extraordinary service he had been in. This was in Aberfan, a place suddenly known across the world on account of the terrible disaster which occurred there on October 21, 1966. The register had just been marked that morning in the village school when, at 9.15 A.M., a great heap of coal slurry which over-shadowed the building suddenly slipped and, with a rumble like thunder, engulfed nearly a whole generation of the local children. One hundred and sixteen died, along with twenty-eight adults. The coal-mining areas of South Wales knew something of disasters but a tragedy of this nature, above ground, took the community into an abyss of sorrow from which it seemed it would never recover.

Dr Lloyd-Jones was asked to preach on the first anniversary of this disaster, November 15, 1967 in the Welsh Presbyterian church, Capel Aberfan. All denominations, however, gathered for these services on the afternoon and evening of that day. In the evening the Welsh

Baptist chapel, Smyrna, across the road was also packed for worship and to hear a relay of the sermon. The evening message was one of glorious comfort for believers from the words of Romans 8:18-23, 'For I reckon that the sufferings of this present time are not worthy to be compared with the glory which shall be revealed in us.' At the conclusion of a profoundly moving service, the Rev. Wilfred Jones, the Vicar of Aberfan, came forward to tell the preacher that this was the message for which Aberfan had been waiting. Two years later a woman wrote a postcard to say she would never forget those services at Aberfan and many others confessed the same. 'I have heard the eminent preachers of all the churches,' said one Anglican hearer, 'but have never heard a sermon or address to compare with what I heard at Aberfan.'

* * *

At Westminster Chapel the expository and evangelistic ministries continued in the manner now familiar for so long. There were many young people present whose own parents had once been youngsters under the same ministry. Except at holiday periods, there were never visiting preachers at the Chapel. Dr Lloyd-Jones was as regular as Big Ben and almost — it seemed — as fixed in his pulpit as the great clock was above the Houses of Parliament. But those who supported him most in prayer did not take the ministry for granted. Another postcard writer sent him this anonymous message: 'Thank you a thousand times for that most wonderful message last Sunday evening! May the Lord graciously bless you, and preserve you to continue this most vital ministry in London.'

By the summer of 1966, ML-J had been through Acts 5 and 6 on Sunday evenings and he commenced chapter 7 on October 16. For the morning sermons he was in John 4. A year later, on October 8, 1967, he began Acts 8 in the evenings but was still in John 4 for the general sermons he was preaching on the Christian life. In the Romans series he concluded his expositions of chapter 12 on Friday, November 11, 1966. The next Friday he started on Romans 13 and remained with that chapter to May 26, 1967. He resumed the series at Romans 14:1 on October 10, 1967.

The press still took notice of Westminster Chapel from time to time. The *Observer* magazine for March 19, 1967 carried a survey of preachers and congregations. The reporter of the service at Westminster Chapel was still mystified, as others had been, at what he found:

On ordinary Sundays you have to hunt for vacant seats in the lower galleries and the central area.

Lloyd-Jones is the last, in London anyway, of the great oratorical preachers. People call it 'Hell and damnation tub-thumping' when they think they have to be funny about it.

You could call his message seventeenth-century Puritanism.

His sermons start quietly. The variations in delivery come later. Slow, slow, quick, quick, slow. He has a Bible in front of him and can locate texts like a computer. Nobody so much as coughs . . .

After hearing him preach many people go to him for help and get it. In private he is quiet and kind. Whether it's what he says, or how he says it, *something* is terribly convincing.

As usual, the beginning of another year's work at Westminster Chapel in September 1967 brought the arrival of a number of new students at the Chapel from various parts of the world. Joan Gibson, arriving from South Island, New Zealand, made her way there for the first time on October 1, 1967. The following week she wrote home:

Last Sunday I did the double. Heard John Stott in the morning and the Doctor at night. I sat up in the balcony at Westminster Chapel and just imagined you thriving on it. There were all and sundry there — black, white, brown, old, young, mothers, fathers, kids and even a dog sitting up the front with his head on his paws! He is a guide dog for a young blind man who has been converted. The Doctor is small, wizened, glasses and wears a black gown which he pulls across and then clutches — but not for long because he then starts to wave his arms around. While I was there he dealt with, 'I am what I am by the grace of God.' 'A repetitive expositor', according to the Principal! I was tickled pink and determined to go back.

As Dr Lloyd-Jones entered upon the new year of ministry at Westminster Chapel in 1968 he had, as usual, no long-term preaching programme. He had been preaching in the Gospel of John on Sunday mornings since 1962 and his method was to stay on a passage for as long as it continued to supply him with fresh and relevant material. On the first Sunday morning (January 7), from the starting point of the Samaritan woman as a new person in Christ, he preached a sermon on the subject of how his hearers should examine themselves. His two main heads were:

(1.) Self-examination with reference to the past, Is your knowledge of Christ the greatest thing that has happened to you? Is your greatest rejoicing in what he has done for you? Has this knowledge been increasing? (2.) Self-examination as we look to the future, What is your greatest desire? How do you face the unseen possibilities (a) Immediate: disappointment, loss, illness, accident, sorrow? (b) Ultimate: death and eternity?

These questions say much about his own view of life. On the following Sunday morning he continued on the theme of the new experience of the Samaritan woman with respect to her witness to others. His main point, over several Sundays, was that her testimony was spontaneous, there was something within her which was urging and compelling. 'The idea of training people to do this is new and modern and really belongs to the cults.' 'The best workers are always the best Christians — best in knowledge and understanding, best in experience, best in life, those most filled with the Holy Spirit.' From the passage he demonstrated the reasons why witness is spontaneous and then went on to show that this is because of what the gospel does *in* Christians, 'what they are is more important than what they say'. In what were to be, unknown to him, his last two Sunday morning sermons in the pulpit of Westminster Chapel (Feb. 18 and 25) his sermons were summaries of what he saw as the priorities in Christian character.

He resumed Romans on Friday, January 12, 1968, taking up verses 15 and 16 of chapter 14 and, of course, there was the usual routine of other mid-week activities. The church meeting of January 18 was to prove his last such meeting. It dealt with normal matters of membership, including the deaths of a much-esteemed retired missionary, Phyllis Wright, and another lady, Martha Wright, who had been a member of the church since 1912. The members' meeting was followed by an address from a former member of the Chapel, Dr John Tester of the Edinburgh Medical Missionary Society (who had gone to Nazareth from Westminster in 1952).

On the first Sunday evening of the year, January 7, he had preached on the passage in the Acts of the Apostles at chapter 8, verse 26, recording the conversion of the Ethiopian eunuch through the witness of Philip. The first words of verse 26 gave him his theme for the first sermon, 'And the angel of the Lord spake unto Philip, saying, Arise, and go . . .' The world is not *man's* world — angels, unseen powers, a supernatural realm! 'Oh, what a message to start a new year with!' he told the congregation that night. 'How I thank God that I am not dependent upon what men are going to do in this coming year . There is God, and he knows all and he is illimitable in his power! The initiative is always with God and we never know how he will act.'

The next evening sermon dealt with the kind of man the Ethiopian eunuch evidently was — moral, religious, yet dissatisfied. On the following Sunday evenings the different parts of the passage were expounded in relation to the theme of what it means to become a Christian. His first two sermons had dealt with common stumbling blocks in the way of being converted, first, the failure to realise the supernatural realm and, second, the danger of being religious without being a Christian. For the third Sunday night (Jan. 21) he took the fundamental problem indicated in the eunuch's acknowledged inability to understand the Scriptures (*Acts* 8:30, 31): 'the Christian message is something that cannot be understood by the natural man'. To make the Christian message acceptable to unregenerate man, to take out the offensive and make it 'intelligible', is to deny it.

The main theme the following Sunday night was that Philip could speak with authority because Scripture is a revelation from God, containing good news from heaven:

> I have no other authority as I stand in this pulpit. The authority of the cults is the authority of experience. They talk about experience, they recommend experience, that is what they have got to offer. That is not the case here. This is exposition of the truth and we have no other authority. My dear friends, let me put it as plainly and as simply as this: standing in this pulpit tonight on the 28th of January 1968 I am doing nothing different from what Philip did with the Ethiopian eunuch.

In February 1968 his work was interrupted by a bout of influenza, and those who attended the Chapel on Sunday, February 11 had the unusual experience of not finding him in his pulpit. He was back for the next Friday night and, although somewhat struggling in health, there was no sign of it in the preaching. He was having much liberty in his Sunday evening evangelistic preaching. On February 18 and 25 (which was to be the last Sunday night he stood as the pastor in the Westminster Chapel pulpit) his subject was the depth and the profundity of the human problem which required the death of the Son of God before the lost could be saved. Men must know the horror of sin, and their own guilt, before they can understand the cross of Christ: 'It is no use saying to people, 'Come to Jesus.' They do not come to Jesus: why not? They have never seen any need of Jesus.' Man is rebellious, lost, miserable, defenceless under the power of sin. And so he closed his Sunday ministry preaching the death of Jesus Christ as the only means by which man may be saved and reconciled to God.

The week following Sunday, February 25, he worked as usual, preaching in Bedford on the Tuesday. He was conscious of being unwell but put it down to the after-effects of his recent influenza. On the Friday he had interviews in his vestry at Westminster with people requiring help and advice, starting at 4.45, prior to the evening meeting at 6.30 P.M. It was to be the 372nd occasion of his preaching from Romans and he had come to the word 'peace' in the statement, 'For the kingdom of God is not meat and drink; but righteousness, and peace, and joy in the Holy Ghost.' His closing words that night were to conclude his twelve-and-a-half years in the exposition of Romans, 'God willing, we will go on to consider the other great characteristic next time — "joy in the Holy Ghost".'

I am not sure at what point Dr Lloyd-Jones knew that he would not be able to preach on the following Sunday, March 3. He was probably hoping for some improvement in the abdominal discomfort from which he was suffering, but at 8 A.M. that Sunday morning Mrs Lloyd-Jones had to ring his assistant, Edwin King (who lived outside London at Chesham, where he supplied a church), indicating that he was needed at once for the Westminster pulpit. It was becoming clear to ML-J that something was seriously wrong: the following Thursday, March 7, he was admitted to the Royal London Homoeopathic Hospital where he underwent major surgery the next day for an obstruction in the colon — a condition brought about by cancer.

No one, outside his immediate family, knew the nature of his illness. The Christian press for the following week simply announced that he was ill and in hospital. In a note to Philip Hughes, on March 13, Bethan Lloyd-Jones said: 'He is making good progress so far and pleasing the doctors. He cannot yet deal with any correspondence. He has been very ill. He sends his love and covets your prayers.'

Many different fears and hopes were entertained. I recall having to go to the Chapel during the week of his operation. I was to take a wedding a few days later, which he had hoped to conduct, and preparation for this required a mid-week visit to the premises. With time to spare, I entered the vast church through the door behind the pulpit, the rows of empty pews facing me, and wandered down an aisle to the far end where I took a seat, alone, in the shadows beneath the encircling gallery. The silence was full of the memories of many years, of congregations assembling on warm summer evenings and in their wet shoes and overcoats in the depths of winter, of times of thunderous praise and others of great stillness when such hymns as

He lovèd me, and gave Himself for me

were sung at the administration of the Lord's Supper. Thousands had been here who knew something of what Moses knew when he was told 'the place whereon thou standest is holy ground'. But then my thoughts were interrupted as I observed another figure, tall although bent with age, entering the auditorium from the same direction that I had come and, not seeing me, she stopped beneath the pulpit and stood motionless looking up at its empty desk and closed Bible. It was Margaret Smith who had spent long years as a missionary in Peru. She was now, in her latter years, one of the brightest of the many single ladies whose lives contributed so much to the congregation and for whom Westminster was their true home. As she stood motionless, supposing herself to be entirely unobserved, nothing could have expressed more eloquently the feelings of multitudes. I think we both sensed that it was the end of an era. I did not doubt that Margaret Smith was praying. It was an intercession that went on far beyond London.

When news spread that the operation had been successful and that he should be able to resume work by September there was great joy at Westminster Chapel. People began to speak of counting the weeks until his return, and one of his regular hearers wrote to say that he was 'the only preacher she could understand'. This he especially prized on account of the fact that its writer was only eleven years old! I think it must have touched him deeply for another reason: he knew that he would not be returning to Westminster. On the evening before his operation on March 8, seeing some apprehension in Bethan as they talked together, he assured her of his confidence that the operation would be successful. At the same time, he added, their lives would not be the same again, for he believed this was God's answer to the question when his pastorate should be concluded. There would be other ministries but his work at Westminster Chapel was done. For several years he had struggled with this question and he now believed that his guidance was clear.

Early in April 1968 ML-J left hospital and, with Mrs Lloyd-Jones, went to convalesce at Hedingham Castle, the beautiful home of Musette Majendie in Essex. He returned to London before the end of April and called a deacons' meeting on May 29. It was then that they heard of his decision to retire at the end of August, with no resumption of his ministry before then. And as he came to Westminster, without any recognition service, so he wished to leave. There would be no farewells, no speeches, no presentations. 'He talked to us for a little while,' writes Geoffrey Kirkby of that meeting, 'and I for one felt that we were experiencing all over again something of that which took place at Miletus when Paul said his farewells to the elders of the church at Ephesus. The Doctor then prayed with us but the emotion of the occasion was too much for him and he stopped and I believe someone else carried on. I am sure that we felt the same emotions stirring us as did the Ephesian elders and we would fain have fallen on his neck and kissed him.'

Many letters came to him as the news of his resignation spread. In a few cases they came from those who had been with him through the thirty years at the Chapel. One man, of eighty-three years, wrote of memories at the Chapel going back to the First World War and could recall that his attendance began in the year 1911. At the other extreme there were letters from those who had only recently found their way to Westminster. One lady wrote of her praise to God for the assurance of salvation given to her in the last month of his ministry. Some converted under his ministry told him of it for the first time. A letter from a man in Switzerland read:

I feel it to be my duty to tell you that on the occasion of one of your Sunday evening sermons in 1954, I have been convicted of my sin and brought into the glorious light and joy of Christ's redeeming grace. I have not told you this before — please forgive me — but the Lord knows! He also knows the great numbers of young men and women from all over the world who have found *life* at Westminster Chapel.

A doctor in Sheffield wrote: 'I felt I would write on this particular date as it was on this day ten years ago that I was converted under your ministry at the Chapel.' 'It was through Marilyn and Westminster Chapel', wrote another, 'that I was led to the Lord.' 'I owe it you', said a correspondent from the Channel Islands, 'that I am a Christian.' There were multiplied testimonies from Christians of what they had learned from his ministry, including a letter from Jim Packer on September 26, 1968 with the words:

I should have written to you long since to say, first, how glad I am to know you have recovered so fully and, second, how I felt at the news that you were leaving Westminster Chapel. God gave you a truly momentous ministry there, and it gives one pause to think that it has ended. It is not given to many of us to change the course of things in the Christian world to the extent that you have been used to change it, nor to restore so much of its true value to so much of our debased Christian verbal coinage. I shall always be grateful myself for the understanding of the meaning of preaching which you gave me — not by talking about it, but by doing it — during the winter of 1948/9, when you peregrinated on Sunday evenings through Matthew 11. I was at Oak Hill, teaching, at that time, and was able to get in fairly regularly. I recall both my mystified fascination as to what you were at when you started in on verse 3 and my sense, by verse 30, that whereas I had never before grasped what preaching really was, I knew now. Incidentally, my sister, who was at Bedford at that time, thinks she became a Christian about verse 29! For me, your preaching of the gospel from the Gospels remains the finest thing of all in your pulpit ministry. This is the time to say thank you, and I say it from my heart.

TWENTY-NINE

A World Pulpit

Acomplete recovery was to follow the months of convalescence in the summer of 1968. From Friday, March 1, 1968, the day when he preached to his congregation at Westminster for the last time, another thirteen years exactly were to be given him.

The main part of his active ministry for the future was clear to him as he reflected on it in those quiet months of 1968. He spoke of it in a personal letter to the members of Westminster Chapel on May 30:

> The moment I realised that I had to undergo an operation, I felt that God was saying to me, 'This is the end of one ministry and the beginning of another.' I said that to my dear wife and colleague before the operation, and, ever since, this conviction has deepened and become more and more clear. I am already past the age at which most people retire today. I have completed 30 unbroken years in the ministry of Westminster and given the best years of my life to it. This has meant that I have refused invitations from various parts of the world to lecture at colleges and seminaries and to address conferences of ministers, etc., etc. But, and perhaps most important of all, it has meant that I have only been able to publish but little of what I have preached at Westminster. Great pressure has been brought to bear on me to publish more. I cannot imagine what my life will be like without preaching three times each week at Westminster Chapel — apart from my summer vacation. But when God calls, he is to be obeyed in spite of all natural feelings. I know that you dear people will understand. If you do not, then my ministry has been in vain.

For the most part his people did understand and rose to his vision.[1] Letters received from the congregation, instead of complaining at what they had lost, expressed the belief that the world needed to read what they had heard. ML-J repeated the same point to Philip Hughes in a letter of July 6, 1968: 'I have felt increasingly that I must put into book form more of the material that I have accumulated — for example, I am anxious to print what I have tried to do on the Epistle to the Romans among others.'

The first fulfilment of this desire came with the publication of *Romans Exposition of Chapters 3:20 to 4:25* in 1970. Its preparation had taken a good deal of his time the previous year, part of which had been spent in the United States. Simultaneously Bethan Lloyd-Jones had started preparing his sermons on Ephesians and the first volume, *God's Way of Reconciliation: Exposition of Ephesians 2:1-22,* came out in 1972 in 480 pages. How such serious books of this size would be received in a market unused to such material was uncertain. Some reviewers in the religious press could be expected to be hostile. What he had published thus far had seen criticism as well as praise. His sermons entitled, *Spiritual Depression: Its Causes and Cure,* published in 1964, were described by one reviewer as a 'hefty volume' in which there was 'nothing intellectually adventurous, no theoretical ranging into new worlds . . . It is rather dreary matter.' Many could not have agreed, for the title needed three reprints within two years. Yet ML-J favoured some caution. There was no parallel in the twentieth century to support the idea of the publication of consecutive expository sermons in a large series. This was part of the reason why the Romans and the Ephesians publications did not start with the first chapters of those letters. There was no announcement of the thirteen volumes that were to follow on Romans, and the seven on Ephesians, simply because there was no fixed programme. In the event there was to be world-wide demand. The *whole* Romans series was even to be published in the languages of Brazil and Korea.

The year 1969 when all this work was beginning, also saw the origin of another of one of his most influential books. The occasion for it was the 'six very happy weeks' he had spent that year at Westminster

[1] Some took the view that the benefit of reading him would be rather confined to those who had sat under his ministry and could put his voice to his written words. Time would prove them very wrong.

Theological Seminary, delivering addresses on 'Preaching' at the invitation of Edmund Clowney. He spoke, as he always preached, from a skeleton of notes, and the recording became *Preaching and Preachers,* in some respects, perhaps, his most important book. His freedom from dependence on paper in speaking was illustrated on this same visit to the States when he spoke at Grace Baptist Church, Carlisle, Pennsylvania. During the first of three meetings a storm broke and the thunder and lightning seemed to be right on top of the church. When about three-quarters of the way through his address, all power and lighting failed, leaving him, his desk and the entire gathering in darkness. These conditions continued for some five minutes, with ML-J proceeding throughout without the slightest pause or reference to what was happening. His third address at Carlisle, on 'The Responsibility for Evangelism', remains one of the most valuable of all recordings made of his speaking.

The main change in his timetable from this date, was the time now given to the editing of the accumulated manuscripts of his Westminster ministry. For the rest of his life a major part of his working hours in private went into the preparation of this material for the press. When one reviewer wrote, 'It is an apparently easy transition for his preaching to be reduced to print' he was quite wrong. First, ML-J would edit and revise transcription taken down from tape recordings. His changes were so numerous that the MS then had to be retyped. The retyped version was then passed to another editor (often S. M. Houghton) whose notes and comments would require a second reading of the entire manuscript by ML-J, who of course took the final decisions. He found the whole process arduous work — more tiring, he would sometimes say, than the initial preparation of the sermons. Paperwork for ML-J lacked the stimulus which he found in preaching. He found 'getting going' in the mornings harder than it used to be and would sometimes stir himself by putting on a cassette of rousing music before beginning a day's work on his manuscripts! Brief summaries of his doings to Philip Hughes would contain such sentences as the following, 'I have had a very busy time preaching in various parts of the country and trying at the same time to correct MSS, but I am feeling well' (Dec. 15, 1972). The desk work was, however, by no means all drudgery. There were times when he became 'lost' afresh in the truths before him and the work then became 'most exhilarating'. The dozen years following his 'retirement' became the most important of his life in terms of the output of his books.

A question he faced while in the States in 1969 had to do with his choice of publishers. His prolonged stay in the States that year gave him the opportunity to talk with American publishers who would handle the North American market but he thought hard on who should publish for Britain and the rest of the English-speaking world. The preparation of his work, under his direction, would be more in the hands of a UK publisher than an American one. His earlier policy in Britain had been to spread his titles among various publishing houses. He had not confined himself to the most conservative of his publishers, the IVF. Now, however, with the ecumenical question a critical issue, he was more concerned to aid those institutions most likely to be most dependable in the years which lay ahead. It was this consideration, principally, which led him to give the publishing of his *magnum opus* on Romans to the Banner of Truth Trust in 1969, and his volume on Ephesians chapter 2 to the Evangelical Press. The second volume was later given to the Banner of Truth when he determined to put the whole Ephesians series in their hands. He endorsed a copy of a Romans volume to me in 1973 (as the surviving founding trustee of the Banner of Truth Trust) with the words, 'To my very dear friend, Iain Murray, and now my publisher.'

For the six years 1970–75 Dr Lloyd-Jones concentrated on the preparation of Romans for the press with a new volume in the series appearing every year. The *Exposition of Chapter* 5 came out in 1971 in 384 pages. He regarded it as 'the key chapter of this great Epistle, absolutely essential to any true understanding of chapters 6-8'. *Exposition of Chapter* 6 was out in 1972, *Chapter 7:1 to 8:4* in 1973, and two further volumes on Romans 8, in 1974 and 1975. The reception given to these volumes across the world was beyond all expectation. A reviewer in *Christianity Today* (Oct. 8, 1971) welcomed the first volume with the words: 'This is no average book. Nor will you read it indifferently. It is the kind of book that will grip your mind and heart . . . it has been a long time since I have read a book I enjoyed so thoroughly as this.' W. J. Grier in the *Evangelical Presbyterian* (Jan. 1971) described it as 'glorious exposition' and, referring to those 'who wondered if he should not have continued his fruitful ministry at the centre of the great Metropolis', he observed, 'If there was any doubt about the wisdom of that decision, it vanishes when one reads the first volume on Romans from his pen which has just been issued.'

After the publication of the sixth in these Romans volumes, subtitled, *The Final Perseverance of the Saints,* there was to be a major delay in the series. The main reason for this was that his attention was now being given to his work on Ephesians. The Banner of Truth Trust published *Life in the Spirit, An Exposition of Ephesians 5:18 to 6:9* in 1974. Subsequent volumes came out in 1976, 1977, 1978, 1979, and 1980, Only one volume remained to complete the whole Ephesians series and this was issued in 1982, the year after his death.

In terms of literary output the 1970s were thus, unquestionably, the most important decade of his life.

Some reviewers were of the opinion that the contents of these books was admirable for the 'twice-born' but of doubtful help to the 'outsider'. Yet the fact is that 'outsiders' were reached by the books as they had been by the original sermons. Not a few have owed their conversion to them. An Annual Report of the London City Mission records how a woman left her husband and her children only to return later when 'she had been converted through reading a sermon of Dr Martyn Lloyd-Jones'. A prisoner in Wormwood Scrubs, London, wrote to say how a copy of *Romans, Atonement and Justification,* loaned to him by a visitor, had been used to open his eyes and bring him to repentance. A student at Reading University heard Dr William Sargant lecture on 'The Mechanism of Brainwashing and Conversion' and then, being convicted by ML-J's reply to Sargant, became a Christian. A Scottish emigrant to Durban, South Africa, found herself 'a failure in every way'. 'Unhappiness and loneliness drove me deep into the pit', she later confessed. In that state of mind she was loaned one of the Lloyd-Jones' volumes which brought her to understand how someone with 'absolutely nothing' could be reconciled to God. 'For the first time in my life I wept with *joy.'*

Another conversion, which affected several lives, occurred in the Midlands of England. A man had been a member of the Watchtower movement for eighteen years when, as he later wrote to ML-J:

> Your book has lit a fire that has spread far wider than myself. About three weeks ago my wife and I were disfellowshipped from the local congregation of Jehovah's Witnesses, this is the ultimate punishment that can be handed out, to a 'backsliding' Witness. We are

now free and feel every day the work of grace within us. I can never express the joy we feel and the peace of mind. Your book came to me about two-and-a-half years ago. I thought it strange that a man not of my faith should give me such a book. Now looking back I see so well the providence of God in the matter. It was only a few weeks later that I sat down one evening to read a few pages and arose a changed man. In your writings you stressed the true state of man before God and I saw myself for what I was. Over the next few months a great change began to come upon me . . . Now I can tell you that the Lord has opened the eyes of two more souls and one of these is my dear wife.

A man browsing in a public library in Stoke-on-Trent picked up a volume by ML-J of whom he had never heard and wrote to the Banner of Truth Trust to ask where he could obtain more. One reader of the books wrote to testify to how he had been delivered from the fear of death; another — an Anglican vicar — to say that their message had kept him from suicide. A lady wrote from Georgia, 'I am filled with thanksgiving that I have found your books . . . May you cast a shadow throughout the world.' An American tourist on a cruise in the Black Sea discovered *Studies in the Sermon on the Mount* in the ship's library and was so impressed that, on returning home, he bought fourteen copies to give to his fellow elders. He could later write to ML-J: 'The response in our church has been quite remarkable.'

The refrain in so many of these letters was the same. It was not praise for the preacher or his style but thankfulness to God for the life-changing power of the truth. In the words of a correspondent in Texas, 'God so opened up his sovereign grace to me through reading your books'; and of a college student in Georgia, 'You have opened my eyes to many of the great doctrines of Scripture.'

A different judgment of the ML-J volumes was inevitable from those with no enthusiasm for his theology. Verlyn D. Verbrugge, reviewing the Ephesian volume entitled *Christian Unity* in the *Calvin Theological Journal* (April 1983), complained of 'a severe negativism which pervades the book on anything other than staunch sixteenth-century Protestantism'. He was disturbed by the preacher's reference to the 'heresy of Roman Catholicism' and to 'liberal Christianity'.

The first review of the Romans series to appear in the *Church of*

England Newspaper voiced similar censure. James D .G. Dunn wrote: 'His stern unyielding dogmatism is rather off-putting; and too frequent over-simplifications seem to betoken a mind anxious to press the diversity of the New Testament gospel within a single dogmatic mould . . . In his often fiery polemic one detects something of the old anti-scholarship bias of an older generation of evangelicals.'

'As years went by,' Christopher Catherwood has written, 'Martyn Lloyd-Jones . . . acquired an unfortunate, negative image in the eyes of many.'

In ML-J's mind the issue came down to differing attitudes to Scripture. He regarded the elements of warning and of opposition to error were essential parts to any true commitment to the Bible and, therefore, believed that the 'disapproval of polemics in the Christian church is a very serious matter'. Accordingly he expected no approval from those who accepted the prevailing attitude which put 'love' first and treated arguments over doctrine as unchristian. It was that very attitude, he believed, which was responsible for the removal of the note of authority from the pulpit: the charge of 'dogmatism' and the dislike of reproof and correction were criticisms of Scripture itself.

One of the main characteristics of ML-J's ministry was thus both an offence to those who were supporters of the spirit of the modern pulpit and an inspiration to those who believed that a return to authority in preaching was a great need. The latter were profoundly thankful for the very thing with which the first group found fault.

If the influence of Westminster Chapel's pulpit was powerful in the 1950s, it was also more limited in its range. Twenty years later, although ML-J's work at Westminster was done, that pulpit had become a world pulpit as the books gave light and assurance to the multiplying numbers among the nations who were coming to love the doctrines of grace. Those who said Lloyd-Jones 'became increasingly a voice in the wilderness' during the 1970s were speaking from a very narrow standpoint.[2] Their judgment may be corrected by the lines of Arthur Clough,

> Far back, through creeks and inlets making,
> Comes silent, flooding in, the main.

---

[2] McGrath, *Know and Serve God,* p. 127

* * *

Before leaving the subject of books something must be said on the series of Dr Lloyd-Jones' sermons on the 'baptism of the Spirit'. They constituted one of the last titles which ML-J prepared for publication and, not without controversy, came out as two paperbacks after his death with the titles, *Joy Unspeakable,* and, *Prove All Things.*[3] It has been said that his publishers, the Banner of Truth Trust, declined to print these sermons. That is not the case. ML-J's understanding of baptism by or with the Spirit was published by them in two major volumes which both appeared in 1978.[4] The sermons on the subject published posthumously were not offered to Banner.

The controversy that followed the publication of these sermons had to do with whether or not they were to be seen as supportive of the charismatic movement. Forewords added to both paperbacks seemed intended to give that impression; they included such statements as, 'God led him [Dr Lloyd-Jones] to welcome (though not uncritically) many aspects of the rising charismatic movement and to see its fundamental compatibility with historic evangelicalism.' Again, 'he believed that all the gifts of the Spirit existed today'.[5] The words were meant to gain readers at a date when charismatic thinking was sweeping through many churches as a tidal wave in the 1980s.

The question is, what was ML-J's intention in preaching these sermons and later wanting them published? If they were not intended to support the charismatic movement what were they for? The answer is that he wanted to state and safeguard an important truth about

---

[3] (Kingsway, Eastbourne, 1984; 1985). The split into two books was not for reasons of size, for the sermons were not published consecutively in the author's own order; instead the eight sermons with the cautionary note were taken out of their original order in the series, and kept back to the second book. This was put right in the cloth, one-vol. edition *Baptism and Gifts of the Spirit* (Grand Rapids: Baker, 1996).

[4] *Romans 8:5-17* and *Ephesians 1:1-23.*

[5] His position was not that the extraordinary gifts of the apostolic age existed today, but that Scripture gives us no authority to assert that they could never be. He did not believe that the extraordinary gifts of the apostolic era *had been* restored to the church.'I have never been satisfied with any speaking in tongues that I have heard.' 'I have never spoken in tongues.'*Fight of Faith*, p. 690 . He believed that God might heal miraculously, but not that the gift of miraculous healing was a present part of the church's ministry.

the work of the Holy Spirit which he had believed and preached long before the world ever heard of a charismatic movement. But from whom did it need safeguarding? That question cannot be rightly answered without knowing the date when the sermons were preached in the years 1964–65, twenty years *before* their publication. In those years he was concerned to address teaching coming from two quarters, namely, from those who had no place for any extraordinary enduement of the Spirit (for the individual Christian or for the church), and from those who were identifying Christ baptizing with the Spirit with receiving 'tongues' and other miraculous gifts.

He differed with both these views and meant to oppose both. An example of the first he saw in John Stott's paperback, *Baptism and Fullness* which appeared in July 1964. ML-J read it and, without naming Stott, quoted it critically in his sermon series on the subject which began in November of that same year. Stott's argument was that the only Spirit baptism is the one which happens objectively to every Christian in union with Christ and at regeneration (*1 Cor.* 12:13). Lloyd-Jones certainly believed that every believer becomes a temple of the Holy Spirit at regeneration, but he held that the indwelling of the Spirit is not the same as full assurance or with being 'filled with the Spirit'. Acts 4:31, for instance, was not describing the same thing as 1 Corinthians 12:13.[6] He wanted to emphasise that there is *more* of the Spirit to be received *after* conversion, and believed that failure to see this was one reason for the little interest in revival as an extraordinary 'outpouring of the Spirit'. He noted that Stott's treatment said nothing of revival, and the same omission was common in other contemporary authors. He feared it was an omission which encouraged an acceptance of existing spiritual conditions and hindered prayer for something greater.[7] Far from this being new to his

---

[6] The latter refers to a single event; the work of Christ 'baptizing with the Holy Spirit'(John 1:33) is on-going, hence the ground for on-going prayer for 'the supply of the Spirit of Jesus Christ'(Luke 11:13; Phil. 1:19). The Spirit is 'not in all persons, nor at all times, in the same measure' (Westminster Larger Catechism, Q. 182).

[7] This subject is too large to be dealt with here. In fairness to Dr Stott it should be said that he rectified his absence of reference to revival in a later printing of *Baptism and Fullness* (1975), and, as he once told me in a personal letter, he 'prayed for the Holy Spirit every day'. Some of the difference here was probably verbal rather than real. Of ML-J's teaching on the baptism of the Spirit, with which I can only partly agree, I have written at some length in *Lloyd-Jones: Messenger of Grace* (Edinburgh:

thought, we have seen him believing it throughout his ministry. It did not arise out of his experiences in the August of 1949. Preaching before that date, he said on June 12, 1949, 'I am charged by certain people with being nothing but a Pentecostalist.' In fact, as noted earlier, the convictions he held on Christ baptizing with the Spirit belonged among the churches centuries earlier.

The danger of the second view was of a very different kind. Here ML-J's thinking needs to be followed closely, for to say the sermons show he was supportive of the charismatic movement is to misread them. There was *no* 'charismatic movement' in England when these sermons were preached (Nov. 1964 – June 1965). There were only the incipient beginnings, an excitement among a few young clergy for whom 'Spirit baptism' meant the gift of tongues and other extraordinary gifts. In a letter to his friend R. G. Tucker, ML-J wrote on November 19, 1964, 'I think we shall be in the "Tongues Movement" for a while' (meaning that he feared it would not be a passing phenomenon). In 1964 no one knew what it might become.

While disagreeing on the tongues issue, he was glad that there should be a new interest in the Person of the Holy Spirit and, knowing that a work of God may start even where there are many imperfections, he warned against premature negative judgments. But he also warned against the danger of confusing claims for tongues and other miraculous gifts with a powerful work of the Spirit bringing fresh life to the church. He pointed out how that wrong identification had happened in the time of Edward Irving, and ended in tragedy.[8]

By the time the excitement took the name of the 'charismatic movement' his criticism was definite. In a sermon on January 28, 1966, when 'experiences' were taking first place among the advocates of the new thinking, he said: 'They say that doctrine does not matter. What matters is that a man has got the Spirit.' This became still more explicit: 'There is a factor which to me is a very serious one at the present time and that is what is known as the charismatic movement . . .

Banner of Truth, 2008), chapter 7.

[8] He also remembered that R. M. M'Cheyne called Irving 'a holy man in spite of all his delusions and errors'. While some were to object to the subtitle of Arnold Dallimore's book, *The Life of Edward Irving, The Fore-Runner of the Charismatic Movement* (Banner of Truth, 1983), charismatic writers have themselves supported that designation — unaware, it seems, of the sad conclusion to Irving's life and ministry.

The teaching of this movement is that nothing matters but "the baptism of the Spirit". You can believe Roman Catholic doctrine or be Methodist or be without any doctrine if you like; it does not matter.'[9]

As this quotation shows, the charismatic movement coalesced with ecumenism. Charismatic leaders, wrote Peter Hocken, had seen an outpouring of 'ecumenical grace' so that people 'holding together apparent opposites in the one mystery of Christ' can be one.[10] The Anglican evangelical *Nottingham Statement* of 1977 noted with approval, 'We see a particular ecumenical significance in the charismatic movement.'

However, ecumenism was not the only reason why, as the charismatic movement developed, it did not have Lloyd-Jones' support. He saw it as endangering the whole nature of church life. If 'apostles and prophets' were restored, 'this means', as one of their leaders affirmed, 'that *men* — rather than particular doctrines or structures — must become prominent again.'[11] Further, if the extraordinary spiritual gifts were once more claimed to be present, then the nature of Christian worship had to be changed. All must now 'share'; 'Listening to the Spirit today', took precedence over the preaching office. He pointed out at a Westminster Fraternal on July 1, 1974, that, whereas the ecumenical movement had made too much of church structures,

> There is a movement which is opposed to all these church structures. The desire is for something 'new' and 'living'. . . the Jesus movement, the new charismatic movement. There is little interest in what happens to the old structures. It is an anti-church movement with an impatience with the old structures and forms; there is a call for house churches, a dislike of church buildings, a preference for small units. The interest is in phenomena and experiences. The very existence of the church in the old form is at stake.

He said this, not because he was opposed to things new, but because he knew from history what happens when the role of biblical

---

[9] From three addresses, 'What is an Evangelical,' *Knowing the Times,* pp. 312-14.

[10] *One Lord, One Spirit, One Baptism* (Exeter: Paternoster, 1987), p. 99.

[11] '*Church Adrift,* David Matthew, 1985, p. 220. A revival of apostles had, of course, occurred earlier in the century in one branch of Pentecostalism: 'There is a church known at the present time as the Apostolic Church. They claim to have apostles and prophets among them. We could easily show that they are not scriptural' (ML-J on Romans, March 18, 1966).

offices in the church are set aside (as the Quakers had done), and when Sunday services are turned into a 'general meeting' at which 'anyone can get up'.

At Bala in June 1977 he said that the revival which the charismatic movement claimed to be, lacked the primary marks of such sovereign movements of the Spirit as had awakened the church in times past:

1. Revivals always have common features and therefore we can test what is being talked about at the present time. The trouble with the charismatic movement is that there is virtually no talk at all of the Spirit 'coming down'. It is more something *they* do or receive: they talk now about 'renewal' not revival.

2. The tendency of the modern movement is to lead people to seek experiences. True revivals humble men before God and emphasize the person of Christ. If all the talk is about experiences and gifts it does not conform to the classic instances of revival. And the true *always* leads to evangelistic concern and outreach.[12]

In the light of these statements, and more which could be given, is it credible that ML-J, at the same time as he was saying these things would have prepared his 1964–65 sermons for publication if he thought they were favouring charismatic thinking? He wanted the sermons in print for quite a different reason: to safeguard the true, and to show how it differed from what was being promoted as the work of the Spirit.

In the 1980s it suited charismatically inclined publishers to link Lloyd-Jones with the charismatic movement, and it was pointed out that twenty years earlier he gave counsel to a few young men who later became charismatic leaders. But he was ever encouraging *all* young men who came to him for help, and the reality is that the emerging charismatic leaders soon found that Lloyd-Jones was not their supporter. A rumour that he favoured the new thinking was early discovered to be false by some who had hoped it was true. After

---

[12] In relation to his own unusual experiences in 1949 it is valuable to note why he did not speak of them. Answering a question, 'Should we not make such experiences known?' he replied that it is teaching that must always be first, and while preachers may indicate in a general way their knowledge of these realities, it is the people's consciousness that they are speaking from experience which makes their words convicting. There is, therefore, no need for a preacher to introduce his own personal experience directly. See *Romans, 8:5-17, Sons of God*, pp. 367-8.

reading what ML-J had said in an address to the Annual Meeting of the Evangelical Library (Dec. 5, 1963), David G. Lillie wrote to Michael Harper on August 23, 1964:

> I don't know how widely it was intended that this address should be publicized, but it is, to me, a very painful revelation of the Doctor's real position in relation to the things of the Holy Spirit, and it is quite different from what I had been led to think. He presents what he terms a 'recrudescence of interest in gifts of the Spirit' in a wholly unfavourable light, and sets over against this the revived interest in the Reformed theology as being the thing which really matters and which alone can meet the spiritual need of serious, intelligent and spiritual people.[13]

Let it be noted, the Library address to which Lillie refers was given *before* ML-J started the baptism of the Spirit series.

It would be a great mistake to think that Dr Lloyd-Jones' convictions on the church's need, and the preacher's need, of the power of the Holy Spirit has simply to do with the title I have discussed. Setting aside differences which arise out of the interpretation of a few particular texts, the main thing in his book, *The Baptism and Gifts of the Spirit*, was the main thing in his life. It could be summed up in the words of George Smeaton:

> The apostles who had received the Holy Ghost on the first resurrection day continued with one accord in prayer and supplication for the promise of the Father (*Acts* 1:14). They prayed for the Spirit though they had received the Spirit. They waited for more of the Spirit that they had in compliance with their Lord's command. This is the true attitude of the Christian church in every age. And the history of the apostles shows that not once, but on many occasions, they were partakers the baptism of the Spirit and fire.[14]

---

[13] This explains why authors favourable to the charismatic movement make little or no referenece to ML-J.

[14] George Smeaton, *The Doctrine of the Holy Spirit*, p. 52

33: At the British Homoeopathic Congress, Margery Blackie (Physician to the Queen) presents ML-J to Queen Elizabeth, Oct. 22, 1970.

THIRTY

The 1970s

The pace of Dr Lloyd-Jones' life slowed somewhat, but not dramatically, in the 1970s. While his overseas visits ended, his last being to give three addresses at the IFES Conference at Schloss Mittersill in Austria in 1971, he continued to preach in many parts of Britain regularly, if not as frequently, as in former years. By that date his connection with the student work of the IVF, which became the Universities and Colleges Christian Fellowship (UCCF) in 1975, was far less. He had given his last major IVF address at Swanwick in 1969 when he spoke of the dangers in the church at Corinth as present in the contemporary scene. It was never published and one can only wonder whether the reason may have been the same as operated in the non-publication of his London Bible College address in 1958. His stand on ecumenism had received a mixed reception from some senior advisers of the Fellowship. There were some within the IVF, and especially those professionally involved in teaching theology in universities, who believed that a 'scholarly', non-partisan approach to their subject could yet win greater influence. Throughout the 1970s there were numbers, mainly connected with the Church of England, who believed that 'the move to regain the high ground with the mainline denominations gathered momentum'.[1] ML-J's question was never answered, 'How was fraternizing with those who deny the gospel at the denominational level consistent with denying it at the

---

[1] McGrath, *Know and Serve God*, p. 127.

student level?' Such questions did not arise in the Christian Medical Fellowship (CMF, the medical side of IVF) where Douglas Johnson continued to exercise leadership. He had retired as General Secretary of the IVF in 1964, to be succeeded by Dr Oliver Barclay who, until his retirement in 1980, continued to value ML-J's counsel. On the big issues the three men thought alike.

Perhaps the only new commitment which Dr Lloyd-Jones was to take on, temporarily at least, in the 1970s was a connection with television. Far from being in a hurry to speak on either radio or television he had declined opportunities to speak on the former when the BBC imposed unacceptable limitations. He was not prepared to turn sermons into sermonettes and accordingly it was only in Wales — where BBC Wales were willing to broadcast full-length sermons — that he was heard preaching on the radio in Britain. He may have been on English television only once or twice before January 6, 1970, on which date he spoke on the ecumenical movement and other subjects in the programme 'Viewpoint'. Later that same month, on January 25, he was interviewed again by BBC television in a programme entitled 'All Things Considered', when he debated the meaning of Christian conversion with Magnus Magnusson. When the interviewer asked, 'Why are there so few conversions?' he was clearly surprised by the answer, 'Ultimately, this is the will of God.' Such unusual television interviews arrested attention and comment was widespread. Writing in the March issue of *Dedication,* its editor reported that a junior BBC executive had told him, 'Dr Lloyd-Jones speaks with divine authority, we hope to have him taking part again in our programmes.'

He appeared again in a programme entitled 'Fact or Fantasy' screened on April 12, 1970. This time he was with three others and again the main subject for discussion was religious conversion. Two members of the panel, a psychiatrist and a marriage guidance counsellor, argued that it was an experience of the natural type, most predictable in adolescents, and akin to falling in love. When these explanations of how people become Christians had been well aired, ML-J stepped in with such a response that a viewer wrote to BBC television:

> I have never before written to the BBC but I was so impressed with the programme last evening that I feel I just have to commend

you for it. I could have listened all night. May I particularly say how helpful I found the comments of the elderly minister. Why haven't we seen him on TV before? He seemed so sincere, so under-standing, so sure of his ground and yet so humble. Quite unlike many of the religious experts who always seem so keen to make an impression. Please may we see much more of this man on TV?

This programme had been Dr Lloyd-Jones' third television appear-ance in a few months. In a review of the April 12 programme, Morgan Derham commented humorously in the *Life of Faith* on April 18, 1970: 'We shall soon have the liberals protesting that the BBC is favouring the evangelicals! Once again the BBC Sunday evening reli-gious television programme included Dr D. Martyn Lloyd-Jones.'

His next appearance was more unusual. Oliver Hunkin, a BBC television producer, had noted that 1970 was the bicentenary of the death of George Whitefield and sought ML-J's involvement in a twenty-minute programme recorded, not in a studio but from sites connected with Whitefield's ministry. ML-J was the narrator and spoke 'live' to the cameras as he stood on a grave top in Islington churchyard and in similar places. 'The Awakener' was shown in colour on September 30, 1970. It was not an entire success to those of us who knew him, for although ML-J could speak freely on Whitefield without a script, the role of the professional commentator talking only to a camera was unfamiliar to him.

His last TV appearance of which we have any record was on the BBC 1 programme 'The Open Persuaders' (Dec. 5, 1972) when the interviewer was the well-known Joan Bakewell. She had familiarized herself enough with some of his writings to know he was not the usual 'Christian', and wanted to press him why he should differ so much with others in speaking as he did on sin and on the exclu-siveness of Christianity. In answer to her questions ML-J spoke of the uniqueness of Christ and of Scripture as revelation. Bakewell wanted to know why he thought a 'sense of sin' was necessary in order to be saved, and she put it to him that as sin was not of any immediate concern to many people, how could his point of view pos-sibly prevail? 'It certainly could', ML-J responded and explained that the modern indifference was caused by ignorance. 'Let people hear the truth about themselves, let them hear the Ten Commandments, and then they would be ready to listen to the message of the New

Testament 'which I maintain is only represented by the evangelical standpoint'.

In a continuation of the discussion with Joan Bakewell, after the filming ended, she confessed that this was a kind of Christianity which she had never met before. All the clerics whom she had previously interviewed had been concerned to assure her that she was a Christian. ML-J was the first to tell her she was not.

It would be intriguing to know why this programme — the best of all he had done — brought his television work to an end. Perhaps the reason lay simply in that very fact. Whatever the reason, the end of invitations to appear on television certainly did not trouble ML-J who was convinced that, next to the pulpit, it was *books* which could most effectively spread the Christian faith.

At this date ML-J often had another audience who saw a very different side of him. With the burden lifted of having to practise a strict economy of time through ten months of the year, there was now more leisure with the family than he had formerly enjoyed. His second daughter Ann had married Keith Desmond in 1965 and their third child, Adam Martyn, was born on May 18, 1971. This completed the circle of grandchildren: of the Catherwood children at this date, Christopher, Bethan Jane and Jonathan were sixteen, twelve and nine, and the Desmond girls, Elizabeth and Rhiannon, were three and one respectively. They all came to share more of 'Dadcu's' time, their name for him being a Welsh variant on Grandpa. From infancy they lived near him (the Desmonds in an apartment in the same house),[2] and were used to wandering in and out of his presence at will. The Catherwoods moved home from Ealing to an old country house at Balsham, Cambridge in 1964, and many weeks would be spent there by the grandparents each year. Dadcu entered into all the children's interests with enthusiasm. If he was at home and free, when such programmes as 'The Waltons' or 'The Little House on the Prairie' were on the television, he would watch with them as they much preferred. Whatever appealed to them, or concerned them, had his attention whether it was the finer points of wrestling, problems at school, or on the lawns at Balsham where the young people were greatly impressed by how he could hit the croquet ball straight

---

[2] The Lloyd-Joneses had moved in 1965 from Mount Park Crescent in Ealing to 49 Creffield Rd, in the same district; it was the first and only home of their own.

for twenty yards! Remembering his own experiences at that age, he believed that teenage years possessed difficulties which merited much sympathy and understanding from adults. He was never dismissive of their problems.

The enjoyment of the grandchildren also figured largely in the decisions on joint family holidays. The attraction of the sports centre at Aviemore, for example, took the Catherwoods to that area of the Scottish Highlands on two occasions in the 1970s, while the beaches of Cornwall and of the Isle of Wight drew the younger Desmonds. Dr and Mrs Lloyd-Jones entered fully into these and other holidays.

* * *

I turn now to the area which received the greatest amount of his time and concern in these latter years, namely, the encouragement and guidance of ministers whose witness would continue when he was gone. Without the care of a particular congregation, he was now more than ever the helper of others. He was constantly available to men individually to give advice by interview, phone or letter.

The 1970s have been represented as supposedly 'something of a scorched-earth era' among those on the Lloyd-Jones' side of the division of the previous decade.[3] He saw it differently. In many churches it was a period of new beginnings, a period when the main effort of numbers of pastors was going into the rebuilding of local congregations. Although some, who had been enthusiastic for the doctrinal recovery of the late 1950s and early 1960s, wavered when they did not see the results which they had expected, others hung on, and faced the slow uphill work of establishing congregations where people would see the Word of God and prayer as foundational to spiritual prosperity. ML-J's concern and affection for these men were unbounded and his visits to hundreds of congregations and manses gave renewed hope and unforgettable encouragement. Even more than the help of having him in their pulpits was the long-term strength gained from being able, perhaps late into the night, to speak to him of how various problems should be approached and dealt with.

In such visits, and at such gatherings as the Westminster Fellowship and the ministers' conferences of the Evangelical Movement of

---

[3] C. Catherwood, *Martyn Lloyd-Jones: Chosen by God*, p. 56.

Wales, there was no question of ML-J giving indiscriminating support. The closer men were to him the plainer he would speak, and there was no tolerance or sympathy if he ever found self-pity or unbelief among them. On one occasion at the Westminster Fellowship, when the subject for discussion was, 'Why are we not experiencing greater blessing?' he said with vehemence: 'We are never promised automatic blessing. Look at the sufferings of the men involved in 1662! Get rid of the idea, "If I do this, God will give the blessing." God knows when to give blessing and when not to. We are not fit to have it. He couldn't trust us to have it. There is the sovereignty of God in this.'

He was ever insistent on the need to raise the standard of preaching. 'It is a great grief to me to hear true words coming out of a pulpit that lacks authority.' There should be compassion and emotion: 'When have you and I last preached with tears?' he might ask us. But more thought was also needed in preaching and for that he pressed the necessity of constant reading. 'Most of the great men of God have been great readers. Daniel Rowland was always reading and in the study. As I get old I read more than ever.' 'What do you take on holiday with you?' he challenged the fraternal one summer. 'I take my Bible and a whodunit book', replied one of the men. 'Is *one* enough for you', said ML-J dryly, and he went on to tell the speaker, 'You are making a great mistake.'

One of his greatest desires was to see pastors brought more closely together. The difficulties in the way of that wider unity were immense. Given the breakdown of the denominations, with their incapacity to exercise any discipline, and the disarray of the evangelical organizations, 'The problem ahead', as he said in the Westminster Fraternal on April 5, 1971, was 'how there should be control without denominationalism'. This difficulty was increased by the failure of the superficial optimism with which many had greeted the work of the British Evangelical Council. Before the end of the 1960s doubts were surfacing among BEC supporters and there were signs — later to be fulfilled — that a number of participating churches were going to revert to giving their main interest to their own more restricted groupings. The *English Churchman,* hitherto sympathetic, in its issue of November 7, 1969, wrote: 'The BEC is not a Church body, and apart from the closer fellowship there appear to be very few, if any, signs of brethren in the evangelical nonconformist denominations working towards visible church unity at the local level.'

ML-J often mourned in private the lack of 'big men' with the vision to see what was needed. He had said all along that secession from mainline denominations was not an end in itself. At a Westminster Fellowship, April 5, 1971, he said,

> It was only part of our idea to separate ourselves from ecumenism. I am not sure that we are clear about this, and our people are not. Facing it will lead to a tremendous upheaval. I am not sure you can persuade your people to face this without some great movement of the Spirit. All this work done by movements should be done under the church or under a fellowship of churches. I do not mean the FIEC, I mean something more like the BEC. There needs to be control which is church based but not a 'denomination'. The church must sanction everything which happens.

He continued to give major help to the BEC and yet, by declining to attend and to speak at every annual conference, he deliberately stepped back from the leading role. At this period he was deliberately seeking to reduce men's dependence on him. For the annual BEC two-day Conference in the 1970s he spoke in 1970, 1971, 1973, 1977 and 1979.[4]

While his preaching journeys continued to be spread over the British Isles their greatest frequency was in Wales. His engagements diary for 1974 shows that he was in the Principality in seven months of the year (sometimes for separate visits within the same month). In 1975 there were only six out of the twelve months of the year when he was not to be found in Wales for one preaching engagement or another and the percentage remained the same as late as 1978. It was in Wales, too, that he made the one exception to his rule, by this date, that residential conferences were now too tiring for him. For many pastors the two-day Ministers' Conference in Bala every June was the high spot of the year and not least because ML-J was always there. The venue was Bryn-y-groes, amidst lawns and trees, overlooking the beautiful Bala Lake. Originally built as a family home, it had all the air of a family as men crowded its rooms and 'the Doctor' presided in the spirit of love so reminiscent of what is written of the Apostle John in old age.

[4] For these addresses see: D. Martyn Lloyd-Jones, *Unity in Truth.*

One of my unforgettable memories is of the 1974 Bala Conference. It began at 5 P.M. on Monday, June 24 with an address on Bible
Translations. Then after an evening meal, ML-J chaired a discussion
on the subject. He seemed both tired and old — not surprisingly,
perhaps, as he had preached several times in the preceding days. But
when he led a further discussion, the next evening, the change was
remarkable. He was obviously refreshed and spoke as though he were
several years younger. The subject was prayer and he presided, sitting in a chair in the crowded front parlour of the house — with
its low ceiling and little white-framed windows looking out on the
sunshine of the early evening. Discussion finally gave way to his own
impromptu address, delivered with much authority and fervour, on
our need of a great 'sense of God'. Prayer had declined because the
belief that we could truly know and enjoy God had declined. Our
chief failure as ministers was the failure to bring people into the presence of God. Our conviction that 'God deals familiarly with men'
was too weak. 'The two greatest meetings in my life were both prayer
meetings. I would not have missed them for the world.' All this and
much more he said seated and, just when it seemed that his flow of
speech and spirit must be concluded because anything else would
have to be an anticlimax, he rose to his feet and, moving behind his
seat as though it were a pulpit desk, continued without any interruption and still more forcefully and rousingly for a further ten minutes!
While books and tapes may give some idea of what ML-J was as a
preacher, no such helps exist to give a real impression of what he was
as an 'exhorter' on such unrecorded occasions as these.

* * *

I close this chapter with a summary of principles which he urged
especially on ministers at this period:

1. *A whole view should be taken of any situation, putting the main
thing before details.* He especially warned of the danger lest a multi-
plicity of subjects and problems distracts from the great issue of the
gospel itself. The nature of evangelical Christianity must be kept at
the centre of attention.

2. *The negative should never be allowed to displace the positive.* If
the negative and the denunciatory begin to take the chief place in a

man's thinking and message, the result is never profitable. We should never major in criticising the errors or practices of others. He would remind us that the upsurge of discontent which had contributed to the rise of the charismatic movement was related to real deficiencies in the churches. A deeper analysis was needed, and it was ever his policy to seek to educate and win those who might be supporting something for lack of knowledge of anything better.

3. *The thought of the extraordinary work of God in revival ought never to lead us to neglect the truth that the Holy Spirit is present to grant us sufficient aid for the work to which he calls us.* Christians are not responsible for the extraordinary but they are responsible for their personal obedience and for such reformation of the church as is required by the Word of God. Faith in the possibility of revival in the future, if it is true faith, will not lead to passivity in the present. This point came into one of his 1977 BEC conference addresses when his subject was Elijah's 'repairing of the altar of the Lord that was broken down' and the consequent giving of fire from heaven (*1 Kings* 18:30-40). Christians, as Elijah, must be ready to fight, to work and to pray: the altar must be repaired; truth must be restored. Such is the call to reformation and here we are responsible.

After the BEC address to which I have just referred, he mentioned to me that he had deliberately made no reference to revival because there was need to emphasize *present* duty. We are to 'rejoice in the Lord *always*'.

4. *There is need to preserve balance, moderation and self-examination in all matters of controversy.* ML-J constantly urged the need for care and discriminating distinctions and he sought to exemplify it in his practice. Thus, while he broke off public co-operation with the Anglican evangelicals who condoned the Christian standing of fellow denominationalists who were false teachers, there was no blanket condemnation of all Anglican evangelicals. A number remained his close friends and he had no hesitation in speaking for them when he was invited. He could say in his BEC conference address of 1977:

> There are many good honest men in the Church of England who are filled with grief and with sorrow. They have expressed their disagreement, they have expressed their fears and I, for one, not only know a number of them, I am praying for them because they are men who want to serve God in a true and in a right way.

5. *There needs to be both the consciousness of the speedy approach of the end of time — the coming judgment and glory — and of the duty of one generation of Christians to anticipate and prepare for the needs of the next.* He held these two truths, content that the New Testament found no contradiction between them. 'The end of all things is at hand' (*1 Pet.* 4:7), has to be balanced with, 'The end is not yet' (*Matt.* 24:6). Both entered largely into his whole outlook. Like C. H. Spurgeon, he lived for the next age as well as for his own, and it was this, as much as anything else, which put any thought of retirement out of his head. That is why the chief part of his time in the 1970s went into the preparation of books and into the encouragement of the men who would be continuing the battle when he had gone. Part of his dislike of paperbacks was his belief that their publishers were thinking only of the present. Books ought to be made to last!

ML-J had a profound sense of the providence of God in history. 'Do not waste too much of your time in worrying about the future of the Christian church' was his counsel to younger men.

'I feel like Griffith Jones of Llanddowror', he said to me the month before his death. He knew I would understand the reference. The preacher to whom he referred, born in 1683, was significant not so much for what he achieved as for what he did in preparing the way for others. He was 'the morning star' of the great awakening of the eighteenth century in Wales. ML-J went on, 'I thought I was going to see a great revival but I am not complaining. It wasn't God's time and this preparatory work had to be done.' If he had done anything to prepare the way for other men that was enough.

THIRTY-ONE

_____

'Dying ... He Worshipped'

When Dr Lloyd-Jones entered upon his eightieth year on December 20, 1978, his engagements diary for the following twelve months was nearly as full as usual. But to his friend, Philip Hughes, he wrote on May 1, 1979: 'I have had a bad winter. I believe I had a virus infection on my lungs and afterward I had to go into hospital for a small operation. I have actually not preached since the first Sunday in February, but I am now beginning to make real progress.' He was at the Westminster Fellowship on July 5, looking pale and aged yet saying nothing of his condition. After summer months with the family at Balsham, he resumed some engagements in the autumn, including a fifty-first consecutive annual visit to Water Street Church, Carmarthen, where he preached twice. On October 11 he preached from Romans 1:14 at the opening of a third year in the life of the London Theological Seminary and in the three following weeks he preached eight times, including engagements in Cardiff, Llanelli and Manchester, where his visits to the Free Trade Hall were always keenly anticipated. When the BEC Conference met in London he preached at the final evening meeting, November 7, 1979, conscious, I think, that it would be his last time in the pulpit at Westminster Chapel. He seemed to abandon any care to conserve his limited strength and preached with considerable animation and physical vigour.

When I saw him at his home in Ealing on November 23, he was quieter than I had ever known him and he confessed to being somewhat weary. For the first time he talked to me of his doubt whether his work could continue, but this in a calm and confident tone far removed from gloom. He had heard of a clinic in Florida with treatment which might be obtained to improve his condition and he had hopes of going there, perhaps at the end of December. If the treatment was successful then he would carry on his work, 'but if not', he paused slightly and I am not certain of the conclusion of the sentence. I believe he said, 'Well, I shall do what I can . . .' His calm acceptance of *either* alternative affected me. In the event, he put aside any thought of a transatlantic journey for medical help. His last engagements in 1979 were the Westminster Fellowship on December 3 and a meeting of the Evangelical Library committee on December 4. As he passed his eightieth birthday on December 20, 1979, for the first time since he had been in the ministry, he possessed an almost blank engagements diary for the year that lay ahead. He knew that public work was almost done.

I was at this time living in Scotland and, although we spoke on the phone, did not see him again until I was back in Ealing on March 3, 1980. It was a lovely day in early spring and I found him sitting in his favourite armchair in the sitting room, dressed in one of his normal dark grey suits but with thinness and weakness giving a marked change to his appearance.

In an interview with Carl Henry for *Christianity Today,* the previous September, he had expressed the intention of employing such time as he had left mainly in writing. The preparation of his Ephesians series was nearing completion but while he anticipated further volumes on Romans they were not his priority. Rather, as he said to Dr Henry, 'I am now ready to commence a spiritual autobiography.' This was a project about which he had spoken before, yet in the ensuing autumn and winter of 1979–80 he decided that he would not do it. Instead he gave me a far greater responsibility than he had ever done before. While I had kept notes for some time for a possible biography we had never actually discussed it seriously. Only at this stage did he commit himself to give me all the help he could in the setting down of a record which, as he charged me, should be for God's glory only.

A new dimension thus came into our conversations from this period and I arrived on March 3 with various questions ranging from,

'Why was Llangeitho also called Capel Gwynfil?' to, 'Who was the author of the anonymous attack on him in the *British Weekly* in 1953?' At this and at other times we talked not so much of any one period in his life as of the main turning points and the key factors.

I believe that one reason why he gave up thought of an auto-biography had to do with assessment of the right use of such time as remained to him. There were members of his family in special need of his support and encouragement; others, also, could still be helped by letters and phone calls. These activities, however, were now linked in his mind with a still greater duty. It came home to him with much conviction that time to prepare for death was very important: he needed such time and believed that its right use was now his chief work as a Christian. This subject came to the fore in an unforgettable way in our meeting on March 3, 1980. In the early part of the con-versation, as we spoke from 10.45 A.M. until 12.30, he answered my queries and gave some valuable comments. But what was uppermost in his thoughts did not lie in the past at all. The big thing before him was that all Christians need a pause from the activities of life in order to prepare for heaven. Referring to words of Thomas Chalmers on this subject and also to his own present condition, he went on:

I am grateful to God that I have been given this time. I agree with Chalmers absolutely. We do not give enough time to death and to our going on. It is a very strange thing this: the *one* certainty, yet we do not think about it. We are too busy. We allow life and its circumstances so to occupy us that we do not stop and think . . . People say about sudden death, 'It is a wonderful way to go.' I have come to the conclusion that is quite wrong. I think the way we go out of this world is very important and this is my great desire now that I may perhaps be enabled to bear a greater testimony than ever before.

Death is not something to slip past, it should be victorious. I am grateful, therefore, for this experience. Maybe this present trouble [referring to his physical condition] is to give me this insight. All my ministry I have used the words 'short uncertain earthly life and pilgrimage'. One of my first sermons was on 'For here have we no continuing city,' and I remember the second half of that sermon, 'but we *seek* one to come' (*Heb.* 13:14). In my youth we moved such a lot. There were just nine years at Llangeitho before we moved to London. My brother died in 1918, my father in 1922. When I entered the ministry I had not lived in any house beyond twelve years. Until Port Talbot it was constant movement and change.

He went on to recall that he had often preached that death is a tremendous thing — to go out of this world and to leave all that one has ever known behind — and his ministry, he confessed, had not been without instances of the power of that message. 'But,' he added with much feeling, 'I can see that it should have been even more emphasized. What is this brief span in the context of eternity!'

All this was not said with an air of sadness nor with the slightest degree of resignation to the inevitable. His whole attitude was one of thankfulness and expectation, 'looking for and hasting unto the coming of the day of God' — and this as something which belongs to all Christians: 'People are so idiotic — they think of death only in terms of age. In 2 Corinthians 4:18 the emphasis is on "looking", "we *look* not at the things which are seen", I am quite certain we are leaving out the experimental emphasis. Christianity is faith but it is not *only* faith.'

In the course of this conversation I spoke of the glorious death of a Christian known to me who had been like Bunyan's 'Mr Fearing' in his lifetime but passed on with great joy. To a brief account of this I added the comment, 'How wonderful it would have been if he had *lived* like that.' The Doctor responded at once and with a definite element of disapproval: 'But don't underestimate dying! *Death* [with great emphasis] is "the last enemy". Men may live well who do not die victoriously.'

In his prayer before we parted he asked for more of what he already knew, 'that we might rejoice in hope of the glory of God'. As I left him at the front door, and it closed behind me, his smiling face remained silhouetted through the glass in the sunshine until I was out of sight. It was no more than the usual way in which he parted with friends, but as I returned to Scotland it seemed very possible that this would be my last view of him.

The next time we spoke was on the phone on March 13, 1980, when I asked advice on an address I was seeking to prepare on 'Is Calvinistic Evangelistic Preaching Necessary?' He took this up with enthusiasm and in a few sentences clarified the whole theme. Referring to a current controversy at a theological seminary in the United

States, he pointed out how, allegedly, it had arisen out of a concern to correct the stress which modern evangelism put on justification. He did not agree. The diagnosis was wrong. The superficiality of modern evangelism was not the result of an over-emphasis on justification, it was because it did not preach the law, the depth of sin and the holiness of God. The gospel was being preached in terms of the offer of a friend and a helper. *The* characteristic of Calvinistic evangelism, he insisted, is that the majesty and glory of God is put first and not some benefit provided for man. Such preaching does not treat sin merely as some kind of sickness but as an affront to God, as lawlessness, and its great concern is that men should see themselves in relation to the glory of God. Modern evangelism pays lip service to regeneration but it does not really believe in it. True Calvinistic preaching shows the complete helplessness of man and regards the humbling of man as the main part of its work. If that is left out, the true glory of salvation cannot begin to be measured.

This reminded me of a strong intervention he had made at the 1978 Westminster Conference after the Puritan preacher John Preston was blamed for 'preparationism' and John Bunyan was thought needlessly kept in the 'slough of despond' by inadequate teaching at the time of his conversion. To set aside the need for conviction of sin prior to conversion, and to call it 'preparationism', was fundamentally at variance with what he believed about true evangelistic preaching. Sinners need to be 'awakened', not in order to be qualified for salvation, nor to 'prepare themselves' (a thing Puritans were wrongly accused of believing), but because it is God's general method to bring men to faith by first causing them to know their need of Christ.[1] It was not enough, he affirmed, simply to tell men to believe in Christ, and he continued:

> I entirely disagree with that. It fathers easy believism and decisionism. Bunyan went through that agony not because of 'preparationism' preaching, *perhaps* partly, but I would say that was not his problem at all. It was *Scripture* which convicted him . . . Look at the difference between Nettleton and Finney. Nettleton tended to leave people under conviction. Finney did the exact opposite. I would defend Nettleton without any hesitation at

[1] For his serious difference with Dr R. T. Kendall on this subject see, *The Fight of Faith*, pp. 722-26.

all. When people came to me under conviction I would not brush it aside. It is no use telling them, 'It's all right.' They have got to see it from Scripture. It may take time. I am never unhappy about people whose conversion took a long time, in fact I am happier with them. I do believe in the possibility of instantaneous conversion but we must not standardize. There are great variations . . . It is not enough that a man says, 'Yes, I believe.' The *whole* man is involved in conversion. Jesus preached *regeneration* to Nicodemus. The preaching of regeneration shows the need for justification. The lack of experience among our hearers is due to the lack of the preaching of regeneration.

These words were a summary of his own evangelistic preaching, and as he was speaking during that phone call of March 13, 1980 I did not believe we would ever see him in a pulpit again. He had not been anywhere in public since early December, nor was he expected to be. It was, therefore, with some amazement that we heard he hoped to preach in Glasgow on Friday, May 9, 1980. This last visit to Scotland he fulfilled, preaching on Psalm 2, beginning with the words, 'Why do the heathen rage, and the people imagine a vain thing?' I cannot attempt to describe the sermon which took the best part of an hour. The tape is available and should be heard by every reader of these pages. The frail, dying man was, in truth, an ambassador from heaven. Knowing the message he had to deliver, and the time he would need, I believe he tried to husband what strength he had but there was no holding back. The message took over the man and every last vestige of energy was poured out in both word and action. The divine wrath, of which the Psalm speaks, was to him a terrible, present reality and he asked the congregation:

Do you still believe in the wrath of God? There are people in England — evangelicals — who think modern man needs entertainment. There is a mania for singing, for drama, for mime. 'People cannot take preaching', it is said, 'Give them singing. Teach them how to dance.' In the name of God I say that is to do violence to Scripture. The church is not here to entertain. It is here to call people to 'be wise', to 'be instructed' (verse 10). It is not just an appeal to 'come to Jesus' — they are to be 'instructed', taught. People are dying through lack of knowledge. We are not here to be popular, but to tell the naked truth: 'Serve the Lord with fear, rejoice with trembling' (verse 11).

The final verse of the Psalm was alive with light and power as he pleaded, with failing voice, 'Kiss the Son, lest he be angry . . . Blessed are all they that put their trust in him.'

The service over, he sat pale and exhausted on the bottom steps of the pulpit while old friends gathered to greet him for the last time. The next morning, Saturday, he was driven south into North Wales where on the Sunday evening he preached in the little chapel at Llanymawddwy, close to Brynuchaf, the home of his friends, John and Mari Jones. It was a final visit to a place so dear to him. The next week he preached twice at Aberystwyth. Some 400 were present for an afternoon Welsh service when his text was, 'And Jacob was left alone; and there wrestled a man with him until the breaking of the day' (*Gen.* 32: 24). 'Here', he said, 'is the essence of Christian experience. It is *personal,* during the recent months of illness I have had to consider how a man feels when he is left alone and can do nothing.' But, further, 'in our loneliness there is Another with us. Fellowship with God is the only worthwhile thing in life and it makes us new.'

In the evening of the same day some 800 people crowded the Baker Street Congregational Church and ML-J preached again on Psalm 2. The sermon included one personal reference. He recalled coming to Aberystwyth in 1911 in a horse-drawn trap, with other children from his school in Llangeitho, to see King George V and Queen Mary lay the foundation stone of the National Library. They had reached their destination at 10.30 A.M. and had to wait until after 2 P.M. for the arrival of the king.

As in Glasgow, it was a very sobering sermon, preached, in the words of the Rev. Geoffrey Thomas, 'with wonderful authority and simplicity'. During May his condition deteriorated and there were only a handful of further engagements to be fulfilled. They included two Westminster Fellowships, and a last sermon at Barcombe in Sussex on Saturday, June 7.

The next Tuesday, June 10, 1980 he had to return to hospital for a check on his worsening condition. There were by this time regular hospital visits for periods varying from a day to a week and generally for chemotherapy treatment.

At this time when weakness and nausea were becoming so much a part of daily life, his spirit was bright with gratitude. 'God's great kindness' became his main theme. There was thankfulness for 'a long life and remarkable health', 'for Bethan', for all that was past (including, in all seriousness, 'The best thing I ever did was to refuse to go on committees . . . I have known many men ruined by committees'). Speaking to me on the phone on June 27 he said: 'I have nothing but praise in my heart. I am more aware of the goodness of God than ever before and that I am "A debtor to mercy alone."' That line of Toplady's he often quoted and, if he had ever been asked to reduce his biography to one sentence I believe it is the one he would have chosen.

It was in connection with the grace of God to him that he mentioned how moved he had been to read reviews of new biographies of two eminent Cambridge men, G. M. Trevelyan, Master of Trinity (whom he had met in 1941–42), and J. D. Bernal, the eminent physicist. 'These reviews', he told me, 'turned out to be a tremendous blessing to me. Here in Trevelyan is human nature at its best and it came to me with such force: Why did God ever choose to look upon me? Why *me* in contrast with these men and the despair in which they died?'

When I next saw him on July 26, 1980 at his home in Ealing, he had waited for seven hours at the hospital the previous day without being admitted. But he was in wonderful spirits and remained thankful for everything. 'I have no complaints', he declared in reference to the experience of the previous day. His conversation flowed. He began by speaking of how God times the encouragements he sends to us and then went on to talk of the great importance of the command which Christ gave to his disciples on witnessing their first success, 'Notwithstanding in this rejoice not that the spirits are subject unto you; but rather rejoice, because your names are written in heaven.' 'Bear that in mind', he said solemnly. 'Our greatest danger is to live upon our activity. The ultimate test of a preacher is what he feels like when he cannot preach.' Our relationship to God is to be the supreme cause of joy. To lean upon our sermons or words of testimony from others is 'a real snare for all preachers'. 'We cannot lean on them.' He then went on to speak again of death and of how it was to be faced without fear. Two things were needed. First, face it as a fact. We must all die. Second, Christians are able to be unafraid because God gives assurance that they will not be left alone and the company they possess at their departure will include that of angels, he affirmed, quoting Luke 16:22, 'the beggar died, and was carried by the angels into Abraham's bosom'. Adding, 'I believe in this ministry of angels, I think more and more of it.'

> Our greatest trouble is that we really don't believe the Bible and exactly what it says. We think we know it but do we really appropriate it and actually believe it is true *for us?* That is Christianity to me. 'Our short, uncertain life' is the most difficult thing to realize. We do not put the emphasis as the New Testament does. We are not meant to despise this life but we are certainly meant to keep it in proportion — 'our light affliction, which is but for a moment' (*2 Cor.* 4:17). We have to take these statements *literally.* They are facts, not merely ideas. That is what I feel you people have got to emphasize more and more.

From these and similar words it was evident that he was still preaching to himself ('more and more I can see that ministers *must* preach to themselves', he said in passing). Another subject upon which he clearly enjoyed meditating upon was the way in which some of the Christian men and women whom he had known had died. Spurgeon once said: 'If I may die as I have seen some of our church members die, I court the grand occasion. I would not wish to escape death by some by-road if I may sing as they sang.' ML-J felt the same. He vividly remembered, for instance, the home-going of William Thomas, one of the early converts at Sandfields. When dying from double pneumonia, Thomas suddenly threw his arms upwards and with radiant smile left this world exulting in the clear recognition of his Saviour.

His prayer before we parted on July 26 was mainly praise for God's exceeding goodness and care — 'the hairs of our head are numbered' — and petition, 'Shed abroad thy love in our hearts that we may rejoice.' Such words as, 'Have pity on thy church', and pleas for colleagues in the work of the ministry were also rarely absent from these short prayers at the conclusion of conversations. 'Now I can pray for you men,' he told me as I left, 'and am doing so. People say to me it must be very trying for you not to be able to preach — No! Not at all! I was not living upon preaching.'

To Philip Hughes, ML-J wrote on September 20, 1980:

> You will be sorry to hear that my health has not been at all good this summer; I have not been able to preach or to do anything else

since the beginning of June. I have to go into hospital every three weeks for a few days' special treatment and it tends to leave me somewhat weak. However, I thank God for his great kindness and mercy to me over these long years and for the privilege of being able to do some work in his glorious kingdom. I am happy to be in his gracious hands and to be content with his will whatever it may be.

We met again in October and November 1980 for lengthy conversations on the biography. I was now beginning to produce some draft chapters which he was ready to go over but the main thing for me was to have down on tape his understanding of the more crucial areas of his life and ministry with which I knew I would have to deal. This was the more necessary for those years in which his thought had been unfamiliar to me.

As he looked back he was convinced that nothing of significance in his life had happened according to his own plans. Things *he* had thought to do, he said, such as going to the Theological College in Aberystwyth in 1925, and then serving permanently in Wales, had not happened, while his life had witnessed a succession of things of which he had never dreamed: 'I found myself living a kind of life I had never imagined for a moment.' He had never intended to preach around the country, or to be a teacher of students or to publish any books. 'When I went to Sandfields if anyone had told me I was going to do what I have actually done, I would have told them they were mad. My only thought was to be an evangelist in a local mission hall. There is only one explanation — the sovereignty of God! the guiding hand of God! It is an astonishment to me.'

We talked about the right framework and structure for the biography and after an interval of a few days he came back to me with this suggestion: 'I think I have got the key to it. From Sandfields, and for the rest of my life, I was confronted with a series of problems.' These, he explained, together with their answers, could well provide the divisions for a number of chapters. He went on to outline what he had in mind. There were the early problems such as the constant calls to preach away from his own church, his relationship to medicine when he was at Port Talbot, and the expectation of his denominational leaders that he would fit into the typical Welsh Presbyterian mould. Then there were the unexpected consequences of the study of Warfield (which put him into the role of a teacher), the problems of the war years at Westminster when the work seemed to have no future, the incompatibility between his convictions with those prevailing in English Nonconformity and — in many ways the greatest problem of all — his concern to be a helper to an evangelicalism whose traditions had diverged so much from the evangelicalism of the past. He reflected a great deal on this latter point. It was amongst evangelicals that he belonged more than anywhere else and yet, from the time of the invitation to be principal of the London Bible College to the Graham crusades and thereafter, he was constantly the outsider.

His divergence from the role which others expected of him would be, he knew, the crux issue in any biography. He posed the question, How did he arrive at the position which so often put him at odds with the religious current of his times? He knew that the answer could be treated in terms of his gifts, his individuality, even in terms of his 'Welshness', but any such treatment, in his view, would be directing attention away from the truth. He could only understand what had happened to him, as already said, in terms of divine providence. God had stopped him from going in ways he would otherwise have taken and constrained him to convictions for which the thought of taking any credit to himself was abhorrent. He was never more in earnest than when he said, 'I am such a sinner that God has always had to compel me to do things.' And again: 'My whole life experiences are proof of the sovereignty of God and his direct interference in the lives of men. I cannot help believing what I believe. I would be a madman to believe anything else.'

From October 1980 I never saw him rise again from his favourite chair. For the next four months this was where he quietly sat, still dressed in a suit, though it hung loosely on him as though no longer his own. I think it was towards the end of the year — on a final hospital visit — that he was told that the time remaining was short and he himself then took the decision to end any further treatment. Although he was progressively weaker, yet all his mental powers were unimpaired and, with scarcely an exception, his phenomenal memory remained. He had slowly lost interest in classical music but his love of good books was unabated and some of the books he enjoyed during the last year of his life must be mentioned. They included a biography of Philip Doddridge; *The Essays and Letters of Thomas Charles* ('definitely one of the most neglected of the spiritual leaders'); *Archbishop Grindal,* by Patrick Collinson; *The Works of Walter Craddock* (the Welsh Puritan); *The Diary of Kenneth MacRae* ('I am enjoying it tremendously'); *Drunk before Dawn* by Shirley Lees; Calvin's *Letters,* and John Owen on *The Glory of Christ.* Of Owen's classic, which he finished in December 1980, he said: 'It has done me great good and been a great blessing to my soul. I feel at times that he tends to go a bit too far. We are not saved by our love to Christ. At times he almost says, "Unless you are longing to be with Christ I doubt if you are a Christian." That is going too far. He was so concerned about glib *fideism* but God justifies the *ungodly.*'

This comment was characteristic of his balance. He longed for more of the *felt* presence of Christ and yet always insisted that our feelings play no part in the basis of peace with God. In this connection I asked him one day if he agreed with Spurgeon's statement that strong faith can exist with little feeling or enjoyment. Emphatically he did, 'Feeling varies a lot. We are not the same from one day to the next.' And he proceeded to quote one of his favourite hymns:

> My hope is built on nothing less
>   Than Jesus' blood and righteousness;
> I dare not trust my sweetest frame

'They come and go,' he interjected

> But wholly lean on Jesus' Name.
> *On Christ, the solid Rock, I stand;*
> *All other ground is sinking sand.*

And then with reference to that hymn's last verse

> His oath, His covenant and blood . . .

he exclaimed, 'Oh, it's the Covenant . . .'

Hymns — Welsh and English — meant a great deal to him. I recall two others about which he spoke and which had often been sung at Sandfields (these were missing in *Congregational Praise*). They were, 'Today Thy mercy calls us', and 'Come, ye disconsolate' with its beautiful closing line, 'Earth has no sorrows that heaven cannot heal'. It might be thought that at the end of such a life ML-J had no sorrows. He had, and they included painful disappointments with respect to men, once close to him, from whom he had expected better things. Yet he also knew, more deeply than he had ever done, that for the praying Christian there is peace in the midst of conflict. Peace is promised for *all* circumstances and its reality shone through his emaciated body and formed a main part of such testimony as he was enabled to give to others.

One former divine says that God always gives to his people the degree of assurance that is appropriate to them. In Dr Lloyd-Jones' case it consisted at this time, and until his death, of quietness, calmness and profound peace. John Owen, who had passed the same way nearly three hundred years earlier, and who also died in Ealing, says in one of his books:

> Our minds in this world are not capable of such a degree of assurance in spiritual things as to free us from assaults to the contrary, and impressions of fear sometimes from those assaults: but there is such a degree attainable as is always victorious; which will give the soul peace at all times, and sometimes fill it with joy.

Such was also ML-J's experience, with the peace deepening towards the end. But it was peace, he wanted to emphasize, *through believing*. All is done by Christ! On this subject he said to me when I was with him on January 19, 1981:

> When you come to where I am, there is only one thing that matters, that is your relationship to him and your knowledge of him. Nothing else matters. All our righteousnesses are as filthy rags. Our best works are tainted. We are sinners saved by grace. We are debtors to mercy alone.

To this I replied that I used foolishly to think that there was something rather wrong about some of the old saints who, when dying, prayed the words that Jesus commended, 'God be merciful to me a sinner'. He proceeded:

> So did I, but it's rubbish. That's where you will come to. I've been brought to that. Daniel Rowland said at the end, 'I am nothing but an old sinner saved by the grace of God.' I say exactly the same.

Then, after a pause, with profound emotion and broken voice,

> God is very patient with us and very kind and he suffers our evil manners like he did with the children of Israel . . . The love of God!

His appearance in his last months combined the utmost gravity with more smiles than, it seemed to me, I ever remembered before; and his face often glistened, especially when he prayed. It so happened that I had been recently reading the words of Abraham Kuyper on Jacob, who, when the end drew near, 'strengthened himself and . . . worshipped'. Kuyper's exposition of Jacob's experience was remarkably parallel to that of this later servant of God. Commenting on the exercise of faith necessary for a dying believer, Kuyper wrote:

> It must not be conceded that on his death-bed a man is permitted to let himself passively be overcome by his distress and by his weakness. In dying, the will, the courage and the elasticity of faith must still struggle against the weakness of the flesh. In this holy moment the spirit, not the flesh, must conquer. And this is what Jacob did. He strengthened himself in order that he might die in a godly manner . . . His mighty spirit shook itself awake. And so he glorified God in his dying. Dying he worshipped. In dying he felt impelled to offer unto his God the sacrifice of worship and adoration; to give Him praise, thanksgiving and honor; to lose himself in the greatness and Majesty, in the grace and compassion of his God; and thus to offer Him the fruit of the lips, in a better fashion than he had ever been able to do in life. Such a solemn worship on one's death-bed is a summary of the worship which we have offered unto God in our life.[2]

True faith and worship are never merely individualistic and ML-J at this period — when he could see few outside his immediate family — remained full of interest in all that concerned the kingdom of God. He still dictated letters to his friend and helper, Miss Pamela Harris, which were sent to friends near and far. Among the last was one dictated on February 1981 to encourage a young minister and another to John Caiger, the Secretary of the Westminster Fellowship, giving suggestions on the future leadership of the fraternal.

Throughout these months his daily care was in the hands of his wife, supported by Ann (who was always close at hand) and Elizabeth. He would often refer with great thankfulness to Bethan and sometimes to the time fifty-five years earlier when, instead of marrying others — as he had feared possible! — she became his wife. As

[2] Abraham Kuyper, *To Be Near Unto God* (1925, repr. 1979, Baker), pp. 324-330.

with every Christian husband, father and grandfather, he had not found it easy to contemplate leaving a much-loved family but he now had assurance that all would be well for them and could say: 'When this illness came, because of my being the one who had made the decisions I was a bit troubled about Bethan and the children after I have gone and tended to worry as to what would happen to them. I have been delivered from it completely. I know that God can care for them very much better than I can and that no longer troubles me at all.'

He continued to give me help with this biography, though, as we spoke of things long past, he was more like an onlooker commenting on someone else's life rather than on his own. He was terribly weak and steadily losing ground. On the phone, on February 13, 1981, he thought he was 'better today', but confessed 'he had not had a very good week'. On February 19, his voice weak and husky, he spoke of being 'much the same'. It was our last conversation, for in the following week he gradually lost the strength and breath with which to speak and communication with the family had to continue by a nod of his head, by a look or sign and one or two very brief notes. Among his last audible words were those spoken to his consultant, Grant Williams, who visited him on February 24. When Mr Williams wanted to give him some antibiotics ML-J shook his head in disagreement. 'Well,' said his doctor, 'when the Lord's time comes, even though I fill you up to the top of your head with antibiotics, it won't make any difference.' His patient still shook his head. 'I want to make you comfortable, more comfortable,' Williams went on, 'it grieves me to see you sitting here "weary and worn and sad"' (quoting Bonar's well-known hymn). That was too much for ML-J. 'Not sad!' he declared, 'Not sad!' The truth was that he believed the work of dying was done and he was ready to go. 'Last night,' Grant Williams wrote to ML-J's local doctor on February 25, 'he refused to take any antibiotic, could hardly talk and I think will die very shortly. I think he is very lucid and knows exactly what he wants to do.'

At one point in these last few days when his speech had gone, as Elizabeth sat beside him he pointed her very definitely to the words of 2 Corinthians 4:16-18 which begin:

For which cause we faint not; but though our outward man perish, yet the inward man is renewed day by day. For our light affliction, which is but for a moment, worketh for us a far more exceeding and eternal weight of glory.

'When I asked him', says Elizabeth, 'if that was his experience now, he nodded his head with great vigour.'

On Thursday evening, February 26, in a shaky hand, he wrote on a scrap of paper for Bethan and the family: 'Do not pray for healing. Do not hold me back from the glory.' The next day he was full of smiles for the little circle who gathered round him and by these, and gestures, he 'spoke' so clearly that we almost forgot the absence of his voice. By rolling one hand over another and pointing, he might request one of us, particularly, to speak, or, clasping his hands together, to pray. On Saturday, still in his sitting-room chair, he slept some hours and at other times appeared to be unconscious. At bedtime it was clear that he was unconscious and, with only Mrs Lloyd-Jones and Ann present, for the first time there was the problem of not knowing how to get him to the bedroom in the front of the house. This need was met by two kind ambulance men who responded willingly to Mrs Lloyd-Jones' call for help and put him to bed. There, a little while later, he came round and knew at once what was happening. To Bethan's enquiry whether he would like a cup of tea he nodded and, while she went to make it, Ann prayed with him. He then drank some of the tea as Bethan and Ann sat with him for about half an hour before sleeping. For over fifty years he had followed M'Cheyne's calendar for daily Bible readings, and one of those readings for the day just ended, February 28, was 1 Corinthians chapter 15. Perhaps the conclusion of that chapter, 'Thanks be to God, which giveth us the victory through our Lord Jesus Christ', or the words of Ann's prayer were in his consciousness as he fell quietly asleep. We cannot know, for his next awakening was in 'the land of the blest'.

As for me, I will behold thy face in righteousness: I shall be satisfied, when I awake, with thy likeness (*Psa.* 17:15).

34. *The burial at Gelli Cemetery, Newcastle Emlyn, March 6, 1981, after a service at Bethel Calvinistic Methodist Chapel.*

35. *The congregation at Westminster Chapel for the Memorial Service, April 6, 1981.*

Index

461

SOME OTHER TITLES BY IAIN H. MURRAY PUBLISHED BY THE TRUST

Iain H. Murray was born in Lancashire in 1931, and was educated in the Isle of Man and at the University of Durham. From 1956 he was for three years assistant to Dr Lloyd-Jones at Westminster Chapel, London, during which time he co-founded The Banner of Truth Trust, which became Dr Lloyd-Jones' principal publisher after 1970. He is married to Jean and they live in Edinburgh, Scotland.

D. M. Lloyd-Jones: The Authorized Biography
Volume 1: THE FIRST FORTY YEARS, 1899–1939
ISBN: 978 0 85151 353 9 | Hardback | 412 pp.
Volume 2: THE FIGHT OF FAITH, 1939–1981
ISBN: 978 0 85151 564 9 | Hardback | 862 pp.

'Martyn Lloyd-Jones, for decades pastor at London's Westminster Chapel, was one of the greatest expositors of the twentieth century. Beyond this, he stood at the center of the century's great events and controversies. In Iain Murray's wonderful two-volume biography "The Doctor" and his ministry are presented and interpreted by one who worked alongside Dr. Lloyd-Jones and knew him well.'
— R. ALBERT MOHLER

ARCHIBALD G. BROWN: SPURGEON'S SUCCESSOR
ISBN: 978 1 84871 139 6 | Hardback | 432 pp.

'The story of Brown's life and ministry is deeply stirring and challenging. It is remarkable that it has been hidden away for so long. Many will surely be thankful for *Archibald Brown, Spurgeon's Successor.* We should do all we can to promote it.'
— SINCLAIR B. FERGUSON

'The biography of Archibald Brown was a rich and instructive gift to my mind and heart. I read it eagerly and thoroughly and found a 'yokefellow' and friend in AGB. Iain Murray's love for and clear conviction concerning true doctrine are in the fabric of his treatments of others . . . I wish I could have heard AGB.'
— JOHN MACARTHUR

MORE IAIN MURRAY TITLES

EVANGELICAL HOLINESS
and other addresses
ISBN: 978 1 84871 319 2 | Paperback | 184 pp.

EVANGELICALISM DIVIDED
A Record of Crucial Change in the Years 1950 to 2000
ISBN: 978 0 85151 783 4 | Hardback | 352 pp.

PENTECOST—TODAY?
The Biblical Basis for Understanding Revival
ISBN: 978 0 85151 752 0 | Hardback | 242 pp.

LLOYD-JONES: MESSENGER OF GRACE
ISBN: 978 0 85151 975 3 | Hardback | 288 pp.

JOHN MACARTHUR
Servant of the Word and Flock
ISBN: 978 1 84871 112 9 | Hardback | 264 pp.

THE OLD EVANGELICALISM
Old Truths for a New Awakening
ISBN: 978 0 85151 901 2 | Hardback | 226 pp.

HEROES
ISBN: 978 1 84871 024 5 | Hardback | 320 pp.

WESLEY AND MEN WHO FOLLOWED
ISBN: 978 0 85151 835 0 | Hardback | 288 pp.

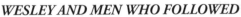

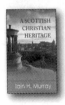

A SCOTTISH CHRISTIAN HERITAGE
ISBN: 978 0 85151 930 2 | Hardback | 416 pp.

The Magazine
The Banner of Truth

NEWS & COMMENT   BOOK EXTRACTS

ADDRESSES   ARTICLES

BOOK REVIEWS

The Banner of Truth magazine is published monthly, 11 issues per year with a double issue normally appearing in August/ September, by the Banner of Truth Trust, and in electronic form as a portable document format (pdf) file.

SUBSCRIBERS REWARDED WITH GREAT RATES!

Magazine Only
1 Year/ 2 Years (postage incl.):
USA $27.50/ $48.50
Australia $35/ $64
UK £15/ £28
Overseas £20/ £35

Electronic Only: 1 Year/ 2 Years:
USA $15/ $23
UK/ Overseas £12/ £22

Electronic (with Magazine): 1 Yr/ 2 Yrs
USA $7/ $12
UK/ Overseas £7/ £13

To subscribe please visit

www.banneroftruth.org/us/magazine/

or contact the appropriate Banner office. Canadian subscriptions are payable in US funds to the United States office.

CONTACT US

Editor: Jonathan Watson | jonathan@banneroftruth.co.uk
Books to be considered for review should be sent to the Editor
at the Edinburgh office.

The Book Fund

How many books do you have? How would you cope if you had only one book, and maybe not even a complete copy of the Scriptures?

To some of our correspondents, one sound Christian book is gold dust, to be treasured and read time and again.

The Banner of Truth Book Fund supplies ministers, missionaries, colleges and seminaries, and needy individuals all around the world with books either free of charge or at heavily subsidised prices.

When you buy Banner books, the proceeds go to support the continued publishing work of the Banner as well as to support the work of the Book Fund. Personal donations can also be made.

A bit of history
Around 1960, just a few years after the Banner of Truth starting publishing books, one of our staff, prompted by the story of Mrs Spurgeon's Book Fund for Pastors, proposed that we did the same thing. The suggestion was adopted and a fund for this purpose has now operated for over fifty years, and hundreds of thousands of books have been sent out all over the world.

An example
To give just one example:
In North America the Book Fund has sent many thousands of books into prisons. What an encouragement to us when we received the following letter—

> I have recently been released from prison. I just wanted to thank you for helping me to grow in wisdom and knowledge of my Lord and Saviour Jesus Christ. You have sent me numerous costly books and they have been an extremely valuable source of encouragement and guidance.

Be a part of it!
There are many more stories that could be told of the work of the Book Fund and the tremendous blessing that books have been to people in all sorts of places and situations—stories of changed lives, changed ministries, and people growing in grace and their love of the Saviour. And you can be a part of it!

www.banneroftruth.org/us/about/the-banner-book-fund/

The Website
Have you visited the new Banner website?

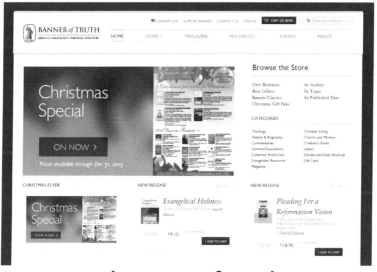

www.banneroftruth.org

- Open an account
- Buy books
- Read articles and reviews
- Subscribe to the magazine
- Consider the daily devotional
- Book for conferences
- Sign up for the Newsletter
- Give to the Book Fund

SOME RECENT BANNER TITLES

J. C. Ryle

New, re-typeset, clothbound editions of
these favorites from J. C. Ryle:

Expository Thoughts on the Gospels — Ryle's popular expositional
series on the Gospels, available individually or as a set (7 volumes).

ISBN 978 1 84871 136 5 (set) | 288–432 pp. per volume

Old Paths — Core doctrines of the Christian faith are discussed
in this much-loved work.

ISBN 978 1 84871 227 0 | 504 pp.

Practical Religion — Clear, concise, penetrating papers provid-
ing guidance on how the Christian believer is to *live*.

ISBN 978 1 84871 224 9 | 472 pp.

New editions of Ryle paperbacks

Warnings to the Churches

ISBN 978 0 85151 043 9
Paperback | 184 pp.

Five English Reformers

ISBN 978 0 85151 138 2
Paperback | 192 p.

Pleading for a Reformation Vision

The Life and Selected Writings of William Childs Robinson (1897–1982)

David B. Calhoun

William Childs Robinson was a teacher and a preacher. He was a teacher who preached in the classroom. He was a preacher who taught in the pulpit. He was a Calvinist and a churchman. He loved and defended the Westminster Confession of Faith because it was, he believed, a faithful expression of the teaching of the Bible. He loved and served the church, his denomination, and the wider church, because he believed that it is 'the kingdom of the Lord Jesus Christ, the house and family of God.' Above all he was a Christian whose words honored Christ and whose life displayed Him.

— David B. Calhoun, Professor Emeritus of Church History, Covenant Theological Seminary, St. Louis, MO

William Childs Robinson was a key figure in the history of Presbyterianism in the South, and in the whole country. When the struggle in the Southern Presbyterian Church was at its height, Dr. Robinson was right there. If you asked the 'founding fathers' of the Presbyterian Church in America, they would all point to him as the stalwart of the faith in those critical days.

— O. Palmer Robertson, Director and Vice Chancellor, African Bible College, Uganda

ISBN: 978 1 84871 356 7 | hardback | 336 pp.

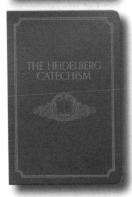